DATE DUE

SUPERVISORY MANAGEMENT

GUIDELINES FOR APPLICATION

Robert C. Lowery
Brookdale Community College

PRENTICE-HALL, INC., ENGLEWOOD CLIFFS, NEW JERSEY 07632

Library of Congress Cataloging in Publication Data

LOWERY, ROBERT C., (DATE)
  Supervisory management.

  Includes bibliographical references.
  1. Supervision of employees. I. Title.
HF5549.L63 1985   658.3'02   84-6993
ISBN 0-13-877176-6

•

Editorial/production supervision: **Joan Foley**
Interior design: **Joan Foley** and **Celine Brandes**
Cover design: **Ben Santora**
Manufacturing buyer: **Ed O'Dougherty**

Printed in the United States of America

10 9 8 7 6 5 4 3 2 1

ISBN 0-13-877176-6   01

PRENTICE-HALL INTERNATIONAL, INC., *London*
PRENTICE-HALL OF AUSTRALIA PTY. LIMITED, *Sydney*
EDITORA PRENTICE-HALL DO BRASIL, LTDA., *Rio de Janeiro*
PRENTICE-HALL CANADA INC., *Toronto*
PRENTICE-HALL OF INDIA PRIVATE LIMITED, *New Delhi*
PRENTICE-HALL OF JAPAN, INC., *Tokyo*
PRENTICE-HALL OF SOUTHEAST ASIA PTE. LTD., *Singapore*
WHITEHALL BOOKS LIMITED, *Wellington, New Zealand*

This book is dedicated to the many hundreds of federal government employees at Fort Monmouth, New Jersey, and Washington, D.C., who had trust and confidence and who supported and stuck by me during a two-year exposé on a cover-up of Department of Army financial mismanagement in the Pentagon.

R.C.L.

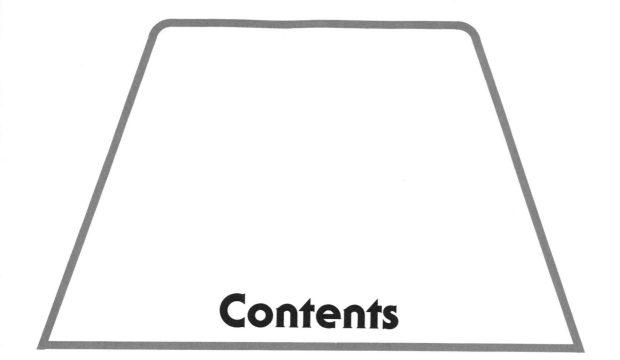

Contents

3   The Fundamentals of Directing and Controlling / 68

4   The Responsibilities of a Supervisor / 102

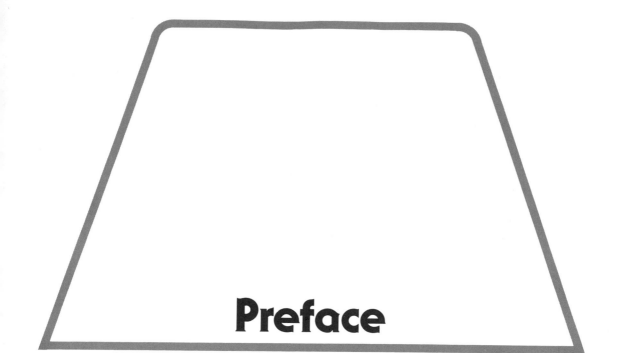

Preface

The United States is a society of many diverse institutions. In addition to our multitudinous government and business establishments, there are numerous charitable, educational, medical and health, professional, recreational, religious, social, and community service organizations—all of which require good management to accomplish their objectives. This book is designed to provide practical guidance for individuals who are involved, or expect to become involved, in management.

The scope of material contained in this book is relatively comprehensive because a good manager must possess knowledge and understanding of how to supervise people and to manage facilities, money resources, computers, information, and time. Doing the *right* things (effectiveness) and doing *things* right (efficiency) require that these aspects of management be properly handled in order to achieve any organizational objective.

Although the book has broad applications, *primary attention is given to first-level supervision.* There are two reasons for the emphasis on supervisory management. First, there are considerably more managers engaged in first-level supervision. Second, the most pronounced area of weakness in management tends to be at the lower levels—the point where people, machines, and other resources must be properly directed in the performance of actual work. One of the reasons why there are so many weak managers is that they so often are placed in their positions without an adequate knowledge of the fundamentals of good management. Managerial skills can be enhanced through obtaining a practical understanding of the principles of how to manage and supervise. The purpose of this book is to help provide a knowledge of the basic skills of how to do the right things under the right circumstances.

I have organized this book into four parts. An understanding of all these parts is a prerequisite for understanding good management. Without this broad foundation in the fundamentals of management, it is very easy to give inadequate attention to the right things or to overemphasize certain aspects of management while ignoring others.

Learning how to manage and supervise is *a building-block process.* It starts with obtaining an understanding of the basic foundations of management and their interrelationships. *Part I* outlines the broad *dimensions of management* by describing what is involved in good planning, organizing, directing, and controlling of the activities of any undertaking. In briefly discussing these fundamentals of management, I have focused attention on five things. These are: (1) the *scope* of each management function, (2) the *importance and interactions* of each function in good management, (3) *ways to implement* each management function, (4) *responsibilities of the supervisor* in handling the fundamentals of management, and (5) *guidelines* for manager use. This first part of the book is a condensation of the most fundamental principles of management that provide the foundation for effective supervision of work activities. Since entire books are devoted to the principles of management, I have designed Part I of this book to do two things: (1) provide a concise review of some of the most pertinent management principles for the reader who has already studied the subject; and (2) provide an outline of selected principles and concepts of management for those individuals beginning their study of management.

Part II covers the *interpersonal relations* in management. Many managers do not do a good job in communicating and in understanding how management actions affect human beings. To help overcome this problem, I examine the principles of effective communication between managers and subordinates. I also discuss the personal interactions between managers and subordinates and how these affect humanistic relations and productivity. Interpersonal relations are probably the most critical area of supervisory management. Human behavior is definitely the cause of a high percentage of managerial problems. Through the use of many actual case studies and supervisory action guidelines, I have attempted to show how to avoid and how to handle the most troublesome problems.

Part III discusses *supervision of the workplace.* It is designed to provide managers with the best ways to accomplish the functions of planning and control, financial management, computer management, and simplification of work methods and procedures. As a manager of managers for many years, I have seen the costly mistakes caused by people who were lacking in these ar-

eas. Many managers do not know how to control their limited financial resources or how to intelligently use computers and computerized management
information. Inability to simplify work activities is both costly and a contributing factor in employee dissatisfaction. Through the use of case studies, illustrations, and action checklists, I have provided the reader with knowledge on
how to improve the supervision of the workplace.

  Part IV addresses *managing time and developing the right attitudes.*
Time is a very restricted and inelastic resource. We cannot control time; we
can only manage ourselves and others in such a way as to make the best use of
it. The final subject covered is managerial attitudes and ethics. Our attitudes
about people, innovation, work, computers, expectations, and ethics can greatly strengthen or weaken the entire management process. The conclusion of
the book deals with preparing for tomorrow's changes in the world of management.

  The reader should take time to think through the case studies, which offer opportunity to apply management principles and concepts. Don't be mis-
led by the simplicity of many case situations.

  One of the facts of "real-world" management is that it is often the simple
oversights and mistakes that cause the major problems in the workplace. Practical application is a significant factor in really understanding good management. Memorizing concepts and terms has little to do with making an individual an intelligent and competent manager. Good management involves much
more than being able to correctly answer multiple-choice questions. *The bottom line in being a good manager is practicality.* It is one thing to have knowledge of management techniques, but it is quite another matter to intelligently
and effectively implement the right things, in the right way, at the right time,
and in the right place. To be truly effective, the concepts and techniques of
management must be individually shaped to fit the needs of each particular
situation. In other words, the "how to do it" is up to the individual manager. I
have attempted in this book to bridge the gap between concept and applica-
ton by providing supervisory guidelines on "do's" and "do not's."

  This book reflects to a considerable extent my personal background as industrial engineer and corporation-wide "trouble-shooter" for Crucible Steel
Company of America, chief of management engineering for the Pittsburgh
Ordnance District, director of programs for the Army Missile Command,
comptroller of the Army Electronics Command, and learning-center chairman
for four diversified college departments. As a manager, I have had to face and
resolve many of the problem situations discussed in this book. I have also seen
firsthand the foolish things that others do as managers. As a college professor
and department chairman, I have come to appreciate the need for a hands-on
approach to teaching management to students and managers. One of the
things I have learned as a manager and as a college professor of management
is that you do not learn how to be a manager by merely reading a textbook on

the subject. To obtain the maximum benefits from this book, take the time to *think things through* and analyze the practical application aspects of each subject area.

As I read my own book, I feel that if I had applied the guidelines I have written I would have been a better manager. Hindsight is usually better than foresight. In this book I have attempted to help managers and students of management to act with foresight rather than with hindsight.

Robert C. Lowery

Acknowledgments

This book is a practical approach in how to manage any organizational situation. I am, therefore, very much indebted to the many practicing managers who shared their thoughts on management with me. I also want to give recognition to the many students of mine at Brookdale Community College who encouraged me to write a nontheoretical book on how to handle the various aspects of supervisory management. Gratitude is extended to Joe Campbell, an artist-illustrator, who worked for me when I was writing a technical book on *Principles and Techniques in the Management of Army Materiel* (1978). Some of Mr. Campbell's ingenuity is reflected in several of the cartoons and charts found in chapters 6, 7, and 10.

R.C.L.

PART ONE

HANDLING THE FUNDAMENTALS

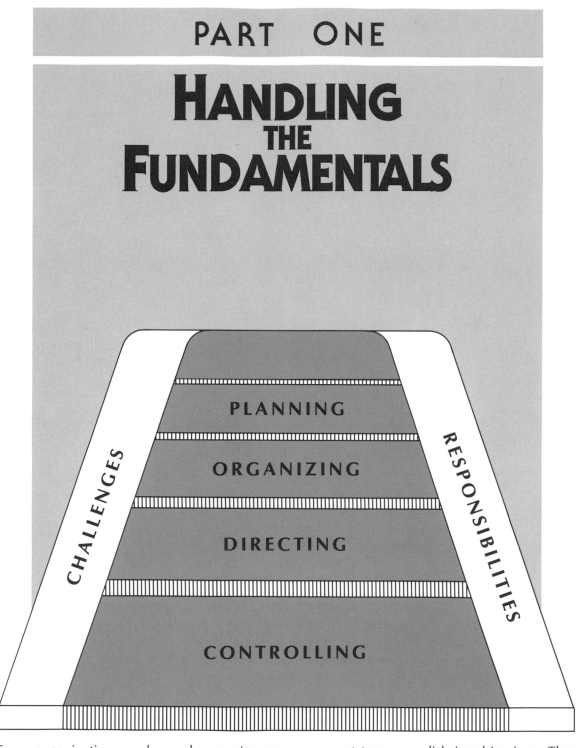

CHALLENGES

PLANNING

ORGANIZING

DIRECTING

CONTROLLING

RESPONSIBILITIES

Every organization needs good supervisory management to accomplish its objectives. The challenges and responsibilities of a supervisor start with planning, organizing, directing, and controlling the activities necessary to achieve organizational objectives.

1

The Challenges of Being a Supervisor

LEARNING OBJECTIVES

The objectives of this chapter on the challenges of being a supervisor are to enable the reader to

1. Identify four major challenges facing management, and describe what makes them especially important for supervisors at this time
2. Relate how supervisors fit into management and why we must change our concept of supervisory management
3. Establish how effective supervisory management involves an understanding of the entire corporate structure
4. Describe how the fundamentals of management are a coordinated and integrated process with many interacting variables
5. Identify the interpersonal, informational, and decisional roles of a manager
6. Delineate the four steppingstones in the management building-block process
7. Describe the three Ts in management

KEY WORDS

Accountability The obligation to explain or justify the performance of assigned responsibilities.

Authority The designated right to act and make decisions on assigned responsibilities.

Controlling The management process of determining progress toward work objectives, identifying deviations and their causes, and initiating action to correct problem situations.

Coordination Ensuring that all work efforts are aimed toward a common objective.

Cost-Effective Accomplishing something at the lowest possible cost and with the greatest benefit.

Directing The management process of assigning, instructing, and correcting people in the work efforts required to achieve objectives and plans.

Effective Doing the *right* things that result in achieving desired objectives.

Efficient Doing *things* right that result in achieving desired objectives with the best methods and procedures and lowest costs.

Humanistic Relations A method of dealing with people that shows an interest in and a concern for the liberty, rights, welfare, and dignity of human beings.

Management The planning, organizing, directing, and controlling of the activities necessary to get something done.

Manager An individual who plans, organizes, directs, and controls the activities involved in achieving the objectives of an organization. Sometimes called administrator, director, executive, general manager, or superintendent.

Organizing The management process of identifying, dividing, and grouping the work activities; and then defining the responsibilities, authority, and accountability of the workers required to best achieve these objectives.

Participative Management A team approach to management problem solving and decision making where managers and subordinates work together to establish objectives, make plans, and determine ways to get jobs done.

Planning The management process of determining the what, when, where, how, who, and why in the accomplishment of work activities.

Principle An accepted rule of action or conduct.

Productivity The quantity of work produced per hour (or other specified period of time).

Quality Control Circle A team of supervisors and workers who study work problems and their causes, and suggest corrective actions.

Responsibility The assigned obligation to perform a certain work task.

Supervision   The act of overseeing the accomplishment of the work to be done.

Supervisor   A manager at the lowest managerial level in the organization hierarchy. Sometimes called foreman, group leader, team leader, project leader, unit chief, section chief, or department manager.

AN EXCITING POSITION

A supervisor's job may at times be frustrating, but it is definitely exciting and challenging. One thing is certain, you won't find the job boring or monotonous. Your day-to-day routine might be described by this poster, published in 1976 by *Supervisor Management* magazine:

> *MANAGEMENT TENDS TO BE*
> *A SERIES OF INTERRUPTIONS,*
> *INTERRUPTED BY INTERRUPTIONS*

Management today, whether in an industrial, commercial, government, or nonprofit establishment, has many new challenges that did not face supervisors in the past. The really effective supervisor meets these challenges while planning for future ones. There are four challenges that tend to be especially important for supervisors at this time:

FOUR MAJOR CHALLENGES

- *Manager-employee relations*
- *Participative management*
- *Productivity and cost-effectiveness*
- *Computer and communication technology*

THE CHALLENGE IN MANAGER-EMPLOYEE RELATIONS

ATTITUDINAL CHANGES

For three hundred years there was a widespread totalitarian attitude on the part of supervisors: "Do it my way or you're fired." Since the 1960s, manager-employee relations have changed considerably and continue to change at a rapid rate. In today's workplace there are certain employee rights and freedoms supported to a great extent by state and federal laws as well as by special interest groups. These rights and freedoms cannot be sidestepped by the supervisor. They must be understood, seriously considered, and intelligently implemented. The supervisor—the manager having the closest contact with the workers—is the individual most frequently confronted with the problem of dealing with changing attitudes of employees. The most likely area of confrontation is in alleged discrimination, where an employee feels that he or she is not being given fair consideration. When these attitudinal situations occur they must be quickly resolved, often by the first-level supervisor, to avoid their becoming agitations that spread to other employees and/or involve outside special interest groups. It is a real challenge to resolve attitudinal problems because the facts are so often "fuzzy" and the individuals involved are usually very emotional about the situation.

LABOR UNION–MANAGEMENT RELATIONS

Another employee area undergoing significant change is labor union–management relations. Inflation with its resulting cost escalation, foreign competition, rising energy costs, greater demands for quality control, and decreasing worker productivity are bringing about attitudinal changes on the part of both labor leaders and managers. The labor relations pendulum over a period of time has swung from the side of management to that of labor unions. There are now many indicators that the gap between labor and management is closing. Participative management between the two groups appears to be more prevalent, with both sides making significant concessions.

THE CHANGING COMPOSITION OF THE WORK FORCE

A third factor affecting manager-employee relations is the changing composition of the work force. Women, older workers, and handicapped persons are becoming more common in jobs once thought to be inappropriate for them. Some are accepted by their peers and some are not. It is a challenge for the supervisor to effectively integrate these groups of workers into a unified work force.

THE CHALLENGE IN PARTICIPATIVE MANAGEMENT

QUALITY CONTROL CIRCLES

A major challenge for today's supervisors is to develop a more paternalistic and participative approach to management problem solving and decision making. In this area of management there is much to be learned from the Japanese concept of quality control circles. These are groups of managers and workers that continuously function to study work processes and problems and how to best handle them. Quality control circles do not wait for problems to occur. They scan the work environment to solve problems before they happen. One key factor in the success of participative work circles is belief in each employee as a valuable "resource" to the organization. A second equally important factor is belief in having individual employees work together with supervisor and peers for the common good of the organization. It is a form of supervisory management based on the development of trust, cooperation, and teamwork.

CHALLENGES TO THE SUPERVISOR

There are many challenges to the supervisor in implementing any form of participative management. One challenge is that it requires the supervisor to have a broad knowledge of management. The individual cannot have "tunnel vision" that only understands one limited aspect of management. The supervisor must see how his or her work activities fit in with those of other managers —both horizontally and vertically within the organization structure. A second challenge is that the supervisor must make an attitudinal adjustment to sharing (delegating) managerial responsibility and authority with subordinates. A third challenge is that of preparing workers for participative management. This requires training, flexibility in job assignments, and reducing outward signs of difference in rank between supervisor and workers. It also means sharing information with workers to create a feeling that everyone is really working from a common base of knowledge. The biggest challenge of all is probably that of implementing participative management when higher-level managers are primarily concerned about short-range time, cost, and profit perspectives.

THE CHALLENGE OF INCREASING PRODUCTIVITY

THE PROBLEM

Productivity is the amount of work produced per hour, or some other specified time period. Unless we solve today's problem of decreasing productivity, our children will be the first generation in the history of the United States to have lower living standards than their parents. For years we have been the most productive economic force in the world. Now, for the first time in our history, the rate of productivity has been decreasing to the point where it has reached *zero* growth.

There are many ways that we can increase the productivity of our industrial, commercial, government, and nonprofit organizations. Historically, we have increased our productivity through (1) capital investment in better tools and equipment, (2) more efficient technologies, (3) improved methods of performing work, and (4) employee incentives that provide benefits for working harder. First-level supervisors have always played a dominant role in getting more productivity from the workers.

THE SUPERVISOR IS THE KEY FACTOR

The supervisor is still the key factor in increasing both the quantity and quality of work produced in the workplace. The question is how? The answer to the question is to be found in how well the supervisor meets the following challenges:

1. Having a positive attitude that knocks down excuses about why we can't become more effective and efficient in the workplace
2. Developing, training, and motivating workers to be effective and efficient in the performance of their jobs
3. Learning how to effectively communicate with and lead others
4. Developing and implementing a positive humanistic relations approach to supervising and handling personnel in the workplace
5. Developing and implementing more effective and efficient methods and procedures for performing required work; simplifying work so productivity is increased and costs reduced.
6. Learning how to manage money resources through effective budgeting and other means of controlling costs and expenditures
7. Learning how to intelligently use computer technology

Above all else, the supervisor needs to develop a strong sense of purpose in the objectives and goals of the organization. If this challenge is met, it will usually have a major energizing impact on the people within the supervisor's organization.

THE CHALLENGE OF USING COMPUTER TECHNOLOGY

THE GREATEST CHALLENGE OF ALL

Mechanization, automation, and computerization of work in both office and production operations is probably the greatest challenge facing managers today. The use of computers is bringing about social and economic changes that are more extensive than those resulting from the Industrial Revolution over two hundred years ago. We now have mini- and microcomputers (1) running equipment, (2) keeping tabs on inventory, (3) performing engineering drafting work, (4) testing products in production, (5) cutting materials, (6) welding, (7) painting, (8) controlling heat and other production processing, and (9) performing tasks that used to be manual operations.

REVOLUTION IN THE OFFICE

Office operations, which have changed little since the invention of the typewriter a hundred years ago, are in the process of being revolutionized. Some believe that the paperless office is achievable by the early 1990s. Others feel that the revolution in office operations is still a long time away because you can't change people that fast. The key to any radical changes in office operations is in the use of more sophisticated computers and communications equipment. There already exists electronic equipment that can type, edit, spell, print, mail, and file letters, messages, reports, and other paper documents. Voice programming of instructions to computers is now an actuality. Microfiche and microfilm (see Chapter 14, Managing Information) have already reduced the number of filing cabinets in many offices. While these advances in the technology of performing office work increase productivity, they create new challenges for office supervisors.

A BIG PROBLEM FOR SUPERVISORS

One of the biggest problems facing the supervisor of computerized operations is the breakup of the traditional working relationships between individuals. This can bring new psychological and sociological problems that can be quite a challenge for any supervisor to handle. Computerization should not intrude on established collaborations between workers to the point where it takes individuals out of their accustomed social environment. Neither should it be the cause of worker over-specialization, which results in monotony. This would be a giant step *backward*. The handling of these problems involving employee satisfaction largely falls upon the first-level supervisor—the manager closest to where work is performed.

WHERE DOES THE SUPERVISOR FIT INTO MANAGEMENT?

To answer the above question we need to first define the terms *management* and *supervision*. In doing so, we should recognize that there are no universal definitions of either term.

MANAGEMENT DEFINED

One way to define *management* is to describe it in terms of what a manager does. The resulting definition is that management involves the coordinated and integrated process of planning, organizing, directing, and controlling the activities necessary to effectively and efficiently accomplish some objective. To be *effective* means that a manager must do the RIGHT things—be capable of getting adequate facts and making correct decisions. To be *efficient* means that a manager must do THINGS right—be competent in accomplishing an objective in the best possible and least wasteful manner. Effectiveness and efficiency can only be achieved through intelligent planning, good organization, humanistic directing of others, and appropriate controls—all of which must be *coordinated* and *integrated* at every step in the management process.

SUPERVISION DEFINED

Supervision can be defined as the act of overseeing people doing work. Supervisors are the *managers* who do the overseeing. They are sometimes called foremen, group leaders, team leaders, project leaders, unit chiefs, section chiefs, or department managers. The term *supervisor* generally refers to individuals in lower-level managerial positions. Higher-level managers are usually called administrators, directors, executives, superintendents, group managers, division managers, plant managers, or store managers. There is very little, if any, practical purpose served in trying to draw a clear distinction between the terms manager and supervisor. All managers, regardless of their level in the organization, must engage in appropriate planning, organizing, directing, and controlling of their particular organizational segment. The managerial role at all levels also includes administrative, technical, and humanistic relations responsibilities.

CHANGING OUR CONCEPT OF SUPERVISORY MANAGEMENT

DIVERSIFIED MANAGEMENT ACTIONS

Supervisory management is a part of every manager's job. To meet the challenges of today's management environment, every supervisor needs to know how to handle the following:

- *Develop effective and efficient plans*
- *Organize work activities and the people to perform them*
- *Lead and develop motivated employees*
- *Control resources and work activities*
- *Communicate with others*
- *Humanistically handle employees*
- *Use appropriate techniques of management*

- *Simplify work activities*
- *Develop and manage budgets*
- *Use computers and management information*
- *Develop constructive attitudes and ethical behavior*

This book discusses all these manager action areas. They are matters of concern at all levels of management. Lower-level managers are especially involved in understanding and being able to handle these diversified management actions. Supervisors are the backbone of any organization because they are responsible for getting things accomplished through the workers. They also are the largest group of people engaged in management.

THE WRONG CONCEPT

Our concept of supervisory management must *not* consider the first-level supervisor as being in a world of his or her own (see Figure 1-1). There must *not* be a gap separating the work activities of the first-level supervisor from those of managers at other levels. Some management students seem to have developed a false concept of supervisory management—that considers the supervisor a low-level manager whose primary concern is hiring, training, monitoring, and evaluating subordinates. This may have been true in the past, but it will not meet today's challenges. For one thing, the guidelines for effective supervision apply to all managers—not just the first-level supervisor. Second, super-

FIGURE 1-1 The wrong concept

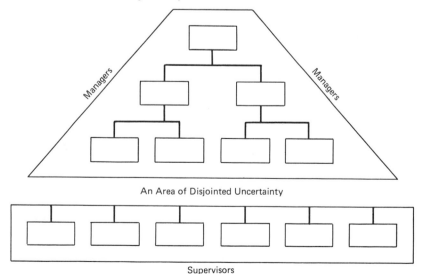

An Area of Disjointed Uncertainty

Supervisors

visory management includes much more than just handling the organizational behavior of people.

THE RIGHT CONCEPT

Supervisors should be part of an integrated management team (see Figure 1-2). The team should be an interconnected group of managers from the top to the bottom of the organization. In addition to handling the interpersonal concerns and many financial and other matters involved in supervision, the supervisor needs to know how management functions at the intermediate and top levels. For example, better use of the organization's limited resources is usually achieved when the supervisor understands how his or her decisions on budget matters affect the total corporate financial plan. Another example is that using computers, developing systems of operational control, and establishing information systems are usually more effective when there is input and understanding at all levels of management.

The first-level supervisor should be as knowledgeable as possible about what's going on in the organization because in the eyes of the workers, their supervisor represents *the management.* Awareness of what is going on throughout the total organization can have two very beneficial spinoffs:

1. Development of capabilities that will enable you to satisfy many of the organizational inquiries of your subordinates
2. Gaining learning experiences that you can apply to enable yourself to become more effective as a manager.

FIGURE 1-2   The right concept

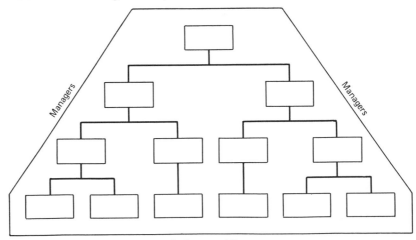

An Integrated Team

LEARNING THE FUNDAMENTALS OF MANAGEMENT

THE IDEALISTIC SUPERVISOR

The idealistic, but realistic, supervisor believes in (1) understanding how the entire corporate structure fits together; (2) knowing the basics of how to plan, organize, direct, and control the achievement of work objectives; and (3) developing the ability to perform in a higher-level managerial position. To achieve these goals, the supervisor must visualize the process of management in both its horizontal and vertical functioning.

THE LITTLE COMPANY THAT DIDN'T MAKE IT

• *UNDERSTANDING THE CORPORATE STRUCTURE*—The management troubles of the former CZI are a good example of the broad scope of things that must be managed in even a very small company. Chuck Zotter, the owner and manager of CZI, was a brilliant individual with many talents, particularly in the field of electronics. As will be seen, he was not very knowledgeable in business management.

In the mid-1970s Zotter applied his engineering talents designing and selling various unique items for a family operated arts and crafts store. Zotter, however, liked to be independent so he established his own little company and incorporated it under the name CZI. In his own company, he started designing electronic items that enabled television stations to present innovative commercial advertisements for their customers. After receiving encouragement for his little business from talking with the manager of a local television station, Zotter borrowed $50,000 to set up his operations. He used these capital funds to obtain tools and equipment, to purchase on-the-market standard electronic components, and to rent office and workshop space.

Within a year after Zotter established his little company, he found himself in deep trouble. The major problem was caused by a technological breakthrough in complex integrated circuits that made most of his purchased parts obsolete. Faced with designing products with his obsolete parts, Zotter found he was unable to sell his work because competitors could build a more sophisticated product at a lower cost. With his back to the wall in product design problems, Zotter had no time to market what he did produce. In June 1983, CZI ran out of cash, was deeply in debt, and Chuck Zotter was an unemployed genius.

The CZI case reflects the fact that there are many complex factors that must be carefully managed in any business undertaking. It sometimes only takes one mistake or misjudgment to cause a potential success to become a failure.

FIGURE 1-3   The corporate management umbrella

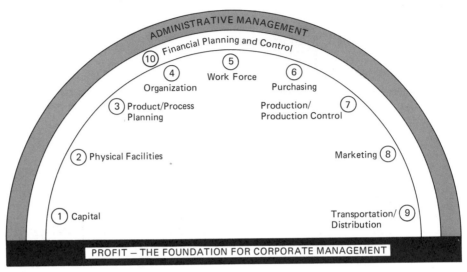

MANY FUNCTIONS MUST BE MANAGED

• *MANAGEMENT IN AN INDUSTRIAL ESTABLISHMENT*—There are
many basic activities that must be effectively managed to succeed in a business
undertaking. The ten basic factors that seem to be the most important in contributing to profit are shown in Figure 1-3. Each of these factors is described in
the paragraphs that follow.

  1.   *CAPITAL*—Cash investment is necessary to establish and operate any
business. Someone must be encouraged to invest money with the expectation
that the business will be financially successful and return dividends. Obtaining
capital requires careful planning; once obtained it must be economically managed and controlled. The case of CZI is a good example of poor management
of capital investment.
  2.   *PHYSICAL FACILITIES*—Most business establishments require some
physical facilities in order to conduct their activities. Facilities such as land,
building, and equipment must be leased or purchased with investors' money.
The obtaining, utilization, and control of physical facilities requires the most
prudent type of management because of the large amounts of money in-

volved. Economic analysis of alternatives to rent or buy, cost analysis of alternative uses of facilities, maintenance, and determination of return on investment are but four of many aspects in the management of facilities.

3. *PRODUCT AND PROCESS PLANNING*—The purpose of a business establishment is to provide a product or service. Management must determine what will be produced and the process by which it will be made. If a product will be produced, it must be designed at a cost that will be acceptable to the consumer. During product design, there must be planning and control of the physical facilities, materials, functions, procedures, work force, and other factors that will be involved in the subsequent production of the product. Process planning must determine the best way to produce the product. If a product cannot be produced at a price attractive to potential customers, this is the same as a failure in product design. CZI is a good example of what can happen when design of a product falls behind the technological state of the art.

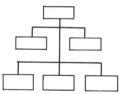

4. *ORGANIZATION*—Organization means defining who is responsible for performing each and every necessary function in producing a product or service in accordance with a process plan. Without organization, few things get accomplished. Ineffectiveness and inefficiency are generally the result when managers fail to organize properly.

5. *WORK FORCE*—An organization without people accomplishes nothing. A trained work force is one of the most vital economic resources in producing a designed product or service. The procurement, development, and

maintenance of personnel are among the most important functions in management. Good humanistic relations are a key factor in the achievement of work output.

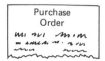

6. *PURCHASING*—The purchasing function is necessary to procure the materials, supplies, equipment, and support services required for the work force to produce a designed product or service. Management must plan and control purchasing so that the right things, in the right quantities, are at the right places, at the right time, and at the right costs. CZI is a good example of what can happen when too many of the wrong things are purchased at the wrong time.

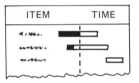

7. *PRODUCTION AND PRODUCTION CONTROL*—A product or service will usually be neither effectively nor efficiently produced unless there is planning and control over its production. Production is the function of providing a designed product or service. Production control is the function of regulating production operations so as to provide the designed product or service in accordance with the process plan or schedule and at the lowest possible cost. It takes management planning, organizing, directing, and controlling to achieve an effective and efficient production of products or services.

8. *MARKETING*—The marketing function is needed to develop customers for a designed product or service and to sell it for a profit. Marketing requires that management coordinate with other vital factors in the corporate structure. Marketing, for example, cannot be performed in isolation from such functions as product and process planning, purchasing, production and production control, and transportation and distribution. It takes good management to plan, organize, direct, control, and coordinate the many functions necessary to successfully market a product or service.

9.   *TRANSPORTATION AND DISTRIBUTION*—It is management's responsibility to plan, direct, and control the transportation and distribution
functions so the product or service gets to the customer when the customer
wants it.

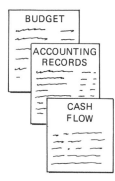

10.   *FINANCIAL PLANNING AND CONTROL*—If a product is to be
produced and sold at a profit, there must be financial planning and control
throughout its entire life-cycle. Every factor shown in Figure 1-3 requires financial management. Lose sight of financial planning and control and you may
lose the entire establishment, as did CZI.

11.   ADMINISTRATIVE MANAGEMENT—Just as an orchestra without
a director generally doesn't play well, a business establishment without effective management cannot function successfully. There must be managers responsible for planning, organizing, directing, and controlling each and every
function in the establishment. Someone must coordinate and integrate the activities of the work force in using the resources to produce and market a product or service, with a financial return to the investors. Administrative management (shown at the top of Figure 1-3) involves the coordination of many
forces, some of which tend to move in opposite directions.

The best organizations know the importance of having all their managers work as a team. This means getting all levels of management involved in such matters as the management of information, work simplification, quality control, and money resources. For team management to be successful, the first-level supervisor must understand the importance of functions and activities beyond those in his or her own organization.

LEARNING THE FUNDAMENTALS

● *UNDERSTANDING THE FUNDAMENTALS OF MANAGEMENT*—The accomplishment of any organization's goals requires managers who know how to plan and organize things and then direct and control the execution of their plans. The steps necessary to develop a plan, to set up an organization, or to establish a system of control are fundamentals of management that pertain to all managers. The principles of how to properly organize work activities and effectively motivate people are also fundamentals of management that concern all managers. It is very important to understand the fundamentals of management and how they apply to managers at different levels in the organization. A very troublesome problem in management occurs when lower-level managers do not understand how management works at the higher levels. The usual result of this is *talking about management teamwork but never achieving it.*

APPLYING THE FUNDAMENTALS

Many of the most important fundamentals of management are discussed in Chapters 2 and 3. In applying these fundamentals in the real world, the supervisor should keep in mind that management is a coordinated and integrated process with many interacting variables. If we were to graphically show the administrative role of a manager it would look similar to the one in Figure 1-4. Every aspect of management revolves around communication and coordination. The arrows in the figure should serve as a reminder that no single phase of management can function in isolation from other aspects.

HUMANISTIC RELATIONS

As we continue to analyze Figure 1-4, notice that the performance of each management function interacts with humanistic relations. Very little planning, for example, can be accomplished without affecting people. Any organizational change has a direct impact on the individuals involved. Some changes can cause people to lose their jobs. The methods employed in directing people can affect the rights, liberty, welfare, and other values that are important to peo-

FIGURE 1-4 The administrative role of a manager

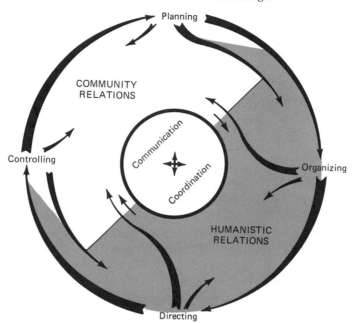

ple. Controlling progress toward achieving work objectives can result in corrective instructions to workers or even disciplinary action. There are very few actions that a manager takes that do not have an impact on people.

COMMUNITY RELATIONS

Community relations are also affected by management decisions. Many companies encourage their managers to give an increasing proportion of their time to community matters—this results in good public relations for the company. Favorable public opinion can have a positive impact on sales of the company's products or services. It can make it easier for the company to employ workers from the community when it is known as a good place to work. The supervisory methods of handling workers is one of the many factors that contribute to establishing a company as a good employer. *People do talk about their supervisor's management practices.*

COMMUNICATION AND COORDINATION

The interrelationships between the four basic functions of management and their interaction on humanistic relations and community relations indicate that the whole management process depends upon effective communication and coordination. The first-level supervisor plays a key role in coordination because it is at this level of management that there is most apt to be a narrow view taken of the whole operation.

THE ROLES OF A MANAGER

MANAGERS ARE NOT REGULATED

A manager must perform many roles beside handling the basic management fundamentals. If you observe how most managers spend their time, you may find it difficult to correlate what they do that relates to the basic functions of management. According to Henry Mintzberg in a 1975 issue of the *Harvard Business Review,* no study of managers has found a standard pattern in the way managers schedule their time. They seem to jump from issue to issue, continually responding to the needs of the moment. The conclusions of Mintzberg's study appear to be true at all levels of management.[1]

The work pace for both chief executives and foremen is unrelenting because of the diversity and frequency of demands placed on them. Many managers simply respond to the pressures of their jobs by working long hours every day. These pressures include attending to scheduled and unscheduled meetings and telephone conversations, participating in ceremonies, seeing important people, settling disputes, getting information, and processing mail.

A MANAGER MUST BE ABLE TO DO MANY THINGS

Managers must play many roles. Good managers are both *analytical* and *conceptual thinkers.* They must be able to analyze and interrelate situations in terms of their constituent elements. This means thinking things through and coming up with workable solutions to specific problems. They must also be able to evaluate things conceptually—in the abstract—and see how all the pieces of the puzzle should fit together. Managers must be *diplomats* in knowing what to say or do to avoid giving offense in dealing with difficult or sensitive situations. It is also often necessary for a manager to be a *politician.* The role of politician involves building supportive alliances and being able to use friendly techniques of persuasion and compromise.

Mintzberg, in the previously mentioned article, comes very close to describing the roles of a manager that are sometimes difficult to relate to the basic functions of management. He identifies ten roles or organized sets of behavior identified with a manager's position.[2] Three of these are identified as interpersonal roles arising directly from the formal authority of the manager. These interpersonal contacts with subordinates, peers, and others tend to give a manager a set of three informational roles. The interpersonal and informational roles of a manager, in turn, provide basic input to a set of four decisional roles. The ten managerial roles are listed below:

INTERPERSONAL ROLES
- *Figurehead role (ceremonial)*
- *Leader role (motivator)*
- *Liaison role (relations with peers and others)*

INFORMATIONAL ROLES
- *Monitor role (solicitor of information)*
- *Disseminator role (sharer of information)*
- *Spokesman role (informer)*

DECISIONAL ROLES
- *Entrepreneur (innovator)*
- *Disturbance handler (responds to trouble)*
- *Resource allocator (decides who gets what)*
- *Negotiator (resolves disputes)*

These ten roles are a good description of how most managers spend much of their time. The emphasis given to a specific role tends to be related to the nature of the manager's functional responsibilities and level of management. For example, staff managers (those who provide services to others) spend much of their time in the informational roles because obtaining, coordinating, and disseminating information are primary staff functions.

The figurehead or ceremonial role of managers is prevalent at the higher levels of management. It is the role of "being seen" at various company and community events as the "official representative" of the establishment. However, at all levels managers may be the figurehead in such events as employee awards and other ceremonial occasions.

Communication and coordination with others are vital in the performance of a manager's interpersonal and informational roles. Employees at all levels—managers and workers alike—appreciate being kept informed of what is going on that affects them.

The decisional roles of a manager are the areas of management that separate good managers from mediocre ones. The most effective manager is constantly looking for new ways to improve things. It often is not easy to change the status quo. It also is not easy to be firm and consistent while at the same time being unbiased and considerate in responding to disturbances in the workplace and in negotiating settlements. Lastly, there are rarely, if ever, enough resources (money, people, facilities, and time) to do everything in the workplace. Therefore the manager must decide upon fair and equitable allocation of resources to those individuals, subunits, projects, programs, and/or functional activities that need them. This is a very difficult role to perform to the satisfaction of everyone.

In most management situations today the typical manager spends a considerable amount of time in interpersonal, informational, and decisional roles. More time is probably spent in these roles than on technical matters.

MANAGEMENT STEPPINGSTONES

MANAGEMENT BUILDING-BLOCK PROCESS

The first-level supervisor who wants to be successful and get ahead should challenge himself or herself to handle the four steppingstones shown in Figure 1-5. The first steppingstone involves having a good knowledge of how to plan, organize, direct, and control the activities of an undertaking. The second steppingstone is communicating and handling humanistic relations effectively to lead and motivate people. It is here that the supervisor links the basic foundations of management to the achievement of productivity through effective interpersonal relations. The third steppingstone requires applying effective management techniques, finding ways to simplify work processes, and exercising control over money resources. These actions are necessary for increased productivity and reduced costs. The fourth step and pinnacle in the management building-block process is attitudinal and ethical behavior. This is very

FIGURE 1-5   The management building-block process

MANAGEMENT STEPPINGSTONES

much a "make-or-break" step in long-term successful management because the manager's attitude is a major factor in style of leadership, humanistic handling of people, and meeting the challenges of tomorrow.

THE THREE Ts IN MANAGEMENT

THINK THINGS THROUGH

The effective manager *thinks things through* before acting. Many supervisors get to where they are through their knowledge, skills, work performance, confidence, and ability to think. Some supervisors, however, are very insecure in their jobs. Behind the appearance of authority and confidence may actually be a scared person—a person who really does not have either faith in themselves or courage to face their responsibilities. Other supervisors look and act like little dictators and think that they can do no wrong. Still others get to where they are by being glib talkers or "apple polishers." Some supervisors allow their emotions—particularly anger, hate, fear—to drive their actions. They may, in their state of instability, act in a hostile or antagonistic way. They may act with vengeance or vendetta. Supervisors who act with a desire for revenge or to antagonize and provoke, have not thought through the consequences of what they are doing. Acting when highly emotional with intentions of hostility or vendetta are not traits of a good manager. These are actions that cause more problems than they solve.

AVOID VENDETTA ACTIONS

The three Ts in management are *Think Things Through*. The first rule to follow in thinking things through is to avoid actions that reflect vendetta or hostility. This means not making decisions when in an unstable or emotional state of mind. Figure 1-6 outlines nine other steps involved in thinking things through. The first positive steps have to do with obtaining and objectively analyzing all the facts of the situation. Since there is often more than one solution to a problem, one should search for and develop the various possible alternatives that will hopefully resolve the situation. After identifying these alternatives, one should evaluate them as to their comparative advantages, disadvantages, costs, and benefits.

After selecting the best potential alternative, the thinking should continue with an evaluation of this alternative's impact on other functions, activities, organizations, worker humanistic relations, community relations, and the total management process. Thinking things through has no place for "tunnel vision"—of only seeing one side of a situation. Thinking things through means not making a final decision until one has accomplished the first nine steps

FIGURE 1-6 Steps in *Thinking Things Through*

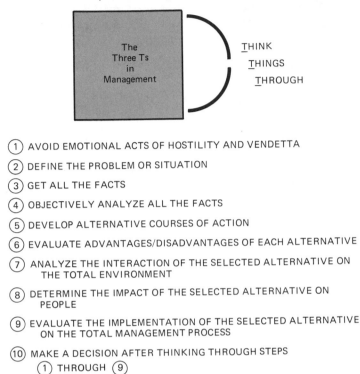

(1) AVOID EMOTIONAL ACTS OF HOSTILITY AND VENDETTA

(2) DEFINE THE PROBLEM OR SITUATION

(3) GET ALL THE FACTS

(4) OBJECTIVELY ANALYZE ALL THE FACTS

(5) DEVELOP ALTERNATIVE COURSES OF ACTION

(6) EVALUATE ADVANTAGES/DISADVANTAGES OF EACH ALTERNATIVE

(7) ANALYZE THE INTERACTION OF THE SELECTED ALTERNATIVE ON THE TOTAL ENVIRONMENT

(8) DETERMINE THE IMPACT OF THE SELECTED ALTERNATIVE ON PEOPLE

(9) EVALUATE THE IMPLEMENTATION OF THE SELECTED ALTERNATIVE ON THE TOTAL MANAGEMENT PROCESS

(10) MAKE A DECISION AFTER THINKING THROUGH STEPS (1) THROUGH (9)

shown in Figure 1-6. Thinking things through involves making certain that the brain is engaged before putting the mouth in gear. As will be seen throughout this entire book, the three Ts apply to every aspect and level of management.

SUMMARY

The attitudes of workers and labor leaders have been undergoing significant changes in recent years. The workers now have certain rights and freedoms not previously available. Various external factors, mostly economic ones, are bringing about a more participative attitude on the part of many labor leaders and managers. These two factors plus the changing composition of the work force present challenging situations in manager-employee relations.

A second major challenge to today's supervisors is the development of a more paternalistic and participative approach to management problem solving and decision making as a means of improving work quality. A third challenge is that of increasing the productivity of the work force so that we can maintain our high standard of living. A fourth challenge, and probably the greatest of all, is to make intelligent use of computer technology in both office and production operations. One of the biggest challenges facing the supervisor of computerized operations is that of adjusting to the breakup of the traditional working relationships among individuals.

Meeting today's challenges in the workplace requires a change in the concept of supervisory management. Most supervisors today must have both an awareness of and the ability to appropriately handle a greater diversity of management actions. This requires the supervisor to (1) understand how the entire corporate structure fits together; (2) know the basic fundamentals of how to plan, organize, direct, and control the achievement of work objectives; and (3) develop the capabilities to perform in a higher-level management position. To be effective on the job, the supervisor must perform many roles, including those of being an analytical and conceptual thinker, a diplomat, a politician, and engaging in various interpersonal, informational, and decisional situations.

Most important of all, the supervisor must *think things through* before acting. These three Ts in management involve making certain that the brain is engaged before putting the mouth in gear.

REVIEW QUESTIONS

1. What changes have occurred in management-employee relations since the mid-1960s and how are they a challenge to management today?

2. Can the Japanese paternalistic and participative approach to management problem solving and decision making work in the United States?

3. What are the challenges of the supervisor in increasing productivity?

4. Why is computerization of work problably the greatest challenge facing managers today?

5. Do you agree or disagree that supervisory management is a part of every manager's job? Why?

6. How can a supervisor realistically become an effective manager?

7. In what ways does supervision revolve around communication and coordination?

8. Describe the process of thinking things through.

A CASE STUDY IN HOW NOT TO MANAGE

From 1980 to 1982 there was considerable personnel turmoil in several New Jersey secondary schools and colleges over employment contracts. Some of the primary factors causing this turmoil were

- Spiralling inflation that had reached the double-digit level
- Increased cost of living that had reached the double-digit level
- Increased school operating costs that had reached the double-digit level
- Policy decisions by government legislators that placed educational cost budget increase restrictions, called "caps," at the single-digit level
- Planning objectives by administrative managers that appeared to give quality education a very low priority and budget cutting a very high priority
- Weak management by some administrative managers that reflected dishonesty and the failure to communicate with employees
- Excessive demands for salary increases and costly fringe benefits by employee associations

One school, in facing these factors, had a complete breakdown in communication between management and employees. The employees, both faculty and supporting personnel, went on strike and the school was closed. The leaders who called the strike arranged to have an organization meeting. There was no planned agenda established for the meeting, which lasted about three hours. During the meeting people were allowed to speak at length without facts. All discussions presented only one side of the issue. Nobody was receptive to taking time to consider alternative actions. Much of the discussion was carried on with a high degree of emotionality because it was directed at personalities rather than facts. No decisions were made. This was due in part to the fact that the group had already made certain vindictive decisions before the meeting and was merely trying to justify its actions.

QUESTIONS

1. What basic management functions were the government legislators performing? What is your evaluation of their performance?
2. What basic management functions were the school administrators performing? What is your evaluation of their performance?

3. What basic management functions were the employee association leaders performing? What is your evaluation of their performance?

4. What factors do you feel contributed the most to the cause of the problem? Why? How well do you think the legislators, administrators, and association leaders applied the three Ts of management? Explain your answer.

NOTES

1. Henry Mintzberg, "The Manager's Job: Folklore and Fact," *Harvard Business Review,* July-August 1975, pp. 49–61. Copyright © 1975 by the President and Fellows of Harvard College; all rights reserved.

2. Ibid., pp. 49–61.

2

Planning Is:
Knowing What To Do
Organizing Is:
Arranging What To Do

The Fundamentals of Planning and Organizing

LEARNING OBJECTIVES

The objectives of this chapter on the fundamentals of planning and organizing are to enable the reader to

1. Describe the following distinct characteristics of the function of management *planning:*
   a. The different types of planning, their characteristics, and their purpose in the management process
   b. The different time spans in planning and their interrelationship
   c. The work efforts involved in the five steps in planning
   d. The elements that can affect the implementation of a plan
   e. The basic guidelines to help achieve effective planning
2. Describe the following significant aspects of the function of *organizing:*
   a. The basic "tools" used in organizing
   b. The line and staff concept and how it functions
   c. The various organization configurations and their use
   d. The basic principles of organizational management and their use
   e. The steps in organizing
   f. The interactions between the employee and the organization
   g. The informal organization and how to cope with it
   h. The management actions that can be taken to improve organization job satisfaction

KEY WORDS

Chain of Command   The hierarchy of supervisors and subordinates.

Delegation   Assigning to others the responsibility and authority for accomplishing work activities.

Departmentalization   Grouping work functions in a systematic and logical way.

Division of Labor   Dividing a work task into specific subtasks so that each person may become more efficient in the performance of his or her job.

Functional Authority   Authority limited to a specific specialized activity or function.

Functions   Work activities to be performed.

Intermediate-Range Planning   Planning for the period of time extending from two to five years beyond the current year.

Job Enlargement   Assigning additional work tasks of the *same level* of responsibility.

Job Enrichment   Assigning additional work tasks of *higher level* of responsibility.

Line Authority   Authority over all work-related activities of subordinates.

Line Organization   An activity that contributes work directly related to the purpose of the organization.

Long-Range Planning   Planning for the period of time extending from two to ten years, or more, beyond the current year.

Matrix Organization   A hybrid organization in which some workers report directly to two supervisors. One is function-oriented and the other project- or task-oriented.

Mission   An organization's reason for existence or main objective for the future.

Objective   The expected goal to be achieved in an organizational undertaking.

Operational Planning   The continuous process of preparing plans, budgets, schedules, and/or forecasts for specific actions on a short-range basis.

Plan   The end product of planning.

Policies   General principles or rules of action for the conduct that managers and employees are expected to follow.

Procedures   The series of steps to follow to accomplish a work activity.

Program Planning   The translation of broad goals of strategic planning into definitive objectives, policies, directives, and work programs to be accomplished within an intermediate-range time schedule.

Short-Range Planning   Planning for the time span of the current year and the next year (the budget year).

Span of Control   The extent of a manager's control: the number of persons who report directly to a manager.

Staff Organization   An activity that contributes work in support of other parts of an organization. Its efforts do *not* contribute directly to the mission or purpose of the organization.

Staff Planning   Providing guidance, instruction, assistance, review, and coordination to the planning efforts of others.

Strategic Planning   Long-range planning by top executives to identify important problems requiring decision for future operations.

Unity of Command   A management principle that each employee should have only one boss.

Unity of Direction   A management principle that each employee should receive only one set of directives from one boss pertaining to the same objective.

A manager's leadership starts with the ability to plan and organize the things that need to be done. Planning, which involves knowing what you want to do and determining how to go about it, is the starting point in management. It is usually quite difficult to intelligently organize, direct, or control anything if there is no plan of action as a guide.

THE FUNCTION OF PLANNING

WHAT IS PLANNING?

LEADERSHIP STARTS WITH PLANNING

As shown in Figure 2-1, planning involves (1) defining the situation, (2) identifying all the actions that must be performed, and (3) determining how the actions should be handled. The end product of planning is a plan—a formulated and orderly method of doing something.

Planning requires thinking things through. Good planning provides the facts for "causative thinking"—thinking that produces an effect or decision, such as choosing the most cost-effective action to take. Poor planning by supervisors can cause worker frustration, dissatisfaction, and low productivity. On the other hand, a well-defined plan of action reflects manager assurance and gives others confidence in performing the tasks to be accomplished. Good planning is essential to the achievement of effectiveness (doing the right things) and efficiency (doing things right). It is a very significant factor in prop-

FIGURE 2-1   The function of planning

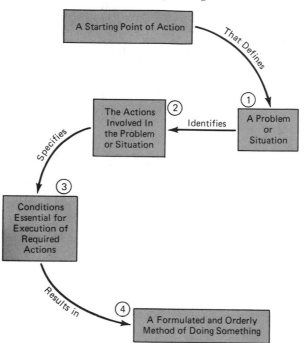

er utilization of people, facilities, materials, and money resources. The planning process helps in minimizing the risks and uncertainities in decision making.

TYPES OF PLANNING

Every manager must do some planning. The type of planning, however, varies considerably at the different levels of management (Figure 2-2). At the top level of management the planning is primarily long-range in time and strategic in scope. At the middle levels of management the planning is primarily intermediate-range in time and program-oriented in scope. At the lower levels of management the planning is mainly short-range in time and operational or functional in scope.

FUTURE LONG-RANGE OBJECTIVES

• *STRATEGIC PLANNING*—Strategic planning is the top executives' long-range plan of action for identifying important problems. It is a continuous and systematic process of making current risk-taking decisions on future courses of action. Strategic planning anticipates the future and is concerned with new

FIGURE 2-2 Characteristics of different types of planning

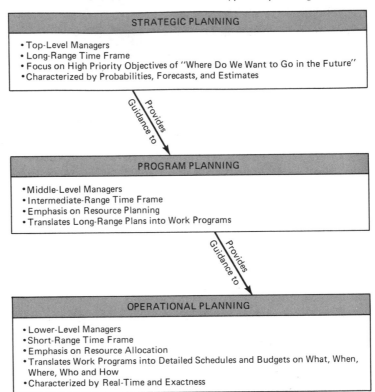

and different businesses, techniques, processes, products, services, markets, and/or concepts of management. The term *strategic* implies that this type of planning covers only those activities, functions, and programs that are of the highest priority.

The nature of strategic planning is highly variable and follows no single course of direction. It usually focuses on one part of the organization rather than on the whole and relies heavily on external information. Strategic planning usually starts with an objective(s) of the business. It then seeks to establish two things:

- *What must be done* now *to attain tomorrow's objectives?*
- *What* new and different *things need to be done to attain tomorrow's objectives?*

Soul-Searching Analysis

The answers to these questions require critical anlaysis of the organization. It means searching for the answers to other questions such as

- *What are the current objectives that need to be changed and why?*
- *What current and/or new products or services should be given priority attention in the future? Are there some current products or services that should be discontinued?*
- *How can current competence be strengthened in the future? In what new areas should competence be developed?*
- *Where can the greatest competition be expected in the future? How should competition be challenged?*
- *What can be done to strengthen relations with current customers and to develop new customers?*
- *Should new business resources be acquired externally or developed internally?*

The primary focal point here is: What direction are we going now and where should we be going in the future?

A PLANNING TRANSLATION AND BRIDGE

- *PROGRAM PLANNING*—Program planning is primarily the middle manager's intermediate-range plan of action. It involves translating the broad strategic planning goals into definitive objectives, policies, directives, and work programs to be accomplished within a specific time schedule. It is a crucial link in the transition of broad long-range goals into detailed courses of action. Program planning provides a bridge between strategic and operational planning.

To visualize how program planning performs a transitioning function, assume that we have a long-range plan to extract essential life-support food and minerals from the bottom of the ocean. The intermediate-range planning would develop the various programs that must be accomplished to achieve the long-range plan. Such a plan would include programs for the following:

- *Design and development of the "mother ship" to take people to the ocean surface worksite and to bring back to land the extracted products.*
- *Design and development of the means of getting workers to the ocean floor and returning extracted products to the "mother ship."*
- *Design and development of a computerized working robot capable of extracting products from the ocean floor.*
- *Development of international laws to clearly define the rights to mine the oceans and to state for whose benefits.*

The function of program planning is to provide a basis for management control. The control aspects include planning for those actions necessary to assure that resources are obtained, allocated, and used both effectively and efficiently in accomplishing strategic objectives. Program planning also includes evaluation of the cost-effectiveness of the alternatives for accomplishing broad strategic goals. Probably the most decisive aspect of program planning lies in the work programs that are developed. When these programs are clearly defined, they provide management with a clear picture of what the program will produce in benefits and what it will cost in resources.

DETERMINING WHAT, WHEN, WHO, WHERE, AND HOW

● *OPERATIONAL PLANNING*—Operational planning is primarily a first-level manager's short-range plan of action. It is a continuous process of preparing plans, budgets, schedules, and/or forecasts for specific commodities, products, projects, programs, or functional activities. Operational planning involves the very specific and detailed determination of *what* must be done, *when* it must or can be done, *who* should do it, *where* it should be done, *how* it should be done, and the *resources* it will take to do it.

An operational plan subdivides a work program into logical work units, assigns tasks to work stations, and defines the flow of work among work stations. Such plans must be coordinated between functional activities and be consistent with the corporate strategic plan. Operational planning deals in real time and exact data. It also involves converting detailed administrative plans into financial terms and requirements for budget formulation and control purposes.

THE TIME SPAN FOR PLANNING

PLANNING IS A CONTINUOUS PROCESS

Two of the more difficult aspects of planning are (1) selecting the proper time span and (2) determining the best type of plan required for a specific task. One of the complicating factors is that planning takes place within a specific but moving period of time. Figure 2-3 shows how planning moves from long range to intermediate range to short range and on out into the future. Because time does not stand still, a long-range plan developed four years ago, for example, must be continuously evaluated and adjusted to meet current and future needs.

PLANNING AND DECISION MAKING

The complexities of the changing environment plus new technological and managerial concepts require organizations to develop long-range as well as short-range plans. A lengthened time span for managerial decisions is necessary to systematically explore the future uncertainties, costs, and risks of alter-

FIGURE 2-3 The time span in planning

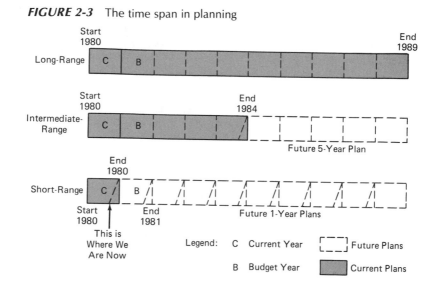

native courses of action open to management. The time span for planning is determined by such factors as

- *The size and diversity of the organization.*
- *The resources of the organization.*
- *The complexity of the organization's programs and operations.*
- *The leadtime required to accomplish programs.*
- *The degree of competition from others.*

STEPS IN PLANNING

START WITH OBJECTIVES

Planning must start with an understanding of the things that should be done (Figure 2-4). This involves knowing the purpose of the organization, the major objectives to be achieved, and the most troublesome problems that might interfere with accomplishing the objectives. The setting of objectives at various levels of management establish the framework for the entire system of planning and, in fact, for the entire management process.

DETERMINE THE CURRENT STATUS

The second step in planning is to determine the current status of things in relation to the desired objectives. In other words, where do we stand right now

FIGURE 2-4   Steps in planning

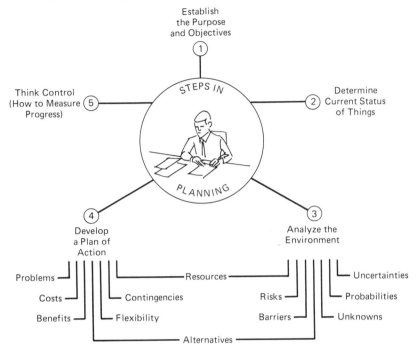

in relation to where we want to go? What are the current facts of the situation? What available resources—facilities, equipment, materials, people, and money—do we have now in relation to what we need? What are the current limitations, such as policies and regulations, that may impede our planning actions? The significance of this step in planning is that before going forward we need to know where we are now.

ANALYZE THE ENVIRONMENT

The third step in planning is to determine how to get from where we are to where we want to go. This step involves identifying the significant factors in both the internal and external environment that can affect our planning. It means analyzing the current situation in relation to the desired objectives. For example, what additional resources are needed? What policies and/or regulations must be changed or prepared? What possible uncertainties and unknown factors may be encountered in the future? What are the probabilities of certain events happening or not happening? What changes can be expected? How can flexibility be injected into planning for the future? What contingency plans should be provided in case uncertainties and unknowns become actual situations? These questions have to be addressed in this third step in planning.

DEVELOP THE PLAN

The fourth step in planning is to develop a plan of action for getting from where we are to where we want to go by using the facts and information obtained in Step 3. This step involves (1) developing alternative courses of action, (2) establishing the beneficial and harmful aspects of each alternative, (3) determining the costs—facilities, equipment, materials, and people—needed to carry out each alternative, and (4) outlining the what, when, where, who, and how of everything that must be done to carry out the selected alternative.

THINK CONTROL

The fifth step in planning is to set up a system for measuring actual accomplishment against what was planned. How can we identify and bring timely attention to troublesome situations before they become major problems? How can we determine the status of costs, time schedules, and quality of performance? This step is important because a plan is usually only as good as our ability to control its implementation.

ELEMENTS AFFECTING THE SUCCESS OF A PLAN

PLANNING REQUIRES CAREFUL ATTENTION TO MANY THINGS

In developing a plan, the manager must consider many elements that affect its successful implementation. These elements are not necessarily within the plan itself. As an example, take the element of "morale." This element is not contained within the contents of a plan. However, if for some reason there is low morale on the part of the people who have to implement the plan, things may not get done.

Particularly in operational planning, managers should determine the status of the following essential elements that can affect the success of a plan:

- OBJECTIVES—*Objectives identify intention to accomplish something. They are the foundation on which the plan is based.*
- POLICIES—*Policies are the principles and general guidelines for achieving objectives. They are general rules of action that tend to contribute significantly to the image of the organization.*

- PROCEDURES—*Procedures establish the series of steps that must be followed one after the other in the accomplishment of an objective.*
- FUNCTIONS—*Functions identify the kind of actions, activities, or phases of work required to accomplish an objective.*
- ORGANIZATION STRUCTURE—*Organization structure is the identity and grouping of functional relationships in such a way as to enable people to best accomplish tasks.*
- PHYSICAL FACTORS—*Physical factors are capital facilities, equipment, and materials required to accomplish functional activities.*
- HUMAN FACULTIES—*Human faculties are the skills and knowledge of people required to accomplish an objective.*
- CONTROL—*Control is the management process of determining progress, deviations, and corrective action to ensure that plans are being carried out. A good plan provides for its means of control.*
- BUSINESS IDEALS—*Business ideals establish the ethical criteria or rules of conduct relating to human actions. Ethics pertain to the rightness or wrongness of certain actions as well as the motives and ends of such actions. Long-term and lasting plans reflect high moral principles and values.*
- EXECUTIVE LEADERSHIP—*Executive leadership is the stimulation and direction of the work force in the accomplishment or execution of a plan. A plan, therefore, should identify who is responsible for providing the leadership to motivate and direct the work force.*
- MORALE—*Morale reflects the mental attitude of the people involved in carrying out a plan. If the morale is low, it is very likely that worker output will be lower, error rate will be higher, performance costs will be higher, and waste will be greater. Realistic planning cannot ignore the morale of the people who are to carry out a plan.*

A GUIDE FOR EFFECTIVE PLANNING

PLANNING IS RARELY PERFECT

One of the main things to remember in planning is to recognize that no planning method can forecast the future with absolute certainty. Futhermore, no decisions for action can be expected to always achieve every aimed-for result. A manager must be willing to accept that sometimes the formal long-range planning process may not pay off. It may even be disruptive and harmful. Effective planning for the future is an extremely difficult task.

For an organization to succeed and to stay ahead, particularly in uncertain and inflationary times, it must plan. The following are some basic guidelines that can help in the achievement of effective plans.

- *Define the mission of the undertaking in clear, understandable, and specific terms to provide purpose and direction for the people involved in the plan.*

- *Develop specific objectives so that people know exactly what the organization is going to do and then assign responsibility for achieving the objectives.*
- *Develop both long-range and short-range plans with a step-by-step approach as to how objectives are to be achieved.*
- *Develop plans on a participative basis wherever possible.*
- *Establish alternative ways of achieving objectives and seek to determine the least costly and most effective or beneficial one.*
- *Consider the principal elements that can affect the implementation of plans and provide for their inclusion.*
- *Identify potential barriers in resource limitations, uncertainties such as changes in the economy, and problems that may be encountered in the implementation of plans. Provide for alternative or contingency plans to handle barriers that may occur.*
- *Avoid unnecessary details and schedules in the plan. Identify and focus on the most significant aspects of the plan. If you get a "handle" on the things that "drive" the plan, you usually don't have to worry about the details that won't have much impact one way or the other on the plan.*
- *Coordinate the plan with all organizations and key individuals that are involved in its implementation.*
- *Establish how to measure progress and control implementation of the plan. Keep in mind that precise and measurable goals make it easier for subordinates to develop their own plans.*
- *Provide for flexibility and changes.*

PLAN FOR BOTH TODAY AND TOMORROW

Planning has an impact on the entire management process as well as being a key factor in establishing a manager's leadership image. Good planning results from following the basic steps of planning, analyzing the various elements that can affect implementation of plans, and planning for tomorrow as well as today.

THE FUNCTION OF ORGANIZING

WHAT WOULD YOU HAVE DONE?

THE CORPORATE APPROACH

A large corporation was awarded a multimillion-dollar contract to produce a highly complex piece of equipment for one of the military services. The strategic importance of the equipment was of such magnitude that it was necessary to give it significant management attention throughout the entire corporation, so the company created a project manager. The project manager was assigned responsibility for overseeing all actions relatable to the new military equipment. With this responsibility the project manager was given full line authority to act and make decisions.

One of the first major problems that the company had to resolve was that of organizing itself to provide the management attention needed to produce the equipment on time and within the contract's budget. In order to minimize organizational and personnel turbulence, the company put the new project manager into the existing organization structure. This was accomplished by setting the project manager up as a top-level equipment-oriented organization. The chief operating executive then directed all functional organizations to assign "dedicated" employees to work for the project manager. For example, the program director in charge of staff planning and control was required to assign a given number of staff planners, budget analysts, and cost analysts to work full time for the project manager. However, control over their promotions and numbers remained with the program director because they were still part of his organization. This policy enabled the company to keep both personnel strength and salaries from getting out of hand. It also provided for an orderly transition of personnel to and from the project manager in accordance with workload demands.

The Military Approach

The military service responsible for the life-cycle management—development, procurement, production, supply, and maintenance—of the new equipment also established a project manager. However, the military service did not superimpose him within the existing organization structure. A separate, independent, and almost totally self-contained project manager organization was established. It functioned like a subsidiary corporation with its own engineering, procurement, supply, maintenance, and supporting staff operations. The staffing of the new organization came primarily from existing functional organizations. The director of planning, for example, found many of his staff planners, budget analysts, and cost analysts transferred to the project manager organization because of the offer of or opportunity for promotions.

Several years later, when the project was successfully completed, the corporation was able to readjust its work force with a minimum of organizational and personnel turmoil. The military service, however, had to undergo a "reduction in force," reduce the salaries of many employees, and incur other personnel turbulence in order to readjust its work force.

This case is one that involves the same problem situation, but with two different organizational approaches taken in its handling. What approach would you have taken? Did your analysis of this case give you insight on the importance of the function of organizing?

WHAT IS ORGANIZING?

ORGANIZING INVOLVES WORK ACTIVITIES AND PEOPLE

The function of organizing involves the orderly and logical arrangement of work activities and the effective assignment of people in the accomplishment of work objectives. It is simply the process of arranging responsibilities so that everyone knows "who does what." Good organization is important to effective management because it

- *Defines workers' responsibilities, authority, and accountability*
- *Facilitates coordination of functional activities by defining and grouping relatable functions in the same organization*
- *Avoids duplication of work efforts*
- *Reduces confusion in the accomplishment of an objective*
- *Reduces friction and tension among the workers and thereby generates better morale*
- *Facilitates training of employees*
- *Reduces the likelihood of overlooking important projects and deadlines*
- *Contributes to worker job satisfaction by reducing uncertainity in the workplace*

THE RAILROAD THAT COULD

Good organizational planning can be a significant factor in business success. A good example is the Union Pacific Railroad's organizational planning. In the 1970s the Union Pacific Railroad had become a highly diversified and profitable company without a huge debt. It achieved its diversification without diluting the stockholders' equity in the business and without the helter-skelter acquiring of other business interests that caused grief with so many other conglomerates. Good sound management decisons appear to have been the key to their success in a time when practically all U.S. railroads were in serious trouble.

GOOD ORGANIZATION PHILOSOPHY

One of the actions taken by the Union Pacific was to properly organize itself into three major operational parts: railroad, energy, and land operations. In expanding their operations in each of these areas, the company adopted a partner philosophy that they could develop their business faster and make greater profits by "joining hands" with others than by attempting to do things alone. Union Pacific granted leases and moved into a joint venture with Stauffer

Chemical for the development of the Union Pacific's huge reserves of trona (a rocklike substance used for making glass and detergents). They joined up with Mono Power Company, a subsidiary of Southern California Edison, in the production of uranium. Union Pacific teamed up with the Standard Oil Company of Indiana in the drilling and production of oil and gas. The railroad also went into coal mining which paid off twice—once in mining its billions of tons of coal, and secondly in transporting the coal over its rail lines.

Good Operating Philosophy

The Union Pacific also exercised good management discretion in investing money to keep its rolling stock and equipment in excellent physical condition. This had greatly improved the efficiency of its railroad operations. Last, and most important, the Union Pacific Railroad's management group made an early decision to not enter into any business expansion unless they knew something about it and unless it fitted into their operations. The Union Pacific appears to have done a good job in establishing (1) the objectives it wanted to achieve, (2) the policies to guide the organization in accomplishing its objectives, and (3) the organization structure to achieve its objectives.[1]

BASIC "TOOLS" USED IN ORGANIZING

Organizing Involves Documentation

The three basic management "tools" used in organization planning are: (1) organization charts, (2) job descriptions, and (3) organization manuals (Figure 2-5).
 • *ORGANIZATION CHARTS*—An organization chart is a diagram of the hierarchy or chain of command of management officials. Properly constructed, an organization chart with its boxes, solid lines, and titles can provide the following useful management information (Figure 2-6):

1. *DIVISION OF WORK*—Each box on the chart represents a subunit responsible for performing certain specific functions.
2. *CHAIN OF COMMAND*—The solid lines on the chart indicate who reports to whom (upward) in the hierarchy.
3. *TYPE OF WORK PERFORMED*—Descriptive organizational titles within the chart's boxes indicate the broad functional responsibilities of each subunit.
4. *GROUPING OF WORK*—The organizational titles within the boxes on the chart indicate how the organization is set up (e.g., by functions, products, processes, geographical areas, or other patterns).
5. *LEVELS OF MANAGEMENT*—The organization chart, by its structure, indicates the top, middle, and lower levels of management.

FIGURE 2-5 Basic "tools" used in organizing

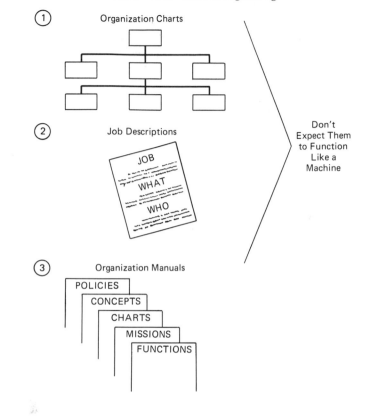

ORGANIZATION CHARTS HAVE LIMITATIONS

Although important as a guide for helping people visualize the parts and patterns of the organization, an organization chart has significant limitations. One limitation is that each person's interpretation of the chart may vary according to his or her assumptions on the meaning of the titles and short descriptions. A second limitation is that the chart cannot reflect the comparative importance of each part of the organization. A third limitation is that the chart cannot show the functional interrelationships between parts of the organization, such as the involvement of the purchasing manager with the production manager. A fourth limitation is that a chart cannot show the content of responsibility allocated to a given position, nor can it show "shared responsibilities" between parts of the organization.

Because of its limitations, the organization chart should be supported with (a) clearly defined mission and functional narrative statements, (b) written concepts of management that define functional interrelationships, and (c) good job descriptions.

FIGURE 2-6 Organization chart

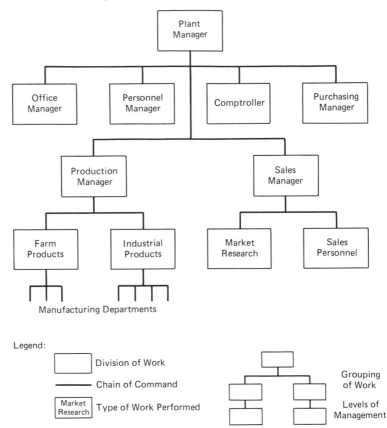

- *JOB DESCRIPTIONS*—A job description is a statement of the objectives of a position in terms of (a) responsibilities, (b) authority, (c) accountability, (d) relationships to subordinates and superiors, and (e) standards of job performance. Job descriptions are guidelines that instruct employees what to do on their jobs.

- *ORGANIZATION MANUALS*—An organization manual is a handbook of significant items of information pertaining to organizational operations. There is no standard table of contents or structure for an organization manual. As a general practice, a good organization manual contains (a) organization-wide standing policies, (b) broad concepts of operational management, (c) organization charts, (d) statements of purpose, and (e) functional statements for all major organizational units.

One should not expect organization charts, job descriptions, and organization manuals to function like machines. Even with many rules and a formal organization hierarchy of functions and managers, how people respond with an organization is affected by many factors. These factors include employee personal apathy, manager favoritism, attitude regarding acceptance of objectives, interpretation of instructions, personal relationships with others, motivation, leadership, problems with semantics, and allotted performance time.

LINE AND STAFF RELATIONSHIPS

The distinction between line and staff organizational units and their respective authorities is a cause of considerable administrative confusion in management. It is important, therefore, to define the line-staff concept and point out how it can be flexible.

LINE ORGANIZATIONS ACCOMPLISH THE OBJECTIVES

- *LINE ORGANIZATION*—A line organizational unit is an activity that contributes directly to the purpose of the total organization. The statement of objectives of an organizational unit defines the purpose and major work activities required for its accomplishment. The organizational elements directly engaged in performing these activities are referred to as *line organizations.*

    There is flexibility in determining whether or not an organization is a line element. For example, in an organization with an objective of manufacturing and selling products, the major line organizations would include the production operations and the sales department. In a retail establishment, the line organizations would include the buying, selling, and distribution functions. In a research laboratory, scientific investigation and engineering development would be line activities. As one can readily see, there is no universal pattern for identifying line organizations. It depends on whether the organization's work activities contribute directly to the purpose of the organization.

STAFF ORGANIZATIONS SUPPORT THE OBJECTIVES

- *STAFF ORGANIZATION*—Staff organizational units do *not* contribute directly to the purpose of the total organization. They exist to offer advice, assistance, support, and to serve other organizations in accomplishing the objective of the total corporation. Staff members should assist, not direct, line personnel. There are many specialized staff organizations. They include such activities as: accounting, cost analysis, maintenance, legal services, personnel management, planning assistance, safety, security, statistical analysis, and other supporting services. The primary tasks of staff personnel are to guide, assist, advise, serve, coordinate, consolidate, and evaluate the specialized functions for which they are responsible on an organization-wide basis.

LINE AUTHORITY EXISTS IN ALL ORGANIZATIONS

• *LINE AUTHORITY*—Line authority is the exercise of direction over all work-related activities of subordinates. Line authority exists within each and every organization, whether line or staff. The controller, for example, is a staff manager who exercises line authority over the budgeting, accounting, auditing, and other subunits of the controller organization. To the controller, budgeting, accounting, and auditing are line functions because they contribute directly to the controller's financial management objectives. The controller directs the work of these functional subunits with line authority. To others outside the controller, budgeting, accounting, and auditing are staff functions because they do not contribute directly to the objectives of the outside organizations. The controller exercises functional authority in performing these staff functions with other organizations.

FUNCTIONAL AUTHORITY IS LIMITED

• *FUNCTIONAL AUTHORITY*—The increasing size of organizations and the rapidly changing environment impose significant problems on human capabilities for work and knowledge on the part of line managers. The line manager is usually so occupied with day-to-day operating problems that there is little time for the many staff functions that are also necessary to get jobs accomplished. As the result of these pressures on the line manager, the role of staff, as strictly advisory, has changed radically. In most large organizations today, a limited command authority called "functional authority" has been given to staff managers. Functional authority is command authority *limited* to a particular activity or function rather than general authority over the operations of an organization. The functional authority cuts across departmental lines to govern a specified staff activity wherever it may be found. Following are examples of functional authority:

1. The chief accountant in the corporation home office prescribes certain accounting procedures to be followed throughout the entire company in all plants and departments.
2. The chief maintenance engineer sets certain specifications and standards to be met in various steps of a manufacturing process.
3. The personnel department prescribes the methods for on-the-job training of all new employees.

LINE AND STAFF MUST WORK TOGETHER

• *TEAMWORK*—Line managers have line authority for tasks that contribute directly to the purpose of the organization. Staff managers have functional authority for the specialized tasks that support line managers in accomplishing their activities. It takes both line and staff managers working together as a

FIGURE 2-7 Line and staff relationships

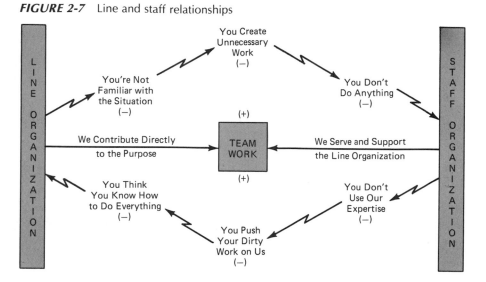

team to have a successfully functioning total organization. As indicated in Figure 2-7, many line and staff managers spend considerable time complaining about one another. The problem is generally caused by a lack of understanding of the respective roles played by both types of managers in the achievement of corporate objectives. The problem can be resolved through mutual understanding and appreciation of each other's purpose in the total organization.

IS THE LINE AND STAFF CONCEPT OBSOLETE?

In many ways the line-staff concept has become obsolete since the time many years ago when it was developed and used by military organizations. It is often difficult to define whether or not an organization is contributing directly or indirectly to the accomplishment of the mission of the establishment. Much more important than determining whether a certain function is line or staff, is to develop explicit written purpose and function statements that clearly define the responsibilities and authority of each organizational element.

ORGANIZATION CONFIGURATION

THERE IS NO ONE BEST WAY TO ORGANIZE

There are many different configurations for reflecting the parts of an organization. The various ways that the subunits of an organization can be formally structured depends upon the type, scope, and size of the establishment. Generally speaking, most organizations are structured in one of three major ways:

1. By functions
2. By divisions:
   ● by project
   ● by product
   ● by geographical area
   ● by customer
   ● by process
   ● by type of equipment
3. By functions and divisions (the matrix organization)

Within either functional or divisional organizations there can be organization by time sequence of operations, by account number, by type of performance incidence, by number of persons per organizational unit, or by some other logical subdivision.

ORGANIZATION BY FUNCTIONS

● *FUNCTIONAL STRUCTURE*—Organization by functions brings together in one department all those work-force elements engaged in one activity or several related activities. As indicated in Figure 2-8, examples of functional organizations are the sales department, the purchasing department, and the maintenance department.

FIGURE 2-8   Organization by function

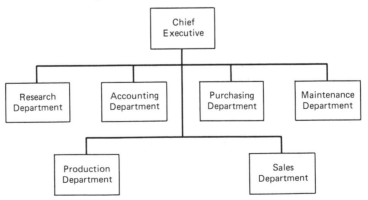

ORGANIZATION BY DIVISIONS

• *DIVISIONAL STRUCTURE*—Organization by divisions is generally found where there is considerable diversity of products, processes, services, or highly critical and/or costly operations involved. Divisional organizations are, to a considerable extent, self-contained and self-supporting. Each division usually has direct responsibility and authority for most of the line and staff functions necessary for it to conduct its operations. Divisional organizations are sometimes semiautonomous such as the Plymouth, Dodge, and Chrysler divisions of the Chrysler Corporation. Each division to a very large extent designs, produces, and markets its own products.

The divisional structure has many different patterns of organization. Some of these organizational patterns are illustrated in Figure 2-9 and briefly described here:

- Organization by project *occurs where a project manager is assigned responsibility and authority for the management of all activities necessary to develop and/or produce a major item of equipment. A project manager may also be assigned the task of managing the construction of a major physical structure.*
- Organization by product *occurs where a product manager is assigned responsibility and authority for producing a specific product or family of products. The primary distinction between a product manager and a project manager is that the latter is responsible for a more important and usually higher-risk/higher-cost item.*
- Organization by geographical area *occurs where a division is given responsibility and authority for all activities in a specified region or territory, such as southeastern United States.*
- Organization by type of customer *occurs where a division is given responsibility and authority for all activities pertaining to a particular class of customers, such as government agencies, industrial firms, or retail consumers.*
- Organization by process *occurs where a division is given responsibility and authority for a specific manufacturing operation, such as spinning, weaving, or printing in a textile company.*
- Organization by equipment *occurs where a division is given responsibility and authority for producing a final product that involves a specific type of equipment, such as the coke plant of a steel company.*

TWO-DIMENSIONAL ORGANIZATION

• *MATRIX STRUCTURE*—The matrix organization structure, as shown in Figure 2-10, is a two-dimensional combination of functional and divisional management. The most common type of matrix organization involves the establishment of a project manager to manage a significantly important item *within* an existing basically functional organization.

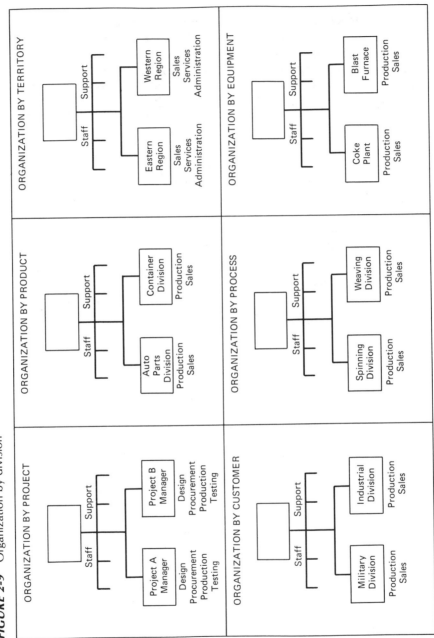

FIGURE 2-9   Organization by division

ORGANIZATION BY PROJECT

Staff   Support

Project A Manager
Design
Procurement
Production
Testing

Project B Manager
Design
Procurement
Production
Testing

ORGANIZATION BY PRODUCT

Staff   Support

Auto Parts Division
Production
Sales

Container Division
Production
Sales

ORGANIZATION BY TERRITORY

Staff   Support

Eastern Region
Sales
Services
Administration

Western Region
Sales
Services
Administration

ORGANIZATION BY CUSTOMER

Staff   Support

Military Division
Production
Sales

Industrial Division
Production
Sales

ORGANIZATION BY PROCESS

Staff   Support

Spinning Division
Production
Sales

Weaving Division
Production
Sales

ORGANIZATION BY EQUIPMENT

Staff   Support

Coke Plant
Production
Sales

Blast Furnace
Production
Sales

FIGURE 2-10 The matrix organization

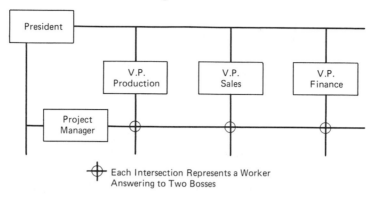

A matrix organization is a hybrid one in which some workers report directly to two superiors (see Figure 2-11). In engineering development, for example, the dotted line in the figure shows that there is a group of workers who are assigned to give dedicated support to the project manager—who is *one* of their bosses. Also notice that these workers still have their parent organization boss, the director of engineering development, who is their second boss. In the matrix organization it is not uncommon for workers to receive contradictory directions from their two bosses. The matrix organization obviously violates the organizational principle of unity of command—that a worker should have

FIGURE 2-11 A functional and project manager organization

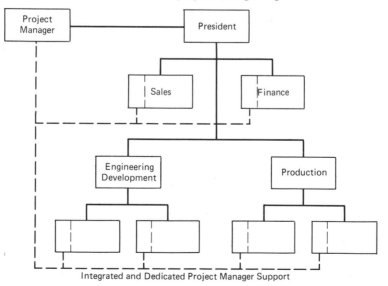

only one boss. This dual boss situation can be a cause of worker frustration and manager "warfare." Effective top management guidance and direction can, however, greatly minimize some of these personnel problems that are inherent in the matrix organization.

Matrix Organization Guidelines

In setting up a matrix organization one should realize that the concept of project management superimposed on a functional organization is not compatible with the traditional concepts of line and staff organization. Many companies do not need a matrix form of organization. For example, the simple functional organization works very well for companies which produce only one product or one group of related products. When a company determines that it really needs to adopt a matrix form of organization, it should consider the following guidelines:

- DIVERSITY OF PRODUCT LINES—*The greater the diversity of product lines, the more difficult it is for functional managers to give sufficient attention to the significantly important products. A project manager can coordinate and give full attention to the high-risk and/or high-cost products that are significantly important to the company.*
- SIZE OF THE COMPANY—*The larger the company, the greater is the need for integration across functional lines. The matrix organization can provide for such integration pertaining to products that are considered the most significant in the company's strategic planning.*
- TOP MANAGEMENT DEDICATION—*The chief executive officer (CEO) of the company must believe that the matrix organization is necessary and "sell" it to subordinates.*
- BALANCED AUTHORITY—*The chief executive officer (CEO) in a matrix organization must balance the authority between project managers and functional managers. The simple facts of the situation are that both types of managers are needed to effectively accomplish the company's strategic plans. The CEO must also be prepared to resolve quickly the major conflicts that are bound to occur between the two types of managers.*

The matrix organization is a method of managing that requires a great deal of skill. If set up only when needed and in accordance with the proper guidelines, it can increase the effectiveness and flexibility of a business operation.

PRINCIPLES OF ORGANIZATION

Achieving Organizational Effectiveness

There are certain principles of management that can be used to help achieve effective organization in any type of enterprise. For example, there is the principle of *span of control* that says there is a limit to the number of subordinates that one manager can effectively control. The principle of *delegation*, as another example, states that a manager cannot personally perform every task for which he or she is responsible. A good manager, therefore, must delegate both responsibilities and authority to subordinates. If these and other principles are intelligently applied, they can help managers avoid many problems.

Henri Fayol, a French industrialist, came to the conclusion that there were principles of management that embodied scientific truth.[2] Most of his principles, developed in 1916, are still good "rules of thumb," as he called them, for today's manager. The following summary listing of the most important classical or traditional principles of organization are, to a considerable extent, a reflection of the principles that Henri Fayol developed over sixty-five years ago:

- THE PRINCIPLE OF OBJECTIVES—*There must be a purpose for the organization to exist, and there should be interrelated and clearly defined organizational goals and job goals.*
- THE PRINCIPLE OF EFFICIENCY—*The organization should be established to do things right, by having good work methods and procedures, so that objectives can be attained at the lowest possible costs and with the greatest benefits.*
- THE PRINCIPLE OF SPECIALIZATION—*The work of each person in the organization should be clearly defined and confined to a single function with related functions grouped under one boss.*
- THE PRINCIPLE OF SPAN OF CONTROL—*The number of subordinates reporting to a supervisor should be limited to that number that can be effectively and efficiently managed and controlled. If the span of control is too broad (too many subordinates), it tends to result in the inefficient use of supervisors because they are overextending themselves and the workers are undercontrolled. If the span of control is too narrow (too few subordinates), it tends to result in underutilized supervisors and overcontrolled workers.*
- THE PRINCIPLE OF SHORT CHAIN OF COMMAND—*The chain of command (levels of management) should be as short as possible. The longer the chain from top management to first-line supervisors, the greater the chance that directives and reports will be distorted on the way from and to the many levels of command.*
- THE PRINCIPLE OF BALANCE—*There should be a reasonable balance in the size of various units within the organization. The organization should achieve a reasonable balance between centralization and decentralization of decision making. There should also be a reasonable balance between standardization and flexibility of procedures. It is also important to achieve a good balance between the principle of span of control and the principle of short chain of command.*
- THE PRINCIPLE OF UNITY OF COMMAND—*Each employee should be accountable to only one boss.*
- THE PRINCIPLE OF UNITY OF DIRECTION—*There should be one manager issuing one set of directives pertaining to the same organizational objective. Different functional managers with interrelated input to the same objective can issue conflicting directives if they do not coordinate their instructional ef-*

forts. The principle of unity of direction is intended to prevent this situation from happening.

- THE PRINCIPLE OF DELEGATION—*Decisions should be made at the lowest competent level with both responsibility and authority assigned as far down the organization structure as possible. The amount of information available to subordinates is a key factor in delegation.*

- THE PRINCIPLE OF RESPONSIBLITY—*Someone must be answerable for performing tasks with delegated authority that is commensurate with the responsibility for getting the job done. A manager is responsible for the actions of subordinates. One can delegate to subordinates but cannot abdicate responsibility. A manager is always accountable for assigned responsibilities, including those that have been delegated to subordinates.*

- THE PRINCIPLE OF AUTHORITY—*Someone must make decisions down through the chain of command. The chain of command or authority is sometimes referred to as the* scalar principle *(Figure 2-12). This principle says that responsibility and authority should have a one-to-one relationship. If someone is given responsibility for doing something, they should have the authority to make decisions on that responsibility. Conversely, if someone is given authority they should also be given some responsibility. In the scalar principle, responsibility and authority flow downward and accountability flows upward.*

FIGURE 2-12   The scalar principle

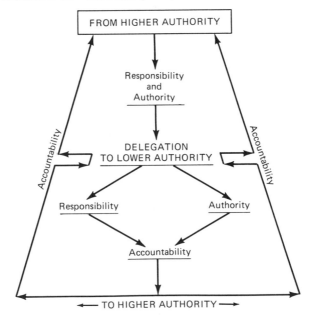

Delegation of *responsibility* and *authority* should flow in an unbroken line from the top to the bottom of the organization. *Accountability* should flow upward from the bottom to the top.

- THE PRINCIPLE OF ACCOUNTABILITY—*Each member of an organization should render reports on the discharge of his or her responsibilities. It is an individual matter that cannot be relieved through delegation.*
- THE PRINCIPLE OF COORDINATION—*The individuals in an organization should work together toward common goals by communicating with each other.*
- THE PRINCIPLE OF "GANGPLANKS"—*Dotted lines should be thrown across an organization chart to authorize lower-level supervisors to work across lines of authority with their peers on important and timely work matters. There is no way that an organization can function either effectively or efficiently if every organizational crossover work matter has to go up, over, down, and around the formal organization chain of command.*
- STABILITY OF TENURE OF PERSONNEL—*Managers and subordinates need time to learn their jobs. If the organization or assignment of personnel is changed too frequently, there is a loss of learning and training and usually an increase in worker frustration. Some changes are inevitable. Managers, however, should carefully evaluate the potential results before making organizational changes so as to maintain maximum stability consistent with good personnel management.*

CARRYING OUT THE PRINCIPLES OF ORGANIZATION

PRINCIPLES MUST BE JUDICIOUSLY CARRIED OUT

The principles of organization are good rules to follow because they are practical and realistic. They must, however, be judiciously carried out. For example, the principle of specialization requires considerable caution in its implementation. This principle can be carried too far, as it has been in some manufacturing production lines and certain types of office work. Overspecialization ignores human nature. It can cause boredom and monotony, which frequently results in carelessness in the quality of work output.

SPECIALIZATION

The principle of specialization is not easy to carry out because it is often difficult to clearly establish when one function leaves off and another related function begins. It is equally difficult at times to determine which jobs are sufficiently related to be grouped together. The principle of functional specialization can also conflict with the principle of unity of command. The line authority of the boss and the functional authority of the staff can have the effect of receiving instructions from more than one manager.

DELEGATING

The principles involved in delegating responsibility and authority to subordinates, but still holding the delegating manager directly responsible for any subordinate failures, places unrealistic pressures on the manager. These pressures may well be a factor in the reluctance of some managers to delegate. Authority can be fully delegated. Responsibility can only be partially delegated because of the fact that the ultimate responsibility remains with the person who has assigned work to someone else.

SPAN OF CONTROL

Carrying out the principle of span of control can conflict with the principle of short chain of command. As one strives to keep the number of subordinates under a supervisor to a manageable number, it tends to increase the number of levels of command in the organization. Another problem in implementing the principle of span of control is determining the magic number of subordinates that can be effectively and efficiently supervised. Some of the factors that must be considered in establishing the span of control are

- *How complex or simple are the functions being performed and supervised*
- *How many and how varied are the functions being performed and supervised*
- *The physical work location of the subordinates in relation to that of the supervisor*
- *The physical layout of the work area*
- *The intelligence, training, and capabilities of the subordinates*
- *The capabilities of the supervisor*
- *The type and condition of equipment and tools available to the work force*

In summary, there are limitations and problems in implementing the principles of organization management. However, the principles are still *good rules of management* and can help in the achievement of effective and efficient work activities.

STEPS IN ORGANIZING

KNOWLEDGE BEFORE ACTION

The proper approach to organizing is to know the important factors involved: understanding the interrelational aspects of purpose, objectives, policies, functions, procedures, and costs. It also means knowing (1) the basic tools used in organizing, (2) line and staff authority relationships, (3) different organizational configurations, and (4) principles of organization management. With this

FIGURE 2-13 Steps in organizing

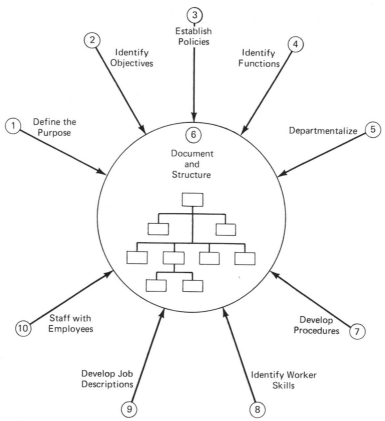

knowledge, and by following these steps in organization, (Figure 2-13) good organization should result:

1. Define the *purpose* of the organization.
2. Identify and establish the major *objectives* that will influence the organization structure.
3. Identify and establish the major *policies* that will guide the total organization.
4. Identify the *functions* that must be performed to accomplish the mission.
5. *Departmentalize* the functions by dividing and grouping similar and related activities into organizational units.
6. Formalize and document the *structure* of the organization mission and functions.
7. Develop *procedures* for carrying out organization functions.
8. Identify *skills* needed to perform organization functions and procedures.
9. Prepare *job descriptions* to include the delegation of responsibility and authority.
10. *Staff* the jobs with the right people.

FIGURE 2-14 Matrix responsibility chart
(a quick way to find out what is really happening)

GENERAL RESPONSIBILITY CHART XYZ COMPANY Date _____	President	Production Manager	Sales Manager	Comptroller	Purchasing	Engineering	Maintenance	Product Design	Quality Control	Planning	Personnel		
Product Design	FD	CC	CC	CC	CC	CC	CN	PW	CN	CN	CN		
Develop Production Plans	DC	FD	CC	CC	CC	CC	ED	ED	CN	PW	CN		
Hire, Transfer Personnel		ED	ED	ED	ED	ED	ED	ED	ED	ED	PW		
Product Pricing	FD	CC	CC	CC	ED	ED		ED		PW			
Provide Plant Maintenance		CC				CC	PW		CC				
Purchase Materials		CC		CC	PW	CC		CN	CN				

Legend:	PW Perform Work	SW Supervise Work	CC Compulsory Consultation	CN Compulsory Notification	DC Discussion of Critical Matters	ED Exchange of Data and Views	FD Final Decision	

In setting up an organization it is often helpful to construct a matrix responsibility chart (Figure 2-14) to establish where different types of work activities are now performed or should be performed. A matrix responsibility chart will also show areas of overlapping responsibilities, duplication of work, and "empire building."

AN ORGANIZATION SHOULD PERFORM WORTHWHILE FUNCTIONS

Organizations exist to discharge some worthwhile function. The people within an organization need a discipline that makes them face up to reality. Managers need to recognize that no organization can perform indefinitely without modification and redesign to include the elimination of elements that have outlived their usefulness. Holding on to functions and organizations that are not cost-effective causes serious problems. For example, organizations tend to apply "Parkinson's Law"[3] by expanding work so that it fills the time available for its completion, even though the work is not cost-effective. The key point is to not let unnecessary functions get a foothold in the organization.

EMPLOYEE AND ORGANIZATION INTERACTIONS

ORGANIZATIONS TEND TO IGNORE INDIVIDUALITY OF PEOPLE

- *THE INHUMAN ORGANIZATION*—An organization tends to reflect a structured, regimented, and somewhat inflexible way of life. Individual rights and human differences seem to be given minimal consideration in the formal organization. For example, the purpose and functions define the work to be performed and where it will be done. Job descriptions tell the worker what must be done on the job. Performance evaluations are based on how well the worker performed the tasks defined in the job description. These aspects of organization seem to ignore the individuality of the person on the job. The feelings, emotions, values, and behavior capabilities of people are not really reflected in the organization structure and job descriptions. Principles of organization focus attention on things that will make the organization more effective and efficient, but give little evidence of concern for human nature and motivation.

PEOPLE DO NOT COME IN STANDARD MOLDS

People, on the other hand, are not structured in neat standard molds. Most people have conceptions of things they value in achieving a state of personal satisfaction. These values vary considerably with different people, and may even vary from time to time with the same individual. People also differ in their behavior capabilities because they have different physical and mental capabilities as well as different response and experience abilities.

For an organization to be effective, individuals must hold jobs they are capable of performing. To obtain maximum productivity from the people within an organization, the organizational environment must also satisfy some of the expectancies that individuals have that influence their behavior on the job.

ORGANIZATION STRUCTURE CAN MOTIVATE, CONSTRAIN, OR FACILITATE HUMAN BEHAVIOR

People often form expectancies of the consequences of their behavior. The combination of expectancies plus individual needs and efforts influence worker performance. One group of writers on this subject express the view that the organization structure can motivate, constrain, or facilitate human behavior.[4]

- *First, the organization's structure can affect the expectancies that individuals have, and thus influence behavior through* motivational *effort. The things that can affect expectancies are: the design of the job, the career advancement potential, and the type of work measurement system.*

- *Second, the organization structure may make it difficult for individuals to translate their desires and values into job performance. A person may want to perform in a certain way, but may not have the necessary information, access to the appropriate individuals, or the authority to do so. In such cases, the organization structure serves to* constrain *behavior.*

- *Third, the organization structure can aid people in translating intentions and effort into action. By providing information, access to individuals, authority, and resources, the organization serves to* facilitate *individuals in performing their tasks.*

HUMAN NEEDS AND ORGANIZATIONAL DEMANDS MUST BE CONGENIAL

In summary, the organization can have a significant impact on employee satisfaction, motivation, and productivity. To achieve these desirable objectives, the organization must attempt to match human needs to organizational demands. Two things that can help match human and inhuman aspects of organization are (1) recognition of the influence of informal groups upon employee behavior, and (2) recognition of ways to provide for employee satisfaction.

THE INFORMAL ORGANIZATION RESULTS FROM SOCIAL RELATIONS

- *THE INFORMAL ORGANIZATION*—The informal organization reflects the relationships that develop among people. It exists wherever two or more people get together and interact with each other. The informal organization tends to give workers some sense of protection and a feeling of belonging which the much larger formal organization usually cannot give. Informal groups operate within the formal organization and are the result of social relationships developed in contacts with others in the organization. These contacts take place during working hours, such as in the daily work routine, the coffee break, and the lunch period. Contacts also take place after working hours in such places as the car pool, the bowling league, the golf course, the shopping center, the local tavern, and other places of social activity. The informal organization is not a part of any organization chart, functional statement, or job description. Yet it can structure worker behavior just as rigidly as formal directives issued by managers.

As indicated in Figure 2-15, the informal organization has both positive and negative aspects. Whether management feels that the informal organization is good or bad for the enterprise, it cannot abolish such groups because it did not set them up. Unlike the formal organization, which was created by management and can be changed or abolished, the informal groups are established from the association of people and will exist as long as people work to-

FIGURE 2-15 Informal organization

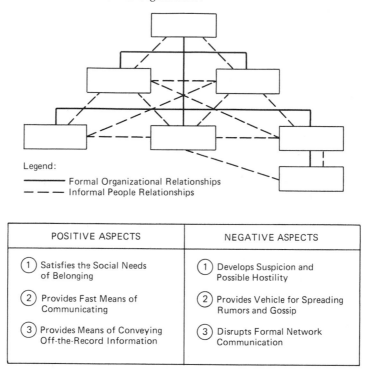

Legend:
———— Formal Organizational Relationships
— — — Informal People Relationships

POSITIVE ASPECTS	NEGATIVE ASPECTS
(1) Satisfies the Social Needs of Belonging	(1) Develops Suspicion and Possible Hostility
(2) Provides Fast Means of Communicating	(2) Provides Vehicle for Spreading Rumors and Gossip
(3) Provides Means of Conveying Off-the-Record Information	(3) Disrupts Formal Network Communication

gether. The wise manager learns to both recognize the existence of and to work with and through informal groups.

DIVISION OF WORK INTO SPECIALIZED TASKS IS GOOD—IF IT'S DONE RIGHT

• *THE ORGANIZATION AND JOB SATISFACTION*—One principle of organization is specialization. It involves the grouping of similar or related activities for purposes of making jobs simpler and easier to control. It further involves the breakdown of work into limited tasks to be performed by each worker. If fully carried out, specialization results in the work of each person being limited to a single function or work task. This principle can help prevent worker frustration by preventing the person from being assigned a diversity of unrelated tasks requiring several skills.

AVOID OVERSPECIALIZATION

The principle of job specialization should be handled with care to avoid overspecialization. Jobs should be designed to maximize productivity. This is generally achieved by effective division of work. There is a paradox, however, that job specialization in its objective of optimizing productivity may result in increasing boredom. When jobs become too simple and routine, they require only slight worker attention. This type of situation can result in employee "horse play," inattention to the job, too much socializing, and sometimes "skullduggery" that results in loss of quality production. As an example of what can happen, a group of workers in a New Jersey food processing plant built a small bomb. The bomb accidently exploded and hospitalized one of the workers. During the investigation that followed, the workers stated that they were not dissatisfied with the company but were bored with their jobs.

MANAGEMENT CAN CORRECT OVERSPECIALIZATION

Some workers are very content with highly routine work. Others become very bored and dissatisfied with jobs that are overspecialized. Some workers adapt to the endless sameness of their jobs through drugs, liquor, and sabotage.[5] For the dissatisfied worker there are at least four management actions that can be

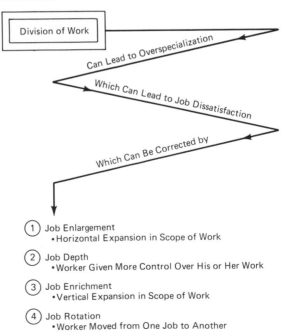

FIGURE 2-16 Job specialization & employee satisfaction

Division of Work

Can Lead to Overspecialization

Which Can Lead to Job Dissatisfaction

Which Can Be Corrected by

1. Job Enlargement
   • Horizontal Expansion in Scope of Work
2. Job Depth
   • Worker Given More Control Over His or Her Work
3. Job Enrichment
   • Vertical Expansion in Scope of Work
4. Job Rotation
   • Worker Moved from One Job to Another

employed to correct the consequences of overspecialization. As shown in Figure 2-16, these actions are job enlargement, job enrichment, job depth, and job rotation.

- JOB ENLARGEMENT—*Job enlargement involves the* horizontal expansion *of the scope of a job through the assignment of different and more varied tasks at the* same level *of difficulty and responsibility. Job enlargement reduces the frequency of repetition of certain tasks.*
- JOB ENRICHMENT—*Job enrichment involves the* vertical expansion *of the scope of a job through the assignment of more varied tasks at a* higher level *of difficulty and responsibility. Job enrichment may involve detailing a worker to a higher-level job to gain experience for possible promotion. Such details usually give the worker an increase in pay.*
- JOB DEPTH—*Job depth involves expanding the extent to which a worker can control his or her work. Expanding the depth of a job generally results in allowing workers to set their own pace and to develop their own methods for getting the job done. It gives the worker* more authority *in what they are doing.*
- JOB ROTATION—*Job rotation involves expanding the scope of work by* moving a worker *from one job to another. Job rotation can reduce the frequency of repetition in performing certain jobs. It can allow a worker to both gain experience on other jobs as well as eliminate the boredom of doing the same job day after day.*

COMPUTERIZATION AND DEHUMANIZATION

The ongoing expansion in computerization of office, manufacturing, and service operations can easily lead to varying degrees of dehumanization of the work efforts of people. A good example is the job dissatisfaction that came to James Keith, an educated, knowledgeable, and experienced sales and service representative for PWC, a large corporation engaged in the marketing of a dynamically changing line of consumer products. Computerization of inventory status and automatic determination of the quantities of various products to be shipped to various customers caused too many items to be shipped, with resulting expensive returns to PWC. The computerization of merchandising greatly reduced the decision making of the sales and service representatives who were geared to meet the personalized needs of each customer. The computerization also left James Keith in the reduced status of a traveling clerk with very little decision-making authority. His customers became frustrated and angry when the wrong products in the wrong quantities were shipped to them and the costly mistakes were "blamed on the computer."

Managers at all levels must seriously evaluate the potential dehumanizing effects of computers in the workplace. Such evaluations must be considered in organizing for the future so as to provide enriched jobs for well educated, trained, and capable employees. Organization is a very dynamic and sensitive element in management. A key factor in organization is to match human needs to organizational demands. Without this matching there is bound to be job dissatisfaction and loss of productivity on the part of the people who are to do the work.

SUMMARY

PLANNING

Planning and organizing set the stage for effective and efficient management —doing the right things at the lowest possible cost and with minimum personnel turbulence. Planning establishes what is to be done; when, where, how, and why it is to be done; and who is to be responsible for doing it. It means thinking about the future as well as the present. Good planning involves many things, such as

- *Establishing the purpose and objectives of what is to be accomplished*
- *Determining the current status of things in relation to the objectives to be accomplished*
- *Analyzing the total environment of things that must be accomplished to get from where you are to where you want to go*
- *Developing a plan of action for getting from where you are to where you want to go*
- *Determining how you are going to monitor and control the implementation of the plan of action*

Planning requires considerable thinking things through. It is the lack of sufficient planning that causes many businesses to fail and turbulent personnel situations to occur in the workplace.

ORGANIZING

Organizing is the management process of identifying, dividing, and grouping the work activities; and then defining the responsibilities, authority, and accountability of the workers required to accomplish the work objectives. Good organization is important because it lets people know "who does what." This facilitates coordination, avoids duplication of work effort and reduces confusion, friction, and tension among the work force. Organizations tend to be a structured, regimented, and somewhat inflexible way of life. People, however, are not structured in neat standard molds. They differ in their value of things and in their behavior capabilities. Organizations have significant impacts on employee satisfaction, motivation, and productivity, The organization, therefore, must attempt to match human needs to organizational demands. A manager can help bridge the gap between employee and organizational interactions by having a good understanding of informal organizations, job enlargement, job enrichment, job depth, and job rotation.

REVIEW QUESTIONS

1. Why is planning not a quick one-time snapshot of things?
2. Discuss the soul-searching analysis aspects of strategic planning.
3. How does program planning provide a bridge between strategic and operational planning?
4. Discuss how the efforts of staff planners and operational planners supplement one another.
5. Describe the concept of line and staff organization and how it can function effectively.
6. Your planning clerk has submitted a complaint to you, the supervisor, about receiving a directive from the chief of the budget branch of the controller's office. Discuss the propriety of the situation in terms of what you are going to say to your planning clerk and to the controller's office.
7. What is a matrix organization and under what circumstances might it be used?
8. Describe the inhuman organization and how to cope with it.

A CASE STUDY IN PLANNING

Assume that you are a member of the Board of Directors of a local nonprofit community service organization. The primary responsibilities of the Board are to (1) participate in the development and approve the program objectives for the organization, (2) develop ways and means of financing the organization's programs, (3) hire and supervise the manager and professional staff of the organization, and (4) oversee the accomplishment of the organization's objectives. After attending several Board meetings it becomes apparent to you that all of the unpaid Board members are conscientious and well-meaning individuals but most appear to be lacking in their ability to effectively make plans for the organization. As a means of improving the situation you obtain Board approval to present a two-hour training session on the fundamentals of planning at a special meeting. Develop an outline of what you are going to cover in the training session. Describe why you think your coverage of the subject will improve the quality of planning by the Board.

A CASE STUDY IN ORGANIZING

As chairman of the Board of Directors of the above nonprofit community service organization, it has come to your attention that there are several informal groups operating within the organization. The situation is shown in the accompanying chart. In situation A, Helen Merry and Paul Welsh are in the same car pool. They frequently transact organizational business even though they work for two different program group leaders. In situation B, Betty Boyd and the manager go to the same church. It has been reported to you that they frequently discuss organizational work problems at a coffee hour after church on Sundays. Betty Boyd's program group leader is aware of this informal get-together.

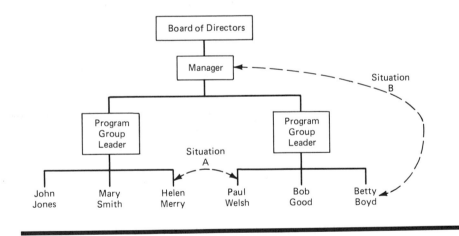

QUESTIONS

1. Evaluate what you think is good and what is bad about situations A and B?
2. As chairman of the Board, do you intend to do anything about either of these situations? If so, what? If not, why?

NOTES

1.   Robert J. Flaherty, "The Great Big Railroad that Could," *Forbes,* June 1, 1977, pp. 37–42.

2.   Henri Fayol, *Industrial and General Administration,* trans. Constance Storrs (London: Sir Isaac Pitman & Sons, Ltd., 1949), pp. 20–37, p. 69.

3.   C. Northcote Parkinson, *Parkinson's Law* (Cambridge, Mass.: The Riverside Press, 1957), pp. 2–12.

4.   D. A. Nadler, J. R. Hackman, and E. E. Lawler, *Managing Organizational Behavior* (Boston: Little, Brown, 1979), pp. 183–84.

5.   John F. Runice, "By Days I Make The Cars," *Harvard Business Review,* May–June 1980, pp. 106–15. Copyright © 1980 by the President and Fellows of Harvard College; all rights reserved.

3

Directing Is:
Leading and Motivating
Controlling Is:
Keeping on Top of Things

The Fundamentals of Directing and Controlling

LEARNING OBJECTIVES

The objectives of this chapter on the fundamentals of directing and controlling are to enable the reader to

1. Understand the function of directing
2. Describe the following qualities that affect leadership:
   a. The most significant characteristics of a leader
   b. The contrasting styles of leadership
3. Describe the following aspects of motivation:
   a. The major variables affecting motivation
   b. The most practical theoretical approaches to motivation
   c. A systematic approach for modifying human behavior
4. Understand the following practical considerations in the function of controlling:
   a. Ten reasons why the function of controlling is important
   b. The steps involved in the development of a control system
   c. Management principles providing basic prerequisites for an effective control system

KEY WORDS

Authoritative Leadership   A leadership that is self-ruling and dictatorial, making unilateral decisions without the participation of others.

Consultative Leadership   A leadership that seeks advice, guidance, information, suggestions, and recommendations from others.

Content Theories of Motivation   The theory that people are motivated according to their needs.

Eccentric Management   A leadership characterized by the beliefs that management is best achieved through putting workers under pressure or placing trust in a small exclusive group of people. The two most common styles of eccentric management are probably management by crisis and management by clique.

Group Dynamics   The active forces that exist when groups of people get together.

Job Content   The characteristics of a job, such as responsibility and potential for growth.

Job Context   The characteristics (such as pay and working conditions) found in the job environment.

Leadership   The act of showing the way and guiding others in the achievement of an objective.

Management by Exception   An approach to management that emphasizes that the most important actions be accomplished first and then gives priority attention to these actions.

Motivation   Whatever causes a person to act or behave in a certain way.

Participative Leadership   A leadership that has others take an active part in the development of objectives, plans, and work methods prior to making a decision.

Process Theories of Motivation   The theory that people are motivated according to their expectancies.

Role Perception   The inclination of people to see other individuals as they want to see them or as they expect them to be. Role perception exists when people stereotype other people according to age, sex, race, national origin, or other factors and then attribute certain characteristics to everyone who falls within the group.

Theory X   A human behavior theory formulated by Douglas McGregor that assumes people to be lazy, to dislike work, and to be driven to work only by coercion or threatened disciplinary action by the supervisor.

Theory Y   A human behavior theory formulated by Douglas McGregor that assumes people have a psychological need and desire to work and will seek responsibility in the right work environment.

Plans and organizations are controlled through the management process of directing. Directing the implementation of a plan or the smooth functioning of an organization involves leadership that motivates people in the performance of their assigned responsibilities. Good leadership requires knowledge of plans, organization structure, and the means of controlling people, things, and time. The leadership and motivation of people—the key elements of directing—provide the linking pin that ties together the management functions of planning, organizing, and controlling.

THE FUNCTION OF DIRECTING

A SHOCKING CASE OF DIRECTING

GETTING PEOPLE TO DO THINGS WILLINGLY

Directing involves getting people to do what you want them to do and to do it willingly. In November 1978 the civilized world was shocked by the leadership of Jim Jones, a religious cult leader, who motivated and directed over nine hundred people to willingly commit mass suicide near Georgetown, Guyana. Parents gave poison to their children and then drank Kool-Aid and cyanide to die beside them. The cult members were routinely instructed in suicide by Jim Jones, who believed in the need to destroy their "utopia" community if it was ever in danger of being broken up by outsiders. When it was threatened in an investigation by a U.S. Congressman (Leo J. Ryan), Jim Jones directed that the members of his cult kill themselves—and they did.

The shocking thing about the incredible Guyana mass suicide is that it so closely followed certain management principles of motivation and leadership. For example, most writings on human motivation state that people do their best when they know what is expected of them. Jim Jones instructed his followers that suicide was expected of them if their promised "utopia" was ever threatened. When it was threatened, they did what was expected of them.

Another disturbing thing reflected in the Jim Jones cult case is the extent to which people can be so greatly influenced by a charismatic leader. Adolf Hitler is probably the best example of charismatic leadership—in the wrong direction. He led the German people into the most devastating war in the history of mankind. Under Hitler's leadership, his followers also engaged in human genocide that systematically exterminated millions of Jews—men, women, and children—just because they were Jewish.

No Simple Answers in Leadership

There are no simple answers as to why people allow themselves to commit mass suicide or to destroy others under the charismatic leadership of individuals such as Jim Jones and Adolf Hitler. It is somewhat frightening at times to see the impacts that leadership and motivation can have on people. Great leaders in the right direction are relatively hard to find. Dr. Werner von Braun, probably the world's greatest missile and space scientist before he died in 1977, was a very effective leader in motivating others in the achievement of our efforts to get to the moon and back. He was also a community builder and leader in getting people to do beneficial things for others. Of more recent date, Margaret Thatcher, Prime Minister of Great Britain, reflects many traits of a strong and good leader. She is intelligent, strong-minded, competent, very courageous, and appears to be honest. She also shows an understanding of the value of people and their needs in convincing them to do what is necessary for their country.

WHAT IS DIRECTING?

Directing Involves People Interactions

Directing involves assigning, instructing, and correcting people in their work efforts to accomplish some objective. As seen in Figure 3-1, directing involves

- *Styles of leadership*
- *Humanistic relations*
- *Group dynamics*
- *Managerial attitude*
- *Motivation of others*

Style of Leadership

Directing entails the providing of leadership in the assigning, instructing, and correcting of the work force in their work efforts. The style of leadership exercised by a manager in performing these tasks can influence worker motivation and productivity. The authoritative leader, for example, is dogmatic and insists on asserting his or her opinion to the exclusion of the judgment of others. Authoritarian leaders often assert their opinions in an arrogant manner. Adolf Hitler was an authoritarian leader. Many of the major blunders made by the

FIGURE 3-1   The function of directing

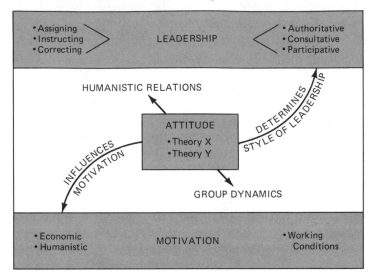

Germans in World War II were caused by the impractical strategic decisions of Hitler. The war might have turned out quite differently if he had consulted more with his professional military staff.

The consultative leader seeks advice or information and asks for guidance from others when making decisions. The participative leader goes one step further and has others actively share and take part in the forming of objectives and plans, and the methods by which they can be accomplished.

MANAGERIAL ATTITUDE

A manager's attitude tends to be a major factor in determining the individual's style of leadership. If a manager has a Theory X attitude,[1] he or she thinks that people dislike work, are lazy, avoid accepting responsibility, and must be told what to do. This type of attitude usually results in an authoritative style of leadership. On the other hand, if a manager's attitude follows Theory Y,[2] he or she thinks that most people like meaningful work, seek responsibility, find purposeful work to be enjoyable, and don't need to be rigidly supervised. This type of attitude usually results in either consultative or participative leadership.

The attitude of a manager is also reflected in the consideration of people as human beings. Achievement of good humanistic relations is very closely related to the manner in which a manager assigns work, instructs subordinates in how to perform it, and corrects them when something goes wrong. The manager who is a good leader and treats employees as human beings usually has few problems in group dynamics—the active forces that exist when groups of people get together.

There appears to be a close relationship between how people are treated as human beings and their motivation to perform work. The manager's attitude toward subordinates tends to be a significant factor in the motivation of workers. Good leadership means knowing how to direct others through a positive attitude that understands humanistic relations and group dynamics.

LEADERSHIP: A KEY FACTOR IN DIRECTING

Directing is the area of management that tends to be the most personal and influential factor in getting workers to accomplish work in the right way. Directing people can lead to doing the right things or doing the wrong things. It is a very significant and sensitive function because it involves integrity and ethical conduct. Getting people to do the right and honorable things requires the right kind of motivation through good leadership.

LEADERSHIP IS AN ART AND A SCIENCE

● *THE NATURE OF LEADERSHIP*—A leader is a person who goes before, shows the way, and guides followers in the achievement of an objective. It is a controversial subject as to whether leadership is a science or an art. Some people believe leadership to be an exact science that can be understood and practiced by anyone. Other people hold that no amount of learning will make a person a leader unless the individual has the right natural qualities. A careful analysis of the nature of leadership indicates that it is both an art and a science. It is a science in the sense that there are effective guidelines, principles, and techniques that can be learned and applied in leading people. Leadership is also an art because a person must use common sense and exhibit understanding and consideration of human behavior that is not found in guidelines and principles. There are many variables of human nature that make the exercise of leadership more of an art than a science. Support for this statement can be found in Part II of this book which discusses the subject of *Interpersonal Relations* in supervisory management.

● *THE CHARACTERISTICS OF LEADERSHIP*—There is no one characteristic that can be used to describe a leader. The same leadership trait, for example, that turns some people "on" will turn others "off." A leadership trait that may be desirable in the production department of a manufacturing plant, may not be desirable in the sales department. There are, however, some leadership characteristics that are desirable in any situation.

HONESTY

One universal leadership characteristic is genuine honesty. The leader who is sincere and straightforward is generally trusted and respected by subordinates. There is also a high correlation between the honest leader and the one who is fair with and considerate of others. When a leader is dishonest, followers tend to be suspicious, apprehensive, and insecure. Honesty is a good foundation upon which to build the basic character of a leader.

COURAGE

A second significant characteristic of leadership is courage. This quality is reflected in the ability to face difficulty with firmness and without fear. There are two kinds of courage—physical and moral. The true leader must have both. Courage is a product of development of self-control, self-discipline, knowledge of one's job, and confidence. With reference to self-discipline, only those who can discipline themselves can expect disciplined performance from others. The courageous leader is loyal to the organization and the people in it, shows a readiness to accept responsibility, and a willingness to admit mistakes. It indeed takes courage to admit that you made a mistake. Courage minimizes fear and maximizes sound judgment under pressure. It also facilitates innovation of new things or methods without which a leader is really not a leader.

COMPETENCE

A third important characteristic of leadership is competence. This has many forms. The most obvious reflection of competence is that of technical knowledge in the specific functions for which one is responsible. Technical competence is more important at the lower levels of management. At the higher levels, competence in the form of superior general knowledge of overall operations is more important. At each level of management there should be competence in the ability to effectively abstract significant facts and information without taking them improperly out of the total context of the situation. There should also be competence in the ability to conceptualize situations and to integrate different facts into a coherent frame of reference. The ability to abstract and conceptualize requires another form of competence, namely intelligence. Other areas where competence is needed are (1) keen understanding and appreciation of organizational objectives and (2) ability to stimulate others in the accomplishment of objectives.

ETHICAL BEHAVIOR

A fourth and very important leadership trait is having a code of ethical behavior. This characteristic has two forms. One involves a commitment to fair dealing with others and an accompanying sensitivity for the rights, dignity, and other values of people. The second form involves personal adherence to high ethical standards of conduct in the performance of managerial responsibilities. Ethical behavior means acting in accordance with honorable motives, rules, and standards of personal conduct both on and off the job. For example, very few people respect a leader whose personal conduct reflects such acts as collusion, falsification of travel expenses, sexual harassment of subordinates, acceptance of bribes, or other immoral behavior.

OTHER LEADERSHIP CHARACTERISTICS

As shown in Figure 3-2, there are other characteristics often considered as personal attributes of a leader. These traits include

- *Pleasing* personality *that impresses people*
- Charismatic qualities *that influence other people to follow the leader*
- *Pleasant-sounding* voice
- *Outward* appearance *that conveys the impression of intelligence, self-confidence, and status or esteem*
- *Socially accepted* manners *and ways of acting or doing things*

FIGURE 3-2   Characteristics of leadership

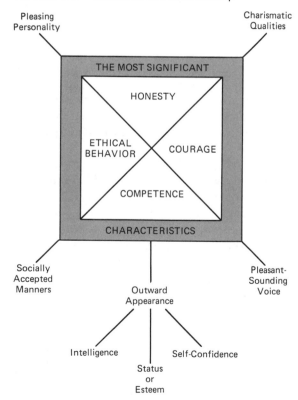

Unfortunately, some followers tend to be overly influenced by the leader's charisma, outward appearance, or even the individual's pleasant-sounding voice. While these are desirable traits for a leader to possess, they are much less significant than honesty, courage, competence, and ethical behavior. The attraction, for example, of the handsome, six-foot-tall football hero may quickly dissipate when subsequent actions of the individual show that the person is not really a true leader. We have already seen how the charm of the charismatic leader can direct people in exactly the wrong way. Effective leadership is derived from those significant characteristics that motivate people in the right direction.

ATTITUDE INFLUENCES LEADERSHIP

•   *STYLES OF LEADERSHIP*—There are many different leadership styles of directing people. The attitude of the manager towards subordinates is a very significant factor in the determination of style of leadership.

AUTHORITATIVE MANAGEMENT

The authoritative style of leadership reflects a person who is self-ruling, dictatorial, and makes unilateral decisions without any consultation with or participation from others. Some authoritative leaders have such an egotistic attitude that they believe the decisions they make are in the best interests of others. Other authoritative leaders reflect an attitude that they really don't care whether their decisions are in the best interests of others. Except where time is a very critical factor or there are situations involving safety, security, or emergencies, authoritative leadership is not recommended as a long-term method of directing others.

General Eisenhower used to demonstrate the art of leadership with a piece of string. He would put it on a table. Pull, he would say, and it follows wherever you wish. Push it, he said, and it will go nowhere at all. Leading people is very similar because it depends on getting them to follow you. The really good manager does not have to push or force most people very much. Managers who prod rather than lead rarely get the best out of their workers.

TEAM MANAGEMENT

A highly recommended style of leadership is team management. This type of manager believes in the values of joint cooperative action in decision making. This can be accomplished through either consultative or participative leadership. A consultative leader is one who seeks advice, guidance, information, suggestions, and recommendations from subordinates and others prior to making management decisions. A participative manager is one who involves others in the development of objectives, plans, and work methods prior to making management decisions.

ECCENTRIC MANAGEMENT

Some managers engage in what might be called eccentric management. The two most commonly found styles of eccentric leadership are probably management by crisis and management by clique. In *management by crisis* the manager believes that workers are better motivated if placed under pressure to get work accomplished. A major problem in this style of management is that it disrupts and often brings other work efforts to a screeching halt, creating employee frustration in the process. The urgent situation may require an unreasonable amount of effort to resolve. Meanwhile, other crises have developed. Once engaged in "firefighting" a crisis, you will find yourself at least one crisis behind.

Management by clique is a system of managing through a small, exclusive group of people, usually close past associates or personal friends. This is negative leadership because it implies: I trust one group but not others. One bad effect is that it causes frustration, irritation, and a feeling of personal prejudice on the part of those employees who are not a part of the clique. A second negative effect is that it closes the door on constructive ideas, suggestions, and recommendations from those not part of the clique. Management improvement is limited to the human resources available within the clique. This can result in carrying past mistakes into the future. It also is a negative motivator of people who are *not* in the clique.

ORIENTATION MANAGEMENT

Many researchers have studied the results obtained by managers who are task-oriented versus those who are employee-oriented. The optimum or most favored situation is where management emphasizes maximum concern for both production and people.[3] The *employee-oriented manager* tends to motivate rather than control subordinates. Employees are encouraged to perform tasks through group participation, and in an atmosphere that is friendly and trusting with respectful relationships among group members. The *task-oriented manager* directs and closely controls subordinates. The primary concern is getting work done rather than developing good humanistic relations with subordinates. Studies at the Ohio State University, conducted over a period of years, showed less worker absenteeism and fewer accidents under supervisors who scored high on consideration for their subordinates.[4] Other studies conducted at the University of Michigan showed that supervisors who were employee-oriented had higher productivity than supervisors who were task-oriented.[5] The many studies conducted show that democratic leadership produces higher employee satisfaction and productivity than autocratic leadership. Conversely, leaders who give high emphasis to the organization structure and the tasks to be done have the highest grievance and turnover rates among their workers.

MOTIVATION OF PEOPLE

Motivation refers to whatever moves a person to action or to behave in a certain way. Understanding the aspects of motivation is a challenge for all managers. For one thing, there is no single system for effectively motivating everyone in a steady consistent manner. This means that a manager must work with and through people to establish the best way to motivate them. It involves developing some understanding of why people behave as they do so that they can be influenced to perform in ways that the manager finds desirable.

● *MAJOR FACTORS AFFECTING MOTIVATION*—A good starting point in learning how to motivate people is to have an understanding of the major factors that affect motivation. These factors fall into the following four clusters (Figure 3-3):

— *The individual characteristics of* the person
— *The characteristics of* the job
— *The characteristics of* the work situation
— *The characteristics of* the supervisor

CHARACTERISTICS OF THE PERSON

The characteristics of the person are reflected in the individual's human needs, interests, values, intelligence, abilities, and attitude toward the job, the work situation, and the supervisor.

CHARACTERISTICS OF THE JOB

The characteristics of the job are reflected in such human satisfiers as the assignment of important responsibilities, a sense or feeling of achievement, and the potential for personal growth of the individual. When these job content factors are satisfying to the worker, one usually finds a motivated individual.

Job context factors—such as pay, working conditions, and supervisory leadership—can have various impacts on different people. A 1950 study of job attitudes by Frederick Herzberg showed that these job environmental factors do not really motivate people. If the job context factors are good, they only prevent people from being dissatisfied. However, Herzberg's study[6] was conducted with two hundred engineers and accountants and should not be projected as necessarily reflecting the reactions of all people in nonprofessional jobs. Some workers do appear to be motivated by the pay of the job and the kind of treatment received from their supervisor.

FIGURE 3-3 Major variables affecting motivation

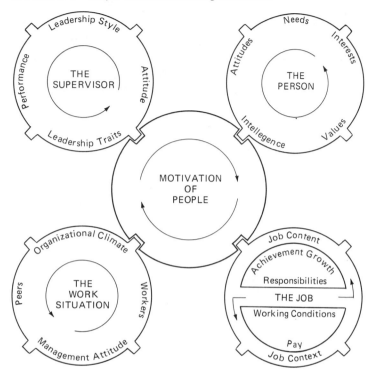

CHARACTERISTICS OF THE WORK SITUATION

The characteristics of the work situation are reflected in the effectiveness of the organization structure, personnel policies, attitudes of management and workers, as well as the generally prevailing environmental climate of the workplace in terms of standards, directives, pressures, social conditions, and treatment of employees. Management, with its power to reward or punish, plays a critical role in determining the job attitude and performance of subordinates. Inconsistencies such as failure to notice outstanding work by some individuals while praising mediocrity in others is usually very damaging to employee motivation. Approval of actions by one's peers can also affect motivation and job performance because most people desire the friendship and approval of the people with whom they work. They therefore tend to behave in a way that gains the approval of their peers. Management attitude as to honesty and fairness is still another factor affecting the organizational climate. When employees say, "This is a good place to work," you will usually find a preponderence of motivated people.

CHARACTERISTICS OF THE SUPERVISOR

The characteristics of the supervisor are reflected in style of leadership, attitude, leadership traits, and overall management performance. These characteristics are often reflected in how the workers conduct themselves. A supervisor's negative attitude toward innovation, for example, will tend to result in subordinates who also fight changes in the workplace.

PERIODIC EVALUATION

The many variables affecting worker motivation should be periodically evaluated by management. The evaluation should start with management's appraisal of its own attitude and that of others in the organization. The evaluation should also include organizational policies, procedures, and programs that af-

FIGURE 3-4 Motivational concepts

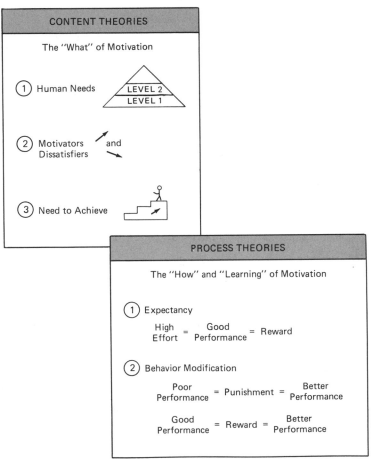

fect employee motivation. Practices considered to have an adverse effect on motivation should be changed to help create a work environment that is conducive to the development of employee satisfaction.

● *APPROACHES TO MOTIVATION*—For many years managers accepted the simple approach to motivation that workers were primarily driven by the economic factor of more money—that they would normally increase their productivity if paid an incentive wage. Psychologists, however, have demonstrated that motivation is much more complex than this. Today there are many theoretical approaches to motivation. Underlying these approaches are various managerial assumptions and attitudes about the nature of people. These motivational concepts tend to fall into the following two groups (Figure 3-4):

1. Content Theories of Motivation
   a. The Human Needs Theory
   b. The Motivator—Dissatisfaction Theory
   c. The Need to Achieve Theory
2. Process Theories of Motivation
   a. The Expectancy Theory
   b. The Behavior Modification Theory

An understanding of these theoretical concepts can help managers perceive the "what," "how," and "learning" processes that are inherent in motivation. The manager with a good comprehension of the fickle nature of motivation is usually in a better position to effectively motivate people.

WHAT MOTIVATES PEOPLE

● *CONTENT THEORIES OF MOTIVATION*—The content approach to motivation focuses on *what* motivates people. It stresses the importance of understanding the factors within individuals that cause them to act in a certain way. Three things can be learned from the content theories of motivation:

1. Individuals have *inner desires* that cause them to act in a certain way. The motives that prompt people to action vary considerably, for one reason or another, from individual to individual.
2. Individuals have *tensions and "drivers"* that pressure them to fulfill some human need. There are many needs such as food, security, achievement, and recognition and they vary considerably from individual to individual. The ways *in which* these needs are translated into action also varies considerably among individuals.
3. Individuals are *not always consistent* in the ways they respond to or act on their needs at different times.

SATISFACTION OF NEEDS

● *THE HUMAN NEEDS THEORY*—A.H. Maslow was one of the earliest theoreticians to reason that human beings have an inner desire directed toward satisfying unfulfilled needs.[7] Maslow's self-actualizing model (Figure 3-5), is

FIGURE 3-5   Maslow's theory on the hierarchy of human needs

SOURCE: Adapted from A.H. Maslow, "A Theory of Human Motivation," Psychological Review 50 (1943): 370–96, American Psychological Association.

based on the reasoning that human beings have an internal need that pushes them toward self-actualization (fulfillment) and personal superiority—a position that few ever attain. How far an individual goes in achieving self-actualization is determined by first satisfying lower-level needs, one step at a time. For example, the first needs that must be satisfied are the physiological needs of food, clothing, and shelter necessary for human survival. A person who has satisfied the lowest-level needs, tends to look for satisfaction at the next higher level.

PRACTICAL IMPLICATIONS OF MASLOW'S THEORY

According to Maslow's theory, an individual will be motivated to fulfill the need that is the most powerful for the individual at a given moment of time. There are practical implications in this theory for motivating people. The managers who can establish where their subordinates fit into the hierarchy of human needs are best able to determine how to motivate them. Since the needs of people are not the same, the same motivational approach will not work effectively with everyone.

SATISFACTION AND DISSATISFACTION OF NEEDS

● *THE MOTIVATOR-DISSATISFACTION THEORY*—Frederick Herzberg, a psychologist, devoted many years to the study of motivation in the United States and abroad.[8] Herzberg developed the idea that there are two sets of conditions or needs that affect a person at work (Figure 3-6). He called the one

FIGURE 3-6   Herzberg's theory

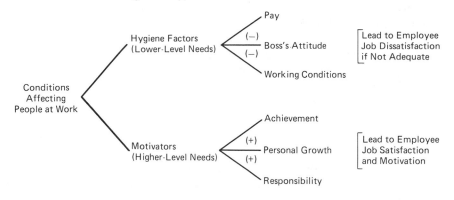

set *motivators* and the other *hygiene factors.* The first group was considered positive and had the power to satisfy employees. These Herzberg called the real motivators. The second group was considered negative and could only dissatisfy or demotivate employees *if not adequate.* Herzberg called these the hygiene factors because he felt they did not really motivate people.

Herzberg's concept recognizes two sets of human needs in the workplace: (1) the *lower-level desires* to satisfy the person's basic needs, such as the amount of pay and the working conditions; and (2) the *higher-level needs* such as achieving status, prestige, and/or growth on the job. The satisfaction or nonsatisfaction of these needs are affected by two sets of work factors—the motivators and the hygiene factors.

HYGIENE FACTORS

The hygiene factors include such things as company policies, administrative procedures, supervision, interpersonal relations, salary, and working conditions. These hygiene factors, says Herzberg, do not tend to be motivators—they only keep workers from becoming dissatisfied. For example, if a workplace is not air-conditioned in the summer, it may lead to worker dissatisfaction. The installation of air-conditioning may eliminate the dissatisfaction but have no effect in motivating the workers to increase their productivity—it merely keeps them from being dissatisfied. Workers tend to become dissatisfied when their wages do not keep up with spiraling inflation. However, a cost-of-living pay increase may result in no increase in their productivity—it just reduces their dissatisfaction in the amount of their disposable income.

MOTIVATING FACTORS

The five most important motivating factors according to Herzberg are achievement, recognition, the work itself, responsibility, and advancement or growth because of the nature of the task. If these motivating factors are not present on a job, the worker won't necessarily be dissatisfied, the individual just won't be highly motivated.

ACHIEVEMENT-, POWER-, AFFILIATION-, AND AUTONOMY-MOTIVATED INDIVIDUALS

• *THE NEED-TO-ACHIEVE THEORY*—The need-to-achieve concept of motivation has been promoted over a period of years by many individuals. This theory is based on the idea that many people have desires to achieve certain goals such as recognition, promotion, and status that don't fit into Maslow's lock-step hierarchy of human needs. The fundamental idea supporting the theory is that the motivation to achieve a particular goal results from three factors (Figure 3-7):

1. The strong *need* or expected satisfaction by the individual to achieve a specific goal
2. The *strength* of or expectation by the individual to achieve the goal
3. The *perceived incentive value* or satisfaction that the individual expects to obtain in achieving the goal

The need-to-achieve theory emphasizes the desires many people have for achievement, power, affiliation, and/or autonomy. *Achievement-motivated*

FIGURE 3-7   The need-to-achieve theory

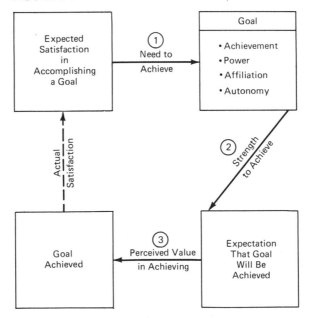

individuals are interested in doing a better job than others, accomplishing something exceptional, or obtaining a promotion. *Power-motivated* individuals have a high need to influence and control other people. *Affiliation-motivated* individuals have a high need to establish and maintain strong and friendly relationships with others. *Autonomy-motivated* individuals have a strong desire to have freedom, independence, and control over their own lives.

There are two important things to keep in mind with reference to individuals that are motivated by their need to achieve. First, they are usually highly motivated to satisfy their needs. Second, some need-to-achieve individuals will stop at nothing to accomplish their goals, particularly those who are power-motivated.

How Are People Motivated?

● *PROCESS THEORIES OF MOTIVATION*—The process approach to motivation focuses on behavioral learning and *how* people are motivated. It stresses the goals or conditions that cause people to be motivated or to change their manner of behaving. A basic consideration in this approach to motivation is the tendency for people to act in accordance with what they believe is likely to occur as the result of their personal conduct. At least two things can be learned from the process theories:

1. Individuals are often motivated by their *expectancies* of what they believe is likely to occur as the result of their behavior.
2. Individuals tend to be motivated by the strength of their *preference* for the expected outcome that will result from their behavior.

People Have Expectancies

● *THE EXPECTANCY THEORY*—The expectancy theory[9] reflects individual differences in how people are motivated. It hypothesizes that the motivation within an individual starts with a desire for something such as the goals of promotion, a new job, the achievement of self-esteem, or the attainment of recognition. From the base point of a specific desired goal the individual seeks to determine how it can be achieved. There is usually an *effort-performance-goal linkage* involved in getting from the desire to the actual achievement of the goal (Figure 3-8). First, the individual perceives the level of effort considered necessary to accomplish a specific goal. Second, the individual perceives that successful performance will lead to the achievement of the desired goal. The most critical elements in the expectancy theory are (1) that the individual will be motivated to produce at a high level where there is the belief that the efforts will result in success and (2) that such efforts will in fact obtain the desired goal. The process hinges on the accuracy of the individual's perception that the desired goals are possible within the organization.

FIGURE 3-8 The expectancy theory

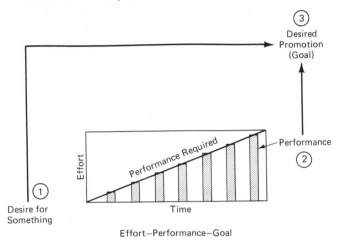

Effort—Performance—Goal

THE ROLE OF SUPERVISORS

Supervisors should help capable and deserving workers to achieve their goals. Incapable or undeserving workers should be counseled regarding what they can reasonably expect to attain based on various levels of work. This is an area where effective career development programs can motivate capable and deserving workers and help develop the less-capable workers to the point where the expectancy theory can realistically come into play. The expectancy theory will usually not be very effective unless individuals who perform at a high level achieve the rewards they deserve. This requires that the manager and the worker be communicating on the same wavelength.

PEOPLE ARE INFLUENCED BY THE PAST

● *THE BEHAVIOR MODIFICATION THEORY*—The behavior modification theory[10] proposes that an individual's present behavior results from past experiences. This theory is also referred to as *operant conditioning theory*. The theory states that human behavior can be reinforced by either reward or punishment (Figure 3-9). For example, if a worker performed in an outstanding manner in the past and received an award (positive reinforcement), there is a good probability that the worker will be motivated to repeat the outstanding performance. Conversely, a worker will tend not to repeat past performance that resulted in disciplinary action (negative reinforcement). The behavioral approach assumes work behavior to be a learned activity. You can learn to do a

FIGURE 3-9 Behavior modification theory (operant conditioning)

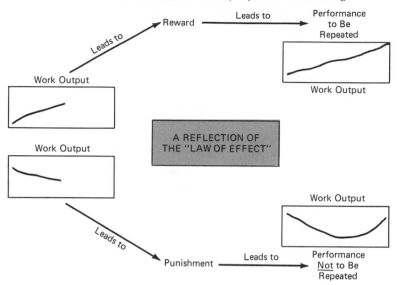

job well or you can learn to do it poorly. Work habits that are the most satisfying tend to come from positive reward and recognition policies.

The behavior modification theory is a reflection of the *law of effect.* For example, the effect of work performance that leads to a reward tends to again lead to the same behavior being repeated with the expectation of receiving another reward. Work performance that leads to punishment tends to lead to a behavioral change to avoid the adverse penalty that is expected.[11]

Both the expectancy theory and the behavior modification theory emphasize the essential linkage between performance and rewards. The two theories differ on one significant point. Expectancy theory is based on the view that an individual's present behavior is a function of *future expectations.* Behavior modification theory is based on the view that an individual's present behavior is a function of *past experiences.*

MODIFYING HUMAN BEHAVIOR

LEADERSHIP

A manager's greatest influence over modifying human behavior is probably to be found in supervisory leadership. Good leadership includes being able to take the right motivational approach at the right time and place. It starts with having a comprehensive understanding of individuals, jobs, and the work situation. Armed with this knowledge, the manager can develop and apply the proper motivational methods to fit the specifics of a given situation.

SYSTEMATIC MANAGEMENT

The management of organizational behavior is best achieved when implemented in a systematic manner. One such approach is shown in Figure 3-10. The action starts with identifying the problem and getting the facts of the situation. Before any action is taken it is very important that the undesirable behavior be clearly identified. Then the frequency with which the problem has occurred should be established. For example, it is not the same thing if the incident is the first occurrence as when it is a frequent occurrence. If the facts show a relatively high incident rate, the situation should be analyzed to establish the cause of the problem. The factors causing the problem may have been a passing situation that has already corrected itself. On the other hand, the facts of the situation may dictate some form of intervention strategy to correct the problem. The corrective action could involve changes in the individual, the job, the work situation, or the supervisor. Whatever changes are implemented, there must be a follow-up action to establish the effectiveness of the intervention strategy. Just because corrective action is directed does not assure its proper implementation or its resolution of the problem.

FIGURE 3-10   Systematic management of behavior

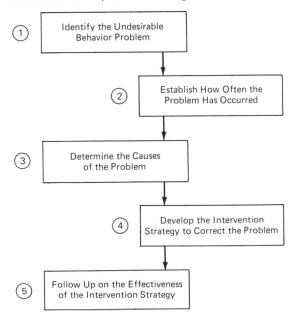

GUIDELINES FOR MANAGING BEHAVIOR

There are certain basic guidelines that will help a supervisor to successfully implement the desired intervention strategy in a behavioral problem:

- *Establish clearly understood performance standards that workers are expected to meet and communicate them to the individuals.*
- *Judge work performance and base rewards or disciplinary actions on facts, not personalities.*
- *Apply positive-reinforcement corrective actions whenever possible and minimize the use of negative techniques such as fear and punishment.*
- *Praise good performance in an objective and consistent manner, and with an awareness that failure to praise good behavior may cause poor work in the future.*
- *Personally communicate specific work performance that is not acceptable, and do it in a private and timely manner.*
- *Be fair by neither underrating nor overrating the work performance of individuals.*

Successful use of these guidelines for handling behavioral problems requires application of the *law of the situation.* First, you obtain and analyze all possible facts, and then you let the facts dictate your decision regarding the situation.

THE FUNCTION OF CONTROLLING

WHAT IS CONTROLLING?

CONTROL IS A COMPLEX PROCESS

Controlling involves assessing work performance to assure that it is adequate and directed toward its intended goal. Control is accomplished through measurement and evaluation of results in comparison with objectives set during planning. To control something means

- *Recognizing and diagnosing problems*
- *Determining what might be causing a given situation to be good or bad*
- *Providing feedback, guidance, and direction to improve things*

Basic to effective control is the establishment of specific (quantified if at all possible) overall goals with subgoals related to schedules and/or costs.

A Case on Communication Breakdown in Controlling

The following case illustrates the importance of controlling all significant aspects of a business operation. The case involves a large ($1.5 billion revenues in 1978), predominately chemical products corporation that became so involved in increasing its profits that it failed to control its employees.[12] This company got itself into trouble on two criminal actions brought about by the U.S. government. One indictment involved the illegal shipment of sporting arms and ammunition to South Africa. The second indictment involved employees dumping excessive amounts of mercury into the Niagara River between late 1970 and the middle of 1977. In both cases the company filed blatantly false documents with U.S. government agencies. On the arms and ammunition case, the employees told the U.S. Office of Munitions Control that the material was bound for Austria, Greece, and Spain. In the pollution case, employees submitted reports showing no deviations above the government limit, which was set at 0.1 pound per day. The company was actually discharging an average of almost 4 pounds per day and on one occasion 330 pounds. Among the factors that caused these two situations were obsession with job security on the part of the employees, and trying to achieve profitable operations in order to avoid a plant shutdown. Insufficient planning for the financial resources required for pollution control was also a contributing factor in the falsification of the pollution report.

This case reflects the importance of effective communication between management and employees on *how* company goals should be accomplished. It also points up the importance of management's checking that goals are being achieved without collusion or manipulation of facts. The pressure to accomplish profit goals can cause hanky-panky behavior on the part of both managers and subordinates. This type of behavior usually defeats its unethical purpose and tends to be very costly in the long run.

Controlling *How* Goals Are Achieved

In this particular case the combined fines may not have damaged the company's treasury to any great extent, but the failure to determine how goals were being achieved tarnished the company's reputation and that of its management. The company had to spend an inordinate amount of time instructing its employees in the importance of complying with all government regulations. Considerable time and money also had to be spent in monitoring newly devised controls to prevent any further cheating by employees. What happened to this company can easily happen to others. The lesson to be learned from this case is don't put pressure on subordinates to attain profits or other goals without controlling how the goals are achieved.

IMPORTANCE OF CONTROLLING

Controlling starts with planning and scheduling of what is to be done, and determining what facilities, materials, people, and money are required for implementation. Through executive action, the supervisor takes those steps necessary to insure that the desired results are attained. A properly designed and effectively implemented control system provides many benefits by enabling the supervisor to

- *Monitor a diversity of functions, operations, and/or products*
- *Control operations that are decentralized and scattered in several work areas*
- *Delegate work tasks to subordinates and determine if they are accomplishing their assigned tasks*
- *Detect problems affecting the organization's performance of its activities*
- *Catch mistakes before they become critical problems*
- *Achieve conformity with regulations, policies, procedures, and organizational objectives*
- *Obtain explanations of the status of operations*
- *Determine needed changes in the organization's performance of its activities*
- *Close the gap between performance and plans*
- *Facilitate dealing with future events*

DEVELOPING A CONTROL SYSTEM

The best control systems are developed on a participative basis involving all levels of management. Participation is important because the specific needs for and types of controls vary by organization and from higher-level to lower-level managers. Only by working together can management develop and operate a coordinated control system that provides the right things to the right people at the right time.

ESTABLISH OBJECTIVES

The steps for developing a control system are outlined in Figure 3-11. Each step in the illustration shows an example of the type of action involved. In *step 1* the objective of achieving customer satisfaction has been established. This is only one of many objectives normally established in a business organization. Others would probably be: (1) shortening production time, (2) increasing sales,

FIGURE 3-11   Development of a control system

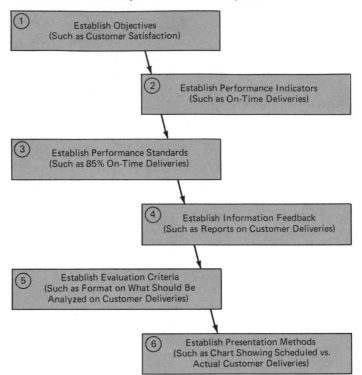

(3) reducing inventory levels, (4) reducing operating costs, (5) reducing labor turnover, and (6) reducing employee grievances.

Establish Indicators

The *second step* is to establish the indicators that will enable managers to measure progress in the achievement of objectives. The example—on-time deliveries—shown in this step is only one of several indicators commonly used for determining customer satisfaction. Other indicators could be: (1) meeting customer quality standards, (2) avoiding overruns on customer costs, and (3) providing timely maintenance services to the customer. In establishing both objectives and performance indicators, look for the most critical ones that need to be controlled. The most significant indicators will enable the manager to both detect deviations and forecast potential problems. Except for the simplest operations, supervisors can neither watch nor control every single action or item. The establishment of too many indicators usually results in an ineffective control system because important things get lost in the details.

ESTABLISH STANDARDS

The *third step* is to establish the standards to be used as a basis for judgment in measuring performance. In the example shown in Figure 3-11, a quantitative standard of 85 percent on-time deliveries was established as one indicator of achieving customer satisfaction. Since conditions change over time, standards established for indicators of performance should be both appropriate and flexible. There are limitations to uniform standards applicable to all organizations even when they perform similar functions. Seldom, if ever, are all environmental and other factors exactly the same. Layout of work, type and age of equipment, quality of materials, workers' experience, and managerial capabilities may vary significantly from one organization to another. In addition, the work efforts of some organizations cannot be quantitatively measured.

ESTABLISH INFORMATION FEEDBACK

The *fourth step* in developing a control system is to establish an information feedback network. This involves determining how information on the performance indicators will be collected, compared against standards, and reported. Whether the information feedback is accomplished manually or by computer, the significant deviations should be highlighted to avoid wasting time and money on matters of minor importance. This will enable the manager to see the problems that require immediate action and avoid dealing with those that can be delegated to subordinates.

ESTABLISH EVALUATION CRITERIA

The information obtained from the feedback system needs to be evaluated. The *fifth step* in developing a control system is to determine the criteria for evaluating information. For example, information regarding the dollar value of inventory on hand has little management use unless it is evaluated in relation to the dollar value of sales to establish the rate at which the inventory is being converted to revenues. Unsold inventory does not bring in the revenues necessary to keep the business viable. It is important to develop standardized formats defining *what* should be analyzed and *how* it should be structured in its presentation.

ESTABLISH PRESENTATION METHODS

The *sixth step* in developing a control system is to establish the methods of presenting the results of the evaluation of information. One of the most effective methods of presenting business information is through well-developed graphic charts. Figure 3-12 gives several illustrations of how such charts can be

FIGURE 3-12 Graphic charting techniques

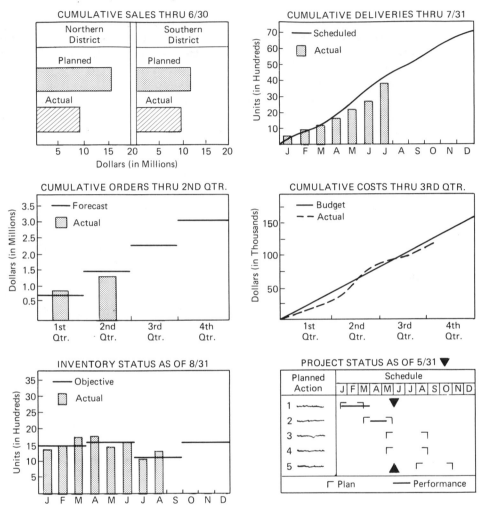

developed. Other methods include statistical reports, narrative reports, briefings, and conferences with superiors, peers, and/or subordinates.

PRINCIPLES OF CONTROLLING

CONTROLS AFFECT TIME, MONEY, AND PEOPLE

There are certain principles of management pertaining to control systems that can save time and money as well as enhance humanistic relations in the work-

FIGURE 3-13 Principles of controlling

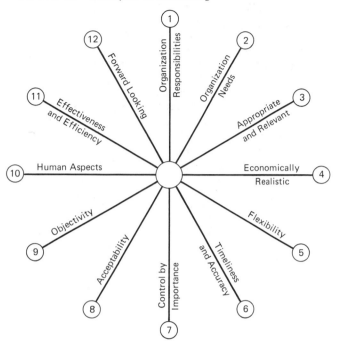

place. These principles are shown in Figure 3-13 and discussed in the following summary listing:

- THE PRINCIPLE OF ORGANIZATION RESPONSIBILITIES—*Build the control system around the functional responsibilities in the organization structure so that it is possible to pinpoint who is responsible for taking corrective action.*
- THE PRINCIPLE OF ORGANIZATION NEEDS—*Structure the control system to meet the needs of and measure the performance of the organization.*
- THE PRINCIPLE OF APPROPRIATENESS AND RELEVANCE—*The information produced by a control system should be simple and focus on those events and results which managers believe to be the most important.*
- THE PRINCIPLE OF BEING ECONOMICALLY REALISTIC—*A control system must justify the expense of developing and operating it. The costs of control usually increase with the preciseness of the measurement of progress. In many situations, approximations are adequate.*
- THE PRINCIPLE OF FLEXIBILITY—*Controls should allow for flexibility that permits reacting quickly to changes. The absence of flexibility can result in situations where the wrong answers are supplied after the problem has been solved.*
- THE PRINCIPLE OF TIMELINESS AND ACCURACY—*A control system should be capable of reporting deviations quickly and identifying potential*

problems before they become critical situations. The quality of information should reflect closeness to reality.

- THE PRINCIPLE OF CONTROL-BY-IMPORTANCE—*Both inputs and outputs of a control system should focus on the strategic control points that are the most critical in the achievement of organizational objectives.*

- THE PRINCIPLE OF ACCEPTABILITY—*Inputs and outputs of a control system must be understood in order for the users to have faith in and thereby be willing to accept the system.*

- THE PRINCIPLE OF OBJECTIVITY—*Objectivity in the development and use of performance information tends to improve both its accuracy and acceptability. The standards by which individuals or operations are to be judged should be known beforehand and verified by external reality.*

- THE PRINCIPLE OF THINKING ABOUT THE EMPLOYEES—*A control system should be established so that it can be viewed through the eyes of the people being controlled rather than only through the eyes of management. The acceptance of controls stands a better chance if management is aware of the personal needs and social pressures of employees and involves them in the design of the system. There will be less employee confusion, frustration, and job dissatisfaction if the system avoids the establishment of too many controls on too many things.*

- THE PRINCIPLE OF EFFECTIVENESS AND EFFICIENCY—*A good control system shows where something is wrong, to what extent it is wrong, who is responsible, and whether it is a part of the working operational functions of the organization.*

- THE PRINCIPLE OF FORWARD LOOKING—*The bottom line in effective control is think ahead and anticipate the problems of the future. After a control system is established, it should be periodically monitored to ascertain if it is accomplishing its purpose.*

SUPERVISION AND CONTROL

Control is achieved through recording the source data which reflects the measurement of progress, deviations, and discrepancies of an operation. These data may consist of direct labor hours, total costs, tonnage produced, items completed, number of documents processed, number and dollar value of sales orders, number and dollar value of engineering change orders, deliveries to customers, actual versus scheduled performance, and so on.

MANAGER INVOLVEMENT IN CONTROL

Very important in getting and using information for control purposes is personal supervision by the manager. Probably the most effective means of controlling an operation is for the manager to personally observe and follow up on the work progress in the place where it is being performed. Personal supervision enables the manager to see the problems firsthand and know the people involved in their solution. A second value in personal supervision is that it shows subordinates that the boss is interested in their work and problems.

Most workers like to see the boss walking through the work area and observing how things are going. Good control starts with good supervision.

SUMMARY

DIRECTING

Plans and organizations are controlled through the management process of directing. The function of directing involves assigning, instructing, and correcting people in the work efforts required to achieve stated objectives and plans. The most important elements of directing are leadership and motivation: getting people to do what you want them to do and to do it willingly.

LEADERSHIP

Leadership involves showing the way and guiding others in the achievement of an objective. It is a science in that there are guidelines, principles, and techniques that can be learned and applied in leading people. Leadership is also an art because it requires common sense, understanding, and consideration that are not found in guidelines. While there are many traits that can be associated with leadership, the most desirable are probably honesty, courage, competence, and ethical behavior.

MOTIVATION

There are many concepts of motivation. Some hold that people are motivated to act according to needs or desires. Other concepts express the belief that people are motivated in accordance with their expectancies. The manager's understanding and attitude about motivation are important. The bottom line is to know enough about your subordinates to determine which concept of motivation best fits each individual.

Good leadership includes being able to take the right motivational approach at the right time and place. Management of organizational behavior is achieved best when it is implemented in a systematic manner—get all the facts and analyze them before making a behavioral modification decision.

CONTROLLING

The function of control involves keeping track of progress toward achieving stated work objectives, watching for deviations in accomplishment of plans, and moving to correct problem situations. The steps involved in establishing a control system are the development of (1) objectives, (2) performance indicators, (3) performance standards, (4) information feedback, (5) criteria for evaluation of information, and (6) methods of presenting performance results. For a control system to work effectively, it must have a minimum of adverse effects on the people who have to live with it.

REVIEW QUESTIONS

1. How is leadership both an art and a science?

2. Do you agree or disagree that honesty and ethical behavior are two of the most significant characteristics of leadership? Explain your answer.

3. In motivating people, why is it a good rule for the manager to get to know subordinates as individuals?

4. Would you agree or disagree that studying the theoretical approaches to motivation is academic "hogwash?" Explain your answer.

5. Why are the beliefs that managers have about motivation important?

6. If you were faced with a motivational problem with a subordinate employee, how would you go about trying to modify the undesirable behavior?

7. Why is the function of controlling a complex process?

8. Why are many control systems not too effective in determining progress or establishing deviations in the accomplishment of plans? Develop a plan that will help make a control system an effective one.

9. In what ways can an effective control system pay for itself?

A CASE STUDY IN DIRECTING

Butch Rice is senior analyst in the Industrial Relations Department of a large steel plant in the Pittsburgh area. His responsibilities include investigation of employee complaints, fact finding regarding employee grievances submitted by local union officials, participation with the director of industrial relations and local union officials in the resolution of employee grievances, and evaluation of employee suggestions. When the director is absent for any extended period of time, Butch sits in his office as the acting director. However, Mr. Wissman, the director, delegates very little authority but prefers that problems requiring decision be deferred until his return. Mr.

Wissman is a very authoritarian manager who operates under a system of management-by-clique with informants located throughout the entire plant, including the switchboard operators. Butch Rice follows this same management practice in his position as senior analyst.

Butch has worked in the same plant for over fifteen years. He has been a laborer, a group leader, a production scheduling clerk, and has served the local union for several years as a shop steward. Butch did not complete high school and has had no formal education or training in management. He got to his current position status through hard work and high performance on the various jobs he held in the plant.

The company had just completed a major renovation and expansion of plant facilities and was obtaining disappointing productivity results. At the corporate level, they hired two recent MBA college graduates and assigned them to work with Mr. Wissman and Butch Rice. The two new employees found Butch to be very uncooperative. Time and again he would express his attitude that "you don't learn how to manage people by reading textbooks and studying management theories." Butch's confirmed conviction was that you learned how to manage through hard work and experience.

QUESTIONS:

1. Evaluate Mr. Wissman's attitude and identify its possible impact on the motivation of Mr. Rice and other subordinates. What corrective recommendations would you recommend to improve Mr. Wissman's management leadership?
2. Analyze Mr. Rice's attitude regarding how you learn to motivate and lead people. To what extent do you agree or disagree with his attitude and why?
3. Do you see any relationship between Mr. Wissman's and Mr. Rice's attitudes and the disappointing productivity results in the renovated plant? Explain your answer.
4. Do you think there were reasons, other than the plant expansion, that caused the two MBA college graduates to be assigned to work with Mr. Wissman and Mr. Rice? If so, what?

A CASE STUDY IN CONTROLLING

MICOM is a billion-dollar-a-year operation engaged in the engineering development, procurement, production, supply, and maintenance of highly technical equipment. The chief executive officer (CEO) of MICOM established a review and analysis system to control the accomplishment of all corporate operations. He had his staff develop management indicators of quantified information that measured how his managers accomplished the objectives and used their resources. The purpose of the management indicators was to enable the CEO to weigh actual performance against established standards, goals, plans, or schedules.

The CEO's staff established 347 management indicators. They included such indicators as the following: major item deliveries, engineering change proposals, travel costs versus approved budget, number of employee grievances, purchase requests over thirty days old, and computer idle time. A monthly meeting was held with top line and staff managers to review their programs against all 347 management indicators. The monthly review and analysis took several days to conduct and involved many more hours of follow-up corrective action. Most of these briefings resulted in the CEO sending out memos as "Noteworthy Achievement" or "Required Management Action" plus special assignments directed to selected managers. Each "Required Management Action" needed a reply sent directly to the CEO. The system involved thousands of hours of work effort in preparation, presentation, and follow-up action but it did produce positive results.

QUESTIONS

1. What is your evaluation of the MICOM control system?
2. What changes, if any, would you recommend?

NOTES

1. Douglas McGregor, *The Human Side of Enterprise* (New York: McGraw-Hill, 1960), pp. 33–43.

2. Ibid., pp. 47–48.

3. Robert R. Blake, and others, "Breakthrough in Organization Development," *Harvard Business Review*, November–December 1964, pp. 133–55. Copyright © 1968 by the President and Fellows of Harvard College; all rights reserved.

4. Ralph M. Stogdill and Alvin E. Coons, eds., "Leader Behavior: Its Description and Measurement," Monograph R-88, Bureau of Business Research, Ohio State University, 1957.

5. Daniel Katz, Nathan Macoby, and Nancy C. Morse, *Productivity, Supervision and Morale in an Office Situation*, (Ann Arbor, Mich.: University of Michigan Institute for Social Research, 1950).

6. Frederick Herzberg, Bernard Mausner, and Barbara Snyderman, *The Motivation to Work* (New York: John Wiley, 1959).

7. Abraham Maslow, *Motivation and Personality* (New York: Harper & Row, Pub., 1954), p. 13.

8. Frederick Herzberg, "One More Time: How Do You Motivate Employees?" *Harvard Business Review*, January–February 1968, pp. 53–62.

9. Martin J. Gannon, *Organizational Behavior* (Boston: Little, Brown, 1979), pp. 173–74. Justin G. Longenecker and Charles D. Pringle, *Management*, 6th ed. (Columbus, Ohio: Chas. E. Merrill, 1984), pp. 285–88.

10. B. F. Skinner, *Science and Human Behavior* (New York: The Free Press, 1953); and C.B. Ferster and B. F. Skinner, *Schedules of Reinforcement* (Englewood Cliffs, N.J.: Prentice-Hall, 1957).

11. W. Clay Hammer, "Reinforcement Theory and Contingency Management in Organizational Settings," in *Organizational Behavior and Management: A Contingency Approach*, eds. Henry L. Tosi and Clay Hammer (Chicago: St. Clair Press, 1974).

12. Hugh D. Menzier, "The One-Two Punch that Shook Olin," *Fortune*, June 5, 1978, pp. 120–23.

4

*Supervisory Management Is:
Developing Teamwork in the
Effective and Efficient
Accomplishment
of Objectives*

The Responsibilities of a Supervisor

LEARNING OBJECTIVES

The objectives of this chapter on the responsibilities of a supervisor are to enable the reader to

1. Relate where and how the supervisor fits into the management hierarchy in terms of responsibilities, management functions, and managerial roles
2. Understand the following aspects of supervisory management that influence a supervisor's effectiveness:
    a. The elements of a supervisor's job that must be consistently and intelligently managed
    b. The desirable relationships between a supervisor and his or her superiors, subordinates, peers, staff assistants, and the union
    c. The change in work style from being a worker to being a supervisor
    d. The tasks involved in the planning and organizing of jobs
    e. The elements of supervisory control
3. Identify the factors that cause supervisors to fail or enable them to succeed
4. Describe the basic criteria for selection of a supervisor and the areas of learning that are significant steppingstones in the development of supervisory abilities

KEY WORDS

Administrative Skills The ability to plan, organize, direct, and control a task, function, project, or organization.

Humanistic Relations Skills The manifestation of interest and concern for the liberty, rights, welfare, dignity, and other values of human beings in the performance of work activities.

Industrial Engineering The discipline that involves research in developing the most effective and efficient methods and procedures for performing work.

Management Hierarchy The successive ranking of managers, one above another.

Staff Assistant An individual responsible for providing technical assistance and support in a specialized functional activity such as accounting, law, or personnel management.

Technical Skills The specialized knowledge in a particular profession, trade, or type of work.

THE CASE OF EDWARD DUNCAN

Edward Duncan is a college graduate with a major in mechanical engineering. He has been employed for several years as a professional engineer by A & S Products, Inc. Three years ago he was promoted to the position of chief of one of the sections in the Engineering Department.

Duncan is a very good engineer and is probably the most capable in his section. Because of his competence in mechanical engineering, he performs many technical tasks himself, often working overtime to complete them. He does, however, closely supervise his subordinates and is able to quickly point out their mistakes.

Edward Duncan is both firm and consistent in the execution of his supervisory responsibilities. He believes, for example, that his subordinates should be at work on time and not leave until the official quitting time. His firm policy on tardiness is that if any employee is late three times within a six-month period, the individual will be docked one hour's pay. This policy is enforced regardless of the reason for the tardiness. The enforcement of this policy may be one factor in the low morale of the workers in Duncan's engineering section, since many other supervisors do not exercise the same firmness in enforcing policies. Employee turnover, complaints, and grievances are very high in Duncan's section. Because the work gets done, Edward's immediate supervisor appears to be satisfied with his performance. However, Edward has not received any special recognition in his periodic performance appraisals.

What is your evaluation of Edward Duncan as a supervisor? Why not write down your evaluation of what's good and what's not good about Edward Duncan's supervisory management? Then you can check your evaluation with the responsibilities of a supervisor outlined in this chapter.

FIGURE 4-1   The difficulties of a supervisor

FITTING INTO
THE MANAGEMENT HIERARCHY

A Supervisor Must Be Responsive to Many Things

To be a supervisor is like being a performing juggler running on a circus high wire (Figure 4-1). Above is higher-level management engaged in setting objectives and issuing orders. Below are the subordinates with their demands and problems. Off on the side representing the workers is the union observing how well the juggling is performed. The superiors are thinking, if not saying, "Don't fail us." The subordinates are thinking, if not saying, "Don't let us down."

A Supervisor Must Communicate, Coordinate, and Cooperate

As reflected in Figure 4-2, a supervisor must communicate, coordinate, cooperate, and help build teamwork between superiors, subordinates, and peers

FIGURE 4-2   A supervisor's responsibilities

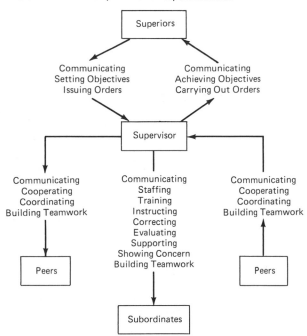

who are supervising other activities in the workplace. Inherent in the responsibilities of a supervisor is the interdependence on others.

A Supervisor Must Satisfy Both Job and Worker Demands

The supervisor is also expected to achieve high production output, maintain good quality of product or service, obtain maximum utilization of resources, reduce costs, and establish a happy, motivated workforce. To be effective, therefore, the supervisor must satisfy many job and employee demands. This involves giving attention to both technical and humanistic relations aspects of the work. Edward Duncan, mentioned at the beginning of the chapter, did not give balanced attention to all aspects of his job. He still spent too much of his time on technical engineering tasks and not enough time in understanding the capabilities, concerns, and problems of his subordinates.

Supervisors are a part of management but they often lose their identity in the precarious balancing act that they must perform. A good supervisor can have considerable influence on productivity, cost reduction, product quality, worker absenteeism, worker morale, and employee relations. The authority, however, that the supervisor may have to carry out assigned responsibilities is often insufficient and/or unclear. Under these conditions, the supervisor is not only on a circus high wire but is there without a net in case a mistake is made.

Primary Emphasis on Directing and Controlling

Figure 4-3 shows where supervisors fit into the managerial hierarchy. A supervisor may be referred to as an operational-level manager, directing workers in the accomplishment of functional work activities. The primary distinction between supervisors and the managers at other levels is in their role in the organizational hierarchy. Managers at all levels have responsibilities for planning, organizing, directing, and controlling. At the middle and top levels, more emphasis is given to the functions of planning and organizing (Figure 4-4). At the supervisory level, the primary emphasis is on directing and controlling.

Technical and Humanistic Relations Skills Required

The roles of all levels of management involve administrative, technical, and humanistic relations skills. Here also, the roles played by managers at different

FIGURE 4-3 How supervisors fit into the management hierarchy

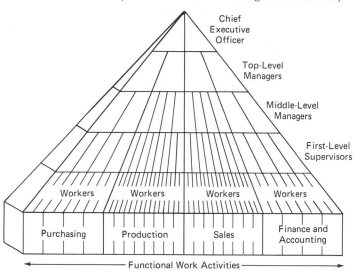

levels vary only in the degree of significance in the application of these skills (Figure 4-5). At the executive management level the primary emphasis is on administrative skills. At the supervisory level the primary emphasis is about equally divided between the technical and the humanistic relations aspects of the job.

FIGURE 4-4 How often supervisors perform basic management functions of planning, organizing, directing, controlling

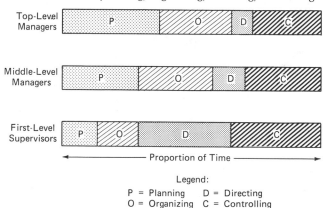

FIGURE 4-5 How often supervisors perform administrative, technical, and humanistic relations roles

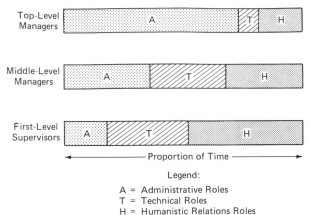

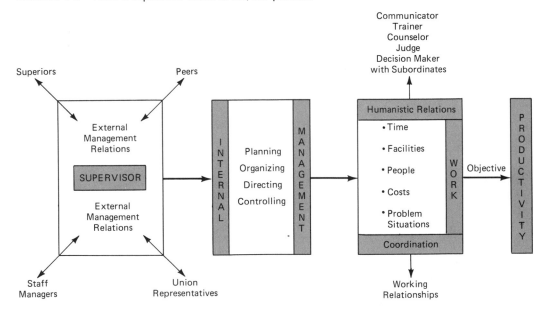

FIGURE 4-6 How a supervisor looks at his/her position

WHAT IT MEANS TO BE A SUPERVISOR

A No-Winner Contest and Very Demanding Job

The first-level supervisor is a very vital link in the management hierarchy. The supervisor stands at the point where management objectives, policies, and directives must be applied and implemented. The role of supervisor is often complex and frustrating because there are so many factors in the job, many of which are beyond the control of the individual in the position. Supervisors often feel they are engaged in a no-winner contest. Figure 4-6 shows the elements that make the supervisor's job a very demanding one.

INTERRELATIONSHIPS IN SUPERVISORY MANAGEMENT

A supervisor must maintain good working relationships with four primary groups of individuals. If the supervisor works in a unionized organization, the number of primary groups is increased to five. As indicated in Figure 4-7, the supervisor is a connecting link involving superiors, subordinates, peers, staff specialists, and the union.

Respect for and Cooperation with Superiors

• *RELATIONSHIP WITH SUPERIORS*—The supervisor is the link between workers and higher levels of management. The supervisor receives guidance, instructions, and directives from middle-level and/or higher-level management. In a well-managed organization there is mutual respect and cooperation between supervisors and superiors. This type of atmosphere in the work environment is an important motivating factor for the supervisor in striving to (1) promote the achievement of company goals, (2) operate according to company policy, and (3) achieve efficiency through the effective use of money, material, and manpower resources. Mutual respect and cooperation are key factors in the achievement of work deadlines, operation within budget restraints, and submission of reports on performance.

Communicating and Working with Subordinates

• *RELATIONSHIPS WITH SUBORDINATES*—If a supervisor expects to achieve success, he or she must get to know the subordinates as human beings.

FIGURE 4-7 Supervisor interrelationships

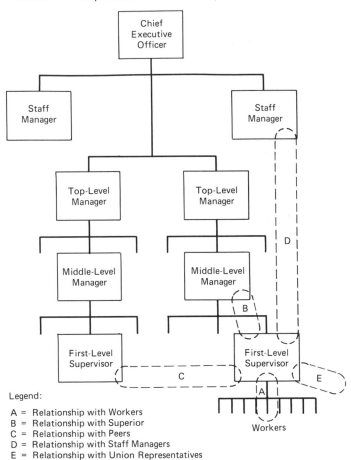

Legend:

A = Relationship with Workers
B = Relationship with Superior
C = Relationship with Peers
D = Relationship with Staff Managers
E = Relationship with Union Representatives

This means communicating and finding out important things about each subordinate. Good communications and showing an interest in subordinates as human beings should be reinforced with actions that show how the supervisor stands behind and supports the subordinates when they are performing according to orders. The supervisor will also stand tall among most subordinates by setting the right example in good behavior, both on and off the job. Every person engaged in supervising others becomes involved in many face-to-face relations with the people they manage. These relationships include (1) placing people on jobs, (2) tailoring jobs to fit the person, (3) providing instruction and training, (4) giving constructive criticism on work performance, (5) evaluating worker performance, (6) handling worker complaints and problems, and (7) taking action to safeguard the health and welfare of workers.

DEVELOPING TEAMWORK WITH PEERS

● *RELATIONSHIPS WITH PEERS*—There are few, if any, work situations where a supervisor does not have to maintain close working relationships with associate peers—the supervisors of other departments. Supervisors should get to know one another as individuals. This will facilitate the teamwork necessary in any work environment. As supervisors help one another, they find that they learn many things from their peers. They also find that cooperation and teamwork usually provide job satisfaction and make the supervisor's job a little easier.

UTILIZING THE SERVICES OF STAFF MANAGERS

● *RELATIONSHIPS WITH STAFF ASSISTANTS*—In most sizeable organizations there has been a growth of specialization that has stripped first-level supervisors of some authority. This increase in staff assistants has occurred in such areas as safety, production planning and control, maintenance, personnel, equal employment opportunity, budgeting, and cost accounting. Each of these staff groups wants to have a say in how the supervisor performs certain functions. Every staff group tends to establish a power base in exercising its particular area of expertise. The supervisor must learn to cope with these many staff assistants. A good guide in this respect is for the supervisor to "join them, not fight them." The responsibilities of every staff assistant are to assist and serve the supervisors in the accomplishment of organizational objectives. A supervisor should work with and take advantage of the services provided by staff assistants. In the event a staff assistant exceeds his or her assigned functional authority (see Chapter 2), the supervisor should tactfully, but forcefully, take corrective action. If the supervisor is not able to correct the authority indiscretions of a staff assistant, the matter should be referred to higher-level management for resolution.

THE GOOD SUPERVISOR HAS FEW PROBLEMS WITH THE UNION

● *RELATIONSHIPS WITH THE UNION*—The best way to establish and maintain good working relations with the union is to be a good supervisor. The supervisor who understands and treats people as human beings does not usually have much, if any, trouble with the union. Supervisors who are respected for their honesty and fairness in working with subordinates are seldom faced with worker complaints and grievances. The reason is that most workers prefer to take their work-related problems to a supervisor whom they trust. When workers feel that they cannot talk things over with the supervisor, it is logical to take their problems to the union. Edward Duncan, mentioned at the beginning of the chapter, would not listen to reason when some of his employees were late to work. For example, he docked an employee for being late a few minutes when the cause was a severe snow storm. The frustrated worker, who had left for work some thirty minutes earlier than normal, felt she had no other choice than to initiate a grievance and take it to the union.

COOPERATION IS MORE PRODUCTIVE THAN CONFLICT

If a supervisor is the "target" of the union, it is probably because the supervisor has failed to develop good humanistic relations with subordinates. In addition to maintaining effective personal relations with subordinates, a supervisor should strive to cooperate with the union and higher-level management in improving the workplace. Working together is much more productive than fighting.

THE BIG CROSSOVER TO SUPERVISOR

SUPERVISION REQUIRES A DIFFERENT STYLE OF WORKING

Most supervisors are promoted to first-level management positions from the ranks of the workers. The changeover from worker to supervisor is a big step (Figure 4-8). It involves a complete change in style of working. If we refer again to the Edward Duncan case, we find that he never really changed his style of working after he became a supervisor. He continued to be an engineer rather than a manager. He frequently was deeply engaged in performing tasks that should have been delegated to his subordinates. While engaged in these tasks, he was not giving sufficient attention to the organization-related concerns of his engineering section.

As a worker, the self-satisfaction of the work itself, along with the pay and fringe benefits, may be the only concerns of the individual. As a supervisor, the primary concerns of the individual tend to shift from self-concerns to company-related concerns such as production, budgets, costs, quality standards

FIGURE 4-8   It's a big crossover to being a supervisor

and time schedules. After the crossover to supervision, the individual may find little time to even think about personal self-satisfaction. As a supervisor, the individual can expect pressures from superiors, peers, workers, and the union. The thinking process in handling these pressures is entirely different from that of a worker.

The new supervisor quickly discovers that there is a big difference between being a worker and doing something yourself versus being a supervisor and telling someone else what to do and what not to do. As a supervisor, you can not rely on your own ability to do a job. You must now rely on getting others to do the job. Knowledge of how to do a job, technical skill, and hard work are not enough to become a good supervisor. One author succinctly expressed this situation by saying that some supervisors are disguised workers trying to get everybody's job done except their own, and in the process jeopardize their own chances of career success.[1]

THINKING THINGS THROUGH

A Supervisor Must Be Management-Minded

A supervisor must be management-minded. This involves diligent application of the three Ts of management—*Think Things Through*. It means knowing and carrying out management philosophies, policies, and procedures while also being alert to where improvements are needed. A good supervisor constantly seeks better ways of doing things. This includes being alert and enthusiastic about constructive changes in work methods and adopting self-improvement as ways of life. Thinking things through is involved in everything a supervisor does. Acting without thinking has no place in good supervision.

APPLYING THE FUNCTIONS OF PLANNING AND ORGANIZING

Planning and Organizing Help Keep a Supervisor on Top of the Job

A supervisor should be on top of the job, not "snowed under" by it (Figure 4-9). Keeping on top of the job starts with planning and organizing. A supervisor should not think that lower-level managers have little responsibility and authority for planning and organizing. It is easy to develop such an attitude, since higher-level managers may have established the primary objectives, policies, and plans as well as the organization structure that the first-level supervisor is expected to follow. Lower-level managers have responsibilities for the detailed planning and organizing that cannot be effectively performed elsewhere in the management hierarchy. Overall effectiveness and efficiency of operations are very much affected by how well the first-level supervisor plans and organizes work activity at the point where it is performed.

FIGURE 4-9 The good supervisor is on top of the job

FIGURE 4-10 The supervisor's role in planning

• *PLANNING*—The supervisor has a dual role in planning (Figure 4-10). The primary role is that of planning the daily, weekly, and monthly work schedules for the workers and the machines in the supervisor's department. A secondary role is that of providing planning input for use in the development of higher-level strategic plans. In the primary role the supervisor is the day-to-day planner for the department. In the secondary role the supervisor is in the position of providing valuable technical information regarding specific functional or operational considerations that may be important to longer-range planning.

PLANNING INVOLVES THINKING BEFORE ACTING

Planning involves thinking before acting. It means looking ahead and preparing for the future. It embraces being knowledgeable of and applying the elements of good supervisory planning shown in Figure 4-11.

Supervisors must plan their own work as well as that of subordinates. The planning must be very certain and specific to avoid confusion and doubt in the minds of the workers assigned to do the work. When workers have a feeling of uncertainty about what the "boss" wants and who is to do it, they tend to respond adversely to the supervisor's leadership. The productivity of a worker may be lowered when there is uncertainty. Planning avoids such "muddling-through" methods of getting work done.

The "boss" who has the attitude, "Tomorrow's another day: I'll think

FIGURE 4-11 Elements of good supervisory planning

(1) KNOW WHAT NEEDS TO BE DONE AND ESTABLISH WORK OBJECTIVES, TIME SCHEDULES, AND STANDARDS OF PERFORMANCE FOR ITS ACCOMPLISHMENT.

(2) AVOID OVEROPTIMISM AND PROVIDE FOR A MARGIN OF ERROR.

(3) AVOID UNREALISTICALLY TIGHT DEADLINES BECAUSE "IF YOU WANT IT BAD YOU WILL GET IT BAD" FROM THE WORKERS.

(4) BE FLEXIBLE, DEVELOP FORESIGHT, AND MAKE PLANNING CHANGES WHEN THEY ARE NECESSARY.

(5) KNOW WHAT YOUR AVAILABLE AND FUTURE RESOURCES ARE IN FUNDS, EQUIPMENT, AND WORKER SKILLS.

(6) DEVELOP AND IMPLEMENT EFFICIENT WORK METHODS AND PROCEDURES.

(7) IDENTIFY SPECIAL SITUATIONS SUCH AS HOLIDAYS AND VACATIONS THAT CAN HAVE AN IMPACT ON PLANNING.

(8) FACE REALITY ON SUCH THINGS AS MAINTENANCE DELAYS AND COSTS.

(9) PROVIDE ADEQUATE COMMUNICATION SO THAT EVERYONE INVOLVED KNOWS WHAT IS GOING ON.

about its problems when they happen," is making sure problems will happen.[2] The effective supervisor thinks before acting. This thinking should involve an analysis that addresses such questions as

- *Do I know what is really required to be done?*
- *Do I have all the facts?*
- *Have I identified and evaluated all the circumstances?*
- *Have I considered all possible alternatives?*
- *Have I coordinated, where necessary, with my peers and the union?*
- *Have I considered advice from all appropriate individuals?*
- *Have I thought through the entire process?*

If the analysis did not score a "yes" on each of the above questions, the supervisor still has some planning homework to do.

ORGANIZING INVOLVES WORK AND PEOPLE

• *ORGANIZING*—Organizing involves determining how the work will be divided and accomplished. It means breaking an objective or plan down into jobs, then subdividing the jobs into tasks, and finally assigning specific tasks to workers with the qualifications to do the work. Effective organizing involves identifying the people who like to and can work alone versus those who like working with others. This requires careful evaluation of people because "loners" usually don't talk about their preference to work alone. It is the socially accepted thing for most people to like to work with others. Careful attention is also needed to assign people who are compatible to jobs where they can work together. These are difficult but important decisions for a supervisor.

It is up to the supervisor to use the existing organization structure to get the required work accomplished. This should be done with the positive attitude that the supervisor is the key individual in the organization and not just an intermediary caught in the middle of a big organizational "quagmire." Most subordinates do not have much respect for a supervisor who constantly complains about being helplessly caught between higher-level management, the union, and workers.

The supervisor should avoid being "organization-happy" in using organization charts, functional statements, and job descriptions as substitutes for leadership in getting people to work efficiently. Of course the supervisor must manage in conformance with these directed aspects of organizational management. To do otherwise would cause considerable problems with other managers and the union. However, organization charts, functional statements, and job descriptions do not cause people to be motivated in the performance of their work. It is through a results-oriented supervisor, who applies a sincere understanding of effective humanistic relations, that people with talents and skills work together and get jobs accomplished (Figure 4-12).

FIGURE 4-12 A supervisor should be result-oriented and have consideration for subordinates

ORGANIZATIONAL TASKS

Supervisory planning and organizing include performing the following tasks where they are appropriate:

- *Obtaining the necessary tools, equipment, and supplies*
- *Developing methods and procedures for the best use of tools, equipment, supplies, and people*
- *Allocating adequate physical space for doing the work*
- *Allocating realistic time for doing the work*
- *Assigning the right people to do the work*

In performing some of these tasks, the supervisor may find it desirable to obtain staff assistance from available experts in other departments. Where the supervisor gets involved in developing work methods and procedures, it is also usually a good policy to coordinate and communicate with the union and obtain their support.

There are tangible benefits to be obtained from supervisory planning and organizing:

BENEFITS FROM PLANNING AND ORGANIZING

- *Maximum use of production capacity of expensive tools and equipment*
- *Effective use of physical work space*
- *Maximum use of the time and abilities of workers*
- *Avoidance of duplication and unnecessary work effort*
- *Avoidance of work bottlenecks*
- *Avoidance of idle time due to lack of materials, poor machine maintenance, and/or workers not knowing what to do*
- *Equal distribution of work to workers according to their abilities*

APPLYING THE FUNCTIONS
OF DIRECTING AND CONTROLLING

It is through directing that a supervisor releases plans and instructions to workers for execution. The exercise of control provides the means of assuring that plans and instructions are being satisfactorily carried out. Directing and controlling are key supervisory roles.

DIRECTING INVOLVES HUMANISTIC RELATIONS

- *DIRECTING*—Edward Duncan, mentioned at the beginning of the chapter, was a good engineer but significantly lacking in his humanistic relations

with subordinates. For example, he was quick to point out mistakes, but seldom praised his subordinates for outstanding work. Even though his firmness and consistency were positive attributes of supervisory leadership, he
should have provided for some flexibility in his directing. He would have
had less employee turnover, complaints, and grievances if he had obtained
and analyzed all the facts and then let the facts of the situation determine
the direction of his decisions.

CONTROLLING IS A LEARNING PROCESS

● *CONTROLLING*—Controlling involves tools and equipment, materials,
methods and procedures, time, costs, and people. Good supervisor control
starts with planning and organizing (Figure 4-13). It also is considerably influenced by the directives of the supervisor. First, the supervisor should carefully
plan the orders issued to subordinates. Second, when an order is issued it
should be thoroughly explained and a check made to be sure the worker understands the order. Third, the supervisor should follow up to see how well the
order is executed. Fourth, in taking corrective action on an order that is not
being satisfactorily executed, the supervisor must obtain all the facts of the sit-

FIGURE 4-13   The elements of supervisory control

uation before making a decision. These facts may reflect that the original order should be modified or changed. Regardless of the care exercised in planning and organizing, it is not possible to anticipate every unforeseen factor. Good control can, therefore, often contribute to one's management learning experience.

The effective supervisor who gets the job done and gains the respect of subordinates, is the one who can be flexible and make changes when necessary. In directing and controlling the work efforts of subordinates, the supervisor should focus on results desired and results achieved. This puts the management functions of directing and controlling on an objective basis which most subordinates tend to readily accept.

HOW TO FAIL AS A SUPERVISOR

DON'T IGNORE SUBORDINATES

Probably the easiest way to fail as a supervisor is *not* give adequate attention to workers or *not* show concern for their needs (Figure 4-14). Some supervisors feel that being concerned about workers is a sign of weakness and may result in challenges to their authority. Showing concern for workers as human beings

FIGURE 4-14   How to fail as a supervisor

does *not* mean giving in to them. Showing concern means being honest, fair, considerate, and objective. The supervisor who meets these leadership qualities can still be tough and say "no" to worker demands and still maintain their respect. An easy way to get into trouble and lose respect of workers is to be tough and *not* be honest, fair, considerate, or objective.

AVOID THE AUTHORITARIAN ATTITUDE

Supervisor attitude, particularly the lack of management-mindedness, is another significant factor that causes supervisors to fail. One author, in a survey of 225 plant managers, states that 56 percent of supervisor failures are due to poor attitude.[3] Poor management on the job, including not thinking like a manager, is another big reason why supervisors fail. Bradford B. Boyd, in his book *Management-Minded Supervision,* states that to be management-minded involves

- *Knowing and supporting management philosophies, policies, and procedures*
- *Adopting constant self-improvement as a way of life*
- *Recognizing the vital role of communication in an organization*
- *Being enthusiastic about change and skilled in initiating it*
- *Understanding the need to know people as individuals and recognizing that motivation is the key to effective leadership*
- *Having appreciation for the management processes of planning, organizing, directing, and controlling*[4]

Attitude toward other people and unreasonableness in methods of doing things can be very damaging to a supervisor's position.

DON'T CLOSE OFF EMPLOYEE SUGGESTIONS

Supervisors with the authoritarian attitude that everything must be done their way close the door to better work methods. Keeping the door open for suggestions, ideas, and recommendations from subordinates can frequently bring about better ways of getting a job done. In addition, consultative or participative management tends to increase worker understanding, acceptance, and motivation for getting things accomplished. Supervisors with the attitude that they are the "boss" and above the subordinates tend to lose respect and worker productivity. Nothing is gained by projecting themselves as superior to other human beings.

ACTIONS CAUSING SUPERVISORS TO FAIL

There are many other factors that can contribute to supervisors' failings:

- *Poor personal relations with subordinates and/or peers as well as with superiors*

- *Tunnel vision in being able to only see one's own little sphere of work activity and nothing else*
- *Failure to communicate with subordinates, peers, and/or superiors*
- *Failure to coordinate work activities with others*
- *Inability to plan and organize things*
- *Supervising too many little things too closely*
- *Trying to do too many things personally instead of delegating appropriate tasks to subordinates*
- *Inability to adjust to necessary changes*
- *Inability to get along with the union*
- *Unwillingness to improve methods of management*
- *Personality defects*

A final reason why managers fail occurs in how they decide on job priorities. It is very easy to spend time on simple tasks that one enjoys while neglecting difficult ones. The trouble with this is that the important tasks are often not the first to get done.

HOW TO SUCCEED AS A SUPERVISOR

KNOW WHAT THE PRIORITIES ARE

A good starting point for becoming a successful supervisor is to know the priorities of what you are supposed to be doing and to give prime attention to the managing of people. To be a supervisor, one must think and act like a manager who (1) knows where he or she is going and (2) fully appreciates the role of workers in getting there (Figure 4-15).

ACTIONS REFLECT ATTITUDE

Attitude is a key factor in being a successful supervisor. The way a person thinks determines how the individual acts. If an individual, for example, is promoted from cost accountant to supervisory accountant, but still thinks like a cost accountant, the individual is not thinking or acting as a manager. The supervisor who "thinks narrow, acts narrow." The case of Edward Duncan described earlier is an example of a supervisor with a limited perspective of his job.

AVOID NARROW-MINDEDNESS

To be a successful supervisor one must think about every aspect of the entire organization being managed. This includes awareness of how one's organizational unit fits in with the functions and work activities of other organizations

FIGURE 4-15 How to succeed as a supervisor

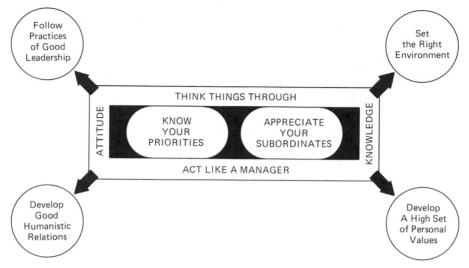

in the total establishment. There is no place for narrow-mindedness in successful supervision—that is, seeing only your own little job.

DEVELOP GOOD LEADERSHIP

A supervisory position is one of the most critical jobs in any organization because it involves directing people in day-to-day operations. This position includes more than assigning jobs, giving intelligent instructions, and following up on work assignments. It also means being a forebearing and sympathetic listener. It includes providing advice and counsel and resolving job-related problems involving subordinates. It means delegating work to others rather than doing everything yourself. It is a constant challenge to find ways of overcoming your own dissatisfactions while motivating your subordiantes to the point where they find job satisfaction. The first important factor, therefore, in being a successful supervisor is to develop the practices of good leadership.

ESTABLISH THE RIGHT ENVIRONMENT

A second important factor in good supervision is to set the right environment for yourself and others:

- *Having a good knowledge of the basic principles of planning, organizing, directing, and controlling and then learning how to put them into actual practice*
- *Developing an understanding of the whole organization, not just your little piece*

- *Setting practical and realistic objectives that can be systematically measured and that can be easily understood by others*
- *Understanding company rules and policies and passing this understanding on to your subordinates*
- *Establishing your organization on the basis of the work effort to be accomplished, not on personalities*

DEVELOP HIGH PERSONAL VALUES

A third important factor in succeeding as a supervisor is to develop a high set of personal values for yourself:

- *Have the courage of your convictions and defend what you feel is right, then be intelligent in the implementation of higher-level decisions once they are made.*
- *Be careful in the assumptions you make about other people. Assumptions tend to greatly influence leadership behavior.*
- *Don't use company policy as an excuse for things you don't want to do or don't know how to do.*
- *Be honest and straightforward.*
- *Admit your own mistakes.*
- *Don't cover up poor performance—either your own or that of your subordinates.*
- *Support your subordinates, even when they make reasonable mistakes.*
- *Be patient and have a sense of humor.*

DEVELOP GOOD HUMANISTIC RELATIONS

A fourth important factor in being successful in supervisory management is to develop good humanistic relations with your subordinates:

- *Don't play favorites with subordinates.*
- *Take pride in your subordinates and defend them.*
- *Strive to get good performance from all of your subordinates.*
- *Don't play the deceptive game of letting subordinates think you agree when in fact you don't.*
- *Give subordinates all possible information that concerns them and their jobs.*
- *Let subordinates periodically know how they are doing in their work performance.*
- *Give subordinates recognition for good work and make certain it is timely and consistently given.*
- *Base subordinate performance appraisals on supportable facts.*
- *Don't allow some subordinates to break rules while "throwing the rule book" at others for the same infraction.*
- *Don't discriminate.*

In summary, the successful supervisor (1) thinks and acts like an effective and efficient manager, (2) knows the work priorities, (3) appreciates subordinates, (4) follows practices of good leadership, (5) sets the right environment for the organization, (6) develops a high set of personal values, and (7) develops good humanistic relations with the subordinates.

THE SELECTION OF A SUPERVISOR

Based on one survey of 225 plant managers, 94 percent of the supervisors were found to be promoted from within the organization. Two-thirds of these plant managers considered a high school diploma a minimum educational requirement and those in technologically advanced companies insisted on college degrees for their supervisors.[5]

What should be the criteria for selection of a supervisor? Should the individual be required to have a college degree? If so, what kind of courses should the individual have taken? Should the selection be based on how well the person has been performing on his or her current job? How about the "yes, sir" person who has done an outstanding job of pleasing their superiors? If you were desirous of becoming a supervisor, what do you think the selection criteria should be?

A BIG DIFFERENCE: WORKER VERSUS SUPERVISOR

Based on managerial training programs being conducted by many industrial, commercial, government, and non-profit organizations, there are indicators that the criteria shown in Figure 4-16 is being increasingly applied in the se-

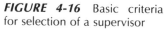

FIGURE 4-16 Basic criteria for selection of a supervisor

lection of supervisors. There appears to be an increasing awareness by higher-level managers that individuals who excel in the performance of a specific working level job do not always make the best supervisors. Edward Duncan is a good example. The highly skilled production worker who is promoted to supervisor often finds the difference between the two positions a very difficult obstacle to overcome.[6] A good supervisor must have a diversity of skills that go far beyond those needed to perform a specific functional job.

SUPERVISORY SKILLS

As reflected in Figure 4-16, if you are desirous of becoming a supervisor your selection should be on the basis of your combined skills in leadership, in understanding and working with people, in technical competence, and in administrative management. It would be a mistake to select you if you do not have all of these skills. The purpose of this book is to help you develop these combined skills.

DEVELOPMENT OF SUPERVISORY ABILITY

SUPERVISORY ABILITY CAN BE LEARNED

To a certain extent supervisory ability can be learned, provided the individual has a flexible attitude. Most of the problems in supervisory management have been experienced by others. This makes it possible to learn many of the *do's* and *don'ts* of management.

FOUNDATIONS OF MANAGEMENT

The development of supervisory ability should start with a good understanding of the fundamentals of leadership and motivation. These abilities should then be applied in performing the basic management functions of planning, organizing, directing, and controlling. The fundamentals of management should be analyzed to gain an understanding of the similarities, differences, and interactions in implementing them at the various levels of management. Teamwork is very important to the achievement of effective and efficient management. To achieve teamwork requires an understanding of how management should function at all levels.

INTERPERSONAL RELATIONS

Armed with knowledge of the foundations of management, the supervisor needs to develop a good understanding and appreciation of interpersonal relations. This includes managerial communications, humanistic relations, supervisory leadership, and ability to handle people. To achieve effectiveness in getting work accomplished through others, the supervisor must be able to communicate, lead, and direct.

SUPERVISION OF WORK

It is a primary responsibility of the first-level supervisor to get the work done. Supervision of work requires development of skills in the use of appropriate techniques of management that will get things done in a cost-effective way. This involves leadership in directing others in the best use of resources—facilities, materials, time, and people. It also includes recognizing the need for and being able to implement work simplification.

ATTITUDE ADJUSTMENT

Good supervisors develop a positive attitude regarding technological changes in tools, equipment, and work processes. They learn to appreciate and handle innovativeness in getting work accomplished. Improvement in the status quo of the organization is a stimulating challenge to the supervisor who shows others the way to better management. For long-term effectiveness in management, the supervisor should maintain an attitude that reflects the highest of ethical practices. To follow principles or standards of management conduct that are not ethical is usually a shortcut to disaster. Some people manage to get by with unethical practices—most do not and their downfall is quite turbulent.

SUMMARY

The position of a first-level supervisor is very difficult, demanding, and challenging. It involves achieving a proper balance between the job demands of high productivity, and the humanistic relations concerns of workers. In meeting these demands a supervisor must communicate, coordinate, and cooperate with superiors, subordinates, peers, staff managers, and the union. The supervisor is a vital link in the management hierarchy because he or she stands at the point where management's objectives, policies, and directives must be carried out. The changeover from worker to supervisor involves a complete change in style of working. The effective supervisor must be oriented toward work results and have a sincere interest in and consideration for the subordinate workers. It is through a result-oriented supervisor, who applies an understanding of humanistic relations, that people with talents and skills work together and get jobs accomplished. A sensitive balance must be achieved between work and people in the process of supervisory planning, organizing, directing, and controlling.

Probably the easiest way to fail as a supervisor is to not give full attention and concern to the needs of subordinates. The successful supervisors, on the other hand, achieve their positions by

- *Thinking and acting like managers*
- *Knowing the work priorities*
- *Appreciating their subordinates*
- *Following practices of good leadership*
- *Setting the right environment in which to work*
- *Developing a high set of personal values*
- *Developing good humanistic relations with subordinates*

The selection of a supervisor should be based on the combined skills of leadership, understanding and working with people, technical competence, and administrative management. To a certain extent supervisory ability can be learned, provided the individual has a flexible attitude. The effective supervisor generally shows ability and willingness to change as time and circumstances dictate.

REVIEW QUESTIONS

1. How is a supervisor like a performing juggler running on a circus high wire without a net?
2. What is meant by the statement that a supervisor must achieve a proper balance between job demands and humanistic demands? What is a proper balance between these two demands?
3. How would you describe the primary distinctions between first-level supervisors and managers at other levels in the organizational hierarchy?
4. Why do many supervisors feel that they are in a no-winner contest?
5. Identify and briefly describe how a supervisor is a connecting link involving five primary groups of individuals.
6. Why is there a big difference between being a worker and being a supervisor?
7. Describe seven benefits to be obtained from supervisory planning and organizing.
8. How is the controlling of people and things influenced by the planning, organizing, and directing actions of the supervisor?
9. If you wanted to be successful as a supervisor, where would you start?
10. If you were responsible for selecting a supervisor, what skills would you look for in the individual?
11. In what ways can supervisory ability be learned?

THE CASE OF JOHN CUMBERLAND AND MARY COLLINS

One year ago John Cumberland, a top-level manager of S & J Products Company, selected Mary Collins to be the manager of the Purchasing Department. The department was organized into five separate areas of buying such as steel products, fuel and lubricants, hardware items, equipment, and office supplies. Collins had a Bachelor of Arts college degree plus two years of experience in the purchasing department before moving into the manager's position. Although she did not have managerial experience, Cumberland felt confident that Collins could do the job. He also thought it would be a "plus" for the company in having its first woman manager.

Collins has not succeeded in being an effective manager of the Purchasing Department despite her drive and hard work. Six months ago Cumberland arranged for Collins to attend a two-week seminar on effective management. The course seemed to have little positive effect on Collins' ability to handle her job. She continued to indiscriminately give unreasonable and unclear work assignments to subordinates. She also discouraged her subordinates from questioning her instructions.

When Collins was first assigned to the position of manager, her peers were fairly tolerant of her mistakes and indiscretions. This tolerance has now changed to one of irritation with Collins and resentment with Cumberland for supporting Collins. The other managers feel that their operations are being adversely affected by Collins' poor managment. Collins' subordinates feel they are having to work harder to compensate for the substandard performance of their boss. In addition, they receive the impact of much of the irritation felt by other managers who depend on the Purchasing Department for service and support.

For several reasons, Cumberland is reluctant to replace Collins. Among the reasons are (1) his emotional involvement in having selected Collins for the job, and (2) his concern that he and the company may be accused of discrimination because Collins is a woman. As of this point in time, Cumberland has a subordinate manager who is a failure on the job and several other managers who are discontented with the whole situation.

QUESTIONS

1. Do you agree with Cumberland's selection of Collins for the position of manager of the Purchasing Department? Why? If you do not agree, what are your reasons?

2.   What is your evaluation of why Colliins has not succeeded in her managerial position? Why do you feel the seminar on effective management resulted in little improvement in Collins' ability to handle her job?

3.   Is there anything that Collins can do to become more effective as a manager?

4.   What do you think Cumberland can do about the situation? What would you do?

NOTES

1.   James Menzies Black, *The Basics of Supervisory Management* (New York: McGraw-Hill, 1975), p. 2.

2.   Ibid., p. 26.

3.   Bradford B. Boyd, *Management-Minded Supervision* (New York: McGraw-Hill, 1976), p. 14.

4.   Ibid., pp. 7–11.

5.   Ibid., p. 13.

6.   Black, *The Basics of Supervisory Management,* p. 1.

PART TWO

INTERPERSONAL RELATIONS

COMMUNICATION

HANDLING PEOPLE

SUPERVISORY LEADERSHIP

HUMANISTIC RELATIONS

The proper handling of human behavior in the workplace is probably the greatest challenge in supervisory management. Most of the interpersonal problems in management can be avoided through effective communication and sincere managerial concern for the people's welfare, dignity, and values.

5

Managerial Communications

MANAGEMENT'S TOUGHEST JOB:
ORGANIZATIONAL COMMUNICATION

Instead of considering effective commu-
nication like a fringe benefit for employees, management must realize that it is only
saving its own neck by accepting communication as a vital and permanent phase of
total management resonsibility.

The most challenging phase of internal communication is the daily involvement of
supervisors in eyeball-to-eyeball relations with employees. Supervisors must be
aware of their impact on workers, even through the seemingly most insignificant
words and actions.

Walter Wiesman
Consultant
Huntsville Chamber of Commerce
Huntsville, Alabama

LEARNING OBJECTIVES

The objectives of this chapter on managerial communications are to enable the reader to

1. Describe the three-way and filtering processes involved in managerial communications
2. Identify the elements of the communication process
3. Describe five principles of good communication
4. Delineate the four steps in effective communication
5. Establish five danger signals that indicate a possible communication breakdown
6. Delineate ways and means of getting ideas across to others
7. Establish the role of the supervisor in managerial communication
8. Depict twelve problems in managerial communications
9. Delineate ways and means of resolving problems in managerial communications
10. Describe the coordination process and its importance in effective management

KEY WORDS

Acronym   A word formed from the first (or first few) letters of a series of words, such as IRS for Internal Revenue Service.

Filter   The term *filter* in the communication process refers to the tendency of each individual to read into a situation what he or she wants to read into it.

Gobbledygook   Vocabulary characterized by jargon peculiar to a particular trade, profession, or group that tends to be unintelligible or meaningless to others.

Reportitis   The tendency of some managers to require detailed reports on anything and everything regardless of their significance in the management process.

Semantics   The different meanings of words or other symbols.

DID THEY REALLY MEAN WHAT THEY SAID?

COMMUNICATION INVOLVES SHARED UNDERSTANDING

Communication is the act of two or more individuals exchanging facts, viewpoints, and/or ideas in order to achieve unity of interest, unity of purpose, unity of effort, and unity of understanding in the accomplishment of some objective. There is a tendency for individuals to fail more often than they succeed in their attempts to communicate with one another. For example, did the writers of the following statements communicate or not? In each case the individual was attempting to summarize the exact details of an accident on an insurance form being submitted to a large property and casualty insurance company.[1]

- *Coming home I drove into the wrong house and collided with a tree I don't have.*
- *The other car collided with mine without giving warning of it's intentions.*
- *I thought my window was down, but I found it was up when I put my head through it.*
- *I collided with a stationary truck coming the other way.*
- *The guy was all over the road. I had to swerve a number of times before I hit him.*
- *I pulled away from the side of the road, glanced at my mother-in-law and headed over the embankment.*
- *I had been shopping for plants all day and was on my way home. As I reached an intersection, a hedge sprang up, obscuring my vision and I did not see the other car.*
- *I had been driving for forty years when I fell asleep at the wheel and had an accident.*
- *I was on my way to the doctor with my rear end trouble when my universal joint gave way causing me to have an accident.*
- *To avoid hitting the bumper of the car in front of me, I struck a pedestrian.*
- *I was sure the old fellow would never make it to the other side of the road when I struck him.*
- *The pedestrian had no idea which direction to run, so I ran over him.*
- *The telephone pole was approaching and I was attempting to swerve out of its way when it struck my front end.*
- *My car was legally parked as it backed into the other vehicle.*

Equally confusing, as well as amusing, is the following quotation taken from a letter to a county department of public assistance: "I want my money as quickly as I can get it. I've been in bed with the doctor for two weeks and he doesn't do me any good. If things don't improve, I will have to send for another doctor."

INTERPRETATION CAN BE COSTLY

In most of these communications it is possible for the receiver to interpret what the sender really meant, but some will require further inquiry. In business management this additional communication interchange decreases efficiency and increases costs of operation, neither of which is desirable. Communication with individuals outside one's organization, such as those described above, can only be partially controlled. Neither the county department of public assistance nor the insurance company had any control over the writing skills of the individuals applying for welfare support or the ones filing accident reports. Effective communication within an organization is another matter because it can be controlled through proper managerial action. This chapter outlines some of the principles and guidelines for achieving effective communications within an organization.

THE COMMUNICATION PROCESS

A THREE-WAY PROCESS

In business management effective communication must really be a three-way process—from the top down, from the bottom up, and laterally between organizational units and individuals on the same level (Figure 5-1). There is no communication without some participation and response on the part of the receiver. Reaching the final goals of an organization depends on a free flow of communication in *all* directions. The managers must make the decisions and

FIGURE 5-1 The three-way communication process

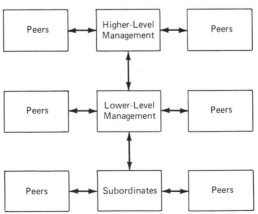

approve the programs of an organization, but these decisions must be clearly understood in order to be effective. Furthermore, at all levels of an organization there must be positive acceptance and encouragement of upward communications—both favorable and unfavorable. It is not sufficient for supervisors and executives to make pious statements that they are always ready to listen, to instruct their subordinates to keep them posted, and to prop their office doors open. Supervisors and executives must be completely sincere and show by actions, not words alone, that upward communications will be acted upon in an objective and constructive manner.

THE FILTERING PROCESS

Perfect communication is very rare because what one person means to write or say is rarely, if ever, the same as what another person understands. As indicated in Figure 5-2, each individual has his or her own personal "filter" which sifts and colors all the incoming information received. It is the individual's perception or understanding of things that causes distortions and misinterpretations to take place. Therefore, instead of getting angry and assuming ill will when someone doesn't seem to understand, one ought to be more tolerant. Conversely, when communication does result in mutual understanding, one should be grateful.

ERRONEOUS ASSUMPTIONS

In analyzing the communication process we need to recognize that words are important but we should be more concerned about the total behavior of the sender and the receiver. This involves recognizing and correcting costly ster-

FIGURE 5-2   The process of communication

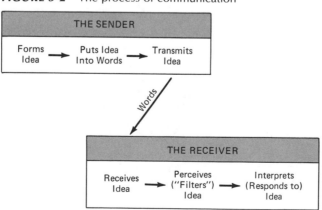

FIGURE 5-3 The elements of communication

eotypes about communication. The following are some of the most common erroneous assumptions about communications:

- No News Is Good News. *This is a poor philosophy. Too often managers react adversely when they hear bad news. The result is that employees are reluctant to tell the supervisor anything but good news.*
- Let Sleeping Dogs Lie. *This is often an excuse for not facing up to a misunderstanding that both parties feel but can't easily express.*
- Subordinates Should Be Seen and Not Heard. *The supervisor or executive who takes this position is cutting off important sources of information.*
- Let the Facts Speak for Themselves. *The trouble is, they don't. People's filters are always at work, making different meanings out of the same "fact." For example, "The boss raced through here angry as the devil," is one person's fact. "The boss raced through here to catch the 4:55 train," is another person's fact.*

- The More Communications, the Better. *Not so! Many managers are "meeting-happy" or suffer from "reportitis" and never see the significant facts from the trivial information that usually goes along with over-communication.*

THE ELEMENTS OF COMMUNICATION

It is generally recognized that the communication process has two distinct elements: (1) the message itself, and (2) the means of conveying the message. As shown in Figure 5-3, the means or physical conveyors of a message fall into three categories. First, there are the written conveyors which have the advantage that they can be checked for accuracy and filed for future reference. Second, there are the oral communications that can facilitate exchange of ideas in a more personal atmosphere and can provide an immediate check on how well the message is getting through. Third, there are the physical gestures, symbols, and signs that tend to provide immediate feedback on whether the message was understood. Regardless of the means there are certain basic principles that should be understood and utilized in the communication process.

ELEMENTS OF GOOD COMMUNICATION

SINCERITY

An essential element of effective communication is sincerity. If it is present, almost any method of communication will work and produce results. Insincerity is probably the greatest barrier to good managerial communications.

UNDERSTANDABLE LANGUAGE

A second element of good communications is understandable and convincing language. Messages must be conveyed in terms that reflect the interests of those involved. Success in communication depends upon gaining acceptance of what is said. The communicator must plan not only what to say but how to tell it so as to gain its acceptance.

COMPATIBLE RELATIONSHIPS

Good communication within an organization requires confidence and mutual respect between members. There must be good face-to-face relationships of individuals and of groups at the various levels of the organization. The fundamental communication in management is the one that exists between supervisor and subordinate. Without a relationship of understanding and acceptance, there will be no true communication. In communication between individuals at the same level, proprietary interests or "fences" must *not* be emphasized. The relationship between peers should reflect understanding and appreciation for the welfare of the *total* organization. When one shows concern for the success of the total organization, there is also an understanding of the roles played by one's peers. Such a relationship tends to indicate teamwork and this, in turn, generally improves communication within the organization.

CHARACTERISTICS OF GOOD COMMUNICATION

Good communication is natural, personal, accurate, timely, sustained, three-way, motivating, dynamic, vital, and sincere. If communication possesses these characteristics it will be listened to and accepted. Good communication will be found in organizations where the management really believes in good communication. Management support and interest in effective communications are basic and outrank the techniques used. In the early days of the United States' efforts in aeronautics and space research and development, the Marshall Space Flight Center (MSFC) in Huntsville, Alabama committed its managers to a behavior science approach to better management. The line managers, largely engineers and scientists, called it an "Impulse for Openness." Figure 5-4 reflects their commitment. After several years of experimentation, MSFC managers credited the experiment with giving them a new perspective on their management responsibilities, a new appreciation of the capabilities of their subordinates, a new facility in the exchange of information, and an atmosphere in which hard work is not only fascinating but fun. The payoffs of the commitment are now a matter of history—putting man on the moon, space vehicles exploring outer space, and the space shuttle.

FIGURE 5-4 Commitment to openness

I believe that every member of the staff is an important person and is a contributing member of a team made up of different and valuable professional skills. We, you and I working together, can individually achieve highest productivity and reward by developing in our interpersonal relations an atmosphere of openness and trust by understanding and using these guidelines:

Value criticism as a compliment and a privilege—give and accept it.

Keep communications open and patiently hear the other person out before responding.

Recognize that defensiveness blunts communications and impedes understanding—don't put the other person on the defensive.

Cooperate, don't compete, with your work partners—volunteer and ask for help.

State your feelings openly in response to an assignment.

In problem solving, confront the problem and the person directly—get conflicts into the open.

FIGURE 5-5 Good communication

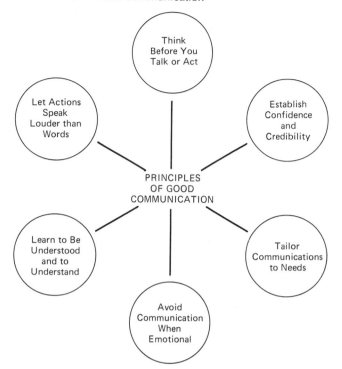

POLICY GUIDELINES

Effective communications are important at all levels of management. It is a critical element of management at the first-level of supervision because a high percent of a supervisor's time is spent in face-to-face dialogue with subordinates. There are policy guidelines or principles of communication (Figure 5-5) that can help managers achieve understanding of their communication efforts:

1. *Think before you talk or act* by developing a clear concept of what you really intend to communicate. This includes determining the true purpose of each communication and not trying to accomplish too much at one time. Plan and outline the important points you want to make. As appropriate, consult with others in planning what you want to communicate. By thinking things through you avoid saying or doing the wrong things.

2. *Establish confidence (full trust) and credibility (respectability)* as a communicator by doing what you say you're going to do or not do. Effectiveness in communication is in direct proportion to the trust and respect others have in the communicator's integrity. Ability to use the right words is not enough. There must be confidence and credibility.

3. *Let actions speak louder than words,* so avoid a tone of voice, facial expression, or gesture that gives others the feeling that you really don't mean what you say.

4. *Tailor communications* to fit the needs and wants of the individual or group involved. This includes being sincerely interested in other people and the things that they value, as well as their problems. Learn when to use the telephone, the informal memo, the formal letter, the group meeting, the report, or the face-to-face dialogue as the appropriate means of communication.

5. *Seek not only to be understood but to understand.* Using words that others will understand and analyzing your own communications from the point of view of the receiving person will help assure your being understood. If you are logical and explain the reasons for what you are doing, you will also stand a better chance of being understood. Being a good listener is the best way to understand the ideas, suggestions, and problems of the receiver of your communication. Here, also, actions speak louder than words, so avoid giving others the feeling that you don't have time to listen to them. Remember that you cannot talk and listen at the same time.

6. Avoid communicating when angry, irritated, or upset, because you may say or do the wrong things.

STEPS FOR EFFECTIVE COMMUNICATION

COMMUNICATION IS INEVITABLE

Communication in the workplace is inevitable. Even if management neglects communication, others such as the labor union do not. The choice is not whether employees will receive information but only whether it will be one-sided and inadequate with possible hostile reactions, or be complete and accurate with friendly reactions. There is much evidence to indicate that people work better, more efficiently, more contentedly, when they know what the objectives are, what the score is, and how they fit into the picture.

Generally speaking, there are four ways people get information:

- *Predisposition of the ideas and attitudes developed since birth*
- *Actual events that have happened*
- *Group pressure*
- *Formal communications*

Formal communications are the principal method that management must use to provide information to workers.

GET ATTENTION

The *first* step in formal communication is to get the attention of the receiver. It is not easy to get the attention of someone who is really not interested in hearing what you want to say. If managerial communications are to register at all, managers must direct them to the known interests of the workers.

- *Security of their jobs and pay*
- *Justice for the workers—both personally and for others*
- *Individual recognition*
- *Group harmony without wrangling and quarreling*

These interests tend to be constants. If managers can relate the details of a communication to one or more of these interests, they can reasonably be sure of having an attentive receiver.

GET UNDERSTANDING

The *second* step in formal communication is to get understanding of what is being communicated. Most people can understand very complicated ideas if they are expressed in simple words. For example, a worker asked his supervisor "What is a gauge?" The supervisor responded: "Why, a gauge is a thing that you put on a piece of stuff to see whether it is just like another piece of stuff." A second problem in getting understanding is the general meaning of words, since some words have different meanings to different people. The best way to overcome this problem is to use the dictionary definition of the meaning that you want to convey. The understanding of a communication will be enhanced if specifics are used and ambiguous generalities avoided. A good practice is to recognize that facts usually need interpretation because people's interests tend to control their perceptions.

GET THINGS TO REGISTER

The *third* step in formal communication is to do everything possible to get the communication to register. One helpful technique is repetition because not everyone grasps an idea the first time it is presented. A second thing to remember is the law of first impressions. It is the first kiss or the first visit to New York City that we tend to remember. This simply means that there is a premium on promptness in communication. Conversely, the idea of completeness is a frequent communication trap. In many situations if we wait for completeness, we will seldom communicate anything to anyone. The important thing is to tell what we now know and do it now. We can always add more information later as it comes to hand.

MAINTAIN CONTROL

The *fourth* step in formal communication is to maintain control over what is communicated. This involves establishing and maintaining a consistent and honest communication policy. The distribution of a factual untruth can cause irreparable damage. While this is something that very seldom happens, it is possible for statements that are factually true to also be misleading. There is a

FIGURE 5-6 Steps for effective communication

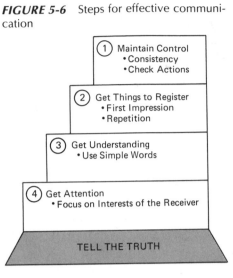

distinction to be made between telling the facts and telling the truth. For example, it can be a fact that your organization has a written and published affirmative action program that specifies no discrimination in wages paid to men
and women who do the same work. The truth, however, shows that 65 percent
(another fact) of the female employees are receiving less pay for performing
the same work.

TELL THE TRUTH

While managers can readily control what their own communications say, they
cannot control what the recipient believes. If their statements are factually
true but conflict with what the recipient sees the managers doing, the recipient will not believe them. Unless the recipient believes what is stated, the
communication effort was wasted, and future communications may not be believed. The most important thing about any communication is that it be dedicated to trying to tell the truth (Figure 5-6).

INTERPERSONAL RELATIONS
IN COMMUNICATIONS

A PERSONAL PROCESS

Communication is a personal process involving the transfer of information
and/or instructions from one person to another. It is a key element in effective
management. Communication is a vital part of the functions of planning, orga-

nizing, directing, and controlling the activities of any organization. At the lower levels of management, usually a high percent of the supervisor's time is spent in interpersonal communication.

A Participative Process

Good communication creates an interest in constructive things and dispels suspicion, rumor, and friction. Good communication is found where the managers of an organization really believe in it. One good way for a manager to show that he or she believes in good communication is to keep subordinates informed by providing for their participation in the planning of the organization's work. There is considerable truth in the adage that workers tend to do best that which they had a part in forming. Various studies that have been made reflect a close correlation between communication and employee productivity.

An Activation Process

The interpersonal aspects of communication dictate two things that must be done:

- *Know how to precisely get concepts and ideas across to others*
- *Give serious attention to the considerations of others as distinct individuals*

Successful management means not only conveying thoughts to others, but also getting action afterward. Managers who follow the principles of good communication will be able to convey their thoughts to others. Understanding people as individuals helps assure getting desired action.

People Are Different

- *COMMUNICATE TO THE NEEDS OF OTHERS*—People differ as to the knowledge they possess, their education, their vocabulary, and their experience. Often people who are highly trained in one field have difficulty in communicating with people who are highly trained in another (the accountant with the engineer and vice versa). Most people unknowingly use words and terms they believe are known and understood by everyone when that is not the case. In communicating one should try to select words and examples that have a universal meaning everywhere and with all people. It is not a bad idea for accountants, for example, to communicate to the maximum extent with other accountants in words that can be understood by nonaccountants. If they follow this practice they will be more effective in conveying accounting information to managers who are not professional accountants.

INDICATORS OF COMMUNICATION BREAKDOWN

● *WATCH FOR DANGER SIGNALS*—In the process of communication between managers and workers, one should be on the alert for the danger signals that indicate messages are not getting across. Some of the most obvious indicators that something is wrong are

- — *The worker performed the wrong task.*
- — *The worker failed to accept responsibility.*
- — *The worker did not recognize the priority of which things come first.*
- — *The worker engages in a labor dispute or strike.*
- — *The manager doesn't hear of problems until they become emergencies.*

If one observes any of the above danger signals this could be an indication of a breakdown in communication.

There are still other danger signals that indicate a possible failure in communication. They include such personal reactions as the following:

- — *The receiver has a look of vagueness.*
- — *The receiver misses the point.*
- — *The receiver changes the subject.*
- — *The receiver says "yes" too often.*

COMMUNICATION SHOULD BE PLANNED

● *HOW TO MAKE IDEAS CLEAR*—In addition to following good principles of communication there are specific things one can do to successfully get ideas across to others. A good starting point is to analyze the frame of mind, the degree of motivation, and the informational background of the listener(s). This action will avoid two common errors in communication: speaking over people's heads and telling people things they already know. From this starting point there should be additional planning before one is ready to communicate.

- — *Determine the exact purpose of the communication.*
- — *Limit the scope of the communication so that it does not cover too much material. Attempting to do too much in one communication—either oral or written—is perhaps the most frequent error made by communicators.*
- — *Organize the material to be communicated under a very few main topics or points.*
- — *Arrange the sequence of points in the communication in an order that will be both logical and easy for the recipient to follow.*
- — *Set up the communication so there is a clear introduction and conclusion. The introduction should give the recipient an overall view of what is going to be in the communication and why it is important. The conclusion should summarize the main points and any action required of the recipient.*

In presenting a communication to the recipient, either orally or in writing, there are still other specific things to do to successfully get ideas across to others.

PRESENTATION TECHNIQUES

1. In the first part of the communication there should be a preview of the purpose, scope, and main points that are being presented.

2. In the main body of the presentation appropriate use should be made of the following techniques:

— *Compare points in the presentation with things that the recipient already understands.*
— *Clarify the purpose of every step discussed in the presentation.*
— *Present clear transitions (continuity) from one part of the presentation to another.*
— *Give examples and illustrations of key points.*
— *Make the main point stand out vividly so that it is easy for the recipient to see the difference between the main point and subordinate ones.*
— *Provide supplemental material to support the main points. If presented orally, provide written handouts. If presented in writing, enclose cross-referenced charts and backup information.*

3. At the end of the presentation summarize the most important points and any action required of the recipient.

In summary, the best way to make ideas clear is to (1) carefully plan the communication; (2) systematically organize the communication into a concise statement of its purpose, scope, main points, and summary; and (3) selectively support the main points with supplementary materials.

IMPRECISENESS DOES NOT CONFLICT WITH TRUTHFULNESS

• *IS VAGUENESS EVER JUSTIFIED?*—Most managerial communications do not benefit from vagueness. There can be occasions, however, when it may be best to be vague. Being imprecise is not in conflict with the importance of telling the truth when we communciate with others. We need to recognize that it is not always in the best interests of all concerned to be blunt and explicit in certain communication situations. For example, what is gained by informing an emotionally disturbed worker that he or she is a lunatic? Since many people have serious emotional problems, we must learn to cope with such individuals. They need to be counseled and helped, not hurt by our brutal integrity. We cannot go on the assumption that no matter how much it hurts, the truth is always good for a person, and that it is a sign of strength and maturity to give and take. If we have to work with a person on a continuing basis, overly straight communication can complicate the situation immensely.

ALLOW FOR FLEXIBILITY IN COMMUNICATION

Skilled managers should develop the ability to vary their language along the spectrum from explicitness to indirection depending on their reading of the person and the situation. In other words, it is not always smart or a matter of honor to "get the cards on the table." A manager needs to use common sense and allow for some flexibility in communication.

THE JAPANESE APPROACH

Japanese managers have proven their ability to achieve high motivation and productivity from their workers. In the book *The Art of Japanese Management*,[2] the authors state that vagueness in communication can cause problems, but it can also serve to hold strained relations together and reduce unnecessary conflict in the work environment. The Japanese use this approach in preventing undue embarrassment and emotional stress to workers who need to be reassigned because of unsatisfactory work performance. It would appear that the Japanese are "conforming with reality," which is one of the dictionary definitions of the word *truthful*.

THE ROLE OF THE SUPERVISOR IN COMMUNICATION

THE CONNECTING LINK

Many, if not most, employees tend to form an impression of the fairness of the whole organization on the basis of the words and actions of their immediate supervisor. It is the supervisor who serves as the connecting link between upper management and the workers because it is the supervisor who interprets upper-management communications to the workers. The supervisor is also responsible for communicating upward to superiors, the problems, feelings, and attitudes of the workers. A supervisor's effectiveness depends to a great extent on his or her ability to be a connecting link in communication.

FEELINGS AND ATTITUDES

Many problems, grievances, and misunderstandings can be prevented when lower-echelon workers think that their feelings are understood by the boss. Too often supervisors are justly criticized because they do not listen to what their subordinates say. They not only fail to listen to words or meanings, but they do not give attention to feelings and attitudes. When this occurs subordinates tend to feel that management is not interested in them. The end result is usually job dissatisfaction and low productivity. There is also a definite relationship between communication breakdown and labor disputes and strikes.

THE KEY PERSON

One of the many major roles of a supervisor is creating a working environment conducive to good communications. Such an environment encourages workers to express themselves and includes a supervisor who carefully listens to what they are saying. The supervisor is the key person in the communication process. The degree to which the supervisor communicates will largely determine the effectiveness of communications within the whole organization. The interpersonal aspects of good supervisory communication are a vital linkage in the entire management process of planning, organizing, directing, and controlling.

PROBLEMS IN COMMUNICATION

THE NUMBER ONE BARRIER

Managers, themselves, are often the number one barrier to effective communication. Too often managers react adversely when they hear bad news. This makes employees reluctant to tell the boss anything but good news. The average employee is not going to talk about anything that might get him or her in trouble. Some managers do not like subordinates to "rock the boat" by suggesting changes that might reflect badly upon the organization. This attitude allows bad conditions to remain in the hopes that they will go away. When a manager only listens to what he or she wants to hear, it creates a breakdown in communication.

LACK OF EMPATHY

Another manager attitude that can block effective communication is lack of empathy or sensitivity to the feelings of subordinates. There cannot be good communication when a subordinate thinks that the boss is incapable of understanding the emotional experiences of other people.

PERSONALITY AND ATTITUDE

Actions that reflect the personality and attitude of the manager can be a third factor influencing communication with subordinates. The difference in rank between superior and subordinate is, in itself, a barrier to communication. It is usually much easier to communicate with others of equal rank. The attitude and perception of the superior towards subordinates can either increase or decrease the chasm caused by differences in position status.

Understanding and Motivation

Employees have barriers of understanding and motivation that cause problems in communication. The supervisor's use of the wrong words at the wrong time can cause a significant barrier in communication. Semantics is also a very significant problem since each person tends to have his or her own meanings of words and symbols. It is a two-way problem that involves both superiors and subordinates. Employee attitude can be a problem. Some individuals don't react well to communication from above. Such factors as work environment, past experience, distrust, emotional matters, or just human nature cause some employees not to want to communicate with their superiors.

Other Barriers

There are other barriers to effective communication that can be found in most any environment:

- *The organizational structure if it has too many bureaucratic levels*
- *The organizational structure if it has unclear definitions of purpose and functions*
- *The physical distance between organizations*
- *The failure to see the need for communication*
- *The tendency of functional specialists to speak a language of their own*
- *The tendency to use acronyms and gobbledygook with the assumption that they are universally understood*
- *The failure to plan and outline important points before communicating*
- *The mental departure not to listen while someone else is speaking*

No Quick Solutions

There are no quick solutions to communication problems. Management does *not* determine when communication takes place. It takes place every time human beings use their natural facilities to listen, read, think, observe, or express themselves. Communication is not an exact science. It is, and will always remain an art.[3] Understanding and applying principles of good communication will help, but cannot be a permanent answer to the problem. One of the best things that management can do is to keep itself perpetually active in the communication process with employees. If management creates a vacuum through silence, the employees will apply the boldest and weirdest imagination to fill it.[4]

RESOLVING PROBLEMS IN COMMUNICATION

THE EFFECTIVENESS OF ORAL COMMUNICATION

To a considerable extent the effectiveness of managers depends on ability in oral communication. No matter how effective written communication may be, much of the information about the organization, its policies, objectives, and plans must be transmitted through oral communication from a supervisor to the subordinates. In oral communication the impact of a manager's personality can be transmitted much more effectively than by written communication. Furthermore, oral communication offers a ready means for the subordinate to communicate "up." Communication is important enough that all levels of management should receive training in it.

COMMUNICATION DEVICES

There are various means and techniques to help management to communicate with its workers. The following is a partial checklist of communication devices:

- Organization charts *showing the work relationships within the organization*
- Committees *that enable managers and workers to participate together in work situations*
- Discussion groups *that allow workers a chance to engage in organizational matters*
- Informational letters and memos *that reflect what is going on within the organization*
- Staff meetings *that enable both line and staff managers to discuss interrelated group work matters*
- Personal contacts *by managers with workers to see and be seen on matters of interest to both*
- Orientation programs *to familiarize workers with new things and important changes in the organization*
- In-house publications *that provide both business and personal information to all employees*
- Bulletin boards *that provide written and picture information to all employees*
- Social programs *that enable managers and workers to get to know one another better*
- Attitude surveys *that give workers an opportunity to express feelings about their work and the things that affect their performance*

- Suggestion boxes *that provide workers an opportunity to suggest management improvements*

HONESTY AND SINCERITY

Honesty, sincerity and being cooperative are basic to good communication. The achievement of these positive approaches to better communication requires a manager to follow certain practices:

- *Always try to be sure that you clearly understand yourself and what you are trying to communicate. This means knowing your own purpose in communicating.*
- *Try to be flexible and adjust to the total physical and human setting in which you are communicating.*
- *Remember that no matter what you say or how you say it, no one ever gets the exact meaning you intend—nor do you get the meaning anyone else intends.*
- *Be alert to the fact that your total personality is communicating as you speak —your tone of voice, facial expressions, and mood.*
- *Try to create the kind of human relations climate which encourages people to ask questions when they don't understand or when they disagree with you.*
- *Keep communication channels open by remembering to preserve the other person's ego.*
- *Encourage the free flow of communication by taking every opportunity to express an honest appreciation of the other person's thoughts.*

BILATERAL COMMUNICATION

Resolving communication problems requires recognizing that it takes two or more to communicate:

- *Anticipate the other person's point of view or reaction to your words and actions.*
- *Develop an awareness of the other person's desires and needs.*
- *Put yourself in the other person's shoes.*
- *Use the vocabulary of the other person.*
- *Analyze the comments of the other person.*
- *Encourage questioning to gain understanding.*
- *Try to understand the other person's reactions.*
- *Admit when you didn't understand something.*
- *Coordinate before you take action.*

SIMPLE GROUND RULES

There are several simple ground rules that will establish reasonably effective communication. High on the list are honesty, simplicity, and consistency. These factors contribute to mutual respect and trust, without which there can not be communication. The challenge to establish credibility clearly starts with top management. The late Edward R. Murrow, when director of the United States Information Agency, had this guiding philosophy:

- *To be persuasive, we must be believable.*
- *To be believable, we must be credible.*
- *To be credible, we must be truthful.*

COORDINATION: A KEY ELEMENT IN COMMUNICATION

MANAGEMENT FUNCTIONS MUST BE COORDINATED

Coordination is the act of *communicating with others* to achieve harmonious interrelationships between functions and organizations. Planning, organizing, directing, controlling, and all organizational aspects of management must be closely coordinated. It is not an easy task because coordination takes time, requires extra effort, and often results in changes in a course of action.

UNNECESSARY COORDINATION SHOULD BE AVOIDED

As reflected in Figure 5-7, the coordination process involves integrating the objectives and activities of *appropriate* organizational units into the larger goals of the total organization. One of the basic problems in coordination is determining the *appropriate* organizational units with which an action should be coordinated. Since coordination takes time and effort, unnecessary coordination that serves no beneficial purpose should be avoided.

IF IN DOUBT: COORDINATE

When is coordination necessary? When is it not necessary? This is not easy to answer. The concerns of various organizational units in a proposed management action can vary from insignificant to considerable involvement. It is, therefore, often difficult to determine who should and should not be included in the coordination process. If a manager is uncertain about coordination on an action, it is a good safe practice to coordinate. Invariably in such questionable situations when a manager decides not to coordinate, the action "boomerangs" back to that manager. The failure to coordinate can cause very sensitive and troublesome management situations to occur.

FIGURE 5-7 The coordination process

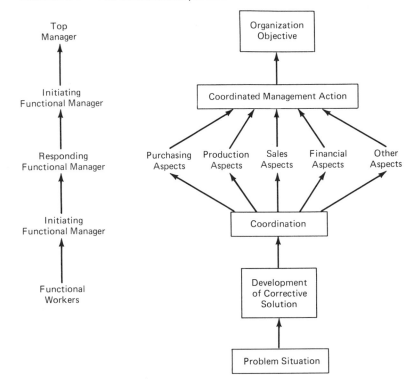

COORDINATION DEVELOPS TEAM EFFORTS

As a general rule of management, coordination should include all organizational units whose functions are involved in the proposed action. Coordination can help develop team effort and avoid irritations or hard feelings between managers. Coordination can also prevent significant matters from being overlooked in the management decision-making process.

AFTER-THE-FACT COORDINATION SHOULD NOT BECOME A HABIT

Usually coordination is accomplished before the fact and prior to an action or decision. There can be *exceptional* situations where coordination is accomplished after the fact. Such coordination, however, should be restricted to emergency situations where time and/or unusual circumstances did not permit before-the-fact coordination. The manager who tends to make a habit of after-the-fact coordination is inviting trouble with his or her peers. Most managers do not take kindly to people who constantly take unilateral actions and then come around after the fact to obtain a concurrence. Frequent after-the-fact coordination can also be an indicator of poor management.

COORDINATION IS A TWO-SIDED PROCESS

Coordination is a two-sided process. The organizational unit initiating a management action should not lose sight of the roles of other organizational units in achieving the total organizational objective. The organizational units with which an action is being coordinated should not pursue their own specialized interests at the expense of either the unit initiating the action or the total organization. It is very easy to criticize the work efforts of someone else, particularly the little insignificant things. *A nonconcurrence in a coordinated action should be reserved for substantive matters, not trivia.* A good manager avoids pursuing his or her own specialized interest at the expense of the total organizational objectives.

DIRECTIVES SHOULD BE COORDINATED

Coordination is particularly important where two or more organizational units are issuing implementation instructions on different functional aspects of the same thing. While serving as a comptroller in the federal government, the author was frequently irritated by the absence of coordination on directives issued by Washington bureaucrats. On March 14, 1973, for example, the author received a directive from the chief of procurement pertaining to the recording of foreign military sales orders in the accounting ledgers. The author was directed to *only record that portion of an order that would be actionable (obligated)* in the current fiscal year. The balance of the order was to be "hidden" in an unofficial reserve account and not be reported until funds were obligated on contracts. The "skullduggery" of this policy was to enable management to show a high percent of obligation of funds in reporting to the Congress. On the same day, March 14, 1973, the author received a directive from the Washington-level comptroller that also pertained to the recording of foreign military sales orders. This letter directed the author to *record the full amount of an order* in the accounting ledgers immediately upon receipt of the order. Failure to coordinate usually results in frustrated and irritated workers, low morale, loss of worker productivity, and manager problems. These adverse factors are particularly prevalent when there is a breakdown in the principle of unity of direction and conflicting instructions are issued to workers.

COORDINATION WITH PEERS

The need for coordination with other managers cannot be overemphasized. Figure 5-8 is an actual example of the "snowballing" effect that was caused by a single maintenance engineer who changed the maintenance concept for an

FIGURE 5-8   An example of failure to coordinate

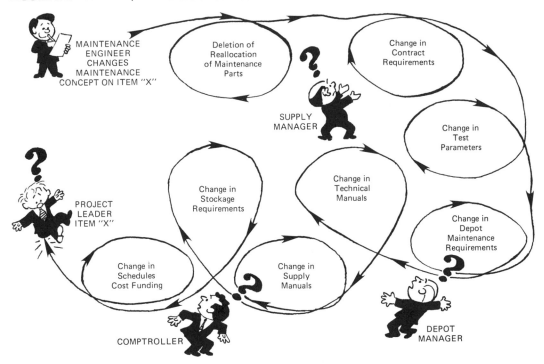

item without coordinating with other involved functional organizations. The illustration is that of an organization involved in research, development, procurement, quality control, supply, and maintenance of complicated communication equipment for various customers. The illustration shows many managers, including the project leader for the item, in a state of confusion and asking the question "what happened?" Before-the-fact coordination could have avoided the confusion which was very costly in time, effort, and use of resources.

The coordination process is an indispensable part of good managerial communications. The failure to coordinate can cause organizational conflict and loss of effectiveness. Coordination is a vital part of managerial communications—of letting the right hand know what the left hand is doing.

SUMMARY

Managerial communications means talking and listening to others involved in the accomplishment of some business objective. Managers at all levels must realize that they are saving their own necks by accepting communication as a vital phase of their total management responsibility. The involvement of human beings is the most important part of managerial communications. A full understanding of the complexity of interpersonal communication is a prime requisite for effective internal communication. Another very important requisite is the active involvement in the communication process by managers at all levels of the organization.

Effective managerial communications must be a three-way process —from the top down, from the bottom up, and laterally between individuals and organizational units on the same level. There is no communication without some participation and response on the part of the individual or group on the receiving end. Perfect communication is very rare because what one person means to write or say is seldom the same as what another person understands or perceives it to be.

One of the best things that management can do is to keep perpetually active in the communication process with employees. Management support and interest in effective communications outrank the techniques used. To a great extent management's effectiveness in communication varies directly with belief in its importance and values. If managers understand people as individuals it will help assure that they get the action they desire. Skilled managers should develop the ability to use common sense and allow for some flexibility in communication.

An understanding of basic principles of good communication will help managers achieve understanding. Two of these principles are thinking before talking or acting and letting actions speak louder than words. Essential elements of effective communication are sincerity, understandable language, and compatible relationships that reflect confidence and mutual respect. There are also several simple ground rules that will establish reasonably effective communication. High on the list are honesty, simplicity, and consistency. Another key aspect of effective communication is to obtain feedback by encouraging workers to express themselves, and for managers to carefully listen to what workers are saying. Ignoring or rejecting feedback is one of the principal causes of failure in managerial communication efforts.

No organization can function well without coordination—the process of communicating with others to achieve harmonious interrelationships between functions. Coordination is a two-sided process involving both the initiating and the responding organizations in a management action.

Oral communications tend to be more significant than other means. Generally speaking, there are four steps in the achievement of effective communication: (1) get attention, (2) get understanding, (3) get things to register, and (4) maintain control over what has been communicated. The most important thing is to tell the truth.

REVIEW QUESTIONS

1. Explain the statement "there is no communication without some participation and response on the part of the individual or group on the receiving end."
2. Explain why perfect communication is very rare.
3. Explain why we should be concerned about the total behavior of both the sender and the receiver in a communication situation.
4. Identify the advantages of oral versus written communications.
5. Explain how sincerity, understandability, and compatibility are essential in effective communication.
6. Explain the communication principle of thinking before you talk or act.
7. Do you agree or disagree that management's effectiveness in communication tends to vary directly with belief in its importance and values? Explain your answer.
8. How can completeness be a communication trap?
9. Why will understanding people as individuals help assure getting the desired action?
10. Do you agree or disagree that vagueness in communication is ever justified? Why?
11. Explain how managers themselves are often the number one barrier to effective communication.
12. Explain how coordination is a two-sided process.

A CASE OF WHO WAS REALLY THE MANAGER?

Mike Jones is a welder who operates a small shop in a Midwest industrial city. He has a reputation for doing quality work and this has enabled him to obtain several sizable maintenance and repair contracts with six manufacturing plants in the area. The workload generated from these contracts has made it necessary to employ four welders and two helpers in the shop.

Due to the increase in business, Mike hired Mary Smith to take care of the bookkeeping and purchasing. After he hired Mary, Mike spent practically all of his time working in the shop, often doing the difficult welding jobs himself. The more time that Mike spent in the shop, the more things Mary found herself doing in the office. First, she started taking follow-up action on delinquent accounts. Then, with Mike's approval, she signed the paychecks to employees and those to suppliers. With Mike's continued absence from the office, Mary found it necessary to accept orders from customers and to arrange the daily and weekly work schedules for the four welders. This also included direct handling of most of the telephone inquiries from customers.

Mary liked her work because she felt that she was really functioning as the general manager of the business. However, she was somewhat disturbed that Mike never took time to praise her for the work she was doing and never gave her either the job title or pay to go with the increased responsibilities she had assumed.

In the process of handling an order from a demanding customer, Mary assigned the job to a welder that Mike thought should have been given to someone else. He immediately came into the office, criticized Mary for what she had done and told her to stick to her bookkeeping and purchasing duties and stop trying to manage the business. At that point, Mary methodically computed her salary to that hour, made out a paycheck for the salary due to her, told Mike to sign it, and then left, crying as she walked out the door.

QUESTIONS

1. Identify the managerial and nonmanagerial functions that Mike and Mary were performing. Who was really the manager? Why?
2. What went wrong between Mike and Mary? Could the trouble have been avoided? How?
3. What do you think Mike should do now that Mary has left? Why?

NOTES

1. Quotes published in the *Toronto Sun* on July 26, 1977.
2. Richard Tanner Pascale and Anthony G. Athos, *The Art of Japanese Management* (New York: Simon & Schuster, 1981), p. 94.
3. Walter Wiesman, *Wall-to-Wall Organizational Communication* (Huntsville, Alabama: Walter Wiesman, 1979), p. 7. Mr. Wiesman, now a communications consultant, was formerly a member of the German "missile team" of the United States Army and the "space team" of the NASA Marshall Space Flight Center.
4. Ibid., p. 3.

6

Humanistic
Relations

DON'T EMPLOYEES HAVE
A *FEW* RIGHTS?

    In an era when so much management time and money is be-
ing directed to technological innovation, it is particularly important that we give equal attention to the human side of this equation. This is as much a business concern as an ethical issue because
a less-than-humane working environment shows up as a concealed
cost on the profit and loss statement.

    More and more studies are confirming that the organizations performing most
successfully are those whose corporate cultures reinforce human dignity and rights.
The issue involved in elevating humanism to a primary business concern is much
more than one of reducing pilferage, absenteeism, or turnover. What is at stake is
nothing less than the return of American business to its preeminent position as an
economic world leader.

    Unless management can untap the vast resources of its workforce at all levels
by inspiring loyalty and stronger cohesion among employees, this national goal will
not be met.

    Managers must recognize that a sensitivity to human needs and employee
rights is no longer a soft issue deserving only minimal attention. Humanism is not
only consistent with maximizing shareholder value, it is the single most powerful
motivational opportunity to generate an outstanding performance. It is in everyone's interest to find ways to coalesce the strategic goals and objectives of an organization with the rights and needs of its employees.

> Those leaders who will accept a humanistic management style, not as a mill-stone but as a milestone in opportunity, will reap rewards of profitability and growth.
>
> Mary E. Cunningham, President
> Semper Enterprises, Inc.
> Osterville, Massachusetts

LEARNING OBJECTIVES

The objectives of this chapter on humanistic relations are to enable the reader to

1. Describe how humanistic relations involve having a strong interest in and concern for the values of people
2. Identify the many factors that interact on the individual worker
3. Describe the effects of poor worker-manager relations
4. Depict the spectrum of personnel management in terms of the procurement, development, and maintenance of personnel
5. Describe the supervisor's role in humanistic relations
6. Establish how supervisors can activate people to work
7. List today's motivational problems in the workplace and how a supervisor can handle them
8. Relate how a supervisor can understand human behavior
9. Identify the revolution in humanistic relations
10. Understand the importance of humanistic relations by analyzing "real world" management situations

KEY WORDS

Grievance   A formal complaint alleging that some unjust act has been committed against a person.

Life-Cycle Management   The management of a product or project from its initial engineering development, through its procurement, production, testing, marketing, distribution, supply, and maintenance.

Open-Door Policy   A manager's practice of making him- or herself readily available to workers for discussion of problems.

Personnel Management   The area of management concerned with procurement, development, and maintenance of personnel.

Work Ethic   The value of exerting effort to accomplish something.

THE PWC CASE

James Keith was a senior sales/service representative for PWC, a large retail and wholesale distributor of records, tapes, and stereophonic accessories. Keith worked in the wholesale division. His job was to take customer-approved budgets for a dynamically changing line of products, determine within these budget restraints the inventory items to be placed in each store, and follow up on sales. The job performance objectives were maximization of sales and minimization of inventory returns. Keith's achievement of these objectives was outstanding in his district.

Keith had been with PWC for over six years, during which time he consistently received superior performance ratings. These reports reflected such statements as

- Decision making—*"Jim makes good, sound, decisions on his own when situations arise."*
- Communicating—*"Demonstrates the ability to communicate with all levels of management."*
- Organizing—*"Organizes and documents all work flow in order to achieve assigned and personal goals."*
- Follow-up—*"Completes all assignments within deadlines."*
- Creativity—*"Is not afraid to suggest and/or implement new ideas."*
- Dependability—*"Jim does an excellent job with very little supervision."*
- Job knowledge—*"Demonstrates a thorough understanding of our system and has an outstanding product knowledge."*
- Leadership—*"Has a good rapport with all of his customers and therefore obtains the necessary cooperation and productivity of others."*
- Motivation—*"Jim always has the drive and motivation to ensure that the job is completed at the optimal level."*
- Overall Evaluation—*"Constantly exceeds requirements with superior quality and quantity of work with results that are frequently exceptional. Jim is a hard working, dedicated representative. His high level of concern in pursuing the job to completion is paying off in sales and limited returns. His high level of performance is definitely an asset to our branch."*
- Employee Potential—*"Employee is ready now for a sales supervisor position."*

In addition to his superior performance evaluations, Keith had been sent to seven different cities in his district to resolve problem situations caused by other sales/service representatives.

HOW INCONSIDERATE CAN MANAGEMENT BE?

On Wednesday September 29, Keith had a meeting with his branch supervisor. They had two arguments. One was about branch personnel getting upset by Keith bringing to their attention such mistakes as their failure to send supplies and information and their shipping of unordered products to his stores. The second matter involved automatic computer-directed shipments of products into stores where the items were slow moving. Keith felt he should have the flexibility of "lining out" products that were not selling after one month, rather than after the computer-directed three months. He stated that the computer-directed shipments resulted in excessive and costly returns plus customer dissatisfaction. At the conclusion of the meeting, Keith's supervisor said "You have the best-looking stores I have seen in my supervised area."

On Sunday October 3, the branch manager called Keith at home and stated "We are going to work on a project in Athens tomorrow. I would like you to meet me at 10:00 A.M. at the airport." On the morning of October 4, at the airport, the branch supervisor said "You may wonder why I am here. Your employment with PWC is terminated and you are to clear your personal items from the company car and give me the keys." "What's the reason?" asked Keith. "Insubordination," said the branch supervisor. When Keith asked for an explanation, the branch supervisor said nothing. Keith called his wife at work to have her come to the airport and pick him up. The branch supervisor then drove away in the company car.

ANOTHER CASE OF INHUMAN TREATMENT

The inhuman treatment of a dedicated employee by PWC is not an isolated case in today's business management. In March 1983, all 120 employees of the Kerr Glass Manufacturing Corporation in Keyport, New Jersey found themselves without jobs, without any warning from the company. When workers showed up for work they learned from an unfamiliar security guard that the plant had been permanently closed. As a matter of fact, movers were already loading the plant's heavy equipment onto flatbed trucks. There was no recent labor trouble at the plant. The State of New Jersey had granted the plant a $1 million loan three years ago to help it maintain employment. As the mayor of Keyport stated upon hearing of the sudden plant shutdown, "I am angry that a major U.S. corporation can operate in such a non-caring manner . . ."

WHAT DOES HUMANISTIC RELATIONS INVOLVE?

STRESSING THE HUMAN BEING'S POINT OF VIEW

Humanistic relations involves having a strong interest in and concern for the human welfare, rights, dignity, and other values of people. It focuses on the importance of people and their capacity for self-realization. In humanistic relations one recognizes that organizations are basically groups of people with various interests and rights, consisting of individuals with different perceptions and values in their lives. The effective manager deals with people in a manner that promotes both individual and organizational goals. This is quite a different management approach from that used by PWC and the Kerr Glass Company.

Humanistic relations stresses the human being's point of view. To achieve good relations with employees one needs an understanding of human behavior. This involves having an awareness of what motivates people, how they are motivated, and the learning process in motivation (see Chapter 3, The Fundamentals of Directing and Controlling). Good humanistic relations are enhanced when the manager has some knowledge of the intelligence, aptitudes, abilities, skills, past experience, perceptions, and driving motives of subordinates. It is difficult to treat people as human beings if you do not know them as individuals with distinguishable features.

Whenever and wherever there is contact between managers and employees, humanistic relations are involved. It is a factor during the recruitment, selection, placement, and training of employees. It continues to be a factor when supervisors issue orders, execute disciplinary actions, give performance appraisals, and take other actions with subordinates. It is in management's interest to get to know their key employees and to develop good humanistic relations. For example, the managers at PWC apparently did not understand the strong points of James Keith. Within five months after they fired him, the company had lost most of the large retail accounts that Keith had managed. Keith on the other hand had successfully relocated himself in a better position with a large investment-oriented corporation.

PERSONNEL MANAGEMENT AND HUMANISTIC RELATIONS

Humanistic relations go beyond the normal field of activities found in personnel management. In personnel administration the primary considerations are applying the techniques of human resource management and interpreting the laws and contracts pertaining to employer-employee relations. Not all individuals employed in personnel management are effective in their humanistic relations with others. They may be conversant with personnel selection, testing, compensation administration, employee benefit programs, and government regulations, but they often fail in their treatment of people as human beings. The situation described next is a good example of how professionals in the field of personnel management can fail in their humanistic relations.

A CASE STUDY IN EQUAL OPPORTUNITY?

Two very capable employees of ECOM were denied equal opportunity during the process of selecting an individual for a relatively high-level position. This particular organization had had frequent cases of inconsistencies in the interviewing and selecting of individuals for various positions. Because of these inconsistencies, the chief executive officer signed and issued a policy that would afford equal opportunity of consideration to all qualified applicants for a position. The policy, prepared by the Personnel Office, clearly stated "Selecting officials will inquire as to the interest and availability of every person on the career referral list. All interested and available candidates will be interviewed."

The above two employees were *not interviewed* for the position so they filed grievances claiming that they had been denied proper consideration for promotion. When they asked why they were not interviewed, the selecting supervisor informed them that there was no legitimate vacancy since the position had been filled. This statement was admitted by the grievants as documentation in the case.

INDISCRETIONS OF THE PERSONNEL OFFICE

The Personnel Office recognized that management was remiss in not interviewing all candidates on the referral list. In an attempt to correct the problem, the Personnel Office decided that the two grievants should be interviewed by the selecting supervisor *after* he had already filled the position. The grievants refused to be interviewed by the supervisor who had already told them that there was *no vacancy* and the selection decision was *irrevocable*. The Personnel Office then tried to deny the grievance by stating that the two employees had "thwarted management's attempt to correct the problem by their refusal to be interviewed."

PERSONNEL MANAGEMENT SHOULD HAVE CONCERN FOR EMPLOYEES

In this situation there are three significant shortcomings reflected in the actions of the Personnel Office. First, there was the failure to enhance the rights and welfare of the employees. Second, there were the actions to cover up the failure to oversee compliance by supervisors of a corporate personnel policy—a responsibility of the Personnel Office. Third, there was the failure to initiate any corrective action against a supervisor who had not complied with a corporate personnel policy—a policy designed to avoid the type of grievances involved in this situation. The actions of the Personnel Office were illogical and reflected a total disregard of good humanistic relations.

INTERACTIONS IN HUMANISTIC RELATIONS

VALUES AND CONCEPTS

Many things affect the individual worker (Figure 6-1). First one must keep in mind that people differ considerably in their values. Some people place high value on the importance of freedom from authoritarian leadership. Others place considerable value on the equal rights they feel are due them by legal guarantees. Personal welfare such as prosperity, good health, happiness, and/ or career success may be what others value. To still others, there is the desire to achieve a feeling of dignity or worthiness. Other things that people value

FIGURE 6-1 Interactions in humanistic relations

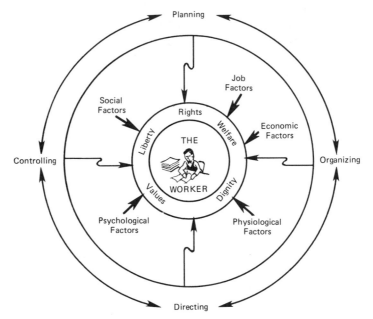

may include fairness, impartiality, independence, honor, justice, honesty, recognition, acceptance, security, and/or money.

People working on any job have something that they would like to obtain from their job. The director of social research for Development Analysis Associates, Inc., a consulting firm, found this to be true after doing a five-month study in which he worked in an automobile assembly production line. The data he gathered indicated that most people want to come to work and be treated with the respect normally accorded to mature adults.[1]

F. J. Roethlisberger and William Dickson, over forty years ago, pointed out the significance of humanistic relations in the work environment. They concluded that each worker "is bringing to the work situation a different background of personal and social experiences. No two individuals are making the same demands of their job. The demands a particular employee makes depend not only upon his physical needs but upon his social needs as well."[2]

INTERACTING FACTORS

The things that the individual worker values are affected by many factors in the workplace. These many interacting factors can be generally classified into the following five categories:

- Job factors *such as working conditions, job evaluations, and quality of supervision and leadership*

- Economic factors *such as wages, training, and promotions*
- Physiological factors *such as safety and job security*
- Psychological factors *such as recognition and acceptance*
- Social factors *such as equal opportunity, teamwork, and friendship*

FUNDAMENTALS OF MANAGEMENT

The arrows in Figure 6-1 also graphically show that execution of the basic
management functions of planning, organizing, directing, and controlling
all have some impacts on the individual worker. At all levels of management there should be an intelligent understanding of how the many
actions involved in performing these functions can affect people in the workplace.

Figure 6-2 illustrates several ways in which a manager can fail in the humanistic relations role. An analysis of this cartoon reflects the following manager shortcomings:

- *Impersonal attitude and actions toward employees*
- *No time for employee personal problems*
- *Unavailability to discuss employee work problems*
- *Quickness to criticize*

FIGURE 6-2   How to fail as a manager

- *Failure to praise good work*
- *Preoccupation with self-importance*

These actions are an invitation to worker dissatisfaction.

IS HUMANISTIC RELATIONS AN IMPRACTICAL MYTH?

The Japanese believe that business organizations should be run as family affairs, with considerable emphasis given to humanistic relations.[3] Some successful managers in the United States believe in this management approach. Pete Peterson, the now-deceased owner-manager of the Wooster Tool and Supply Company in Wooster, Ohio, ran his operations as a family affair. There was outstanding teamwork throughout the plant as reflected in no worker turnover, no grievances, and a happy highly motivated workforce. Mary Cunningham, the president of Semper Enterprises, Inc., in Osterville, Massachusetts also feels that firms should be family affairs. She says "The family model, when you stop to think about it, comes a whole lot more close to the humanistic values that we desperately need to unlock in today's organizations." She has also stated "I am convinced that women will not make their most important contribution by trying merely to imitate men. Women should not try to hide characteristics such as empathy and compassion that society traditionally has labeled feminine." There are limitations in how far very large organizations can be effectively managed as family affairs. But even in a large corporation like PWC, mentioned at the beginning of the chapter, there is absolutely no need for such inhumane and inconsiderate treatment of an employee such as James Keith and others who PWC had also abruptly fired without sufficient cause. Such ruthless, nonhumanistic management practices should not exist in the United States.

THE ENVIRONMENT OF HUMANISTIC RELATIONS

MISSION ACCOMPLISHMENT AND HUMANISTIC RELATIONS

Organizations are not established for the purpose of humanistic relations. They are established to perform specific functions that contribute directly or indirectly to the achievement of the objectives of the organization. However, no organization can effectively or efficiently accomplish its mission without sufficient attention to humanistic relations.

Humanistic relations are influenced by all the actions and conditions in the work environment. As mentioned previously, the basic management functions of planning, organizing, directing, and controlling are all factors that affect humanistic relations. For example:

- *The development or planning of a workload schedule has a direct impact on the people who will fulfill the schedule.*
- *An organizational change may affect the job and/or pay of an employee as well as disrupt the social relations of employees in the work environment.*
- *The methods used in directing an employee to perform a job can turn the person "on" or "off." If properly handled, directing can be a positive motivating factor. If improperly handled, it can cause low morale and decreased worker productivity.*
- *In handling the function of control, low morale and productivity are virtually assured when a manager always criticizes poor performance and never praises or gives recognition to good work.*

EFFECTS OF POOR WORKER-MANAGER RELATIONS

The effects of poor worker-manager relations are charted in Figure 6-3. The absence of such good relations often results in productivity problems with low-

FIGURE 6-3 Humanistic relations—a sensitive factor in management

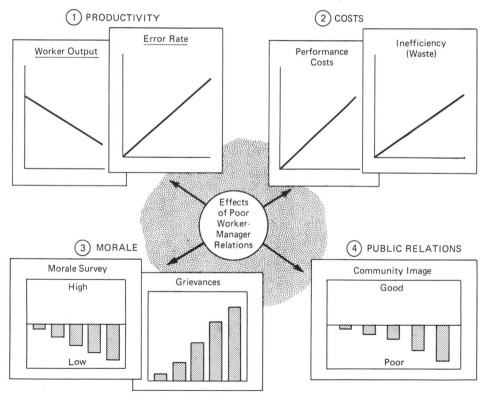

er output and increased errors. It means control problems with resultant inefficiency and high costs. It causes employee morale problems and grievances that will sooner or later adversely affect the manager's as well as the organization's public relations image. All these effects appeared in the reorganization case discussed next.

DID MANAGEMENT FORGET ABOUT THE WORKERS?

INTEGRATED LIFE-CYCLE MANAGEMENT

In the middle 1970s the United States Army Electronics Command was engaged in the integrated life-cycle management of major items of technically complicated equipment. The life-cycle management started with the original concept of the item and continued through the research, engineering development, procurement, production, supply, maintenance, engineering modifications, and ultimate disposal or phaseout of equipment. The primary objective of life-cycle management was to provide for the complete *coordination and correlation* of *all* aspects in the management of equipment from "life to death."

"POWER-HUNGRY" MANAGERS LED THE WAY TO A REORGANIZATION

Several years later, the research-and-development managers felt they did not have enough control over the management of the equipment they were developing. An outside committee of high-level managers from industry was appointed to evaluate the situation. The committee recommended that all Army commodity commands establish research and development as a separate self-contained and independent organization for each major classification or type of equipment. The recommendation was immediately accepted by the Army Materiel Command in Washington.

MANAGEMENT PROBLEMS LED TO A SECOND REORGANIZATION

The then-existing Army Electronics Command, a single agency, was split into four separate autonomous organizations, each with its own specialized staff and operational subunits. From the very start, the split organization caused many serious problems in planning, budgeting, accounting, financing, computer operations, communications, coordination, and transition of equipment from research and development to other stages in the life-cycle management. These problems became so great that within three years the split organizations were again consolidated.

THE TWO REORGANIZATIONS HURT MANY PEOPLE

Many workers were hurt in the two reorganizations. The initial reorganization split certain functions such as centralized planning, budgeting, financing, procurement, and support operations among four organizations. This resulted in salary reductions for some supervisors and many workers because the scope of their responsibilities had been diluted. In several cases relatively high-level managers were reduced in grade and pay. This caused a "domino effect" that reduced each lower grade level and pay in the organization. The downgrading and displacing of people in the job structure was determined by seniority. When the "bumping" process was over, some workers had pay reductions of over 50 percent. In other cases, some nonmilitary veteran workers with minimum seniority ended up working for individuals who were once their subordinates. Many people lost their jobs or had to transfer and relocate to jobs in other parts of the country.

The two reorganizations caused other personnel problems. The first reorganization created considerable duplication of work that enabled some people to get promotions. When the duplication was eliminated in the second reorganization, some individuals lost their short-term promotions and other innocent people had to be demoted because of seniority "bumping." The personnel turbulence caused by the two reorganizations was both harsh and far-reaching.

The first reorganization also caused severe problems of coordination. Workers and supervisors became frustrated. Hundreds of lengthy "memoranda of understanding" were written in attempts to clarify the coordination of the many integrated functions involved in life-cycle management. Some of the better workers and supervisors left their jobs in utter disgust.

A UNION'S ACCOUNT OF THE FIASCO

The National Federation of Federal Employees, one of the unions representing the employees involved in the fiasco, placed an advertisement in a local newspaper stating that the disastrous impact of the reorganization had left many employees and their families with permanent scars. Attention was called to the job losses, the many senseless reassignments, the job transfers, and the immeasurable disruption of work that will never be forgotten by the hundreds and hundreds of employee casualties. "The fragmentation of a single organization into four parts continues," said the union, "to boggle the minds of rational people as to the real underlying reasons for the disaster."

"Power" Versus Humanistic Relations

Throughout the first reorganization, there were many indicators that the top managers directing the changes were more interested in obtaining power than in giving consideration to the humanistic relations aspects of their badly conceived decisions. There was an obvious maneuvering to grab people and money with little thought being given to such problems as

- *The distribution of limited human resources to the point where some managers found themselves without experienced personnel to do the work*
- *The luring of workers between organizations to the point where there was a critical loss of worker expertise in certain vital functional areas*
- *The splitting and weakening of some organizations to the point that they could no longer stand and operate independently or effectively*
- *The quadruplication of workload in such areas as accounting, with fewer people to do the work*
- *The conflict-of-interest situations between managers, with workers caught in the middle*

Inadequate attention to humanistic relations caused damage to employee morale, job satisfaction, attitude towards work and productivity that will last for years.

Lessons Learned

One lesson to be learned from this situation is that people are important because it takes people to get things accomplished, even in a highly mechanized or computerized operation. A second lesson is that humanistic relations are involved in every aspect of management, particularly in planning a reorganization. The top managers of the Army in this case apparently did not care much about the workers' welfare, rights, and other human values. There was a high price paid for this lack of consideration for people and the irreparable damage to both employee relations and work productivity. Hopefully, the reflection of this case here will at least cause some managers and students of management to recognize the importance of considering humanistic relations in decision-making.

THE SPECTRUM OF PERSONNEL MANAGEMENT

Humanistic Relations Embrace All Areas of Personnel Management

A significant portion of the job of most lower-level managers is spent working with and resolving personnel matters. Personnel management embraces three major areas of specialized functional activities. Each of these areas requires the

FIGURE 6-4 The three purposes of personnel management

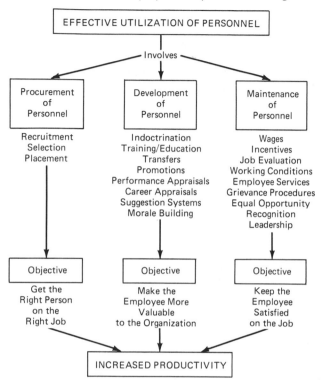

exercise of effective humanistic relations. Figure 6-4 schematically groups these three personnel management functional areas as

- *The* procurement *of personnel with the objective of getting the right person on the right job*
- *The* development *of personnel with the objective of making the worker more valuable to the organization*
- *The* maintenance *of personnel with the objective of keeping the worker satisfied on the job*

Maximum utilization of the work force of any organization can only be attained if workers are

- *Procured who are able and willing to do the work required of them*
- *Placed on jobs related to their capabilities and interests*
- *Developed through education and training to effectively and efficiently perform their jobs*
- *Kept relatively satisfied on their jobs*

PERSONNEL UTILIZATION AND PRODUCTIVITY

A manager must give constant attention to the entire spectrum of personnel management because it is people that make the organization. If they are improperly placed, inadequately trained, and/or dissatisfied, the best of equipment and work methods will probably not increase their productivity. Conversely, there is both a logical and practical expectation that the effective utilization of personnel will have a direct impact on worker productivity. The remainder of this chapter plus the following two chapters will focus on pertinent personnel management actions that will enable managers in achieving the objectives shown in Figure 6-4.

SUPERVISOR'S ROLE IN HUMANISTIC RELATIONS

THE CASE OF BILL SMITH

Bill Smith, a former army sergeant, is supervisor of a large group of office workers. The composition of his work force is approximately 60 percent women and 40 percent men, with 7 percent black workers.

Bill is a very hard working and conscientious supervisor. He does not ask anything of his subordinates that he wouldn't do himself. This fact probably accounts for why he sets high production standards for his workers. To facilitate achievement of these standards, he has developed good job descriptions that clearly define each worker's responsibilities. Bill has also done an effective job of delegating responsibility and appropriate authority to his subordinates.

Bill Smith is very firm and consistent in demanding that his subordinates perform in accordance with the responsibilities in their job descriptions. He is also very consistent and firm in insisting that all work be accurate and completed on time. He gives appropriate recognition to those employees who perform in an outstanding manner. The employees in Bill's branch will tell you that he is an equal employment opportunity supervisor. He does not discriminate.

The employees in Bill Smith's branch, however, are not happy on their jobs. There are a few exceptions, but not many. This dissatisfaction is reflected in an extremely high rate of turnover. The most significant causes of this turnover are probably Bill's temper and his authoritarian style of leadership. Whenever mistakes are made or reports are turned in late, he becomes very angry and often shouts at the person involved. There are very few grievances because Bill only demands that workers perform in accordance with their job descriptions. Rewards are based on performance. Promotions are based on the combined factors of performance and seniority. Although many workers have gone to the union with complaints, there usually has not been enough justification to support formal grievances.

Bill is recognized by his superiors as a hard working and conscientious supervisor who runs a "tight shop." He has received several commendations for his work performance.

What is your evaluation of Bill Smith as a supervisor? Smith is now retired and has been replaced by a very meticulous supervisor who is both employee centered and very calm when things go wrong. What do you think happened to worker productivity after Smith retired?

A Supervisor Must Understand Human Behavior

Some supervisors work with records and reports while others work with materials and equipment. All work with human beings. Whether a supervisor is in a bank, hospital, school, office, retail store, manufacturing plant, research laboratory, or government establishment, he or she must work with people. Every supervisor, therefore, must know the what, how, and why of human behavior in order to maximize achievement in the workplace.

An organization achieves its goals through the workers. A major factor in achieving organizational goals is motivation of the workers. The degree of motivation is greatly influenced by many actions and conditions that affect humanistic relations in the workplace. A basic concern in humanistic relations is understanding the values and expectations that people develop while working on a job. In the case of Bill Smith, he gave his subordinates a feeling of insecurity and exasperation because of his intolerant attitude regarding mistakes. Smith had many attributes of a good leader but he was not sufficiently employee-centered. In the regimentation of the workplace, he overlooked too many of the human expectations that affect motivation. The most significant of these expectations are reflected in Figure 6-5. Note that the more wheels that are in gear, the greater the motivation. When Bill Smith retired, his replacement practiced participative management and operated the branch with considerably less-rigid rules and regulations. The change in organizational climate greatly reduced employee complaints and turnover and increased both the quality and quantity of production. Under the new boss the workers had a feeling of belonging. They could make themselves heard and there was more opportunity to develop a spirit of teamwork.

A Supervisor Must Be Employee-Centered

It is in humanistic relations that the supervisor plays a key role in motivating people to work effectively and efficiently together. The supervisor as a leader must have a strong interest in and concern for the human welfare of the subordinates. A good supervisor needs to achieve the proper balance between being

FIGURE 6-5   Humanistic relations in the workplace

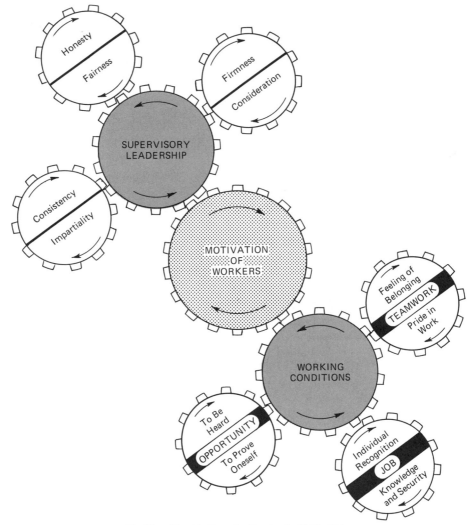

The More Wheel in Gear, the Greater the Motivation

job- or task-centered and being employee-centered (Figure 6-6). This means
spending at least as much time on developing and maintaining group morale,
cohesiveness, and worker job satisfaction as is spent on pushing productivity,
cost reduction, and time schedules. Effective supervision results from giving
proportional attention to both job demands and human welfare demands. The
humanistic relations demands are particularly important since many studies
have shown that supervisors who are employee-centered obtain more productivity than those who are job or production-centered.[4] In the case of Bill

FIGURE 6-6 Achieving a balance between work and people

Smith, both the quantity and quality of work productivity increased when the new employee-centered supervisor took over.

SUPERVISORS SHOULD UNDERSTAND SUBORDINATES

The leadership exhibited by the supervisor is significantly important in keeping the workers satisfied on their jobs. The core of the supervisor's many responsibilities is found in the leader's understanding of and obligation to subordinates. Having an understanding of a subordinate means paying attention to the person as a whole, not just the person on the job. This is significant because an individual's beliefs, habits, attitudes, prejudices, likes, and dislikes are factors that influence the person's abilities as well as actual performance on the job. Getting an understanding of an employee should *not* be carried to the point where it is an invasion of the person's privacy. However, the more a supervisor can establish personal contacts with subordinates, the greater is the chance of satisfying the needs of workers on the job. Personal contact with subordinates removes the "stranger" atmosphere in the workplace. It also helps bring about a more congenial working atmosphere. When the supervisor and the subordinate can exchange thoughts and feelings, a climate is created that encourages employee growth on the job. The smart supervisor strives to develop a work environment that is conducive to the maintenance of worker group spirit. The first-level supervisor is usually in the best position to achieve this extraordinary feat. *Remember,* many workers see more of their fellow employees during the workweek than they see their own families. Good humanistic relations in the workplace is a significant factor in worker satisfaction on the job.

SUPERVISORS MUST DEVELOP INTERPERSONAL SKILLS

The leadership of the supervisor can have an influence on productivity, worker absenteeism, worker turnover, quality of the product or service, morale of the work force, grievances, relations with the union, cost reduction, and many other things. The supervisor must attain results from workers of various ages, educational levels, and with a variety of different attitudes and perceptions. This means that the supervisor must excel in interpersonal skills and be able to handle all types of individuals, many of whom may not be especially dedicated to their jobs or to the organization.

In summary, the supervisor's role in humanistic relations is to maintain a person-to-person approach with workers that creates a satisfying work environment. The supervisor who can develop a good working atmosphere will usually find that it has a positive effect on both employee job satisfaction and productivity.

ACTIVATING PEOPLE TO WORK

COMMUNICATION ACTIVATES AN ORGANIZATION

A primary responsibility of a supervisor is to convert human strength into productive effort. This requires effective communication with others and development of the right mental attitude of the workers. There must be a clear understanding of instructions, orders, and/or information received from superiors. The first-level supervisor must then provide even clearer understanding to the workers (Figure 6-7). If a supervisor is to best serve the organization, he or she must be knowledgeable of pertinent information when subordinates ask questions. The extent to which the supervisor keeps informed of what is going on will largely determine the effectiveness of the communications within the organization.

DAILY CONTACT WITH THE WORKERS

It is a good practice for a supervisor to have some daily personal contact with employees. Many hold periodic meetings with their subordinates. Others

FIGURE 6-7   The connecting link—the supervisor

strive to have an open-door policy where employees are encouraged to come in and discuss things when they wish. Daily contact does not mean that the supervisor stops and talks to every subordinate. It can involve walking through the work area, showing interest and concern in what is going on, and seeing what the problems are on a day-to-day basis. Making it easy for subordinates to see and talk to the supervisor helps prevent breakdowns in communication. This is important because one of the major contributing causes of grievances is the breakdown in communication between the supervisor and the worker.

UNDERSTANDING WORDS, FEELINGS, AND ACTIONS

One way for the supervisor to activate others to work is to listen to what they are saying—not only their words and meanings, but their feelings and attitudes. People tend to mirror themselves through both their words and actions. The smart supervisor gets to know and understand the subordinates through their words, feelings, and actions. Many subordinates know a great deal more than supervisors sometimes realize. It is amazing how much a supervisor can learn from subordinates if he or she encourages them to think and express themselves, and pays attention to what they say. Observation of workers' feelings and attitudes often gives an indication of real trouble spots in the workplace as well as their possible solution. When subordinates feel that the boss tries to understand and act, where possible, on a given situation from their point of view, they usually develop a positive attitude toward the work to be done. In activating others, the supervisor can enlist participation, leave people with an indifferent attitude, or arouse resentment. To achieve positive action, establish effective communications and a work environment of good humanistic relations.

MOTIVATING WORKERS

TODAY'S MOTIVATIONAL PROBLEMS

Supervisors are faced with increasing motivational problems in today's management. For one thing there are many "do-nothing" jobs in plants and offices where most of the worker's time is spent monitoring a machine or a computer. Second, there are many "isolation" jobs in today's mechanized and computerized work environments wherein individuals are required to work alone. Individuals who are subjected to working in isolated situations often tend to be less receptive to supervision. Third, the increased mechanization and computerization of work causes increased discontentment because there may be fewer places to advance in the individual's career development.

HOW TO HANDLE MOTIVATIONAL PROBLEMS

What can a supervisor do when faced with some of the motivational problems in today's management? The answer to this question lies in the supervisor's actions in the following areas of management:

1. Learning and applying the fundamental principles of human behavior
2. Performing an analysis of the human behavior strengths and weaknesses of both self and subordinates
3. Developing and implementing a high quality of managerial leadership

KNOWING THE FUNDAMENTALS OF MOTIVATION

Obtaining knowledge about the fundamental principles of motivation (see Chapter 3) will help a supervisor in using motivational techniques with the greatest results. The supervisor will know, for example, that the use of penalties or other punishment is usually not too effective in getting a worker to adopt a new work method. Positive reinforcement is often much more successful in getting workers to change their behavior. For example, a large insurance company started a program that penalized workers who were frequently late for work. If an employee was late five or more times during a month, the individual lost one-half day of vacation. When this motivational policy brought only limited improvement in tardiness, the company changed to a positive approach. Under the new policy, an employee with a perfect on-time record for any two-month period got an extra one-half day of vacation. An employee who was late to work for unavoidable and supportable reasons was not penalized. After the new policy was implemented, tardiness dropped to a very low level.

ANALYSIS OF SELF AND OTHERS

After obtaining a knowledge of the fundamental principles of motivation, a supervisor should perform a self-analysis to identify his or her strengths and weaknesses in managing others. An analysis of the strengths and weaknesses in the work habits of subordinates should also be made. When a supervisor knows what the weaknesses are, he or she is best able to give attention to their correction. One way to perform this self analysis is to make analytical comparisons with the guidelines for handling people contained in this book.

MANAGERIAL LEADERSHIP

The quality of managerial leadership is a significant motivating factor, in spite of the motivational research studies of some psychologists. Managerial leadership is reflected in how well the supervisor performs the basic functions of management (see Chapters 2 and 3). Following are some of the things that a supervisor can do to help motivate subordinates:

- *Follow the practices of good supervision outlined in Chapters 7, 8, and 9.*
- *Plan and organize the work efforts in the organization in an efficient and effective way.*
- *Carefully select the tasks and goals given to the workers.*
- *Provide adequate incentives, including wage compensation plans, where possible.*
- *Be timely and fair in evaluating work performance.*
- *Reflect personal concern and sensitivity to the feelings and problems of subordinates.*
- *Have knowledge of events, both within and outside the organization, that may affect the work efforts or jobs of subordinates.*
- *Take actions that build the self-esteem and confidence of subordinates.*
- *Maintain two-way communication that assures subordinates that they have a place to go when troubles arise.*

● *Engage subordinates in participative management whenever possible; be open to the possibility of changing your mind on the basis of subordinates' attitudes and ideas.*

THE IMPORTANCE OF GOALS

Of the many things involved in motivating workers, the primary responsibility of the supervisor is to provide clearly defined tasks and goals for subordinates. Having a goal that enables a person to see something ahead in the future is one of the best ways to stimulate motivation and build worker confidence.[5] Conversely, there is no better way to get nothing done than to aim at nothing. A research study conducted by Stephen X. Doyle and Benson P. Shapiro found that salespeople, for example, worked longer hours on their jobs when the task was clear and when they saw a positive relationship between their effort and results. Where there was clarity between task, effort exerted, and results attained, there was almost a 40 percent increase in hours spent selling or in sales-related activities per week.[6]

In work situations involving "do-nothing" or other monotonous jobs, the key to motivating workers lies in the quality of managerial leadership, particularly the personal concerns of the supervisor for the subordinates.

UNDERSTANDING HUMAN BEHAVIOR

A supervisor needs to have a good understanding of human behavior in order to activate people to work. Supervisors who are humanistic-minded in their dealings with subordinates are usually able to achieve high productivity, lower costs, better quality of work, and have less personnel turbulence.

PEOPLE ARE NOT ALIKE

In understanding human behavior it is a good practice to recognize the fact that no one is perfect. Analyze yourself or others and you will find a mixture of both good and bad human characteristics. No two individuals are exactly alike. Furthermore, body chemistry and other stimuli cause individuals to vary in their behavior from time to time.

PHYSIOLOGICAL AND GENETIC CAPABILITIES

Human behavior is determined by many factors. First the limiting factor of the individual's physiological and genetic makeup can constrain certain capabilities of the person. The behavior of some individuals, for example, is limited by their intelligence, reaction time, manual dexterity, physical stamina, and weight-lifting capabilities. Some of these characteristics are difficult to change with training and/or experience. On the other hand, some characteristics such as knowledge can be changed with training. A good supervisor should recognize the physiological and genetic limitations in workers and assign jobs that they are capable of performing. The supervisor should also determine where training and experience can help change the capabilities of an individual.

MOTIVATIONAL NEEDS

Second, human behavior is motivated by the needs of the individual. This means that a supervisor should be familiar with the fact that human beings are motivated by a great diversity of things. Some of these things may be physiological, others psychological, and still others may be sociological.

PERCEPTIONS

Third, human behavior is influenced by how individuals perceive their environment in terms of experiences, future needs, and things that they value. Many workers, for example, tend to behave according to what they think will be acceptable to the boss. This means that they may think one way but act in another way. In so doing they are neither honest with themselves nor the supervisor. A supervisor can modify this behavior by being honest and straightforward, by encouraging subordinates to "call things as they are," and by developing a participative form of planning and decision making. Role perception, which leads to doing what you *think* someone else wants, can be harmful and dangerous. This is because people can end up doing the wrong things because they made a miscalculation in their perception. Honest and frank two-way communication between supervisor and subordinate can minimize this problem.

EXPECTATIONS

Fourth, human behavior can be affected by an individual's expectations of future events. People tend to behave according to what they expect in the work environment. For example, they develop expectations of what kind of behavior will lead to rewards—such as pay increases, promotions, or outstanding performance ratings. When these results do not materialize, the individual may become very disturbed. Irrational behavior may also occur when an individual feels that the rewards received are not enough. If the worker feels an unfair situation exists, there is dissatisfaction and possible irrational behavior.

FIGURE 6-8   Interactions in understanding human behavior

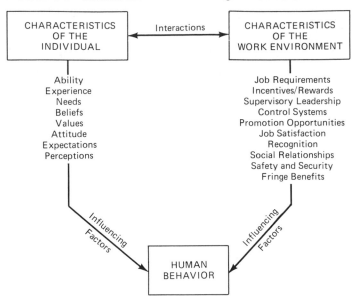

A supervisor can minimize these situations through honest and timely communication that keeps subordinates continually informed on their work performance.

EXPERIENCES

Fifth, human behavior is influenced by how individuals evaluate the things they experience. Most people arrive at the conclusion that they either like or dislike a given experience. When workers have unpleasant work experiences, this can lead to dissatisfaction, absenteeism, tardiness, resignations, and poor work. On the other hand, the more satisfied an employee is on the job, the less the likelihood of undesirable behavior.

MISCONCEPTIONS

Sixth, human behavior can be affected when an individual develops a misconception of something. Effective communication between the supervisor and the worker is the best way to prevent misconceptions.

As reflected in Figure 6-8, human behavior in the workplace is primarily determined by the characteristics of the individual and those found in the work environment.

THE REVOLUTION
IN HUMANISTIC RELATIONS

A CHANGING WORK FORCE

Humanistic relations are more significant today than in the past. One reason is that the workers have changed and are continuing to change. Years ago a high percentage of workers were immigrants who had the old caste system in their blood. These workers viewed U.S. working conditions as far superior to conditions in their home countries. Today the workers are third, fourth, and fifth generations of these immigrants. Most are better educated and no longer willing to accept any type of working conditions. Many have been indoctrinated with the philosophy that we are all created equal. This philosophy is reflected in the attitude that the laborer is as much of a human being as the president of the company, and that the worker should have an opportunity to share proportionately in the combined efforts of labor and management.

SOCIAL LEGISLATION

Social legislation passed by Congress provides a basis for much of the humanistic relations revolution that is being experienced today. Social security, unemployment insurance, and welfare, along with food stamps and similar forms of payment, have changed working from an economic necessity to an alternative life-style for some people. Losing a job today does not mean an instant end to income as a worker.[7] This changing attitude toward work is reflected in a somewhat widespread de-emphasis of the work ethic—the value of exerting effort to accomplish something. Many young workers in particular tend to rebel against the drudgery of routine jobs. Many workers of all ages prefer leisure time to overtime. The changing social conditions have also altered the attitudes of many workers regarding the conditions under which they will work.

EQUAL RIGHTS LEGISLATION

The equal rights legislation of the 1960s and 1970s has generated a new ball game in management. Many individuals with records of irresponsibility have strong attitudes that their "rights" entitle them to preferential treatment in the workplace. If these "rights" are not satisfied to their way of thinking, there are immediate charges of discrimination. Neither the family nor the schools have successfully conveyed the fact that with *"rights"* there must be *acceptance of responsibility*. All individuals in the United States have a "right" to obtain an equal education. However, to obtain that education the person must accept the responsibility for studying and learning how to apply the knowledge acquired. Without the acceptance of responsibility our business establishments will continue to find that many of their workers cannot effectively read or write. This fact is also reflected in a steady drop in the average score on the verbal section of the Scholastic Aptitude Test.

Social Changes

Various other social changes add to the revolution in humanistic relations. High on this list is the growing two-career family with both husband and wife working. Then there is the problem of handling educated workers that are mismatched on jobs because their education is out-of-line with employment requirements. This problem continues to increase as we automate, computerize, and mechanize both office and nonoffice jobs. Our growing "push-button" work environment is quite often out of step with the educational and experience background of the workers.

Management Adjustment

Management must gear itself to addressing the revolt against tradition and the growing emphasis by workers of their individual needs. Too many managers show by their actions that they are insensitive to human needs. Jungle-like hiring and firing are the norm rather than the exception in industry and government.[8] For example, the Asbury Park, New Jersey Housing Authority told about twenty of its employees that it had accepted resignations the workers said they never submitted. The action came about when the employees were trying to negotiate a contract.

In summary, social and equal rights legislation plus changing social conditions are placing high demands on management to give more attention to the concerns of its workers. This involves turning aside "status quo" management and giving attention, where appropriate, to such practices as participative management, flexible working time, job sharing, work sharing, reducing stress on the job, self-management by workers, and other innovative approaches to management as they develop in the future.

SUMMARY

Humanistic relations involves having a strong interest in and concern for the human welfare, rights, dignity, and other values of people. It embraces all of the influencing physiological, psychological, and sociological interactions that affect people as human beings.

There is very little management planning, organizing, directing, and controlling that does not affect humanistic relations. No organization can effectively or efficiently accomplish its mission without giving sufficient attention to humanistic relations because people are involved in most everything accomplished in the workplace. The effective manager handles people in a humanistic manner so both the individual's and the organization's goals are achieved.

The spectrum of personnel management embraces the procurement, development, and maintenance of personnel. The objectives of these three functional areas of activity are (1) to get the right person on the right job, (2) to make employees more valuable to the organization, and (3) to keep employees satisfied on the job. The supervisor who applies humanistic relations plays a key role in the achievement of these objectives. It is reflected in the manner in which the supervisor activates people to work, handles motivational problems, and understands human behavior. Social and equal rights legislation plus changing social conditions are making it more difficult for management to handle workers. "Status quo" personnel management is not the solution to the problem.

REVIEW QUESTIONS

1. Why should a manager get to know the people in his or her organization?
2. What is the relationship between humanistic relations and the administrative management functions of planning, organizing, directing, and controlling?
3. Describe the difference between humanistic relations and personnel management.
4. How do people differ in their concepts of the things that they value?
5. What are the effects of poor worker-manager relations?
6. Describe the spectrum of personnel management.
7. Describe the supervisor's role in humanistic relations and its importance.
8. How can a supervisor activate people to work?
9. Describe today's motivational problems in the workplace and how a supervisor can handle them.
10. What is the revolution in humanistic relations?

THE CASE OF WHERE'S THE PROMOTION?

Joe Larsen is a security manager for a large department store chain. He is responsible for security in the company's largest store. Because of his experience he is called upon to set up security systems and train security managers in other stores in the chain.

When Larsen started to work for the company he was promised a job review for possible promotion in ninety days. The promised job review did not occur. After he asked why there had not been a job review, Larsen was informed that his job would be reviewed after six months rather than ninety days because he had executive status. At the end of the six months there was a problem as to whether the store operations manager or the regional security manager should review his job. Before the question was resolved, the position of the store operations manager was abolished. The regional security manager told Larsen that there was nothing he, the regional manager, could do. Eventually Larsen was informed that the job review wouldn't result in a pay raise because executive reviews only provided guidance and direction. Larsen was then told that his position would be reviewed at the time of all other executive reviews. However, Larsen's job was not reviewed along with the other executives. When Larsen inquired, he was given an official directive that security executives were to be reviewed on their job employment anniversary date. Since Larsen's anniversary date had already passed it meant that his job would not be reviewed for almost another year.

An unhappy Larsen submitted applications for employment with several other companies. When he told his superiors, he was informed that he was a very valuable manager and they did not want to lose him. He was immediately given a "merit" increase in pay instead of a promotion. Larsen was also informed that the company would do everything possible to find him a job with regional responsibilities. Larsen, for personal reasons, decided to stay with the company. Four months later Larsen was notified by telephone that he had received a very favorable job review and would receive a raise in salary.

QUESTIONS

1. Develop a list of the company's actions that reflect poor employer-employee relations.
2. After analyzing the above list, develop a policy checklist of things that the company should do to improve its humanistic relations in the development and maintenance of employee satisfaction.

NOTES

1. John F. Runice, "By Days, I Make the Cars," *Harvard Business Review*, May-June 1980, p. 115. Copyright © 1980 by the President and Fellows of Harvard College; all rights reserved. Mr. Runice, as Director of Social Research for Development Analysis Associates, Inc., a

consulting firm, based his statements regarding how workers like to be treated on data gathered after spending five months working on an automobile assembly plant production line.

2. F. J. Roethlisberger and William J. Dickson, *Management and the Worker* (Cambridge, Mass.: Harvard University Press, 1939), p. 553.

3. W. H. Franklin, Jr., "What Japanese Know that American Managers Don't," *Administrative Management*, September 1981, p. 37.

4. Rensis Likert, *New Patterns of Management* (New York: McGraw-Hill, 1960).

5. "Motivational Programs—Or How You Can Get More Out Of *You*," *Administrative Management*, September 1978, p. 32. Excerpted with permission from Office Administration and Automation, © 1978 by Geyer-McAllister Publications, Inc., New York.

6. "What Counts Most in Motivating Your Sales Force," *Harvard Business Review*, May-June 1980, p. 133.

7. Arnold R. Deutsch, *The Human Resources Revolution* (New York: McGraw-Hill, 1979), p. 17.

8. Ibid., p. 27.

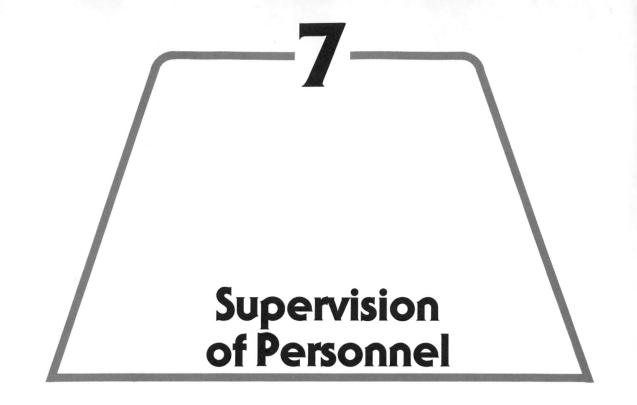

7

Supervision
of Personnel

PUTTING HUMANISTIC RELATIONS
TO WORK IN HANDLING PEOPLE

Supervision is the hub of an organization's personnel management activities. Daily, supervisors interpret and apply policies and practices that affect the welfare of both the organization and employees.

Success or failure of any operation depends heavily upon a supervisor's action or inaction regarding a variety of conditions. Thus effective supervision may be defined as the art of balancing the needs of business with the needs of employees, while never forgetting the ultimate objective, or indeed requirement, of having the best qualified person on each job.

John H. Gauch, Personnel Manager
General Employment, Bell Laboratories
Holmdel, New Jersey

LEARNING OBJECTIVES

The objectives of this chapter on supervision of personnel are to enable the reader to

1. Delineate the responsibilities of the supervisor in job design, job descriptions, job evaluations, and staffing of jobs

2. Relate how job reviews have to do with job enlargement and job enrichment

3. Relate the supervisor's responsibilities to develop personnel through orientation and training as well as job transfer and promotion

4. Establish the supervisor's responsibilities and the guidelines in conducting personnel performance and career appraisals

5. Delineate practical supervisory guidelines for performing the following tasks:
   a. Delegation of responsibilities to subordinates
   b. Giving orders to subordinates
   c. Steps to take when subordinates resist orders from the supervisor
   d. Administering discipline to subordinates

6. Describe how to integrate the goals of the supervisor with those of individual workers and groups

7. Describe how to develop a positive attitude with subordinates

8. Apply supervisory management guidelines to the analysis and resolution of personnel case studies

KEY WORDS

Career Appraisal   The evaluation of an employee's potential future for promotion to a higher position.

Employee Turnover   The number of employees being replaced on jobs within a specified period of time.

Equal Employment Opportunity   The right of every person, regardless of age, nationality, race, sex, or disability to equal treatment on the job.

Job Description   An explicit statement of the duties, responsibilities, and authority of a job.

Job Design   Establishing what a person is required to do on the job and the results expected.

Job Evaluation   The comparison of jobs to determine their relative value to the organization.

Performance Appraisal   The evaluation of an employee's past and current work performance on the job.

Staffing The selection and placement of personnel to perform each job in an organization.

THE CASE OF THE NEW ASSISTANT

Jerry Mohr is the controller of a large corporation. The company has just recently acquired a new line of products by the takeover of another business establishment. The expanded operations are having a significant impact on the controller's workload in such areas as (1) new budgets to be developed, (2) changes in the accounting structure, (3) auditing of accounting records, and (4) economic analysis of the costs versus benefits of various proposed management actions. This expansion has increased the workload in all controller departments and has necessitated a considerable amount of travel for Jerry Mohr.

To help alleviate the workload situation in his own office, Mohr hired a new staff assistant, an economist, whom he strongly felt was the right person for the job. The first nine days after the new employee reported to work, Mohr was tied up in important meetings and unable to orient his new assistant to her job. His secretary and several other employees did what they could to orient the new assistant. On the tenth day Mohr devoted the entire day to orienting the new assistant. It was a complete and very thorough orientation that covered (1) the job, (2) the controller's operations, (3) the company, (4) the products, and (5) pertinent company and controller policies and procedures. Because Mohr hadn't personally hired anyone for quite some time he gave the orientation "off the top of his head" as various thoughts came to his mind. The following day Mohr received a telephone call that his new assistant had decided not to work for him. What happened? What did Mohr do or not do that may have caused the new assistant to not accept the job? Are there any humanistic relations lessons to be learned from this case? Why not write down your answers to these questions and then check them out as you read this chapter.

GETTING OFF TO THE RIGHT START—WITH PEOPLE

People: An Indispensable Resource

Without people, the computers, word processors, mechanical robots, and other automated equipment will not achieve and sustain maximum productivity. Regardless of how sophisticated a piece of equipment is, it must be set up, operated, and maintained by people. If an operator gives a computer the wrong programmed instructions, the computer provides wrong answers in microseconds. If a machinist puts the wrong punched or magnetic tape in an automated milling machine, the machine produces a product that may have to be scrapped. Without trained and properly supervised personnel, the wheels of productivity virtually come to a screeching halt.

Personnel management is probably the most sensitive and important activity involved in the supervision of work and productivity. As seen in Chapter 6, personnel management involves

1. Procuring personnel with the objective of getting the right person on the right job
2. Developing personnel with the objective of making the employee more valuable to the organization
3. Maintaining personnel with the objective of keeping the employee satisfied on the job

Supervisors have considerable involvement in the achievement of these three objectives.

GET THE RIGHT PERSON ON THE RIGHT JOB

• *PROCUREMENT OF PERSONNEL*—The procurement of personnel includes the recruitment, selection, and placement of people on jobs. It is a very challenging task where mistakes can prove quite costly. If the wrong person is selected and placed on the wrong job, both productivity and employee morale will usually suffer (Figure 7-1). Where highly productive equipment is in-

FIGURE 7-1 Getting the right person on the right job

volved with the job, an improperly placed worker can, through incorrect operation, cause costly damage to the equipment. The misplacement of people on jobs can also result in serious accidents and injuries. The presence of a few misplaced workers in an organization can disrupt the entire production process.

Personnel policies that get the right person in the right job result in increased employee productivity—in much the same manner as if an obsolete machine was replaced by a new one. The proper selection and placement of workers contributes to good employee morale, increased quantity and quality of work output, and a reduction in operating costs. The procurement of personnel involves the supervisor in job design, job descriptions, job evaluations, and the staffing of jobs. These management actions will be discussed in the paragraphs that follow.

JOB DESIGN INVOLVES HUMAN AND TECHNICAL ASPECTS

● *JOB DESIGN*—Job design establishes what a person is required to do on the job and the results expected. It is usually accomplished simultaneously with process design—the determination of how a product will be made or a service performed. As shown in Figure 7-2, job design identifies the technical and human aspects involved in performing the job. It also establishes the skills, physical effort, mental effort, and supervision required of the person on the job. Job design is often a complex task to accomplish. Ignore the human aspects, and you may have the extremes of either a monotonous job or a frustrating one that is beyond the capabilities of the average worker to perform. Ignore the technical aspects, and you may have a job that is ineffective and/or inefficient.

ECONOMIC COSTS OF JOB DESIGN

The design of jobs involves many economic factors. First, job design sets the evaluation baseline for establishing a worker's wages. Second, job design that

FIGURE 7-2   The technical and human aspects in job design

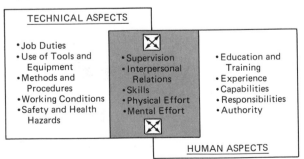

ignores the human aspects can result in the expenses of worker absenteeism, turnover, and "skulduggery" caused by boredom on the job. Third, the technical aspects of job design have a bearing on training, supervision required, material wastage, quality defects, damaged equipment, and tools and equipment needed to do the job.

The scientific management approach to job design involves work flow and procedures analysis, methods of work analysis, and time study. Care must be taken here to avoid job design based on economic factors alone, with workers treated as machines. The best job design represents a good balance between the technical and the human aspects seen in Figure 7-2.

JOB DESCRIPTION: THE FOUNDATION FOR JOB PAY

• *JOB DESCRIPTION*—Job design results in a job description—a written record of the duties, responsibilities, authority, and working conditions of the job. The job description outlines the duties of the job but does not specifically reflect the factors that were considered in the job design. The job description provides the foundation for determining job pay.

RANKING AND CLASSIFYING JOBS

• *JOB EVALUATION*—Good job descriptions are necessary for accurate job evaluation. It is through job evaluation that salary and wage rates are applied to specific jobs. The salary and wage classification of jobs is based on critical evaluation of the degree of duties, skills, work effort, responsibilities, authority, accountability, and work conditions of a specific job. Some jobs are best evaluated by comparing one job with another on a factor-by-factor basis (skill, experience, responsibility, supervision received). Another common evaluation method is the quantitative system of ranking and classifying jobs on a numerical factor comparison basis. This is accomplished by selecting the common factors that are a part of all jobs, relating each factor to a defined weighted quantitative scale, and then rating each job on a factor-by-factor basis. Figure 7-3 is an example of a job evaluation rating summary based on the quantitative system.

SUPERVISOR RESPONSIBILITIES FOCUS ON ACCURACY

• *SUPERVISOR'S ROLE IN JOB DESIGN AND EVALUATION*—The supervisor is responsible for managing the work force. Many other individuals, however, are usually involved in the design and evaluation of jobs. The design of jobs by the scientific management approach of method and time study is usually performed by specialized industrial engineers with input and review by the supervisor and the job occupant. The writing of job descriptions is usually a joint effort of the supervisor and the Personnel Department with input and

FIGURE 7-3 Job evaluation chart

JOB EVALUATION — RATING SUMMARY									
Department					Date				
Job Title									
Job Number									
Job Factor	Max. Points	POINTS							
SKILLS									
1. Education and Training									
2. Experience									
3. Mental Skills									
4. Physical Skills									
EFFORT									
5. Mental Effort									
6. Physical Effort									
RESPONSIBILITIES									
7. Tools and Equipment									
8. Materials									
9. Work of Others									
10. Safety of Others									
11. Money or Funds									
12. Quality of Work									
WORK CONDITIONS									
13. Supervision									
14. Hazards									
Total Points	100								

review by the job occupant. The supervisor is usually responsible for the content and accuracy of the final job description. The final description and evaluation should be signed by the supervisor to show that he or she approves it. After approval of a job description, the supervisor should clearly communicate the responsibilities and performance standards of the job to the employee who must do the work.

Job evaluation for salary and wage purposes is usually the sole responsibility of compensation specialists in the Personnel Department. The reason is to achieve consistency of evaluation throughout the entire organization. The supervisor's key role in job evaluation is to see that the job being evaluated is accurately described in the job description.

THE SELECTION PROCESS

● *STAFFING JOBS WITH WORKERS*—The staffing process involves obtaining the personnel to perform each job in an organization. This process requires considerable planning because personnel needs have to be anticipated in ad-

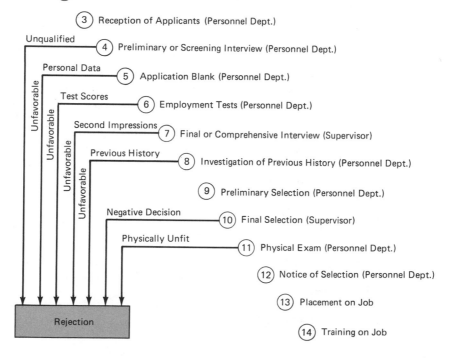

FIGURE 7-4 The selection process

vance of job openings. Staffing procedures vary considerably from one organization to another. The Personnel Department plays a major role in the development of staffing policies and procedures as well as the coordination of the entire staffing process. Some personnel departments make the final selection and assignment of workers. It is usually a better policy to have the final staffing decisions made by the department supervisors where the new employees will work.

Figure 7-4 provides an outline of one procedure for staffing employees to jobs. The action starts with the development of the job description. Actual recruitment is triggered by the supervisor submitting a requisition for personnel to the Personnel Department. The final selection of the worker is the responsibility of the requisitioning supervisor. Figure 7-5 provides guidelines for the supervisor to follow in the staffing of employees to jobs.

THE STAFFING PROCESS AND GOODWILL

In the staffing process the Personnel Department and the supervisor should make every effort to generate goodwill in their contacts with job applicants. Actions such as rudeness, abruptness, and inefficiency in the staffing process can cause better applicants to seek employment elsewhere. Discourteous treatment of job applicants can have other negative results. For one thing an

FIGURE 7-5 Guidelines for staffing of new employees

1. Review applicant's résumé and application before interviewing. Identify areas where you would like additional information during the interview. Avoid asking questions during the interview that are clearly answered in the résumé or application.
2. Plan questions and items you will discuss during the interview.
3. Start the interview at the appointed time. This reduces the applicant's tension.
4. Put the applicant at ease from the start by discussing some neutral topic such as current events or the weather.
5. Let the applicant play a large role in determining how the discussion goes. You will learn more about the individual's attitudes and capabilities, provided you listen carefully.
6. Use questions sparingly. Do not interrupt or change the subject when asking them. Examples of questions you might want to ask are:
   a. Tell me about your past work experiences.
   b. What do you find most satisfying in a job?
   c. What do you feel your strong points are?
7. Avoid asking questions that can give rise to legal problems. These include questions pertaining to marital status, religion, age, disabilities, nationality, or race.
8. Follow your interview plan and don't allow the discussion to drag on to the point where it becomes nonproductive.
9. Conclude the interview by telling the applicant what you intend to do and what the applicant can reasonably expect will happen.

individual selected for a job can start employment with a very negative attitude regarding the organization. Second, improper handling of job applicants can hurt the employer's public relations image in the community.

THE CASE OF THE NEW ASSISTANT

In the case of the newly hired assistant discussed at the beginning of the chapter, Jerry Mohr, the controller, made several staffing errors. First of all, he should have planned his work schedule to be in his office and available to greet his new assistant when she reported for work. Second, he should have planned in advance how he was going to handle the orientation of the new employee. This planning should have identified what he would handle himself, and what his secretary and other staff members would do. Third, before the new assistant reported to work, the Personnel Department should have been contacted, as appropriate, and arrangements made for necessary employment forms, passes, information booklets, and so forth to be available on the first day. Fourth, an orientation checklist should have been prepared identifying all the items of information to be provided and actions to be taken when the new employee reported to work. In not providing for an orderly, well-planned, and scheduled orientation, Jerry Mohr caused his new assistant needless frustration and insecurity. It is no wonder she decided not to work for him.

PERIODIC JOB REVISIONS

- *JOB REVIEWS*—Once a job has been designed and evaluated, it should be reviewed periodically. Job reviews can bring attention to changes in the work process that are not reflected in the job description. Ignoring these changes can result in employee dissatisfaction when the individual feels there is a discrepancy between job responsibilities and pay.

     The periodic job review can also uncover worker dissatisfaction caused by overspecialization. Job situations involving either overspecialization or underpaid responsibilities can often be corrected through job enlargement or enrichment.

REEVALUATION OF JOBS

- *JOB ENLARGEMENT AND JOB ENRICHMENT*—Job enlargement and job enrichment involve an expansion in the scope of a job through the assignment of different and more varied tasks. In job enlargement, the expansion is horizontal—at the same level of difficulty and responsibility. In job enrichment, the expansion is vertical—at a higher level of difficulty and responsibility. Both job enlargement and job enrichment can make the work more interesting and thereby more satisfying to the worker. This is usually accomplished through a structural redesign of the job.

A supervisor watches for jobs that need reevaluation for possible job enlargement or job enrichment. The following action checklist should help a supervisor identify the unenriched jobs:

AN ACTION CHECKLIST FOR UNENRICHED JOBS

1. Analyze the total job. Can the person doing the job tell where work begins and where it ends? Can the person determine what responsibilities are his or hers versus those that are someone else's? Does the job serve a useful purpose? Does the person doing the job understand this purpose? If the answer to any question is "no," the job may need to be redesigned.
2. Analyze the decision-making and control aspects of the job. Is the job of such a nature that a reasonably capable and intelligent person could make decisions regarding the work they are required to do? If the answer is "yes," does the job give the worker such decision-making authority? Is the job holder required to follow prescribed methods and refer *all* unusual situations to a superior for resolution? If the answer is "yes," the job is a possible candidate for job enlargement or job enrichment.
3. Analyze organization charts, job descriptions, job titles, training manuals, and work-flow diagrams to identify unenriched jobs that might be overspecialized. Use these management tools to identify unenriched jobs that have a low degree of decision-making authority and control.
4. Identify areas in which the structural opportunity for unenriched jobs exists. Look, for example, at "trouble-shooting" jobs. Positions entitled *expediter, coordinator, consultant,* and *analyst* may reflect jobs in which the job holder has little or no authority and is not really responsible for anything specific. There is also a good possibility that the coordination and communication functions may have been removed from the line jobs within the organization thereby causing them also to be unenriched.

POTENTIAL SOLUTIONS

Once a supervisor is aware of jobs that should be reevaluated for possible job enlargement or job enrichment, there are at least two potential solutions to the problem. One action is to find additional tasks and responsibilities that will make the job more challenging, interesting, and satisfying. A second action is to establish a system of job rotation. Such a system requires that a person only has to work on a specific unenriched job for a limited period of time before being moved to a second job, to a possible third job, and eventually back to the first job.

With the current state of the art in computer technology, more companies should look into the cost-effectiveness of replacing some of their monotonous manual jobs with robots. The Chesebrough-Pond plant in Clinton, New York, for example, uses a robot to pick jars of skin lotion from an assembly line and place them in shipping cartons.

DEVELOPMENT OF PERSONNEL

MAKE THE EMPLOYEE VALUABLE
TO THE ORGANIZATION

The development of personnel starts with the job interview and subsequent orientation of newly hired employees. It continues when there is a significant change in organizational objectives or an assignment to a new job. Development of personnel should be a continuous process of training and educating employees for such purposes as learning new skills, improving present skills, transferring to more satisfying jobs, or advancing to higher-level positions. Other elements of a good employee development program include periodic objective appraisals of past work performance and future career development. There should also be participative opportunities for employees to express their suggestions for improvements in the work environment.

Personnel development is important because an untrained employee is usually a liability and has a tendency to

- *Produce less*
- *Waste more materials and supplies and damage more finished work*
- *Cause more breakdowns of equipment and breakage of tools*
- *Interrupt the work of other employees*
- *Require more supervision*

Properly planned and conducted orientation, training, and educational programs can be very cost-effective. The benefits of higher productivity, improved quality of work output, increased worker satisfaction, and reduced operating costs can more than compensate for the costs of the personnel development program (Figure 7-6).

FIGURE 7-6 Developing workers

MAKE THE PERSON FEEL WELCOME, COMFORTABLE, AND ACCEPTED

● *INDOCTRINATION OF NEW EMPLOYEES*—Positive motivation of a new employee is usually enhanced when the supervisor or properly designated person explains the responsibilities of the job, gives instructions on how the job is to be performed, provides assistance in helping the new employee learn the job, and takes time to answer questions. In addition to telling the new employee what is expected on the job, the supervisor or a properly designated person should orient the individual regarding the following matters:

1. When and how the individual will be paid
2. Policies and procedures regarding overtime and other premium pay
3. Policy and procedures concerning tardiness and attendance
4. Policy and procedures for reporting sickness
5. Policies and procedures regarding safety, security, and identification badges
6. Policies and procedures regarding parking and parking permits
7. Policies regarding dress and personal conduct
8. Policies regarding fringe benefits
9. Location of facilities (lunchroom, drinking fountains, first aid, lockers, restrooms)
10. Where to go for help on questions pertaining to the job

The orientation should conclude with a tour of facilities and an introduction to co-workers.

DETERMINING TRAINING NEEDS

● *PERSONAL GROWTH TRAINING*—The supervisor should constantly be on the alert to determine when and where employee training and development is needed. Some of the situations that indicate a need for training are

— *New work methods and procedures*
— *Low productivity*
— *Excessive scrap, errors, or rework of output*
— *High operating costs*
— *Excessive overtime*
— *High employee turnover*
— *Low morale*
— *Promotion of deserving employees*

The training and development of personnel requires careful planning. First, training plans should focus on those workers who most need the training or are most deserving of training that could lead to job advancement. Second, the training plan should allow for the time required to obtain necessary materials and/or equipment if the training is to be given in-house. Third, the training plans should provide for the systematic instruction that will provide the benefits desired. Last, the training should be scheduled so that it can be completed without interruptions.

WAYS OF TRAINING

There are many ways that employee training can be executed:

1. On-the-job training
2. In-house discussion conferences
3. Out-of-house discussion conferences
4. Apprenticeship or intern training programs
5. In-house classroom training
6. Out-of-house classroom training
7. Off-the-job reading programs
8. Programmed instruction using textbooks or teaching machines with logical subject sequencing that the trainee must follow
9. Computer-assisted instruction

Figure 7-7 shows a trainee of Prudential Property and Casualty Insurance Company in Holmdel, New Jersey, using a centrally located desk computer to get instructions on how to handle certain types of insurance transactions. Computers can be very practical and cost-effective in employee training programs. They can be used for drill and practice in work exercises, problem solving, simulation of problem situations and their solutions, and individual tutorial instruction.

FIGURE 7-7 Computerized training at Prudential Property and Casualty Insurance Company in Holmdel, New Jersey

Rules of Training

There are certain basic rules to be followed in personnel development situations where the supervisor or a properly qualified in-house person gives the training:

1. Know the people being trained in terms of their interests, ambitions, schooling, aspirations, and motivation.
2. Recognize that each individual's learning ability is different—some are fast learners, others are slow learners. Take time to find out why the slow learner is having trouble.
3. Learn how to motivate individuals so they want to learn. You can't force people to learn when they don't want to.
4. Establish the right environment for training to include privacy, minimum noise interference, adequate lighting, and comfortable working space. Company conference rooms can be a good psychological setting for employee development programs.
5. Give the "big picture" first and then discuss the detailed parts of the total task.
6. Inform the trainee why the instruction is important.
7. Discuss and then demonstrate how things should be performed.
8. Allow time for the trainee to practice how things should be done.
9. Don't cover too much material at one time. Too much information will only confuse. Space the training so the trainee can absorb the information.
10. Emphasize and illustrate the key points with visual aids and examples.
11. Put the trainees on their own in a gradual step-by-step process.
12. Be patient and avoid becoming irritated.
13. Use words that are familiar. Carefully explain new terms.
14. Let the trainees know where they stand. Everyone likes to know "How am I doing?" People left in the dark tend to become tense and frustrated. This tends to impede their ability to learn.
15. Make effective use of praise—it is one of the best motivators.
16. Expect ups and downs. There is a plateau in learning when there is little noticeable improvement.
17. Evaluate and follow up by testing the trainees.

Most people are anxious to do well when they are first assigned a job. Approval of their work efforts is particularly important during the early stages in employee development. Good training affects the future. The individual who gives the training must have a desire to teach and enjoy it. Trainees must feel that the instructor wants to help them, is interested in their development, is patient when they make mistakes, and is pleased when they do well.

BOTH Supervisors and Workers Need Training

The ideal training program should include educational programs for both supervisors and workers (Figure 7-8). Inadequately trained group leaders, project leaders, and other supervisory personnel do not usually command the respect of their subordinates. Furthermore, supervisors without adequate training often lack confidence in themselves. This situation can cause person-

FIGURE 7-8 A formula for developing workers

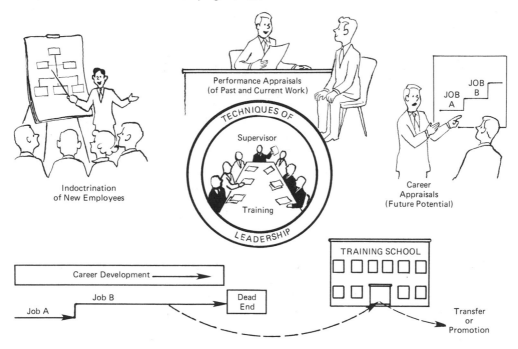

nel turbulence that literally tears an organization apart. A poorly trained supervisor, who doesn't know how to handle people, can so adversely affect employee morale that the productivity of the entire organization is lowered. It is vitally necessary that all supervisors be trained in methods of good leadership, employee humanistic relations, and techniques of instructing.

The ability to perform a mechanical or technical operation in a superior manner is no guarantee that a person is capable of supervising that operation. (Remember the Edward Duncan case at the beginning of Chapter 4.) Many organizations, however, choose their supervisors on the basis of operational work performance without giving them any training in the fundamentals of supervision. This is where "The Peter Principle" is so often affirmed. This theory maintains that people are promoted to their level of incompetence by moving them one notch beyond the level of their ability.[1] Managers who lack training in the fundamentals of supervision are probably the largest known cause of employee turnover, absenteeism, and grievances—all of which add up to decreased productivity.

TRAINING SHOULD BE SELECTIVELY GIVEN

Some supervisors, because they have developed a training program, think that the instruction should be given to all of their subordinates, irrespective of the level of their skills, education, and experience. A more sensible and cost-effective approach is to give the training only to the people who need it or who have the greatest potential for job advancement. In any training program it is important to

1. Explain to the trainee why the training is being given
2. Explain the reason why to employees who have not been selected for training

Training and educational programs are a significant element in the development of improved attitudes, skills, and work performance of both managers and workers. Since these programs are expensive they must be carefully planned and executed. To obtain the maximum benefits, training and educational programs should be custom made to meet the specific needs of the organization and the individuals.

DEAD-END JOBS EQUAL UNHAPPY WORKERS

● *TRANSFERS AND PROMOTIONS*—Training and educational programs should consider the importance of developing employees to the point where they can be transferred or promoted to higher level or better jobs. Employees who feel that they are working on dead-end jobs with little or no chance of advancement are generally unhappy. This unsatisfactory personnel environment can be minimized through carefully planned programs of promoting qualified employees and training and/or transferring other deserving employees with an outlook toward promotion.

The transfer of personnel can involve a job change without a change in pay. The positive aspects of a personnel transfer action are as follows:

— *It can remove an employee from a conflict-of-interest or personality situation.*
— *It can place an employee in a work environment where there are greater opportunities for promotion.*
— *It can place an employee in a work environment that is more in line with the individual's education, training, and/or experience.*
— *It can place an employee in a work environment that is more in line with the individual's social interests.*

DON'T CREATE OVEROPTIMISM

The promotion of personnel involves a change in job with an increase in pay and/or status. The positive aspects of promotion are obvious. Career appraisals—evaluations of an employee's potential for promotion to a higher-level job—are used by some organizations as a systematic means of developing employees for promotion. An objective career appraisal will not only identify the employee's positive capabilities for promotion, but will outline a constructive course of training and education to strengthen any weak areas. Extreme caution should be exercised in career appraisals to not create overoptimism regarding the chances for promotion. Often there are factors relating to promotions that are beyond the supervisor's control.

In summary, a well-thought-out program for employee transfers and promotions can enable qualified and deserving employees to see "light at the end of the tunnel." The important things to consider in such programs are objectivity, fairness, and equal treatment.

LET EMPLOYEES KNOW HOW THEY ARE DOING

● *PERSONNEL PERFORMANCE APPRAISALS*—Factual and unprejudiced performance appraisals can be a good way of developing employees to become more valuable to the organization. A performance appraisal objectively evaluates an employee's past and current performance on the job. It is a plan for the systematic and periodic review of an individual's work performance and effectiveness. Employees who are not periodically given performance appraisals may not know if their work is satisfactory or unsatisfactory. Properly conducted appraisals are often a major factor in rewarding deserving performance through salary increases and/or promotions. Improperly administered appraisals can be very damaging to employee morale and productivity (Figure 7-9).

Performance appraisals are frequently based on trait ratings that use spe-

FIGURE 7-9   Employee appraisals should examine total work performance

cific distinguishing characteristics pertaining to the job. The first step in such appraisals is to identify the traits that are considered to be good performance indicators for each job level. The second step is to relate or judge the individual's past performance and/or future potential against the traits for the job.

Be Honest, Fair, and Objective in Employee Appraisals

One of the benefits of employee appraisals is that it forces direct communication between the supervisor and the employee. However, there are several problems to overcome in employee appraisals:

— *The "halo" effect wherein one or two personal traits improperly influence the evaluation of all traits or performance factors*
— *The problem of semantics where words have different meanings to different people*
— *The time required to prepare and conduct a good performance or career appraisal*
— *The problem of human error in judging people*
— *The problem of evaluating people when the perfect appraisal system has not been and probably never will be developed*
— *Supervisory inconsistency in both attitude and realistic assessment of an employee's performance and potential for advancement*

Use Facts, Not Opinion

Most people want to know how they are doing on the job. They also like to know what their opportunities are for advancement. Periodic performance and career appraisals can help satisfy these desires. It is very important that all appraisals be based on the facts of behavior and performance. Because of the many problems just mentioned, appraisals can either help develop a more effective and efficient employee or turn the person "sour" on the whole management process. The determining factors will be the objectivity, honesty, fairness, and consistency by which the supervisor appraises the employee.

Honesty and Accuracy

One of the major problems in performance ratings lies in the inconsistency of attitude among raters. Some supervisors inflate all their ratings because it's an easy thing to do, and gives them a certain amount of goodwill with subordinates. Other supervisors render true and accurate ratings that may actually prevent a deserving employee from getting promoted. This can happen when a deserving employee receives a good performance rating from a conservative supervisor, and some undeserving employee receives an unjustified higher rating from another supervisor. The illusion of accuracy in performance appraisals is one of the disconcerting aspects of such rating systems.

GUIDELINES FOR PERFORMANCE APPRAISALS

Following are some guidelines for supervisors to consider in performance appraisals:

— *Base performance on a review of the entire rating period and avoid being influenced by very recent actions.*
— *Don't focus too narrowly on either a few peaks or valleys in performance. Examine the total work performance of the individual.*
— *Don't be unduly influenced by some conspicuous personality or behavioral trait of a subordinate. This will act as a "halo" and tend to obscure factual judgment of the individual's overall capabilities. Avoid either positive or negative "halo" ratings because liking or disliking a person may have no relationship to actual work performance.*
— *Base performance on clear measurement criteria. Since many job descriptions are unclear, it may be necessary to use other measurement factors.*
— *Conduct the appraisal objectively based on facts and avoid subjective value judgments that may be either too lenient or too tough.*
— *Substantiate significant performance deficiencies with specific examples.*
— *Remember that most people know their deficiencies and that highly critical performance ratings may cause the person to backslide rather than improve.*

In summary, performance appraisals should be handled discreetly and objectively so as to result in the positive motivation of the individual. Poorly conducted appraisals can leave deep scars in a person's self-esteem which may impair the individual's performance for a long time.

ENCOURAGE PARTICIPATIVE MANAGEMENT

• *EMPLOYEE SUGGESTION SYSTEMS*—The basic idea behind a suggestion system is that an employee on the job is often the logical person to suggest improved methods for doing the work. An employee may have practical ideas for speeding up production without sacrificing quality, as well as ideas for new tools and simplified methods of performing a job task. A suggestion system where employee ideas can be judged and the individual adequately rewarded can result in net operating savings of considerable magnitude.

Encouraging employees to make suggestions causes the individuals to feel that they hold a recognized place in the organization. It can also stimulate the employee's interest in both the job and the organization. The development of ideas is a stimulus in itself to most employees. The adoption of the best suggestions has a wholesome effect on the general morale of employees.

PROBLEMS WITH SUGGESTION SYSTEMS

There are two major problems in suggestion systems. One problem is the time it takes to evaluate the worth of a suggestion. Because of other priorities, it is very easy for a manager to set this evaluation aside. The longer the time span between the submission and its evaluation, the greater the harm to the suggestion program. Employees are quick to conclude that it doesn't pay to submit suggestions because nobody ever looks at them.

A second problem of suggestion programs is the tendency for some supervisors to act negatively toward adoption of a suggestion from a subordinate. Their reaction is an expression of "Why didn't I think of that?" The truth of the matter is that some suggestions can be viewed as an adverse reflection on management.

Despite the problems, it is good management to make the opportunity available to employees to suggest policy, procedure, and methods improvements. A good suggestion system is a form of participative management in which both managers and workers can reap benefits.

HANDLING PEOPLE AT WORK

Keeping employees satisfied on the job is no easy matter. People are motivated by many different stimuli such as the recognition illustrated in Figure 7-10. What may influence or stimulate one person may have no effect on another. The same individual may be motivated one day and "turned off" the next day by the same stimulus. The work performance of people can be affected by many factors:

- *Adequacy and reasonableness of the wages received*
- *Accuracy of job evaluations in measuring the relative importance of job characteristics and responsibilities*
- *Working conditions such as lighting, heating, ventilation, safety, and cleanliness of the work environment*
- *Employee services provided in eating facilities, parking facilities, sanitation facilities, medical services, insurance programs, educational programs, recreational programs, and information services*
- *Honesty and integrity of equal opportunity in transfers, promotions, and educational programs*

FIGURE 7-10 Keeping workers satisfied

- *Fairness reflected in the handling of employee complaints and grievances*
- *Objectivity, consistency, and fairness in the administration of recognition and worker incentive programs*
- *Quality of the supervisory leadership*

Most of these factors tend to reflect the extent to which management cares about the employees. Also very important in employee job satisfaction is the way the supervisor handles such tasks as delegation, giving orders, administering discipline, and dealing with group dynamics.

DELEGATION IS A FORM OF PARTICIPATIVE MANAGEMENT

● *EFFECTIVE DELEGATION*—A key element in a supervisor's relationship with subordinates is delegation of responsibility and authority. This is a form of participative management. The act of delegation gets both supervisor and subordinates involved in accomplishing work objectives. It means entrusting someone else with doing something that needs to be done.

A supervisor must delegate tasks, jobs, and/or projects to workers because he or she cannot do everything. It is difficult for some supervisors to overcome the psychological barriers of having workers set their own goals, take actions on their own initiative, and participate in work decisions. Many supervisors feel that they are losing control when they delegate responsibility and authority to workers. It is even more difficult to delegate a job to a subordinate when you feel you can do it better yourself. Difficult as it may be, a supervisor must delegate *appropriate* work to subordinates because the supervisor cannot be running around trying to do everyone's job.

BENEFITS OF DELEGATION

Failure to delegate may mean you are doing somebody else's work. The supervisor who delegates increases his or her effectiveness in getting things done. Some of the benefits of delegation are

— *Your department will function more smoothly, particularly when you must be away at meetings or for other reasons.*
— *You free yourself to concentrate on the most urgent and important work problems and situations.*
— *You will get more suggestions on how the operations in your department can be improved.*
— *You will be able to train your subordinates in handling problem situations.*

As a starting point in effective delegation, the supervisor should develop a delegation chart (Figure 7-11). The list of tasks reflected in a delegation chart will vary according to the type of work being performed and the scope of authority that has been delegated to the supervisor. In developing a delegation chart it is important to

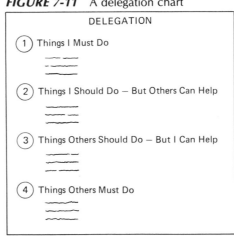

FIGURE 7-11 A delegation chart

— *Know to whom you can and cannot delegate*
— *Know the right things to delegate*
— *Know how much to delegate*

WHAT TO DELEGATE

Routine time-consuming tasks should be delegated to others to save the supervisor's time for nonroutine things. For example, subordinates can be delegated such supervisory tasks as

— *Maintaining certain records*
— *Preparing production reports*
— *Coordinating the collection and processing of reports and communications between work stations*
— *Checking reports for errors*
— *Preparing requisitions for supplies and materials*
— *Obtaining clarification of operational reports*
— *Having an experienced worker train a new employee to do certain work*

In delegating tasks such as those just listed, the supervisor must periodically follow up on how well the task was performed. For example, the supervisor should check to see if the new employee received sufficient training. It is also important in delegation that the supervisor minimize interrupting employees once they start working on the delegated assignment.

In delegating responsibility the supervisor must also delegate *appropriate* authority necessary to carry out the responsibility. For example, an employee given the assigned task of preparing a department budget should also be given the authority to question data that appears to be inaccurate or inconsistent.

WHAT NOT TO DELEGATE

There are certain tasks that *should not be delegated* to a subordinate worker:

— *Disciplinary actions*
— *Praise and rewards for work performance*
— *Changes in work methods and procedures*
— *Human relations problems*

The supervisor should *never* "pass the buck" to a subordinate in a situation where the supervisor wants to avoid sticking out his or her neck. The supervisor must also remember in delegating tasks to others not to renounce or relinquish all responsibility. If something goes wrong, the supervisor is still accountable and must take the consequences for a wrong decision.

DELEGATION GUIDELINES

There are certain policy guidelines that can help make delegation effective. These guidelines should be applied by managers at every level in the organization:

1. Delegation should be practiced at every level of management.
2. Subordinate managers should be encouraged to delegate and must be given a feeling of job security when they do. This is particularly important since the reason some managers hesitate to delegate is that they fear they might lose their position.
3. Managers at all levels should know the capabilities of their subordinates so as to not delegate responsibility that exceeds those capabilities. This means knowing the strengths and weaknesses of people based on their proven records of performance. With this kind of information, work can be delegated to people where application of their strengths can produce results.
4. Responsibilities should not be delegated without giving the subordinate the necessaray resources to do the job.
5. Subordinates should know the exact results that are expected to be achieved in their delegated tasks.
6. Subordinates should see the delegated assignment as a step forward in their career development.
7. Subordinates should be assured that they will receive assistance when they encounter problems.
8. Once a task is delegated and fully understood by the subordinate, the individual should be given appropriate freedom to get the job done. Excessive supervision can easily destroy the positive aspects of delegation and cause it to become ineffective.
9. Managers should be prepared to accept some mistakes when they delegate. Firmness, fairness, and understanding in the handling of mistakes made by subordinates usually results in a concerted effort to avoid repetition of the mistake.
10. Performance of managers should be evaluated on *both* their own work accomplishments and on how well they are developing their subordinates through effective delegation. It is a manager's job to convert human strength into productive effort. Effective delegation of work to subordinates is one way to convert potential strength into actual responsibility for using that human capability.

TOLERANCE TOWARD MISTAKES

In delegating responsibility to a worker the supervisor should maintain a tolerant attitude regarding a reasonable number of mistakes. Some mistakes will be made. *The only person who does not make mistakes is the person who does nothing.*

● *BEHAVIOR PATTERNS IN GIVING AND RECEIVING ORDERS—* Orders are issued to get something done or to prevent something from happening. Good communications are vitally important in giving and receiving orders. If an order is to be effectively carried out, the person giving and the person receiving the order must see things the same way.

A Supervisor Must Understand Human Behavior When Giving Orders

The person giving an order must have an understanding of human behavior to successfully communicate that order to another person. With some people orders must be given in an authoritative way. However with most people, orders are best received, understood, and executed if they are given in a consultative or participative way. The key is to have an understanding of the disposition and state of mind of the person receiving the order. If the person is inclined to have a Theory X attitude and doesn't like to work, the order may have to be given in an authoritarian way. On the other hand, if the person has a Theory Y attitude and likes to work, the order should generally be given after allowing the recipient to participate in the decision-making process. It must be recognized that there are emergency, accident avoidance, or security situations that dictate the authoritarian method of giving orders to a subordinate.

A Supervisor Should Know Workers' Capabilities Before Giving Orders

A supervisor should know workers' capabilities before issuing orders to them. This avoids giving an order to an individual who cannot execute the order because it is beyond the person's mental, physical, or skill capabilities. It also avoids giving an order that insults the intelligence of the very capable individual. A supervisor should be flexible in giving orders because some workers like to be told in fine detail exactly what to do while others like freedom in getting the job done. People differ considerably in their attitudes and capabilities for performing work. The giving of orders should recognize these differences.

Guidelines in Giving Orders

Figure 7-12 reflects guidelines a supervisor should follow when issuing orders to subordinates. Note that the behavioral attitude of the supervisor plays an important part in the reaction that can be expected from the recipient of the order.

Reflect Confidence

First, the supervisor should reflect a position of confidence when issuing an order. How can one expect a subordinate to enthusiastically carry out an order if the supervisor's approach is negative and reflects a lack of confidence in what the subordinate is being asked to do?

FIGURE 7-12 Guidelines in giving orders

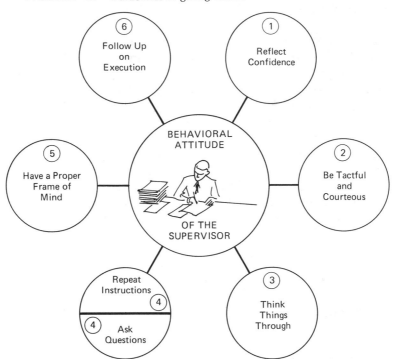

BE TACTFUL AND COURTEOUS

Second, the supervisor should be pleasant, courteous, and tactful when issuing orders. Nothing is gained, except resentment, if the supervisor gives an order in a rude and dictatorial way. There is nothing wrong in phrasing an order to sound like a request. A supervisor may be surprised at the results when an order is issued by saying "Will you try to . . .", or by saying "I would appreciate it if you would . . ."

THINK THINGS THROUGH

Third, the supervisor should plan and think through orders before they are issued. Don't expect others to be mind readers about what they are expected to do. The supervisor should be specific and avoid ambiguity. This includes clearly explaining the reason for new orders or significant changes in old orders. There should be a good reason for issuing an order. If not, the order probably isn't necessary.

Repeat Instructions and Ask Questions

Fourth, the supervisor should repeat instructions to be certain that they are understood. The subordinates should also be given a chance to ask questions. If the order is complex, technical, and/or subject to different interpretations, have it repeated back to be certain that it is understood. The supervisor should not assume that orders are understood. Remember that some workers are hesitant to either question an order or have the boss repeat it. The understanding of orders will be enhanced if the supervisor is careful and avoids issuing conflicting instructions.

Have a Proper Frame of Mind

Fifth, the supervisor should be in the proper frame of mind when giving orders. The tone of voice and use of body gestures are important factors in communicating orders. Supervisors should not put themselves in difficult situations by issuing orders when they are emotionally upset and angry. They will regret it.

Follow Up on Execution

Sixth, the supervisor should make it a practice to follow up on the execution of orders that are given. Many things can happen, and the only way a supervisor may find out how things are going is through periodic follow-up. Remember that some workers are reluctant or even afraid to tell the boss about any of their problems.

• *HOW TO HANDLE RESISTANCE TO ORDERS*—Most subordinates in a work situation willingly comply with orders if the supervisor handles the situation in a humanistic manner. However, some workers tend to resist, or even refuse, to do what they are asked to do. How do you handle this problem? Well, it is not easy. For one thing there is the understandable tendency for some supervisors to lose their tempers. This is probably the worst thing that can happen because it usually does not resolve the problem; it only makes it worse. The supervisor should try to remain calm and collected and take steps to find out why the subordinate is resisting or refusing to carry out the order. There may be a good reason. For example, the subordinate may feel that the order requires work to be performed that is not in the individual's job description.

Allow Time To Resolve the Problem

Figure 7-13 shows some recommended steps for a supervisor to take in situations where a subordinate resists carrying out an order. First, think things

FIGURE 7-13 How to handle resistance to orders

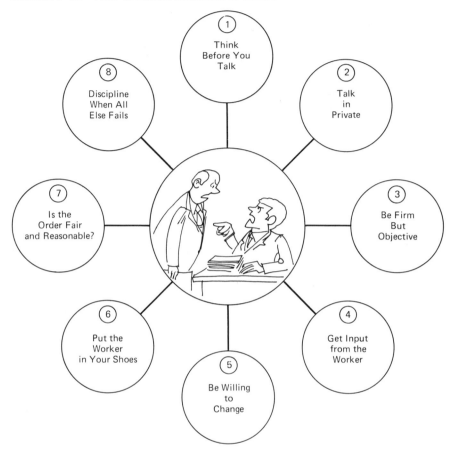

through before you talk. This will give you time to organize what you want to say and do. Second, talk to the subordinate in private. It is a matter between you and that person. Third, take a firm position but be objective and willing to listen to the subordinate's point of view. Fourth, try to find out what the subordinate thinks should be done. Fifth, revise the order if the subordinate presents facts that justify such action. Sixth, if there are insufficient facts to revise the order, try to get the subordinate to see the situation from your position. In other words, put the subordinate in your shoes with the expectation that the individual will change his or her position. Seventh, find out if the order was fair and reasonable from the point of view of the subordinate. If not, obtain the reasons why. Eighth, take disciplinary action if the order is found to be fair and reasonable, and the subordinate cannot present facts to justify a revision of the order.

UNION PARTICIPATION

In a unionized organization, the worker may request or demand that a union representative be present when you talk to your subordinate. Grant the request, even if the management-union contract does not specifically dictate it. If it is necessary to take disciplinary action, invite the employee's union representative to be present. You may be surprised to find that the union representative is on your side.

● *ADMINISTERING DISCIPLINE*—Worker complaints and grievances are actions of dissatisfaction directed against management and supervision. Sometimes the shoe is on the other foot, and the supervisor is dissatisfied with a worker. The dissatisfaction can lead to the supervisor taking disciplinary action against a worker.

DISCIPLINE SHOULD BE A POSITIVE FORM OF MOTIVATION

A supervisor can look at discipline in a negative way—as punishment—or in a positive way—as constructive criticism and training. The purpose of discipline should be the motivation of workers to meet established rules, regulations, and standards of job performance. To achieve this, it is usually better for a supervisor to think of discipline in the positive sense as a form of improving the subordinate's work efforts. If a worker observes the rules and exceeds the standards of performance, consideration should be given to some form of reward such as recognition or, if possible, advancement. If a worker does not observe the rules and constantly falls short of the standards of performance, the individual should be appropriately penalized. The objective of the disciplinary action should be to allow the worker to learn what performance and behavior are acceptable (Figure 7-14).

Disciplinary action can be executed in many ways. In any form it is an unpleasant task that supervisors must perform. A supervisor, therefore, should resort to disciplinary action only after all other corrective actions have failed. For one thing it is difficult to avoid worker dissatisfaction with the handling of disciplinary action. One reason is that the supervisor is not only the person who bring charges against the worker, he or she also usually acts as judge and jury.

The need for taking disciplinary action can be considerably reduced through effective supervisory leadership. When workers feel that they have a good leader who is fair and considerate, they tend to get more satisfaction in their work and are less inclined to break rules.

HOW TO ADMINISTER DISCIPLINE

Where disciplinary action is necessary, good supervisory management can help to effectively bring about the necessary corrective action without harm-

FIGURE 7-14 Disciplinary action can be a learning experience

ful personal aftereffects. The following is a checklist of things to do in administering discipline:

1. Inform workers at the start of their employment of the rules and standards of performance with which they must comply.

2. Don't go into a meeting with the worker and have your mind already made up as to what action you are going to take.

3. Obtain and objectively analyze all the facts of the situation before you take any disciplinary action. You may find that you are partially responsible for the situation.

4. Don't discuss the situation with the worker when you are upset or angry.

5. Approach the situation with the positive assumption that most workers want to do the right thing and that there may be extenuating circumstances involved.

6. Give the worker a chance to explain his or her side of the issue. For example, you may be able to ask the worker to express how he or she is doing on the job and thereby let the individual bring up the subject.

7. Tactfully criticize performance with facts and, to the maximum possible extent, avoid personal censure of the individual. Personal verbal attacks on the individual usually accomplish very little except hostile confrontation that diverts attention from the primary issue of work performance.

8. Follow the practice of progressive disciplinary actions starting, where possible, with an oral warning, to a written warning, to a temporary suspension, and finally to discharge.

9. Make a written memo of the facts and the action taken and give a copy to the worker. It will help eliminate misunderstanding.

10. Control extreme outbursts of your own personal emotions by being calm and even-tempered. Sometimes, however, an occasional show of displeasure will indicate to the worker that you are both human and really dissatisfied with the work being performed.

11. Don't take a disciplinary action unless you intend to fully implement it. One of the worst things a supervisor can do is to make a disciplinary decision and then not carry it out. It is equally important to avoid making a decision that would not hold up under an appeal action by the worker.

12. Apply the principle of impartiality. If the same facts apply to a situation, be consistent in the disciplinary action that is taken.

As has been mentioned many times, the best way to administer discipline is to be a firm, consistent, fair, honest, and considerate leader who operates within authority limitations.

FIGURE 7-15   There is collective force in group dynamics

GROUP DYNAMICS: A COLLECTIVE FORCE
IN THE WORKPLACE

● *HANDLING GROUP DYNAMICS*—A supervisor not only has to handle be-havioral situations involving individual workers, but must understand and work with the forces of group dynamics. The term *group dynamics* applies to the interactions among members of a group, and with their attitudes, beha-viors, and relationships with people outside the group, including their supervi-sor. It is a dynamic situation because things are constantly changing. A group can present mass resistance or full support of a management-directed action. They can be extreme conformists or nonconformists. They can bring collective pressure to bear either for or against something. The nature of group dynam-ics is such that it can virtually make or break a supervisor (Figure 7-15).

Group dynamics is found in both formal and informal work groups. For-mal work groups are teams of employees assigned by the supervisor to work on certain activities or accomplish specified objectives. Informal work groups are formed spontaneously among employees who work near one another or who have common personal interests such as riding together in a car pool or playing on the same bowling team. Informal groups are inevitable whenever people work together. Formal groups can usually be controlled by the supervi-sor; informal groups cannot.

A SUPERVISOR MUST INTEGRATE
DIVERGENT GOALS

A supervisor must strive to integrate three sets of goals in the work environ-ment. These include the goals of the supervisor, of the individual worker, and of the informal groups. While this may at first appear impossible, it can usually be achieved if the supervisor does the following things:

— *Don't ignore either the individual worker or the informal organizations be-cause their support is essential to the accomplishment of the supervisor's goals.*
— *Don't try to break up informal organizations because it can't be done. If at-tempted, there will be undesirable confrontation.*
— *Don't try to join informal organizations because it can cause distrust of the supervisor by other employees who are not members of the group.*
— *Show sincere consideration for the values and goals of the individual work-ers in the organization.*
— *Recognize the existence, values, and goals of informal groups in the organi-zation.*
— *Share your own experiences and knowledge with all of your workers.*
— *Listen to suggestions, complaints, and reports that come from members of in-formal groups.*

> — *Engage both individuals and informal groups in participative management by getting them to share with others their knowledge and information on how to attain the goals of the organization.*
> — *Provide sound direction, guidance, and facts to assist both individuals and informal groups in agreeing with your inclinations.*
> — *When it is not possible to integrate the goals of the supervisor, the individual workers, and the informal groups, openly explain the final decision and the reason for it.*

A supervisor must be guided by the fact that without group support the chances of success in any undertaking may be slim. It is up to the supervisor to recognize when group action is going off in the wrong direction and to take firm steps to correct the situation. The steps for keeping group work activities on the right track should start with the proper issuing of orders by the supervisor to individual workers. If individual workers are effectively supervised, there is little chance of problems with the forces of group dynamics.

DEVELOPING A POSITIVE ATTITUDE WITH SUBORDINATES

DEVELOPING A PHILOSOPHICAL ATTITUDE

Attitude is the propensity or inclination to look at specific things in a particular way. A supervisor's attitude toward subordinates is a key factor in effective supervision. The supervisor's attitude regarding subordinates should be a constructive one that starts with developing a positive philosophy toward people. Such a philosophy should reflect the following things:

- *That people are human beings with feelings and minds which reflect things that they value*
- *That people are a very tangible asset and should be treated with consideration*
- *That most people expect to work, want to work, and will obtain satisfaction from work that is performed in a good work environment*
- *That workers look to their supervisor for guidance, direction, and support*
- *That the behavior of people is caused by both heredity and environmental factors, and while little can be done regarding heredity, the supervisor can exert correctional influence regarding the work environment*

SUPERVISOR'S PERSONAL CONDUCT

The personal conduct of the supervisor tends to reflect the individual's attitude toward subordinates. Therefore, it is important for a supervisor to do things that show concern and sensitivity for employees. Some of the things that a supervisor can do are

- *Be aware of his or her own biases and prejudices and control them.*
- *Let subordinates know where they stand by keeping them informed about changes that may affect them, and by giving them timely and constructive appraisals of their work performance.*
- *Go out of the way to help and support subordinates, particularly when something goes wrong.*
- *Give praise when it is appropriate and see that it is timely.*
- *Be tactful, courteous, and understanding.*
- *Be willing to learn from subordinates.*
- *Be firm, but also be consistent and fair.*
- *Don't discriminate or play favorites.*

The supervisor plays the dominant role in the procurement and development of personnel, as well as in the maintenance of a satisfied work force. It starts with participation in the selection of employees, their orientation and training on the job, and continues in the day-to-day handling of such matters as delegating work, issuing orders, administering discipline, and other supervisory actions.

SUMMARY

Personnel management is probably the most sensitive and important activity involved in the supervision of work and productivity. It involves (1) getting the right person on the right job, (2) developing personnel so that they are more valuable to the organization, and (3) keeping employees satisfied on the job. The procurement of personnel involves the supervisor in job design, job descriptions, job evaluations, and the staffing of jobs. An important responsibility of the supervisor is seeing that the jobs of subordinates are accurately described in the job descriptions.

In staffing personnel on jobs, the final selection decision should usually rest with the new employee's supervisor. Well-planned orientation of new employees is important in getting them started to work with a positive attitude toward both the supervisor and the organization.

A supervisor should be alert to subordinates working on unenriched jobs. Timely action to make jobs more interesting through job enlargement or enrichment can help achieve greater employee satisfaction. Development of personnel is a continuous process. It starts with indoctrination of the new employee. As the employee continues to work in the organization, the supervisor should determine when and where further training and education is needed to improve attitudes, skills, and work performance.

Training and education programs are not the only means of developing personnel. Programs that encourage promotion of qualified employees and transfer of deserving individuals for the purpose of giving them experience that can lead to promotion, can be very effective in developing personnel. Factual and unprejudiced performance appraisals are another way of developing employees to become more valuable to the organization.

The work performance of individuals can be affected by many factors. Most of these factors tend to be a reflection of the extent to which management cares about and is considerate of the employees. Also very important in employee job satisfaction is the way the supervisor handles such tasks as delegation, giving orders, administering discipline, and dealing with group dynamics. If individual workers are effectively supervised, there is little chance of problems with the forces of group dynamics.

The supervisor's attitude toward subordinates is a key factor in effective supervision. It should start with a positive philosophy toward people and be reflected in actions that show concern and sensitivity for subordinates.

REVIEW QUESTIONS

1. Discuss the primary objectives of effective personnel management and the involvement of the supervisor in their achievement.
2. How is the supervisor involved in job design, job descriptions, job evaluation, and the staffing of jobs?
3. What are the consequences of poor staffing practices?
4. How can a supervisor assess the jobs that should be reevaluated for possible job enlargement or enrichment? What actions can a supervisor take to make jobs more satisfying to workers?
5. How is an untrained employee a liability? What can a supervisor do to develop personnel to the point where they are assets to the organization?
6. What is a delegation chart? What is its significance?
7. How is effective delegation a form of participative management?
8. Why is an understanding of human behavior important in communicating orders to subordinates?
9. When disciplinary action is necessary, are there any actions that can be taken to minimize harmful aftereffects?
10. Discuss some of the do's and don't's in handling employee performance appraisals.
11. How can a supervisor handle resistance to orders by a subordinate?
12. What are some basic rules that should be followed in personnel training?

CASE STUDIES IN THE SUPERVISION OF PERSONNEL

A.   THE CASE OF NEWTON FOLEY

Newton Foley is an employee of a public utility company. His job does not involve any contact with customers. One day Foley came to work wearing a T-shirt with a decal picture on the front of the garment. Harry Klein, a first-level supervisor in another department, considered the T-shirt decal to be derogatory to the company. In spite of the fact that Foley was not one of his subordinates, Klein ordered Foley to go home and change to another shirt and then return to work. Klein then proceeded to dock Foley's pay for the time it took to comply with the order to change shirts. When Foley returned to work he noticed that another employee in the building was also wearing a T-shirt with the same decal picture. Since the company rule book on personal conduct had no code of dress for employees, Foley filed a grievance with the union. He won the grievance and the restoration of his docked pay.

QUESTIONS

1. What is your evaluation of Foley's conduct on the job?
2. What improper actions do you think Klein took with reference to Foley?
3. How do you think Klein should have handled the T-shirt situation?
4. Do you feel Foley will or will not be a better motivated employee as the result of this incident? Why?

B.   THE CASE OF FRED DORAN

Fred Doran is the supervisor of the receiving department of a large retail store. He has no control over the workload of merchandise moving in and out of his department. The inflow is largely determined by the buyers of the merchandise. They also frequently make unreasonable demands about moving merchandise from receiving to the various sales departments in the store. Many requests are received late in the workday. Doran, however, complies with the buyers' demands even if it means moving merchandise out of the receiving department at quitting time. The workers in Doran's department complain about the constant pressures of "move this, move that."

Doran in turn complains to the workers that he has no control over what the buyers order or their demands for moving merchandise to various parts of the store.

Since the morale is not good in Doran's department, he arranged a bowling contest with the buyers. The receiving department won a smashing victory. The next day, the morale was high in Doran's department. Everyone felt great, but there was no improvement in the work situation. The workers continued to complain about the demands to "move this, move that."

QUESTIONS

1. What is your explanation of why the workers, when they were happy, didn't work harder but continued to complain about the workload?
2. If you were Doran, what would you do to improve the work situation? Why?

C. THE CASE OF HENRY LACKATHINK

Henry Lackathink is a supervisor in the F & A Company. The company has liberal policies regarding employee training and development. Three of Lackathink's employees submitted requests to attend a training program that will require them to travel to a training center in the Pocono Mountains and be away from the job for two weeks.

Hermine is one of Lackathink's best workers and one whom he has in line for future promotion. She has never attended any training programs conducted off the company premises. Because of the heavy workload in Lackathink's department and his dependence on Hermine, he feels that he cannot spare her to attend the two-week training program. Lackathink talks to Hermine and explains why her request cannot be approved. He mentioned how important she is to the department and how he has plans for her future promotion.

Mary is average in her work performance and is not currently in line for future promotion. She has attended one three-day seminar on data processing, approximately one year ago. After considerable discussion with Mary, Lackathink approves her request for the two-week training program.

George is a big talker, a politician, and somewhat of a troublemaker. He is also not a competent worker. George constantly requests approval to attend various training programs. He has attended two one-week seminars in the past nine months. Since George can do very little to ease the burden of the heavy workload in the department, Lackathink approves his request for the two-week training.

Following Lackathink's decisions regarding Hermine, Mary, and George, he notices that there is considerable discontent among other workers in his department. Then Hermine requests a lateral transfer to another department.

QUESTIONS

1. What can Lackathink do about Hermine's transfer request?
2. What do you think is causing the other workers to be discontented? What can Lackathink do about it? What would you do about it if you were Lackathink?
3. What can be learned from an analysis of Lackathink's supervisory practices regarding training and development of subordinates?

NOTES

1. Laurence J. Peter and Raymond Hull, *The Peter Principle* (New York: Morrow, 1969), p. 25.

8

Handling Sensitive Personnel Situations

LABOR-MANAGEMENT:
COOPERATION OR CONFLICT?

Labor and management today have the same important decision to make. Each of us can either add new bricks to strengthen a wall between us, or we can make up our minds to tear down barriers that separate us.

I believe enlightened leaders of both labor and management realize that a better future for all of us requires partnership and cooperation, rather than conflict in labor-management relations.

If we are to successfully meet the challenges of the future, each of us, whether we are a union leader, union worker, corporate executive or middle-management supervisor, must be guided in our relations with each other by two simple words—"mutual respect."

In this age of rapidly advancing technology in every field, management at all levels must not fall into the terrible trap of thinking of their employees as just accessories to their organization's computers and machinery. On the other hand, union workers must remember that their individual performance on the job directly and dramatically affects the success of their employer in business, as well as their own security and success as breadwinners for their families.

Labor and management need each other to be successful, even if it doesn't seem that way sometimes because of a temporary breakdown in communication between them. Promoting better communication must be the goal of both sides, regardless of whether the subject at hand is an on-the-job grievance from an employee or an attempt by management to increase production and profits. We have obligations to each other that must not be trampled as each side exercises its rights.

The decision in labor-management relations is ours. We can work together and respect each other, or we can work at odds with each other and find some day that we no longer have anything to fight over—simply because we will both be out of business.

> Stephen C. Hornik, Vice President
> United Food & Commercial Workers Union
> Local 56 AFL-CIO

LEARNING OBJECTIVES

The objectives of this chapter on handling sensitive personnel situations are to enable the reader to

1. Recognize practical guidelines for performing the following tasks:
   a. Counseling a problem employee
   b. Resolving personnel conflict in the workplace
   c. Achieving good working relations with the union
   d. Preventing grievances
2. Understand the purpose of affirmative action programs and the supervisor's role in their execution
3. Identify five reasons why a supervisor should treat handicapped workers like any other workers
4. Describe the responsibilities of the supervisor in protecting the health and safety of workers
5. Describe the superstructure of labor-management cooperation
6. Delineate the five-step grievance procedure
7. Apply supervisory management guidelines to the analysis and resolution of personnel case studies

KEY WORDS

Affirmative Action   Plans and programs designed to achieve results in the avoidance of discrimination against any person

Arbitration   The use of a third party to make decisions for disputing persons and resolve their differences.

Civil Rights   The rights to full legal, economic, and social equality established by the Thirteenth/Fourteenth Amendments to the United States Constitution and certain Congressional Acts.

Civil Service   Those branches of public service concerned with all governmental functions except the military services.

Conciliation   The use of a third party to bring disputing persons together in order to resolve their differences.

Equal Opportunity   The right of every person, regardless of race, color, sex, age, religion, nationality, or disability, to equal treatment on the job.

Equal Opportunity Laws   The Equal Pay Act of 1963, the Civil Rights Act of 1964, the Age in Discrimination Act of 1967, and the Federal Rehabilitation Act of 1973.

Labor Relations Laws   The National Labor Relations Act of 1935, the Fair Labor Standards Act of 1938, and the Taft-Hartley Act of 1947.

Mediation   The use of a third party to offer suggestions to disputing persons in order to resolve their differences.

OSHA   (Occupational Safety and Health Administration)—A government agency that assists employers in providing a safe and healthy workplace.

Shop Steward   The first-level representative of a union.

THE CASE OF JOSEPH EARL

Joseph Earl was a government civil service employee with emotional problems. Over a period of many years various employees harassed and made derogatory remarks to Joseph Earl about his irrational behavior on the job. Two female employees were afraid of him because he called them "nutty." Some employees laughed and sneered at Joseph Earl and others called him a "nut." In a sworn statement to a police officer, Joseph Earl claimed that a young supervisor called him a "jerk" and threatened to "beat him into the ground." This incident allegedly occurred in a restroom at work. Joseph Earl's supervisors at work appeared to do nothing to stop the harassment that he was receiving. From all indications, they had neither understanding nor concern for Joseph Earl's emotional problems.

One day Joseph Earl called in sick. Approximately three weeks later he returned to work and was requested to provide a medical certification of his illness. Two weeks later Joseph Earl turned in a medical certification stating: "I know my condition so a doctor is not needed. I am sick and disgusted with the way my supervisor treats me." Joseph Earl's supervisor told him his application for sick leave was not submitted in accordance with published personnel policies. He was advised to submit a revised application. Three weeks later, Joseph Earl submitted a revised application. In the space for the physician to sign, indicating that the employee was under medical professional care, Joseph Earl signed his own name and indicated the cause of his illness as "depressed." This application was also rejected by Joseph Earl's supervisor.

When Joseph Earl's application for sick leave was rejected, he wrote a memo and posted it on the office bulletin board alleging that there had been oppressive acts over a fourteen-year period that caused his illness. The memo also stated that his supervisor was denying him earned sick leave. Joseph Earl, through his union representative, filed a grievance charging his supervisors with constant harassment over a period of many years. The grievance was denied at successive levels in the grievance procedure.

Four months later Joseph Earl was absent for two weeks due to illness. When he returned to work he presented a medical certificate stating "A relapse of my depressive state" and signed his name as the attending physician. This certification was rejected by the supervisor and Joseph Earl filed a second grievance. The grievance claimed there had been maltreatment, abuse, and harassment by Joseph Earl's supervisors. The grievance was rejected at successive levels in the grievance procedure because none of the accusations could be substantiated. In both of Joseph Earl's absences he was charged vacation time for his unsupported sick leave. When his accrued vacation time was exhausted, his salary was docked for the hours he was off the job with the alleged illness.

Following the denial of Joseph Earl's grievances regarding his unsupported sick leave, his behavior became more irrational. He posted derogatory signs in the office concerning his supervisors. Through his union representative he initiated three grievances against two supervisors alleging harassment, conspiracy, violation of civil rights, and denial of constitutional rights when they inferred that he be required to see a psychiatrist. The grievances called for disciplinary actions to be taken to reprimand the two supervisors. These grievances were denied because of lack of supporting evidence.

As the reader will find later in the chapter, this is not the end of the Joseph Earl case. Subsequent irrational behavior led to actions to fire Joseph Earl and he was, in fact, removed from the government service. These events and the final outcome will be discussed later. As of this point what is your evaluation of how Joseph Earl's supervisors handled his behavioral problems? As you read this chapter, look for things that you feel might have minimized or even avoided the Joseph Earl fiasco. What is your reaction to the role of the union in supporting Joseph Earl? Do you feel the union may have erred in its handling of Joseph Earl's grievances?

COUNSELING PROBLEM EMPLOYEES

SUPERVISORS SHOULD RESOLVE, NOT CONTRIBUTE TO, PROBLEMS

The Joseph Earl case is an example of a sensitive situation involving a problem employee that required extraordinary handling. This case is not unique in the supervision of personnel because many individuals have emotional problems.

A supervisor must be able to identify and understand problem employees such as Joseph Earl, and quickly determine if professional help is or is not needed. The combination of supervisory understanding, counseling, and appropriate solicitation of professional help may have kept the Joseph Earl situation from getting out of hand. As it was, Joseph Earl's supervisors helped contribute to the problem rather than resolve it.

PROBLEM EMPLOYEES CANNOT BE IGNORED

Problem employees are a part of virtually every organization. Some employees are habitually absent from work, or do not get to work on time, or leave work before quitting time. Other employees may be alcoholics or drug addicts. Some individuals are problems because they are arrogant, uncooperative, nonconformists, or rabble-rousers. These problems have many causes. Whatever the cause, the supervisor cannot ignore problem employees—they can be very disruptive to the overall performance of an organization. The supervisor who cannot handle problem employees may lose the confidence and respect of the other workers.

What can a supervisor do with regard to problem employees? One thing is to avoid hiring them. Some supervisors, however, have little control over the people hired and assigned to their departments because the recruitment function is handled by a staff Personnel Office. In other situations the problem may have developed after the individual was hired. Even with the most careful recruitment of employees, there will still be personnel problems. The causes of some problems may be within the work environment. Other causes may be due to problems within the home or they may be genetic within the individual. Supervisors often find themselves with the job of counseling and trying to straighten out problem employees. If the supervisor takes the right approach in counseling, he or she can often succeed in improving the situation. The wrong approach, however, may make matters worse.

SIGNS OF A TROUBLED WORKER

The starting point in handling problem employees is to recognize the signs of a troubled worker. Some indicators of a person with problems are

- *Irritability*
- *Frequent lateness to work*
- *Increased absences from work*
- *Inclination to have accidents*
- *Excessive use of alcoholic beverages*
- *Sudden change in behavior*

It is important to recognize the signs of a troubled employee and counsel the person before things get out of hand. Failure to do this may lead to no other option than that of taking disciplinary action. This type of action, however, may cause new problems with the employee.

To Counsel or Not To Counsel?

When faced with a problem employee, the supervisor should counsel the individual to determine

- *If this is a problem that he or she may be able to help the employee overcome?*

OR

- *If this is a problem that is beyond the supervisor's capabilities, where the employee may need professional help.*

The importance of arriving at the correct answer cannot be overemphasized. The supervisor who takes action that exceeds his or her capabilities is something like a plumber trying to do dental work. If, after counseling the worker, the supervisor feels that disciplinary action is necessary, the following two questions need to be addressed:

1. Has the individual been given a sufficient chance to correct the problem?
2. Has the supervisor taken the time to find out whether the worker may have problems needing professional help?

Not taking the time to get the answers to these questions could result in taking unjust disciplinary action against an individual (Figure 8-1).

In the Joseph Earl case, his supervisors fired him for disgraceful conduct and creating a disturbance. The disgraceful conduct charge was based primarily on a letter that Joseph Earl wrote to the parents of a young supervisor in his department. The charge of creating a disturbance was primarily based on Joseph Earl's refusal to leave a specific work area when asked by a supervisor.

Post-mortem analysis of this case shows that the disciplinary action taken against Joseph Earl was unjust. His supervisor never informed him as to what was considered an acceptable standard of conduct. As the United States Civil Service Commission stated in response to an appeal by Joseph Earl, the supervisor "was guided by his own personal version of what constitutes a reasonable standard of conduct." There was no evidence that the supervisor's standard was ever communicated to the employee prior to his engaging in the alleged disgraceful conduct.

Joseph Earl was charged with creating a disturbance when he insisted on using a telephone in the area where an office machine demonstration was to be conducted. A young supervisor in Joseph Earl's department informed him that he was a low-level employee and that the demonstration was for management. The supervisor then shouted to another supervisor to "get this thing out of here." According to statements made by other employees, there was an ex-

FIGURE 8-1 A supervisor should avoid unjust disciplinary action

change of shouting between the two supervisors. The U.S. Civil Service Commission, in revoking the disciplinary action against Joseph Earl concluded that the young supervisor created as much, if not more, of a disturbance than Joseph Earl.

Several significant things can be learned from the Joseph Earl case. In the first place, a supervisor should instruct other employees to not make fun of troubled workers but to try and be understanding. Second, a supervisor should take time to counsel problem employees and advise them as to the company's standards regarding acceptable and not acceptable on-the-job conduct. Third, a supervisor should listen to and objectively analyze the facts of an employees' complaint, even when it comes from a problem employee. Fourth, supervisors must control their own emotions on the job and avoid actions that do not reflect good leadership. Last, a supervisor should not take disciplinary action without objectively analyzing all the facts of the situation.

SUPERVISOR SELF-ANALYSIS

There are some guidelines that a supervisor can follow to help achieve successful results in counseling a problem employee. Recognizing the fact that there is a very unpleasant situation to handle, can the supervisor control his or her own temper, emotions, and opinions while trying to get the facts needed to help solve the problem? Is the supervisor aware that trying to resolve the problem is a part of his or her job and cannot be avoided? Does the supervisor recognize his or her own limitations in handling what may be emotional problems? Has the supervisor analyzed his or her own actions to establish any factors that could be contributing causes of the problem employee's behavior? For example, did the supervisor cause frustration by setting unrealistic production goals? Did the supervisor fail to praise the employee for doing an outstanding job on a difficult assignment? Did the supervisor try to motivate the individual by fear?

GUIDELINES FOR COUNSELING A PROBLEM EMPLOYEE

After the supervisor has made the objective self-analysis indicated above, he or she should consider the following guidelines in counseling a problem employee:

1. Put the individual at ease by discussing some current event such as the Super Bowl, the World Series, or a subject of known interest to the person. This allows the employee to set the course of the discussion.
2. Lead the discussion to the problem by bringing up a work situation that involves the employee and then ask the individual how it is affecting him or her.
3. Let the individual express the things that might be bothering him or her.
4. Give assurance of sincerity in trying to help improve the situation and enable the individual to get a fair deal.
5. Obtain the employee's opinion of his or her behavior.
6. Show the employee how behavior can hurt the individual on the job and with peers.
7. Ask for the individual's recommendations on what he or she would do if in the supervisor's position.
8. Try to put the employee at ease by showing how all people have problems of some sort.
9. Don't expect to resolve all problem situations in one counseling session. Where emotional problems are involved it may take several fifteen- to thirty-minute counseling sessions before one observes progress.
10. Recognize your own limitations, but don't be too hasty in referring an employee for professional help. Indiscriminate referral can cause more intensified irrational behavior (as was the case with Joseph Earl).
11. If it appears necessary to involve professional help, consult with them first on how best to approach the individual in getting such help.
12. When counseling a problem employee, arrange that there are no interruptions.
13. When counseling, don't preach or lecture and try to avoid arguing with the person.

A discreetly conducted counseling session with a troubled employee can sometimes help relieve the tension and stress causing the undesirable behavior. An improperly conducted counseling session, on the other hand, can have many adverse results. Joseph Earl's supervisors did not counsel or try to understand him. He responded with memos calling them Judas, nuts, puppets, idiots, pathological liars, and people who should see a headshrinker.

EMOTIONALLY DISTURBED EMPLOYEES

In counseling problem employees, a supervisor must realize that the most seriously troubled workers are those who are emotionally disturbed. These employees may have exaggerated fears, they may not be able to face reality, they may sincerely feel that they have done nothing wrong, or they may really think that the supervisor is "out to get them." Some emotionally disturbed individuals tend to live in a world of imagination, especially when they have feelings of being threatened by something. The sensitive aspect of working with emotionally disturbed individuals is that they can go off in either of two directions. One direction can be adjustment to the real world, and the other is off the deep end. The irrational memos and letters that Joseph Earl wrote were a reflection of what can happen when a supervisor frustrates a person with serious emotional problems.

SUPERVISORS CANNOT IGNORE PROBLEM EMPLOYEES

The supervisor is usually not a professional psychiatrist, yet he or she may have to work with emotionally unstable individuals. Many companies do not have adequately trained specialists in the Personnel Department to help the supervisor with these individuals. Sometimes the only solution is to discipline or fire the individual. This type of action may bring the union to the defense of the employee with a resulting battle that is both costly and disruptive.

UNDERSTANDING AN EMOTIONALLY UNSTABLE PERSON

One of the best actions a supervisor can take with an emotionally unstable person is to try and understand the problem and to get other employees to do likewise. The worst thing a supervisor can do is to convey either by words or actions that the problem employee is "crazy" or a hopeless case. The supervisor should *show humanitarian concern and understanding* through the process of personal counseling previously discussed. If reasonable attempts to help the problem employee have failed, the supervisor should consult with the Personnel Department for assistance, including possible reassignment to a more suitable job.

AFFIRMATIVE ACTION

BEING SENSITIVE TO MINORITIES

A very sensitive area in the supervision of personnel is affirmative action. The Equal Employment Opportunity Commission (EEOC), established to enforce the equal employment opportunity laws, encourages all employers to engage in affirmative action programs. These programs are designed to help all minorities, which include blacks, Spanish-speaking Americans, Mexican Americans, American Indians, all women, disadvantaged young people, handicapped workers, and individuals over forty years of age. Supervisors must take care to treat all minority workers without discrimination. This involves being sensitive to the sometimes understandable impatience of minorities for improvement in their employment opportunities.

ACTIONS COUNT

More specifically, the supervisor must learn to listen to and understand the point of view of minority workers. Since they expect fairness and equality in the workplace, the supervisor must expect some questioning of management decisions by minority employees. Because of past inequalities, some minority individuals may be somewhat resentful and hostile. The primary way to minimize these sensitive situations is for the supervisor to show by *actions* that he or she is treating *all* individuals with the same degree of fairness.

THE CIVIL RIGHTS ACT OF 1964

The *Civil Rights Act of 1964* prohibits employers, unions, and employment agencies from discrimination in hiring, wages, terms of employment, working conditions, job assignments, promotions, training, and use of facilities. This basic equal employment opportunity law states that an employer cannot discriminate against a person because of race, color, religion, sex, or national origin. The basic civil rights law was amended by the *Equal Employment Opportunity Act of 1972* which set up an Equal Employment Opportunity Commission (EEOC) to enforce the provisions of the Civil Rights Act of 1964. This commission, and similar state enforcement agencies relating to state laws, facilitates the filing of discrimination complaints against employers.

THE EQUAL PAY ACT OF 1963

The *Equal Pay Act of 1963* amended the Fair Labor Standards Act of 1938 to require employers to pay the same wages to men and women for doing the same work. This law was revised in 1972 to cover professional and management occupations. The Wage and Hour Division of the U.S. Department of Labor enforces the provisions of the Equal Pay Act.

THE AGE DISCRIMINATION IN EMPLOYMENT ACT OF 1967

The *Age Discrimination in Employment Act of 1967* forbids discrimination against workers over forty years old. The law applies to hiring, firing, promoting, classifying, paying, assigning, or eligibility for union membership. The purpose of the law is to promote employment of older persons based on their ability rather than their age. The Act is an amendment of the Fair Labor Standards Act of 1938 and its enforcement is handled by the Wage and Hour Division of the U.S. Department of Labor.

THE EQUAL EMPLOYMENT OPPORTUNITY COMMISSION

The *Equal Employment Opportunity Commission* (EEOC) encourages business and other organizations to engage in affirmative action programs that achieve *results* in the recruitment and upgrading of minority employees in the workplace (Figure 8-2). An organization that handles any federal government contracts, *must* develop and implement an affirmative action program. Affirmative action programs must specifically define the positive actions that will be taken to ensure that there is no discriminatory treatment of workers. The emphasis in such programs is on *proof of results* in eliminating discrimination. Good intentions expressed in words are not enough. The purpose of affirmative action is to encourage *implementation* of equal opportunity.

THE SUPERVISOR'S ROLE IN AFFIRMATIVE ACTION

The actions of the first-level supervisor are an important element in the prevention of discrimination. First-level supervisors can easily negate the affirmative action policies of higher-level management. For example, a supervisor fires a black person for insubordination while a white person working on a key job, who is also guilty of insubordination, is only given a reprimand. Although the company has a policy that employees can be fired for insubordination, the rule must be applied equally to all persons. The consistency with which a first-level supervisor carries out company personnel policies is a key factor in avoiding charges of discrimination. Many discrimination complaints evolve more from the way the supervisor handles a particular situation than from the rea-

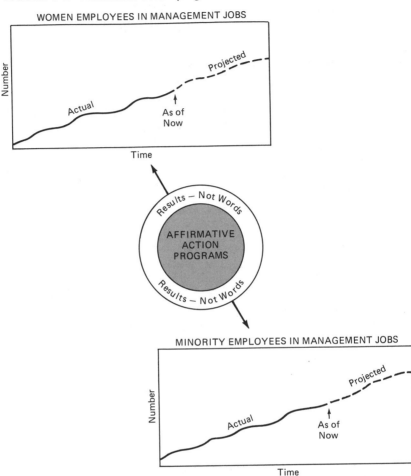

FIGURE 8-2 Affirmative action programs with results

son behind the action. When a company policy is violated and someone is treated differently, there is always the possibility that the person may find cause to file a complaint and charge that the differential was due to discrimination.

AFFIRMATIVE ACTION GUIDELINES

The following list includes important things for the supervisor to remember with reference to affirmative action.

1. The equal employment opportunity laws give rights to workers who suffer discriminatory treatment because of their race, color, sex, religion, age, or national origin.

2. The actions of the supervisor will speak louder than his or her words. The affirmative action program of the supervisor should show by actual statistics and facts what has been and is being done to eliminate discrimination.

3. Compliance with affirmative action programs involves

   - Using selection criteria for job applicants that are based on, and are consistent with, the *minimum* qualifications defined in the job description
   - Identifying all qualified minority applicants from employment files and/or from minority talent-bank files
   - Identifying the applications of all minority persons who apply for the job
   - Certifying as to the positive recruiting efforts made to attract minority candidates and their results
   - Scheduling all qualified minority candidates for interviews provided their applications were received before the closing date for accepting applications

4. Supervisors who violate equal opportunity laws get both the organization and themselves in serious trouble. The violation may cause the organization to pay attorney fees, court costs, and damages (including back pay) for the discriminatory act. These costs are in addition to the time spent in hearings and investigations in handling the situation.

Affirmative action is an established fact in business management today. It must be a part of every supervisor's plans.

SUPERVISING DISABLED EMPLOYEES

THE FEDERAL REHABILITATION ACT OF 1973

The *Federal Rehabilitation Act of 1973* extended the right to an equal chance to work or get ahead on the job to disabled persons. Government contractors and subcontractors must take affirmative action to employ and advance qualified disabled individuals at all levels in the organization.

The reluctance of some employers to hire disabled people is probably based on misconceptions about the dependability and productivity, and the accommodation of handicapped workers. E.I. du Pont de Nemours & Company conducted a study of 1,452 employees with disabilities, including orthopedic difficulties, blindness, visual impairment, heart disease, amputation, paralysis, epilepsy, heart impairment, and total deafness. Among these employees were 562 craftsmen; 334 professional, technical, and managerial employees; 233 machine operators; 224 clerical employees; 83 service workers; and 16 laborers. Here are some of the findings regarding handicapped employees that surfaced from the du Pont study:[1]

DISABLED PERSONS ARE USUALLY GOOD EMPLOYEES

   - *Analysis of safety records indicated that 96 percent rated average or better both on and off the job, with 51 percent rated above average in comparison with the total work force.*

- *Analysis of attendance records indicated that 79 percent had average or better-than-average attendance when compared with the total work force.*
- *Analysis of production records showed that supervisors rated 91 percent of their disabled workers average or better when compared with the general work force.*
- *Analysis of expenditures for special accommodations for handicapped individuals showed that few disabled workers required special work arrangements.*

Properly placed disabled workers tend to have greater job stability and less turnover than nondisabled workers.

Managers who have handicapped and nonhandicapped workers in their organizations state that they work together harmoniously. Handicapped people are like any other people—most are likable, friendly, pleasant, cooperative, and helpful—and, of course, some are not.

Don't Discriminate Between Handicapped and Nonhandicapped Employees

Supervisors with handicapped workers should treat them in the same way that they treat other workers. It is, of course, extremely important that the handicapped worker be placed on a job that the individual is best equipped to handle. Once a handicapped employee is properly placed on the right job and adequately trained to perform the job, there should be no discrimination between handicapped and nonhandicapped workers. Whether handicapped or not, some workers will be productive, and some will not. Supervisory decisions regarding recognition for the productive workers and disciplinary action for nonproductive workers should be the same for all workers.

MANAGING CONFLICT

Some Conflict Is Inevitable

Conflict is inevitable in every organization. People have different sets of values, diverse attitudes, opposing ideas, and divergent interpretations of the same communications. Regardless of their cause and who is involved, a supervisor must be capable of taking timely action to resolve conflicts when they occur. Conflicts that are ignored or pushed aside tend to grow and become very destructive to personnel relations. A supervisor must be able to detect conflict situations as they develop and work on a satisfactory solution.

Methods of Handling Conflict

Mary Parker Follett was a truly creative political and management philosopher with keen insight into human nature. She devoted a lifetime to searching

FIGURE 8-3 Resolving conflict

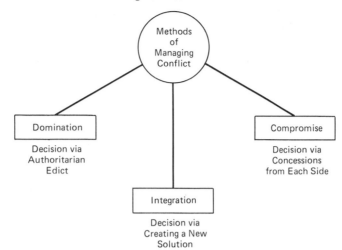

for the true principles of organization which would ensure a stable foundation for the steady and orderly progress of human well-being. Her papers and lectures were not theoretical but practical. This practical management is reflected in her approach to dealing with conflict in the workplace.[2] She outlined three methods as shown in Figure 8-3. They are

1. Domination
2. Compromise
3. Integration

Domination by the supervisor may be the easiest method of resolving conflict at the moment it occurs, but it is not usually successful in the long run. Compromise is probably the most common method used to resolve conflict. Here the supervisor gets concessions from each side, and each party gives up something in order to have peace. Compromise is one of the basic tactics employed by unions when they ask for more and settle for less. The integration method of resolving conflict involves finding a solution in which neither side has to sacrifice anything. Integration resolves conflict through the process of creating something new. Compromise, on the other hand, continues to deal with something that already exists. As a general rule, if the supervisor uses the compromise method, the conflict will probably come up again in some other form.

A CASE EXAMPLE OF RESOLVING CONFLICT

The Comptroller of ECOM, a large government installation, once experienced an abnormal number of employee complaints coming from one particular department. In a follow-up visit to this department on a hot, humid July afternoon, he ran into a figurative "hornet's nest." There were eight window air conditioners, each with four speeds and four directional outlets, and all eight were turned off. The Comptroller asked Bill, the supervisor, why none of the air conditioners were turned on. Bill stated that there was a conflict between Mary, who was too cold, and Jane, who was too hot. In order to settle the argument, Bill said, he shut off all the air conditioners. This decision was typical of Bill's short-tempered authoritarian actions which frequently caused employee complaints to come from his department. In this particular situation, Bill could have used the integration method of resolving the conflict. With the flexibility contained in the four-speed, four-directional-outlet type of air conditioners, it was possible to give warmer air to Mary and others who did not like frigid temperatures, while at the same time directing colder air to Jane and others who liked it cold in the office.

GUIDELINES FOR RESOLVING CONFLICT

There are specific guidelines for a supervisor to follow when using the integration method of resolving conflict:

1. Get the facts of the conflict's dimensions and intensity. Who is involved? What is the conflict about? Remember that rampant emotions can confuse the issues.
2. Bring the differences into the open by giving the participants in the conflict the opportunity to state their views, justify their attitudes, and explain their feelings. This should be done in private interviews with each party involved. Ask such questions as: How do you feel about this situation? How do you think the other persons feels? Why do you feel as you do? Why do you think the other individual feels the way he or she does?
3. Try to de-emotionalize both parties while you evaluate both sides of the issue. The attempt to cool things down should be done by talking to each party separately. Tell each party that you expect them to work together while you are looking into the matter.
4. In analyzing the problem
    *   Find the significant rather than the dramatic features of the controversy.
    *   Break the problem into its various parts and examine each part.
    *   Identify the conflicting issues involved and try to realign them on both sides of the controversy.
5. Identify the options, anticipate the responses from both parties, and prepare your own responses.
6. Select the best option and implement it. In arriving at the decision, don't theorize but take actions that are realistic.

The ability of a supervisor to minimize or resolve the consequences of conflict is a highly valued management skill. The supervisor who can defuse an explosive confrontation not only restores harmony in the work environment but gains a reputation for being a "real" leader.

OCCUPATIONAL SAFETY AND HEALTH

THE PROBLEM OF ON-THE-JOB HAZARDS

Each year, according to the Bureau of Labor Statistics, there are approximately 5,000 work-related deaths in workplaces with 11 or more employees, and about 6 million work-related injuries. The Bureau's data show that roughly 43 million workers lose workdays as the result of work-related injuries. This represents a loss equivalent of a full year's work for about 171,000 employees. In addition, workers in the private sector experience about 148,000 new cases of occupational illness. These figures translate into approximately 1 job-related injury or illness for every 11 workers in the private sector of the economy during every year.[3]

These statistics, while providing an overall picture of the problem of occupational injuries, illnesses, and deaths, tend to cloud the human dimension of the situation. Each of the above numbers represents human suffering affecting not only the victims but their families and friends. The enormous extent of human suffering and grief in these cases is immeasurable.

OCCUPATIONAL SAFETY AND HEALTH ACT OF 1970

The Occupational Safety and Health Act of 1970 was designed to increase employers' consciousness of the need for safety and health in the workplace. This legislative act established an Occupational Safety and Health Administration (OSHA) to assist employers in providing a safe and healthy workplace. In 1980, ten years after the establishment of OSHA, there were considerable charges and countercharges about who was responsible for situations when statistics showed lack of significant improvement in bad conditions. OSHA officials blame industry because the basic strategy of many employers is to oppose rather than comply with regulations to help them improve safety and health conditions.[4] Labor unions vigorously defend OSHA while business establishments attack OSHA as unnecessarily antagonistic and their regulations as time consuming.[5]

Many management officials claim that concentration on compliance with specific OSHA rules inhibits their efforts to improve safety conditions. They point out the fact that OSHA standards fill 1,500 pages of fine print in the Code of Federal Regulations[6] and that many of these standards are ridiculous.[7] Criticism of OSHA could start with the agency's verbose definition of the term *exit*. The agency defines *exit* as "that portion of a means of egress which is separated from all other spaces of the building or structure by construction or equipment as required in the subpart to provide a protected way of travel to the exit discharge." OSHA was also criticized when they ordered the owner of a small business in Indiana to place exit signs over the 12-foot doors at the front and back of his seven-person shop "so in case of a fire a newly hired employee could tell where the door was." Another small business was ordered to have signs printed in both Spanish and English because one of the employees was of Spanish descent. This employee, however, spoke only English.

WORKERS' COMPENSATION CLAIMS

Growing recognition of possible health hazards in the job environment is leading to an increase in workers' compensation claims and to higher operating costs. Changes are also taking place in the legal definition of occupational disease. This term has traditionally excluded all ordinary diseases to which the general public is exposed. In recent years, however, a number of states have amended their workers' compensation codes to include "cumulative injury" as part of occupational disease. This tends to make an employer liable should any continuing circumstances of employment play a part in an illness of any kind. For example, all costs of a cumulative injury claim for a job-related case of emphysema may be charged to the employer even though a two-packs-a-day smoking habit may have been a major contributing cause of the disability. Employers can, therefore, bear a large burden for occupational disabilities which are caused at least in part by factors not related to the job.

PROBLEMS IN OCCUPATIONAL SAFETY AND HEALTH

While the fight over the future of OSHA continues, the supervisor must face the fact that one of management's major responsibilities is protecting the health and safety of the workers. This is a very sensitive and difficult area of management responsibility. It is sensitive in that the lives and economic welfare of people are involved. It is difficult because there are so many factors contributing to the problem. These factors include (1) management and employee ignorance of conditions contributing to safety and health hazards, (2) management's reluctance to spend money, (3) employees' fear of losing jobs, (4) lack of adherence to safety standards, and (5) a government with mixed priorities. Also contributing to the problem is the fact that employees are often willing to risk possible future injury or illness in order not to jeopardize their jobs. Older workers in particular are not eager to make a fuss about safety and health situations when they are forty or fifty years old and have a lot of bills to pay.

SUPERVISOR RESPONSIVENESS

What can a supervisor do to overcome some of the sensitive factors contributing to occupational safety and health problems? For one thing, the supervisor

FIGURE 8-4 A supervisor should be responsive to potential health hazards

can be responsive to worker complaints since reported instances of coughing, nausea, or other physical discomfort may be warning signs of occupational health hazards (Figure 8-4). Second, the supervisor should inform workers of potential hazards and insist on compliance with safety and health standards. Third, subordinates should be encouraged to voice complaints to the supervisor about safety and health hazards. And last, the supervisor should discuss with his or her superiors the need to spend money, where necessary, to correct safety and health hazards in the workplace.

POLICE THE WORKPLACE

The supervisor must give major attention to employee safety and health for two reasons. The first and most important reason is humanitarian—the improvement of the welfare of the workers. The second reason is that employees individually or through their union can make complaints to OSHA. The Occupational Safety and Health Act of 1960 guarantees that any worker, whether a union member or not, has the right to file a complaint without suffering from employer discrimination. OSHA can come in and conduct an inspection which may result in the issuance of citations and fines for alleged violations of occupational health and safety standards. The best action is for the supervisor to police the workplace and provide the stimulus to both workers and higher-level managers to effectively enforce safety and health standards and correct those working conditions considered dangerous to the safety and health of employees.

LABOR-MANAGEMENT COOPERATION

SUPERVISORS OCCUPY VERY SENSITIVE POSITIONS

The first-level supervisor is in a very sensitive position with reference to labor-management relationships. First, there is the matter of being responsive to the policies and practices that higher-level management expects the supervisor to implement. Then there is the fact that the first-level supervisor, as the manager with the most day-to-day contact with workers, must handle many situations that result in either labor-management cooperation or conflict. The first-level supervisor can be a preventer and resolver of conflict or a cause of it.

EMPLOYEE RELATIONS

As reflected in Figure 8-5, the superstructure of labor-management cooperation is dependent on several sensitive relationships that can be easily disrupted. The best way to develop labor-management cooperation is to prevent discord from occurring. If a supervisor establishes and maintains good employee relations there is usually a minimum amount of labor-management conflict. Good employee relations can come about through good leadership and effective supervisory practices.

UNION RELATIONS

Supervisors should establish and maintain effective working relationships with the union. There is nothing to be gained and much to be lost when a supervisor considers the union as an invading enemy. There are situations where union representatives tend to infringe upon management's authority. They may result from the fact that the union representative may not have sufficient information regarding the situation. When someone does not have enough

FIGURE 8-5 The superstructure of labor-management relations

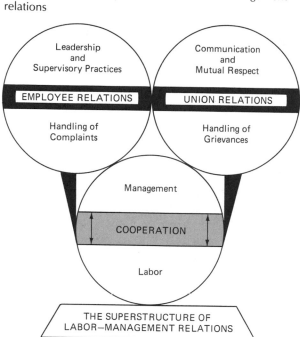

facts about a problem situation, this can result in an arrogant and uncompromising attitude. In the Joseph Earl case discussed earlier, the union representative had not taken the time to obtain all the pertinent facts in the misconduct situation. Without facts to support his case, he was arrogant to the point that a libelous action was threatened by a higher-level manager in Joseph Earl's organization. If the union representative had obtained more facts instead of retorting with libelous statements, he probably could have won the grievance on the grounds of harassment.

HONESTY, FAIRNESS, AND CONSIDERATION

Most union representatives know the facts of the situation and are interested in fairness and honesty. As a general rule, the supervisor who is honest, fair, and considerate toward subordinates will usually obtain cooperation and support from the union. When both management and the union show by their actions that they are honest and are interested in fairness, labor-management cooperation usually results.

There is much more to labor-management relations than just sitting down once every year or two to negotiate the job-related issues and terms of the labor-management contract. There cannot possibly be good labor-management cooperation unless there is continuous communication between the two sides. Management and labor unions have different roles to play in the work environment. Each group, therefore, should strive to see and understand each other's side, and to work together to establish a concept of cooperation that extends beyond collective bargaining on job-related issues.

JOINT COMMITTEES

One way to achieve labor-management cooperation is through joint labor-management committees, plant or office production committees, quality-of-work committees, and other consultative bodies at the plant or office level. These consultative groups can deal with issues and problems of mutual interest without hurting the bargaining rights of either party. Various management and labor groups have successfully formed joint committees to find ways to increase efficiency, reduce waste, improve working conditions, and expand business. Both management and the union can profit from such joint efforts. Labor-management cooperation at the plant or office level is much more intelligent than labor-management conflict that hurts both parties.

Labor-management cooperation can only exist when both parties develop respect for each other. Such cooperation is easier to achieve when management, particularly at the first level of supervision, starts the action by showing consideration for employees. From this starting point, there are many things that a supervisor can do to further develop good working relations with the union:

GUIDELINES FOR LABOR-MANAGEMENT COOPERATION

1. Be familiar with pertinent labor relations laws such as:
   - The *National Labor Relations Act of 1935* which describes the rights and conditions under which workers can bargain collectively through their authorized representatives
   - The *Fair Labor Standards Act of 1938* which regulates wage payments and hours of work
   - The *Taft-Hartley Act of 1947* which imposed certain controls over unions and their collective bargaining methods
2. Be familiar with pertinent equal opportunity laws such as
   - The *Equal Pay Act of 1963* which requires payment of the same wages for all people who do the same job
   - The *Civil Rights Act of 1964* which prohibits discrimination against blacks, women, or people of various religious beliefs or nationality
   - The *Age in Discrimination Act of 1967* which prohibits discrimination against workers over forty years of age
   - The *Federal Rehabilitation Act of 1973* which prohibits discrimination against disabled persons

3. Be familiar with the labor-management contract and with other pertinent personnel policies and procedures of the company.

4. Show an understanding and respect for the role of the union in the company's operations.

5. Be approachable and encourage union representatives to see you whenever they are concerned about labor-management situations.

6. Discuss, within the limits of your authority, upcoming situations that may have an effect on workers or the union.

7. When labor-management problems arise, give immediate attention to trying to resolve them and invite union representatives to participate.

8. Take all possible corrective action within the limitations of your delegated authority and the contractual provisions of the labor-management agreement. Don't take actions that could cause the company to be charged by the union with breaking either the law or the labor-management contract.

9. Immediately refer matters that are not within your delegated authority to higher-level managers.

10. Be firm, consistent, honest, and fair in your relationships with subordinates.

11. Be firm, but calm, if union representatives make unreasonable demands, act indiscreetly or arrogantly, or conduct themselves in a manner that shows lack of respect for your responsibility as a supervisor.

12. Let there be no doubt with anyone that you have a primary responsibility to protect the interests and the rights of the management of your company.

13. Make certain that you have separated a worker's attitude, ability, and performance from the individual's position regarding unionism when you make job assignments, performance appraisals, promotions, or take disciplinary actions. Keep your opinions regarding the union completely to yourself—both on the job and off the job.

14. Don't throw your management position around indiscriminately or take advantage of little loopholes in the labor-management contract. Remember that a general type of contract is usually easier for everyone to administer, if both parties make decisions that are reasonable and equitable.

THE SHOP STEWARD

• *FIRST-LEVEL MANAGEMENT AND THE UNION*—The union shop steward is usually the first-level of representation in a union. It is the shop steward's assigned job to protect the rights of union members just as it is the supervisor's job to protect the rights of management. The shop steward has a right to inform and advise a supervisor that certain management actions against an employee are contrary to the labor-management contract. However, the shop steward has no authority to tell a supervisor how to run the department or to tell any employee what to do on the job. If a shop steward exceeds his or her authority, the supervisor should continue to maintain a constructive approach to resolving the problem while tactfully but firmly informing the shop steward that union authority is being overextended. In taking this positive action with the shop steward, the supervisor must be careful to avoid loss of temper or composure.

COMMUNICATION

The best action a supervisor can take to establish and maintain good relations with the shop steward is to keep the latter informed of what is going on. If the supervisor ignores the shop steward there will be animosity and hostility between them. This will adversely affect all parties concerned—the supervisor, the employees, and the union.

COOPERATION

A supervisor does not give up any rights or authority in being cordial and cooperative with the union. The supervisor who gets to know the shop steward usually finds that they have some mutual problems. Furthermore, the union can often help in solving some of these problems, particularly those involving seniority versus qualification for a job assignment (Figure 8-6).

FIGURE 8-6   Management-union cooperation

HANDLING GRIEVANCES AND COMPLAINTS

WHETHER REAL OR IMAGINARY, GRIEVANCES CANNOT BE IGNORED

A grievance can result from anything about an individual's job that is thought to be irritating or tends to cause an individual to feel that something is unjust. It may exist even though no verbal or written complaint is ever presented. A grievance may be imaginary or based on a lack of knowledge and facts, but it is still a grievance until it is properly cleared up. If a worker only imagines he or she has a grievance, the individual may be just as discontented as if it were a real grievance, and the same careful handling is necessary. This is where the

FIGURE 8-7   Causes of grievances

① SUPERVISORY LEADERSHIP
- Discrimination (Violation of Equal Rights)
- Favoritism (Cliques)
- Failure to Inform (Communication Gaps)
- Handling of Disciplinary Problems
- False Promises (Honesty)
- Lack of Fairness and Consideration
- Failure to Give Credit When Due
- Ignoring Complaints

② PERSONNEL POLICIES AND PRACTICES
- Selection and Promotion of Employees
- Transfers of Employees to Other Jobs
- Layoff of Personnel
- Use of Temporary Employees

③ WORKING CONDITIONS
- Safety and Health Hazards
- Sanitation
- Eating Facilities
- Work Rules

④ PAY
- Shortages
- Inequities
- Fringe Benefits

⑤ PLANNING AND ORGANIZING
- Work Assignments
- Production Standards
- Technological Changes
- Organizational Changes

⑥ VIOLATION OF SENIORITY RULES

supervisor's "open-door policy" can pay off. It affords workers the opportunity to see the boss and express their complaints. It is an effective way to clear up the imaginary grievances and to prevent minor complaints from becoming major grievances.

There is dynamite in neglected or indifferently handled grievances. Poor handling of grievances is doubly dangerous because an accumulation of little irritations and aggravations, which nobody pays much attention to, can finally swell up and burst like an atomic explosion. Whether the cause of a grievance is real or imaginary, if it disrupts the mental attitude of the worker, it is very apt to also disrupt productivity. Not only is the rate of output of the aggrieved worker likely to fall, but through "rabble rousing" or other tactics, the distrubed worker can adversely influence the productivity of other employees.

CAUSES OF GRIEVANCES

● *PREVENTING GRIEVANCES*—The best method of handling grievances is to eliminate the causes. This is easier said than done because of the almost limitless number of factors that cause workers to be upset. A major consideration in avoiding grievances is to be knowledgeable of their causes. Figure 8-7 lists the most frequent causes of grievances from the employee point of view. Once a supervisor knows of the situations that cause grievances, it is easier to take corrective action to prevent them from occurring.

BEHAVIORAL ATTITUDE

The behavioral attitude of the supervisor is a significant factor in preventing grievances. For example, the manner in which a supervisor gives orders to others can be either a contributing action or a preventer of grievances (Figure 8-8). Thinking before you talk or act, being objective, listening to the worker's point of view, and making decisions that are fair and reasonable are all actions that keep grievances from happening.

ORGANIZATIONAL CLIMATE

Third on the list of ways to minimize grievances is to develop a positive and constructive organizational state of mind, as seen by the people in the unit. If workers know, for example, that they can speak their opinions without fear of reprisal, it tends to create a good climate in which to work. Also, if workers know that management is honest and fair, they usually develop a positive state of mind. As another example, if the supervisor encourages participative management with workers and actually uses their good ideas and suggestions, the result is an organizational climate with people probably saying: "This is a good place to work" (Figure 8-9). On the other hand, if the organizational climate is

FIGURE 8-8 Most grievances can be prevented

bad, you will probably find low morale, frequent grievances, and problems with the union.

GOOD LEADERSHIP

A fourth factor in preventing grievances is the type of leadership the supervisor uses to get workers to do what he or she wants them to do. Successful leadership lies primarily in the development of the mental attitude of other people. Workers tend to reflect the attitude of their boss. They will generally do more work and complain less for a leader whom they respect and in whom they have confidence. Good leadership keeps many employee complaints from becoming formal grievances. A supervisor can act as a "safety valve" in keeping complaints from being magnified out of proportion to their seriousness. Some of the things that a supervisor can do to keep grievances from happening are

1. Let workers know that the supervisor wants their honest and frank complaints.
2. Encourage workers to make complaints to the supervisor first, rather than to fellow workers who usually cannot do anything to correct the trouble.

FIGURE 8-9 Creating a healthy state of mind in the workplace

3. Maintain an open-door policy that makes it easy for a worker to make complaints directly to the supervisor.
4. Prove by actions that the supervisor was sincere in wanting workers to make complaints.

Although it is difficult to eliminate all causes of employee grievances, a supervisor can reduce their occurrence by analyzing situations from the viewpoint of the subordinate. Such analysis of irritative situations can often lead to their correction even before workers complain. If a situation is corrected after a grievance has been made, the worker may still hold it against the supervisor for not taking action until the worker pushed the matter.

• *RESOLVING GRIEVANCES*—Second in importance to eliminating causes of grievances are (1) keeping the door open to receive grievances and complaints, and (2) establishing a good procedure for handling employee irritations that have been formally presented to the supervisor for resolution.

When an employee voices a complaint, the individual usually wants several things to happen. Most subordinates like a supervisor who will

- *Listen and try to understand the employee's feelings*
- *Objectively analyze the facts of the employee's complaint*
- *Take corrective action based on the supportive facts of the situation, provided such action is within the delegated authority of the supervisor*
- *Refer a supportable complaint to higher-level management when the corrective action is beyond the delegated authority of the supervisor*
- *Honestly state why no corrective action can be taken if the facts dictate such a response*

THE GRIEVANCE PROCEDURE

Most organizations have established formal grievance procedures. In unionized organizations this procedure is usually written into the labor-management contract. A typical grievance procedure has from three to five steps. Figure 8-10 is an example of a five-step grievance procedure.

FIGURE 8-10 A five-step grievance procedure

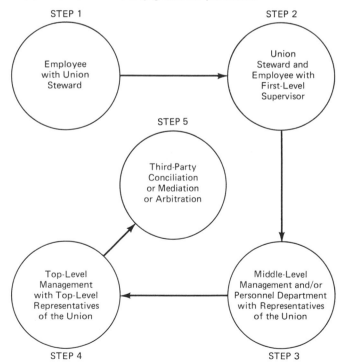

The initial action in settling any grievance should always be between the aggrieved worker and the supervisor. In the majority of cases the complaint can be settled at this level. If the supervisor can take care of the worker's complaint and thereby make it unnecessary for the worker to seek union support, a better relationship will be established between the two parties. A procedure, however, should be established whereby a worker may appeal a grievance to higher authority. This provides the worker with a recourse in the event the individual's grievance is neglected, unfairly handled, or denied by the first-level supervisor.

A high rate of worker productivity can never be obtained if workers have pent up irritations which they are unable to express or which have been improperly handled. Not only will the productivity of the aggrieved worker probably fall, but the individual's unhappy attitude might easily have an adverse influence on the productivity of other workers.

Establishing a formal procedure for handling grievances and explaining all its steps to the workers can relieve some of an individual's frustration when there is an irritation that has not been satisfactorily settled. A formal grievance procedure provides a channel of communication through which a complaint may be aired and an amicable solution obtained. Even though some employees may never use the procedure, the fact that they know it is available to them can be an important factor to good morale.

In any formal grievance procedure, the supervisor should be the person in the key position. To the average worker, the supervisor is not only the "boss," he or she is the organization. The reason for this attitude on the part of the worker is that the supervisor is the management official with whom the employee comes in contact every day.

HOW TO HANDLE GRIEVANCES

When a supervisor is presented with an employee complaint, there are several actions that should be taken. First, and probably most important, is to put the employee at ease, and then listen and show the individual that the supervisor is concerned about the complaint. During this discussion, the supervisor should get the pertinent facts so he or she has a full understanding of the situation. The employee should be asked to recommend a solution. The more the employee talks about the situation, the greater the likelihood that the individual may talk the complaint away. At the conclusion of the meeting the supervisor should summarize the situation and give a direct answer as to what will be done and when. If promised action on the complaint is not forthcoming within a reasonable period of time, the supervisor should keep the employee posted on any progress and, if possible, reasons for any delays. If the facts of the situation do not support the complaint, the supervisor should explain this to the employee. A supervisor should not cause a complaint to dangle when no action is going to be taken. Neither should a supervisor promise something that cannot be fulfilled. When a "no" answer is given to an employee's complaint, the supervisor should explain any appeal procedures the employee can take.

LISTENING AND ACTING

The Joseph Earl case mentioned at the beginning of the chapter is a good example of what can happen when a supervisor does not listen to or act on an employee's complaint. There was no question about the fact that Joseph Earl was an emotionally disturbed employee. He did some irrational things that irritated other employees. However, when he complained in a sworn statement of harassment, his supervisors did nothing about it. They had him removed from his job on the grounds of disgraceful conduct and creating a disturbance. The U.S. Civil Service Commission, in considering the appeal by Joseph Earl of the adverse action taken against him, directed that the removal action be re-voked and that Joseph Earl be returned to his job with pay from the date of his removal. One of the statements made by the appeals officer was that there was no evidence in the record that the supervisor gave any consideration to Joseph Earl's contention that he was harassed by another employee.

DON'T IGNORE COMPLAINTS

A supervisor cannot ignore employee complaints, even those from a "trouble-maker." In Joseph Earl's case, one of the reasons he was reinstated to his job with back pay was that the supervisor took no notice of the individual's sworn complaint to a police officer that he had been called a "jerk" by a young supervisor who threatened to "beat him into the ground."

SUMMARY

A typical work force will include problem employees who flagrantly violate rules of conduct as well as persons who are alcoholics, drug addicts, and emotionally disturbed individuals. The supervisor cannot ignore problem employees because they can disrupt the entire work environment. Through proper counseling of problem employees, the supervisor can usually improve the situation. To properly counsel a problem employee, the supervisor should

- *Know the problem indicators*
- *Know how to effectively counsel problem employees*
- *Know the limitations in handling problem employees*
- *Know when and how to get professional help*

Conflict is inevitable in every organization and for many unavoidable reasons. Three methods of dealing with conflict are domination, compromise, and integration. Compromising, by having each side give up something, does not usually solve the long-term problem. Integration involves finding new solutions where neither side has to give up anything. If a supervisor is willing to work at it, he or she will often find that the integration method of resolving conflict can bring about viable solutions to organizational conflict.

There are many federal laws to protect workers against discrimination because of their race, color, religion, sex, age, national origin, or disability. To help assure compliance with these laws, managers at all levels are expected to develop and implement affirmative action programs. These programs are intended to achieve *results* in the avoidance of discrimination in the workplace. The emphasis is on proof of results and not words. Supervisors who violate equal opportunity laws can get themselves and their company in very serious trouble. A supervisor must also give major attention to employee safety and health—first for humanitarian reasons and second to avoid violation of the Occupational Safety and Health Act of 1970.

The supervisor who is a good leader and treats subordinates as human beings usually has very few labor-management problems. When both management and the union show by their actions that they are honest and are interested in fairness and justice, the groundwork is laid for good labor-management relations. Cooperation between management and the union should be a continuous communication process with mutual respect for each other. The supervisor holds a key position in fostering this cooperative attitude. The supervisor should maintain an open-door policy in regard to hearing grievances and complaints. This policy will help resolve problems before they get out of hand. There should also be a grievance procedure for handling those matters that cannot be resolved by the first-level supervisor. Under no circumstances should a grievance be ignored or allowed to dangle with no action taken. This causes resentment and irritation that are totally out of proportion to the facts of the situation.

REVIEW QUESTIONS

1. In what way is a supervisor in a very sensitive position with reference to labor-management relationships?

2. Describe how labor-management cooperation can be achieved through joint committees.

3. What are the equal opportunity laws, and why are they important in supervisory management?

4. What is meant by the expression that a supervisor acts as a safety valve in employee relations?

5. Why is the open-door policy important in supervisory management?
6. Does a company with a minimum number of grievances need a grievance procedure? Support your answer.
7. What is the purpose of an affirmative action program?
8. Give two reasons why a supervisor should devote major attention to employee safety and health.
9. Since very few supervisors are trained psychiatrists, how can they counsel an emotionally disturbed employee?
10. What justification is there for saying that a supervisor should treat handicapped workers like any other workers?

CASE STUDIES IN HANDLING SENSITIVE PERSONNEL SITUATIONS

A. THE CASE OF ELSIE GOLDSTEIN

Elsie Goldstein is Jewish and an ardent advocate of women's liberation. She has a college degree and is a very capable worker. Elsie has been employed by the Bennett's Company for fifteen years. During this time she has worked in eight different offices. Two of these transfers were to obtain a promotion. Goldstein feels that most of the supervisors under whom she has worked had a prejudice against women. One of Goldstein's promotions came as the result of a grievance in which she claimed discrimination for not having been initially selected for the job.

Because of Goldstein's strong feelings regarding women's rights, the Personnel Office arranged to transfer her to Bill Smith's department where over 40 percent of the employees are females. Since her assignment to Smith's department, Goldstein's work performance has been very good. She has, however, spent a large amount of time talking about women's liberation with other employees. Because of her good work Smith never mentioned that he felt she spent too much time away from her job.

Smith recently promoted one of the women in his department to the position of branch chief. Goldstein was one of the candidates for the position. Prior to announcing his decision, Smith talked to each of the unsuccessful candidates as to why the individual was not selected. A week later, Goldstein and her union representative presented a grievance claiming that Smith discriminated against her because she is Jewish. How can Smith defend himself?

B. THE CASE OF EDWARD MILLER

Edward Miller is a very knowledgeable and highly productive subordinate who works for Robert Laury. He is normally a very dependable worker. However, several times recently Laury noticed the smell of alcohol on Edward's breath and talked to him about it. Edward has also been off sick more in the past six weeks than he had been in the last seven or eight years. His absences have been of short duration and almost never extended beyond one day at a time. This morning when Laury came to work, Edward was again absent. About ten o'clock Laury received a call from Edward, who stated he had a problem and asked Laury to meet him in Room 206 of a local motel. Laury drove to the motel and found Edward getting over a drunken hangover. Edward said that he was at the motel because his wife locked him out when he came home smelling of alcohol. In Laury's discussion with Edward it became apparent that he needed help. Laury mentioned about Edward going to Alcoholics Anonymous for help. Edward said that his wife wanted no part of Alcoholics Anonymous because to get help from them you had to admit that you are an alcoholic. Such an admission was socially unacceptable to Edward's wife.

QUESTIONS

1. What guidelines should Laury follow in counseling Edward?
2. If you were Laury do you feel that this is a situation where you need professional help? Explain your answer.
3. How would you handle the Alcoholics Anonymous situation involving Edward and his wife?
4. If you were Laury and received Edward's request to meet him at a local motel, would you have really gone there? Explain your answer. What would you have done if you were a male supervisor and the employee was a female?

NOTES

1. Robert B. Nathanson, "The Disabled Employee: Separating Myth from Fact," *Harvard Business Review*, May–June 1977, pp. 6–8.

2. Henry C. Metcalf and L. Urwick, *Dynamic Administration—The Collected Papers of Mary Parker Follett* (New York: Harper & Row, Pub., 1940), pp. 7–9.

3. Hon. Joseph M. Gaydos, "In 1979, 4,950 Workers Die on the Job," *Congressional Record*—Extensions of Remarks, December 5, 1980, p. E5323.

4.   Kenneth N. Gilpin, "Little Progress in Job Safety" (The *New York Times*, December 14, 1980), Section 3, p. 3.

5.   Philip Shabecoff, "Labor Worries Over Decline in Its Influence," (*New York Times*, January 4, 1981), Section 4, p. E3.

6.   Edwin McDowell, "OSHA, E.P.A.: The Heyday Is Over," *New York Times*, January 4, 1981, sec. 3, p. F1.

7.   Several highly critical studies of OSHA have been conducted. Among the most critical is a study of OSHA in 1977 written by Professor Richard J. Zechhauser, professor of political economy, and Albert Nichols, both of Harvard University.

9

Supervisory Leadership

DEVELOPING SUPERVISORS
TO MEET THE CHALLENGES OF MANAGEMENT

The first-line supervisor should be the backbone and strength of management by communicating company philosophies and being consistent in executing policies and procedures. Supervisors should be able to accept these responsibilities.

Successful organizations believe in teamwork. One way to achieve teamwork is to establish a flow of communications on a consistent basis from the executive suite to all other levels.

A good supervisor should try to see an answer for every problem. His or her attitude should be that even though it may be difficult, it's possible—not that it may be possible, but it's too difficult. Supervisory leadership involves moral responsibility for motivating others to achieve the human desire to perform well.

ACHIEVED RESULTS ARE LEADERSHIP'S MOMENT OF TRUTH.

Abbie A. Robinson, President
AAR & Associates
Consultants to Management

LEARNING OBJECTIVES

The objectives of this chapter on supervisory leadership are to enable the reader to

1. Delineate practical supervisory guidelines for performing the following tasks:
    a. Developing harmonious and supportive relationships between different manager levels
    b. Problem solving and decision making
    c. Building confidence and cooperation of subordinates in the achievement of organizational objectives
2. Describe two aspects of role perception and how they can jeopardize the accomplishment of work objectives
3. Identify five danger signs of tension and stress and how to cope with them
4. Establish three actions that a supervisor can take to achieve self-development
5. Apply supervisory management guidelines to the analysis and resolution of leadership case studies

KEY WORDS

Biofeedback An electronically recorded technique of obtaining information about vital body functions (blood pressure, heart rhythm, muscle tension, and skin temperature) to determine an individual's stress level (the point at which stress is triggered). Once the stress level is established, avoidance skills are put into practice to help the individual achieve stress reduction when faced with stressful situations.

Encounter Group An informal group of people, usually with similar backgrounds and problems, who engage in rough-and-tumble confrontation where each member airs his or her emotions without holding back, thereby eliminating stressful situations.

Hypothesis An unproved theory presented as a possible explanation for the occurrence of something or as a potential solution to some problem.

Stress Anything that arouses or provokes a person to the point where it disturbs or interferes with the normal functioning of the human body. A stressful situation, such as a frustrating job, can increase blood pressure, pulse rate, and/or muscle tension to the point where it can damage both physical and mental health.

Tension   The reflection of mental or emotional anxiety caused by situations involving suspense, excitement, or a strained relationship between individuals.

Transcendental Meditation   A technique for reducing tension and stress through the act of concentration without interruption for an extended period of time (twenty minutes). The meditation is executed by thinking of some meaningful and pleasant word.

THE CASE OF THE "PIN HEAD" SUPERVISOR

A manufacturing plant in New Jersey wanted to upgrade the managerial abilities of its first-level supervisors, so it brought in a consultant to conduct a training course in supervisory management. At the start of one of the training sessions, the instructor drew the following picture on the blackboard:

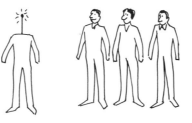

Several of the supervisors asked the instructor why he drew the picture showing them as a "pin head?" "Because that is what you are," responded the instructor. The instructor then called their attention to how they had answered an earlier question on what they considered to be their biggest supervisory problems. "Remember," said the instructor, "many of you gave lack of respect from your subordinates and the union as being one of your biggest problems. The lack of respect from your subordinates may be due to the fact that they see you figuratively as a 'pin head'—a person with a very narrow and limited perspective. For example," explained the instructor, "when we discussed higher-level management strategic planning, you showed no interest in the subject because you felt that it did not involve your department. You again changed communication channels when we tried to discuss staff functions. As a matter of fact, every time we talked about a function that was not part of your job, you indicated your disinterest in the subject. The bottom line is that your subordinates are seeing you for what you are—a 'pin head' who is not informed and cares less about what happens in other plant operational areas. You can't run this plant when you only see your own little functional area and nothing else."

The instructor then discussed the importance of being a leader who sees the "big picture" and has a positive attitude reflecting drive, courage, and persistence in improving the "status quo" (Figure 9-1). When the discussion was concluded, the picture on the blackboard looked like the following:

FIGURE 9-1 Successful leadership

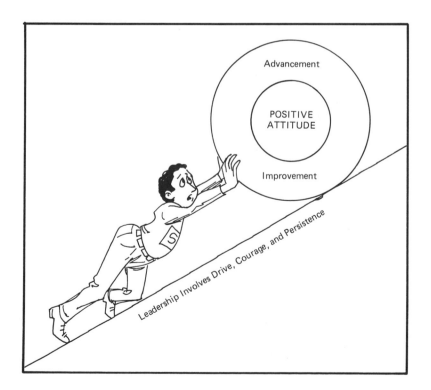

PERSONAL PRACTICES OF GOOD SUPERVISION

Up to this point, we have discussed the responsibilities of a supervisor (Chapter 4) and his or her involvement in understanding human behavior and being able to motivate the workers (Chapters 3, 5, 6, 7, and 8). To be respected and considered as a real leader, it is also very important to be able to handle the following potential problem areas of supervisory management:

1. Getting along with the boss
2. Understanding role perception
3. Dealing with tension and stress

GETTING ALONG WITH THE BOSS

HARMONIOUS AND SUPPORTIVE RELATIONSHIPS HELP EVERYONE

A first-level supervisor cannot have control of a work situation unless there is unity and cooperation with his or her boss. The influence and power that a supervisor has with subordinates is affected by the relationship that exists with higher-level management. If there is a bad relationship it tends to erode the authority of the lower-level supervisor. The power base of a supervisor is greatly enhanced when there is a harmonious and supportive relationship among the different levels of management. Subordinates, for example, tend to have greater confidence and respect for their supervisor when they know that there is a supportive relationship among the different levels of management (Figure 9-2).

Upper levels of management should recognize the difficulties associated with the position of a first-level supervisor and help the latter develop a power base. One source of improving the first-level supervisor's power base of authority, confidence, and respect is for upper-level management to show its personal confidence in the first-level supervisor.

UPPER-LEVEL MANAGER RESPONSIBILITIES

There are various other things that upper-level managers can do to help first-level supervisors perform their functions more effectively. As implied above, they should first become fully aware of the actual working conditions of the first-level supervisor. An awareness of these conditions will give upper-level managers a better realization of the importance of the following things:[1]

- *Keeping first-level supervisors informed about the corporate perspective as it relates to the supervisor's operations*
- *Keeping first-level supervisors aware of upper-level managers' priorities*
- *Educating first-level supervisors about new technological developments that might affect their jobs*
- *Providing feedback on how well first-level supervisors are meeting management's expectations*

LOWER-LEVEL MANAGER RESPONSIBILITIES

Getting along with the boss is a two-way process. The first-level supervisor should try, whenever possible, to recognize at least some of the major problems of higher-level management. Where appropriate, the first-level supervisor should work with superiors on these problems to obtain the best possible results for the company. Various studies suggest that the effective managers

FIGURE 9-2 Harmony and support work best for everyone

take time and effort to manage not only relationships with their subordinates but also those with their bosses. This includes doing such things as the following:[2]

- *Developing a positive attitude in accepting delegation of work from above rather than the attitude of "the boss is dumping work on me"*
- *Seeking information and help from higher-level management instead of waiting for the boss to provide it*
- *Showing initiative and selling oneself to the boss, not by political apple polishing but by conscientious work efforts*
- *Avoiding unrealistic assumptions and expectations as to what the boss is going to do*
- *Developing a relationship of mutual dependence with the boss*

A SAD CASE OF NOT UNDERSTANDING

Harvard professors Gabarro and Kotter tell the sad story of a vice-president of manufacturing and a subordinate manager who could not compensate for each other's limitations.[3] The top-level executive was very effective in everything except working with people. The subordinate manager had an excellent record that included a reputation for working with people but no experience in reporting to a difficult boss. Many misunderstandings developed between the two individuals during a period when the company was bringing out a major new product. As a result of these misunderstandings, planning went awry. A new manufacturing plant was built that could not produce the new product designed by engineering, in the volume desired by sales, or at the cost agreed on by the executive committee. As a result, the company lost several million dollars. Each of the two managers blamed the other for the mistakes. The subordinate manager was fired.

Who was primarily to blame for this situation? Was it the top-level executive who could not manage his subordinates, or was it the subordinate manager with the inability to manage his boss? Gabarro and Kotter felt that the situation could have turned out differently had the subordinate manager been more adept at understanding the top executive and in managing his relationship with him. The subordinate manager not only had a different personality than his boss, he had made unrealistic assumptions and expectations about the boss-subordinate relationships. He did not, for example, recognize the mutual dependence between the two managers. As a result, he did not manage himself both upward and downward.

A SUPERVISOR MUST MANAGE BOTH UPWARD AND DOWNWARD

Subordinate managers cannot assume that the boss will magically know what information or help they need and provide it to them. The effective supervisor seeks the information and help that is needed to do the job instead of waiting for the next higher level manager to provide it. Obtaining information about the boss's goals, problems, and pressures should be an ongoing process because priorities and concerns change.

The supervisor who wants good relationships with his or her superior should also be sensitive to the boss's work style. A supervisor is not going to change either his or her own basic personality or that of the boss. However, the supervisor should be aware of what impedes versus facilitates working with the boss and take actions that will make the relationship the most effective.

UNDERSTANDING ROLE PERCEPTION

DOING WHAT YOU *THINK* SOMEONE WANTS

Role perception is the act of saying or doing what you *think* someone else wants you to say or do. Perceiving the role that you think others would like you to play is somewhat similar to being an actor or actress on a stage. In both cases the individual's human behavior on the job may be quite different from the real person's behavior.

A supervisor should not always believe it when a subordinate agrees with the supervisor on a specific issue. The subordinate may be opposed to what the supervisor wants to do, but nevertheless tries to give the supervisor the impression that he or she agrees with the proposed action. The game of role perception involves saying or doing what the subordinate perceives the boss wants. Authoritarian supervisors and those who do not communicate with their subordinates unknowingly encourage the game of role playing.

PERCEPTIONS MUST BE UNDERSTOOD TO AVOID PROBLEMS

A supervisor can modify the game of role playing by being straightforward, by encouraging subordinates to "call things as they are," and by developing a participative form of planning and decision making. A supervisor must understand role perception because it can jeopardize the accomplishment of work objectives. There can be serious problems when people do the wrong things because they had a misconception of what should have been done.

DISCRIMINATION AGAINST CIVILIANS

There is another aspect of role perception that can cause personnel turbulence in the work environment. It occurs when a supervisor has a preconceived opinion of certain people and things. For example, Colonel Crockett was in charge of an office that included both military and civilian personnel. His perception of military personnel was that they were superior to and more dependable than civilian personnel. His perception of civilian personnel, regardless of their position, was that they were at best only satisfactory in their work performance. Colonel Crockett's attitude regarding civilian workers caused uneasiness, dissatisfaction, and agitation—none of which were conducive to the establishment of a good work environment with high productivity.

DISCRIMINATION AGAINST WOMEN

Sam Jones is another example of why a supervisor must put aside perceptions of people that can be unfair and discriminatory. Jones is the manager of a large office. He has an ethnic background where for generations the male members have perceived women as inferior individuals in the work environment outside the home. Jones' perception of the women in his office is that they are not dependable because they are frequently sick, are lacking in physical stamina, and are emotionally unstable. Government laws and regulations prohibit Jones from discriminating against women in the office work environment. However, with his misconception of women's abilities as workers outside the home, he still manages to make it difficult for women to get fair and just treatment in relation to the men who work in his office. With the exception of two first-level accounting supervisors, there are no female supervisors above middle level in Jones' office of over three hundred employees.

Sometimes one's perception or intuitive judgment of a person is correct, but commonly perceptions tend to be wrong. A supervisor, therefore, must always be objective and base personnel decisions on facts, not perceptions. In summary, a supervisor should understand two things regarding role perception. First is the fact that a subordinate's role perception can influence what the worker does. Second is the fact that a supervisor's role perception can influence the supervisor's attitude and behavior in how he or she treats subordinates.

DEALING WITH TENSION AND STRESS

TENSION AND STRESS HAVE DANGEROUS CONSEQUENCES

Tension, as it relates to human physiology, is the reflection of mental or emotional anxiety. Stress is any stimulus such as fear or the pressure of work deadlines that disturbs or interferes with the body's normal functioning. Trying to draw a distinction between tension and stress does not appear to be purposeful. Both tension and stress can result in many dangerous consequences with physical, behavioral, and other adverse effects.[4]

PHYSICAL EFFECTS

Possible physical effects of tension and stress include increased blood pressure, increased heart beat, and difficulty in breathing. These effects can easily lead to heart attacks, severe migraine headaches, peptic ulcers, ulcerative colitis, skin rashes, and disabling strokes.[5] If stress is strong enough and permitted to last long enough, it can damage both physical and mental health.

BEHAVIORAL EFFECTS

The behavioral effects of tension and stress may be reflected in excessive drinking and smoking, use of drugs, proneness to accidents, impulsive and irrational actions, impaired speech, nervous laughter, stuttering, and trembling. Inability to concentrate and make decisions, frequent forgetfulness, hypersensitivity to criticism, irritability, moodiness, and mental blocks are other adverse effects of tension and stress. Still other problems that can result from tension and stress are absenteeism, poor productivity, labor turnover, and job dissatisfaction.

Our modern business society, in both the public and the private sectors, causes many situations that are emotionally and physically stressful. The pressures of technological progress, the complexity and demands of coping with the confusing economic environment, the harrassment to conform to voluminous and often confusing rules and regulations, and the changing and sometimes disturbing attitudes of workers are but a few of the things that put tension and stress on all managers.

FRUSTRATION

Supervisors must develop an awareness of how some of their actions can cause tension and stress with their workers. For example, one cause of tension and stress is frustration (Figure 9-3) which can be brought about when workers see what their supervisor has done to their hard work. When one works hard to do something and the supervisor unilaterally and indiscriminately changes things, it can give a person the feeling of inadequacy. This feeling, in turn, can cause frustration which becomes a factor in physical disorder or disease. Because of the potential undesirable effects on health and well-being, it is very important that a manager be aware of the harmful physical and mental effects of tension and stress and learn how to alleviate them.

LEARN HOW TO RELAX

One of the best ways to cope with tension and stress is to learn how to relax. There is considerable literature on stress written by medical researchers and

FIGURE 9-3 Frustration

practitioners, clinical psychologists, sociologists, and other medical and behavioral scientists that provide recommendations on how to live with stress.[6] Some of the modern methods for coping with stress include transcendental meditation, encounter groups, and biofeedback.

TRANSCENDENTAL MEDITATION

Transcendental meditation, for example, is used by many managers because it is so simple. It basically involves meditating for approximately twenty minutes, once or twice daily, using a meaningful word such as *God, amen,* or *love,* or some other focal point for achieving concentration. Through meditation, the mind is given a rest and anxious or stressful thoughts are dissipated. This causes the person to feel relaxed and better able to face stressful situations.

ENCOUNTER GROUPS

Methods such as encounter groups involve meeting with a group of usually ten to twelve people and allowing oneself to 'let go' and release pent up feelings without holding back.[7] The objective is a clashing of emotions among members of the group to teach people how to understand themselves and cope with themselves and their peers. *Encounter groups must be conducted by skilled leaders,* otherwise there can be more problems created than solved. For example, serious emotional problems may be revealed during a group encounter session, and there may be no suggested solution. As another example, members of an encounter group usually make a solemn declaration not to talk about any personal or private matters that surfaced during the group discussions. However, some people cannot control themselves from talking after they leave the encounter group. These and other situations can cause serious emotional damage to a person when their defenses are stripped away by others.

BIOFEEDBACK

The biofeedback method of coping with stress uses electronically recorded information about a person's vital functions (blood pressure, heart rhythm, and muscle tension) to enable the person to learn to control these vital functions and thereby reduce stress.

There are certain danger signs (Figure 9-4) that a manager should look for that can indicate a need for some self-searching and possibly some outside

FIGURE 9-4 Tension and stress danger signals

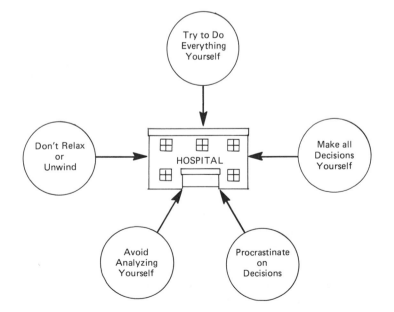

help in coping with tension and stress. Some of these danger signs can be found in the answers to the following questions:

1. Do you delegate responsibility or are you trying to do everything yourself?
2. Do you also delegate authority when you delegate responsibility, or do you make all the decisions yourself?
3. Do you make firm decisions when you have the facts of the situation and after you have spent a reasonable amount of time analyzing the facts, or do you procrastinate the decision making?
4. Do you analyze yourself and objectively view your assets and liabilities and then take constructive action to improve your weak areas, or do you avoid analyzing yourself?
5. Can you work hard on the job and then turn it off when you are away from the office or plant?

If you can't delegate, can't make decisions when you have the facts, can't analyze yourself, and can't relax away from the job, you are a top candidate for a disabling disease. According to a top psychologist at the Menninger Foundation in Topeka, Kansas, a manager must break the pattern of things that cause tension and stress. The solution may lie, says the psychologist, in some combination of meditation, physical exercise, group-participation therapy, or in just learning how to unwind and have fun.

PROBLEM SOLVING AND DECISION MAKING

DEFINE THE PROBLEM

One of the specific skills required of a supervisor is ability to make the right decisions. A very important element in decision making is to clearly define the question or problem. One of the crucial steps is to determine whether there is a need for a decision and why it is necessary.

Problem solving and decision making are involved in every aspect of supervisory management. As reflected in Figure 9-5, thinking things through is the keystone of problem solving and decision making. The process starts with obtaining an understanding of the problem. It is not uncommon to find at this point in the decision-making process that there really isn't a problem after all. Clearly defining the problem, therefore, can save time that otherwise would have been wasted in trying to resolve some difficulty that either didn't exist or could be routinely handled.

ANTICIPATE THE FUTURE

In defining a problem, the supervisor should try to anticipate future difficulties. This will enable the supervisor to take action to prevent problems from occurring as well as prepare for what to do should they arise. Identifying and

FIGURE 9-5 Thinking things through is essential in decision making

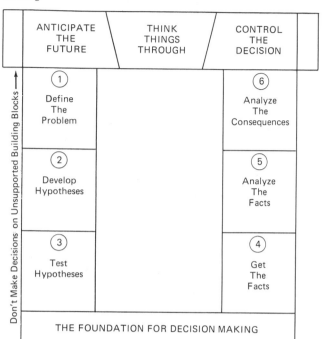

analyzing deviations from past experience is one way to identify problems. A supervisor should be suspicious that something is wrong when significant increases are observed in such things as equipment failures, defective products, costs, customer complaints, absenteeism, labor turnover, or production slippages.

Another way to anticipate and/or define problems is by analyzing deviations from budgets, delivery schedules, and other plans. These deviations can tell the supervisor that something is wrong and that action must be taken to get things back on the right track.

A third way to identify potential problems is to have good communication with others and listen to what they tell you. Open communication with subordinates, peers, union representatives, and others enables them to bring problems to the attention of the supervisor. Talking and listening to people can uncover potential equipment failures before they occur and unsatisfactory working conditions before they become employee grievances.

DEVELOP HYPOTHESES

Having clearly established the fact that there is a potential or actual problem, the second step in decision making is to develop relevant opinions or untested hypotheses as to possible alternative solutions to the problem. Peter F. Drucker, the noted management consultant and writer, is a particularly strong advocate that one must first start with opinions before finding the facts of the situation. Only by starting out with opinions can the decision-maker find out what the decision is all about.

TEST HYPOTHESES

After developing untested hypotheses of causes and solutions to the problem, the third step in decision making is to find out which hypotheses are possible and thereby worthy of serious consideration. Having done this, one should determine what facts are needed to test the hypotheses to see if they would work. This involves thinking through what should be looked at, studied, and tested that will either support or not support the hypotheses.

GATHER FACTS

The fourth step in decision making is to gather relevant facts regarding the situation. The untested hypotheses will help the supervisor in deciding what facts will be needed to make a correct decision.

ANALYZE THE FACTS

The fifth step in decision making is to analyze the facts of the situation in relation to each of the alternative untested hypotheses. The analysis may uncover other alternative solutions. All alternatives should be evaluated from such points of view as

- *Achievement of goals and objectives*
- *Resources available (funds, people, facilities)*
- *Time available*
- *Costs*
- *Expected benefits*
- *Logicalness*
- *Practicality*
- *Ease or difficulty of implementation*
- *Impact on other operations and/or people*

In selecting the best alternative, it may be necessary to trade off the comparative advantages and disadvantages of the various options. Rarely does one alternative have all the advantages and no disadvantages. It is very likely that there will have to be a compromise in arriving at the selected alternative.

ANALYZE THE CONSEQUENCES

The supervisor should avoid the action of immediately moving from selection of what appears to be the best alternative to its implementation. Once the supervisor has selected what appears to be the best alternative, it should be analyzed to determine possible consequences in implementing the decision. The sixth step in decision making, therefore, is to anticipate and determine what problems might or will occur if the decision is carried out. Some of the things that need to be checked are

- *The attitude, willingness, and capabilities of subordinates to implement the decision*
- *The impact, if any, on other functions and organizations*
- *The impact, if any, on community relations*
- *The impact, if any, on humanistic relations*
- *The leadership available to direct implementation of the decision*

CONTROL THE DECISION

After the above six steps have been carefully performed, the decision can be carried out. Effective implementation involves setting up an appropriate system of control to measure progress. The supervisor should be prepared for the fact that implementation of the decision may uncover other problems that will require solution. Problem solving is a contingent type of activity with the supervisor taking timely actions when routines break down or when unanticipated problems occur. It is the supervisor's job to get the system going and to keep it going. Problem solving and decision making are key elements in keeping things going.

SUPERVISOR SELF-DEVELOPMENT

A supervisor must be able to (1) visualize how work can be accomplished; (2) plan and organize the tasks required to do the work; (3) integrate the resources of money, machinery, materials, methods, and manpower; and (4) direct workers in such a way that they will be motivated to work. What can a supervisor do to help develop himself or herself to handle these four things?

SELF-DEVELOPMENT INVENTORY

The first action in supervisory self-development is for the supervisor to take an objective inventory of his or her current knowledge, skills, and abilities. Figure 9-6 is an example of how this can be accomplished. This self-evaluation will

FIGURE 9-6 Self-development inventory

CURRENT JOB RESPONSIBILITIES	EVALUATION		
	Weak	Sat.	Good
Planning & Scheduling Work			
Equipment Technology			
Materials Handling & Control			
Work Methods & Procedures			
Production Control			
Maintenance			
Quality Control			
Training of Personnel			
Motivation of Personnel			
Personnel Relations			
Conducting of Meetings			

point out the supervisor's strengths and weaknesses in management. From this self-evaluation, the supervisor can develop a plan for improving weaknesses (Figure 9-7). The last action is to work the plan and analyze onself to see if weak areas were strengthened.

SELF-DEVELOPMENT PLAN

A self-development plan can be carried out in several ways. For one thing, a supervisor could follow a planned reading and study program at home. Reading, studying, and working the case problems in this book is one way to accomplish some of the needed self-improvement. A second method is to obtain approval to attend supervisory training programs conducted by the employer. A third method is to study and complete courses in management at a local college or technical school.

One thing that any supervisor interested in self-development can do is

FIGURE 9-7 Plan for self-development

AREA OF WEAKNESS	PLANNED ACTION	TIME SCHEDULE

read and study current management publications such as *Administrative Management, American Management Association, Business Week, Forbes, Fortune, Harvard Business Review,* and *Supervision.* Most of these publications are available in local libraries. The important thing about supervisor self-development is that it be continuous. A continuous reading and study program is one way to keep up with the constantly changing concepts and practices of management.

Self-Development Means *DO IT*

Increasing technological advancement increases the demands for better educated, first-level supervisors. A supervisor should not be content with things as they are. Learning is a lifelong process. Supervisors must keep pace with technological advances and obtain a better understanding of new developments in management practices. Evidence of self-improvement is usually helpful in getting promotions. The good supervisor should prepare himself or herself to be able to move on to higher-level positions. Self-development can help a supervisor achieve such advancement. Supervisor self-development, as previously mentioned, can take place on the job, in the classroom, in training programs, and in reading and study programs. The bottom line is *do it.*

FIGURE 9-8 How a supervisor can build confidence and cooperation

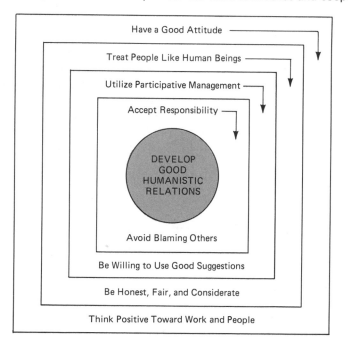

Have a Good Attitude

Treat People Like Human Beings

Utilize Participative Management

Accept Responsibility

DEVELOP
GOOD
HUMANISTIC
RELATIONS

Avoid Blaming Others

Be Willing to Use Good Suggestions

Be Honest, Fair, and Considerate

Think Positive Toward Work and People

BUILDING CONFIDENCE
AND COOPERATION

Employee confidence and cooperation are essential factors in accomplishing organizational objectives. The effective supervisor builds confidence and co-operation within the work force. This task is no minor undertaking, as shown in Figure 9-8. It involves establishing and maintaining a working environment with a positive attitude toward the work, the organization, and the subordinates. It means avoiding the negative "they did it" syndrome of blaming problems on someone else. Focusing attention on how to solve problems rather than on who caused them is a much better approach to building confidence and cooperation. Most important of all in the development of employee confidence and cooperation is the supervisor's attitude regarding the humanistic relations considerations given to the workers.

SUMMARY

The personal behavior of a supervisor should reflect the ability to handle the many headaches that are part of being a leader. A supervisor should strive to get along with his or her boss because everyone comes out ahead when there is a harmonious and supporting relationship. The supervisor's management efforts should be focused both upward to the boss and downward to the subordinates. In working with the boss and the workers, a supervisor should be aware of the serious problems that can occur through role perception. Decisions should be based on facts, not perceptions. A subordinate's role perception can influence what that person does. A supervisor's own role perception can influence his or her behavior regarding the treatment of subordinates.

Tension and stress can result in many dangerous consequences with physical, behavioral, and other adverse effects. A supervisor should be aware of these harmful effects and find ways to alleviate them by learning to relax, to delegate, and to make decisions. Decision making can be easier if the supervisor thinks things through and follows certain logical steps.

The really effective supervisor pursues a continual program of self-development to keep up with the changing work environment. The effective supervisor also builds confidence and cooperation within the work force.

REVIEW QUESTIONS

1. How can upper-level managers help first-level supervisors in performing their jobs more effectively?

2. How can first-level supervisors help themselves in getting along with the boss?

3. Why should a supervisor base decisions on facts, not perceptions?

4. Why should encounter groups be carefully planned and controlled by skilled leaders?

5. In what ways is "thinking things through" the keystone to problem solving and decision making?

6. How can a supervisor develop himself or herself?

CASE STUDIES IN SUPERVISORY LEADERSHIP

A. THE CASE OF FRED WILSON

Mary Jones is a procurement specialist in the purchasing department of a fairly large manufacturing plant. The typing workload has significantly increased in Jones' area of work. She feels that the purchase of a typewriter with stored memory capability would greatly increase the speed of typing contracts and purchase orders that have standard clauses and standard instructions to contractors and venders. Jones, therefore, submitted a request for a new automatic typewriter to her boss, Fred Wilson. Because of the high cost of the typewriter, Wilson said he would have to obtain approval from the controller, a senior-level executive. Six weeks later, Jones asked her boss about when she could expect the approval to purchase the typewriter, as the workload was continuing to increase. Wilson said that he had not yet received approval from the controller. Two weeks later, Jones had neither received the typewriter nor had she heard from Wilson on its status. She was very upset about the situation so she went to see Wilson.

QUESTIONS

1. What do you think Wilson should do when Jones comes in to see him?

2. Can you think of at least three possible alternative actions that Wilson could have taken when Jones submitted the typewriter request eight weeks ago?

3. What actions, if any, do you feel Wilson should have taken during each of the past eight weeks?

4. What is your evaluation of Wilson's manager relations with Jones? With the controller?

B. THE CASE OF GEORGE ALEXANDER

George Alexander has two college degrees and is the manager of a large office. Alexander has his sights set on becoming a top-level manager. As one means of achieving this goal, he goes out of his way to build his own good image with top-level managers. Alexander has perfected the trait of perceiving what his boss likes and then adjusting his behavior to fit the situation. You could say that Alexander is a first-class apple polisher. For example, if he thinks that top-management favors certain policies or procedures, Alexander complies with them even if he feels that they need to be changed. On the other hand, Alexander could care less about complying with policies and procedures that are not emphasized by his boss.

While Alexander can do no wrong in the eyes of the boss, his subordinates have no respect for him. This lack of respect is based on many things, including the following:

1. No consideration, concern, or respect for the needs and goals of subordinates
2. Too busy to communicate with subordinates except to give them authoritarian orders
3. Not willing to listen or to seek suggestions from subordinates
4. Not tolerant of mistakes by subordinates
5. No effort to see the subordinate's side of an issue
6. No support or credit given to subordinates
7. Inconsistency in handling personnel matters such as promotions, performance appraisals, and discipline
8. Not sensitive to good humanistic relations with subordiantes

In addition to these things, Alexander's personal behavior leaves much to be desired. He has used subordinates, without remuneration, to help him repair his house and car. He also has ordered publications at company expense for his own personal use and has acted disgracefully in the area of moral conduct.

Incredible as it may seem, Alexander, with all of his personal behavior and supervisory shortcomings has managed to be the "fair-haired boy" with his boss. He recently was promoted to a higher-level position.

QUESTIONS

1. How do you explain Alexander's recent promotion? Do you think he will eventually achieve his goal of becoming a top-level manager? Explain your answer.
2. Alexander violated almost every guideline for effective supervisory leadership, yet he is moving ahead in the management hierarchy. What can we learn from this situation? Is there or is there not merit in following the guidelines contained in this chapter? Explain your position on this question.

NOTES

---

1. W. Earl Sasser, Jr. and Frank S. Leonard, "Let First-Level Supervisors Do Their Job," *Harvard Business Review,* March-April, 1980, p. 120.

2. Bradford B. Boyd, *Management-Minded Supervision* (New York: McGraw-Hill, 1976).

3. John J. Gabarro and John P. Kotter, "Managing Your Boss," *Harvard Business Review,* January-February, 190, pp. 92–100.

4. See John M. Ivancevich and Michael T. Matteson, *Stress and Work: A Managerial Perspective* (Glenview, Illinois: Scott, Foresman, 1980), pp. 13–14.

5. See Mary C. Gutmann and Herbert Bension, "Interaction of Environmental Factors and Systemic Arterial Blood Pressure: A Review," *Medicine,* November 1979, p. 543.

6. See Herbert Benson, *The Relaxation Response* (New York: Morrow, 1975); and Herbert Benson, "Your Innate Asset for Combating Stress," *Harvard Business Review,* July-August, 1974.

7. In the 1960s psychologist Abraham Maslow started a human potential movement that led to the "encounter group" with its emphasis on rough-and-tumble confrontation among people with similar occupations, backgrounds, and problems. Encounter groups became popular because people liked the idea of airing their emotions without holding back and thereby ridding themelves of their hangups.

PART THREE

SUPERVISION OF THE WORKPLACE

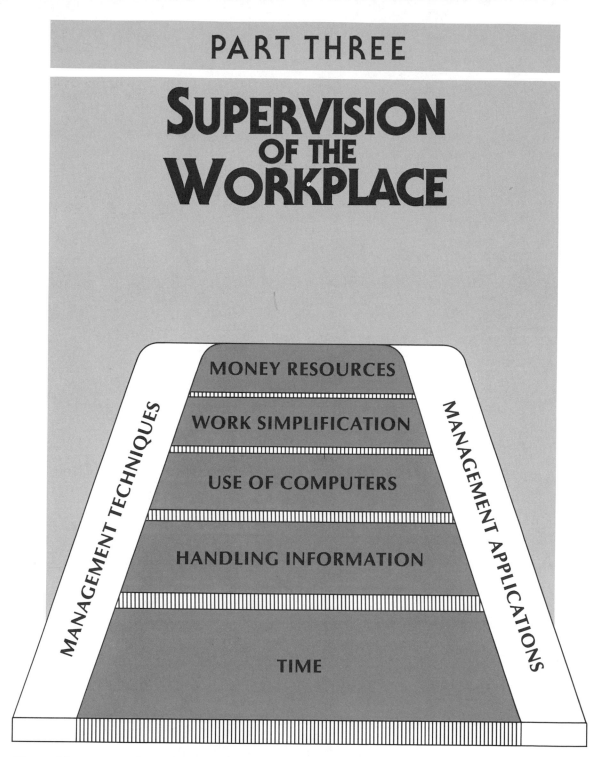

MANAGEMENT TECHNIQUES

MONEY RESOURCES

WORK SIMPLIFICATION

USE OF COMPUTERS

HANDLING INFORMATION

TIME

MANAGEMENT APPLICATIONS

The achievement of maximum productivity is greatly influenced by intelligent handling of budgets, use of computers, management of information, and simplification of work methods and procedures. Supervisors play a major role in these aspects of good management.

10

Techniques in Effective Management

A Memo to Managers:

As managers, we are told that we should be both effective and efficient. To be effective we should always make the right decisions. To be efficient we should get things done with the least effort and cost. But how can we achieve effectiveness and efficiency when we must keep on top of so many things?

Except for the very simplest management situations, we can't really do the best job unless we use some of the proven methods of good management. There are many management techniques that can help us accomplish the results we desire. Participative management, where both the manager and the subordinate look at the problem and its solution, is one technique. In planning and controlling the work efforts of others, there are various charting techniques that can help us keep on top of where we are and where we appear to be going.

The bottom line is to know what the techniques in effective management are and to use them where it is appropriate.

From a Manager

LEARNING OBJECTIVES

The objectives of this chapter on techniques in effective management are to enable the reader to

1. Relate the principles of management and the working climate reflected in Theory Z
2. Recognize the following specialized methods of planning and controlling work activities:
   a. Network techniques of decision trees, PERT Time, PERT Cost, and Critical Path Scheduling (CPS)
   b. Line-of-balance charting
   c. Gantt charting
3. Describe the following management processes:
   a. Management by objectives
   b. Management by exception
   c. Management review and analysis
   d. Quality control circles

KEY WORDS

Critical Path Scheduling (CPS)   An arrow diagraming technique that highlights the critical path of events requiring the greatest amount of time and/or costs to implement.

Decision Tree   A linear (using lines only) means for outlining objectives, alternatives, and consequences of a series of interrelated decisions.

Gantt Chart   A charting technique that shows specific scheduled starting and ending times versus actual work progress.

Line of Balance   A charting technique that shows scheduled versus actual quantities of work produced at each key control point.

Management by Objectives (MBO)   The process of establishing and performing work activities in accordance with clearly defined and integrated goals.

Network Techniques   A logical arrangement of geometric symbols, interconnecting lines, bars, or arrows that show significant operations, occurrences, sequences, and interrelations in the accomplishment of a work program.

PERT   An acronym for a planning network technique called Program Evaluation Review Technique.

PERT Cost   A network charting technique that shows major events and estimated costs for performing a work program.

PERT Time   A network charting technique that shows major events and estimated times for performing a work program.

Proportional Value Distribution   Listing the many things that require management attention and then ranking them in order of importance.

Quality Control Circles   A team of supervisors and workers who study work problems and their causes, and suggest corrective actions.

Review and Analysis   The critical examination of an organization for the purpose of establishing where things stand and where they appear to be heading.

Theory Z   A concept of management formulated by William G. Ouchi that considers workers as the key to increased productivity through the development of trust, discernment, coordination, and intimacy between managers and subordinates.

THE EMC COMPANY CASE

PLANNING FOR A NEW PRODUCT LINE

The EMC Company, a manufacturer of electromechanical components for television, radio, and stereophonic equipment is adding a new line of products. The company would like to market these new products by September 1985. This is a crucial production date to meet because EMC's competitors are expected to market a similar line of products by early 1986.

To manufacture the new line of products will require an expansion of facilities. The expansion project involves

1. Constructing a 600 ft. × 300 ft. one-story steel and cement block addition to an existing building.
2. Tearing out one wall of the existing building, which currently houses the packing and shipping department. This will enable the company to integrate the flow of new products with currently produced products.
3. Purchasing and installing two large production lines of equipment to produce the new products.
4. Purchasing various pieces of noninstalled materials handling equipment, such as forklift trucks.
5. Training employees in the manufacturing processes for the new product.

The expansion project was started on January 5, 1984 and was to cost $4 million. The planned completion date was June 1, 1985. By June 1, 1984 the detailed drawings and specifications for the building and equipment had been approved and contracts awarded for the construction and purchase of major items of equipment.

PROBLEMS IN CONTROLLING

For the first three months of the project, everything moved rather smoothly. During the next nine months the project encountered some difficulties. The problems appeared to be due primarily to layout changes and revisions of drawings and specifications. By May 1985 the project was in serious trouble. A top-level managers' meeting was held on May 21 at the corporate headquarters. The following information was reported at that meeting:

1. Total costs through April 1985 were $6 million.
2. Expected completion date of the building was now projected for the end of November 1986.
3. The connecting wall to the packing and shipping department had already been taken out and the opening covered with plastic materials.
4. The materials handling equipment was delivered on May 1, 1985 and stored outside the main plant building.
5. Two major pieces of production equipment were behind schedule and expected to be delivered and installed on or about December 10, 1985.
6. Employees have been trained in two of the twenty-one manufacturing processes.
7. There have been fourteen design changes in the building and equipment, and eight changes in the planned manufacturing layout and process.

At the May 21 meeting it was announced that the project engineer, Mr. Keller, had been fired on May 18 and that Mr. Foster had been appointed to the position. What do you think may have happened in this case? Where do you think the planning and control might have been inadequate? What would you do if you were Mr. Foster? Can you answer these questions now? If not, look for possible answers as you read this chapter.

MANAGEMENT TECHNIQUES AND EFFECTIVENESS

SELECTIVE USE OF MANAGEMENT TECHNIQUES

A technique is the method by which an individual performs a job. The development and use of good work techniques are a significant factor in effective and efficient management, particularly in planning and controlling work activities. Even the simplest operation can require extensive planning involving facilities, equipment, materials, people, time, and money. And then after a plan of action has been developed, there must be provisions made for its control. Without this, many things just may not get done—as in the case of the EMC Company.

Many different management techniques have been developed to help managers in carrying out their responsibilities. Most of these techniques involve the areas of planning and controlling, and the handling of people. It is important that a manager use and modify only those techniques that are the most suitable and fitting for a particular purpose and situation. If not, it is like buying the wrong size shoes and then wondering why your feet hurt.

THE JAPANESE TECHNIQUE OF MANAGING PEOPLE

JAPANESE PRODUCTIVITY

Japan's productivity figures for manufacturing automobiles, compared to those of the United States, provide just cause for studying Japanese management practices (Figure 10-1). From nearly all accounts, Japan has become the world's most efficient automobile manufacturer. During the period from 1976 to 1981, the output per worker at the Toyota Motor Company in Japan was three times that of one of the major U.S. auto makers. A quality comparison of the final products of the two manufacturers showed Toyota producing 80 percent to 85 percent of their cars with no defects, versus seven to eight defects per car for the U.S. auto maker.[1] In addition to this, the U.S. manufacturer recalled hundreds of thousands of defective cars for corrective repair work. During this same five-year period, Toyota, as well as the rest of Japanese industry, maintained stability in employment. In the United States, automobile plants

FIGURE 10-1 Japanese productivity

THE JAPANESE ADVANTAGE
(All Japanese automobile companies compared with American companies)

		Japan	U.S.
Manufacturing (Machine stamping operations)	Parts stamped per hour	550	325
	Manpower per press line	1	7-13
	Time needed to change dies	5 minutes	4-6 hours
	Average production run	2 days	10 days
Source: Harbour & Associates	Time needed to build a small car	30.8 hours	59.9 hours
Personnel (Average automobile plant)	Total workforce	2,360	4,250
	Average number absent (vacations, illness, etc.)	185	500
	Average absentee rate	8.3%	11.8%

SOURCE: From "The Company That Stopped Detroit" by Steve Lohr. *The New York Times*, March 21, 1982, © 1982 by The New York Times Company, Reprinted by permission.

laid off hundreds of thousands of workers, with unemployment in the industry above 20 percent in early 1982.

JAPANESE STYLE OF MANAGEMENT

To understand the Japanese school of management thought, one needs some knowledge of their culture and way of living. One important factor is that the Japanese community is not a collection of individuals but of family groups. The traditional Japanese emphasis on the family has been transferred to the place of work. Employees tend to stay in the same firm for all of their working life. Within the firm the status system places tremendous stress on seniority with promotions based on length of service. Labor unions are also a part of the firm and not associated with an outside specific trade or skill. All of these factors create a very paternalistic treatment of employees and permanence of employment. The cultural work environment in Japan tends to establish an enviable record of good industrial relations.

THE JAPANESE WAY OF MANAGING

● *PRINCIPLES OF MANAGEMENT*—Following are the primary traditional management principles of the Japanese:

1. Permanent employment of workers with privileges based on length of service
2. Position status based on education, years of service, and job responsibilities
3. Slow performance evaluation and promotion of both managers and workers to discourage the playing of short-sighted management games
4. Employee skill and career development through job rotation
5. Compulsory early retirement (at age fifty-five, except for top-level executives) to create vertical mobility and opportunity for younger employees to advance in position
6. Systematic collection and passing on of information to managers and workers
7. Collective decision making with plans prepared, fully discussed, and accepted by both management and workers
8. Total economic and social concern by employers for their employees, both on and off the job

The principle of lifetime employment is probably a key factor that gives strength to the principle of collective decision making. It stands to reason that people will be more inclined to engage in participative management when the employee feels that "this is my company" and the manager knows he or she will be around to implement "today's decisions." Participative decision making tends to establish and maintain very strong collective values between managers and workers. It appears to give the average Japanese worker a sense of responsibility, that work gets accomplished through teamwork and "togetherness" and that no one can accomplish things alone.

THEORY Z: THE PEOPLE CONCEPT

• *THEORY Z*—William G. Ouchi made an extended study of the management practices of Japanese companies, starting in 1973. He called the Japanese approach to management *Theory Z*—a concept of management that involves workers as the key to increased productivity. The bottom line in Ouchi's concept is that managers need to learn how to supervise people at work so that they can work together more effectively. Theory Z is based on the Japanese management principles outlined in the previous paragraph. William Ouchi feels that Theory Z can work in American business establishments if they carry out a step-by-step integration of certain economic and human principles. These steps start with understanding the conditions that exist in a Type Z organization. The basic Type Z working climate is based on the following values:

1. *Long-term employment*—Most employees work during their entire career for the same company
2. *Trust*—The confidence that personal sacrifices of time, effort, and money will be repaid in the future and there will be equity in the end
3. *Discernment*—The concern of employees to work well together in governing their own workmanship as well as to help others in order to increase productivity
4. *Coordination*—The actions of people that link trust with discernment
5. *Intimacy*—The close personal relationships that reflect caring for, support of, and unselfish attitude toward others

The Theory Z approach to management develops close, harmonious personal relations with effective teamwork and group satisfaction. The emphasis in Theory Z is given to (1) personal contacts between executives and workers, (2) group development, and (3) communication between workers and management.[2]

ACHIEVING QUALITY OF PRODUCTIVITY

• *QUALITY CONTROL CIRCLES*—A quality control circle is a means of achieving high quality of productivity. In Japan, a quality control circle consists of from two to ten employees who are permanently assigned to study problems of production or service. These circles will collect statistical data on the nature of the problem, analyze the data, determine the cause of the problem, and suggest corrective action. Where the problem and its solution are within the circle, the members take the necessary steps to implement their own suggestions. Appropriate recognition and rewards are given for successful implementation. The type of recognition and reward is determined by the importance or innovativeness of the implemented suggestion.

The Japanese emphasize that the fundamental purposes of the quality control circles are to accomplish the following human aspects of organization:

1. Contribute to the improvement and development of the enterprise
2. Respect humanity and build a happy, bright workshop which is meaningful to work in
3. Fully develop human capabilities

The key elements in quality control circles are to thoughtfully combine the statistical and the human aspects of improving productivity. This permits people to think and use their knowledge and wisdom on a supervisory-worker participative basis.

Trust in Management

● *PATERNALISTIC MANAGEMENT*—The Japanese make good use of human resources in achieving a commendable rate of productivity. It is a highly paternalistic and participative form of management in both decision making and problem solving at all levels. Where the Japanese operate plants in the United States, they practice the same techniques of family management. For example, they want their employees to depend on and trust management. The workers appear to readily want to place their confidence in management. In the early 1980s, Nissan Motors of Japan built a truck plant in Tennessee. Many of the workers were given on-the-job training in Japan. When these workers returned to the United States they had a very paternalistic attitude regarding the company and a deeply expressed concern for producing high-quality trucks. They also had no desire or intention of joining the United Automobile Workers Union.

The Japanese style of management instills a strong sense of belonging and group-centered enthusiasm in an atmosphere of job security. Unless workers adopt some of the counterproductive social attitudes and practices of many Americans, the system will continue to pay off in increased productivity, high quality of product, and worker job satisfaction. Maybe we should try it.

NETWORK TECHNIQUES

Logic Diagrams

Network techniques are management "tools" used in planning and control. These techniques take the form of a logical arrangement of geometric symbols, interconnecting lines, bars, or arrows that show significant operations, occurrences, sequences, and interrelations in the accomplishment of a work program. The historical development of network techniques can be traced back to the process flow diagrams used in the early part of the twentieth century.

Logic diagrams can show the characteristics, time constraints, dollar limitations, and decision points of a problem situation involving planning and control. If properly constructed, such diagrams can show on a single page what would take many pages to describe in writing.

PROBLEM CLARIFICATION
AND PROBLEM SOLUTION

• *THE DECISION TREE*—The decision tree, Figure 10-2, is the prototype for most logic diagrams. It is a linear (using lines only) means for outlining objectives, alternatives, and consequences of a series of interrelated decisions. The decision tree diagram is a good initial procedure to follow in systematic problem solving because it can present the dead-end or "disjunctive" paths as well as the continuing or "conjunctive" paths that may be taken. The decision tree diagram demonstrates that the process of finding the preferred solution to a problem is something like going through a maze in which more than one route may lead to the end objective.

One of the things to be gained from making a decision tree is that it forces the analyst to define the problem, outline its scope, identify the decision points, and project the alternative courses of action in searching for the best solution. There is a close relationship between problem clarification and problem solution. The display of a problem in a decision tree can often be very helpful in arriving at the best decision.

PERT—A TIME PROBABILITY TECHNIQUE

• *PROGRAM EVALUATION AND REVIEW TECHNIQUE (PERT)*—PERT is an event-and-time network technique for effective planning and control. It is a technique that shows the probabilities of occurrence of the time required to perform specific events. First, it is concerned with the specific activities or events that must be accomplished to achieve a project objective. Second, it establishes the probable times required to accomplish each activity or event.

The PERT technique is particularly adaptable to planning and control of situations involving uncertainty such as research and development work and the manufacturing of items that have never been built before. In these circumstances, neither the required time nor the costs can be estimated with exactness. Therefore, both project completion times and costs must be estimated on the basis of probability.

THREE TIME ESTIMATES

PERT requires three estimates for each activity involved in a work project. The three time estimates are

1. An *optimistic time* in which everything goes right—a very unlikely situation with an occurrence probability of 10 percent or even less.

FIGURE 10-2 Decision tree

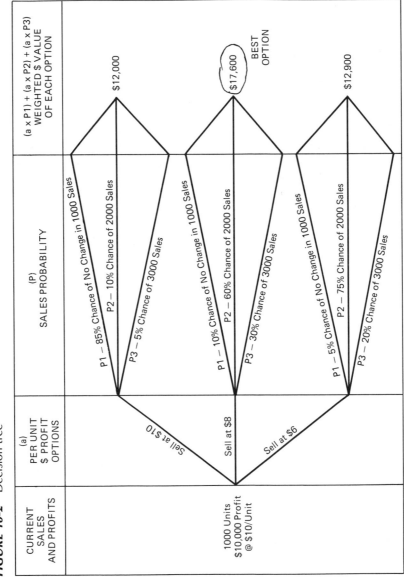

CURRENT SALES AND PROFITS	(a) PER UNIT $ PROFIT OPTIONS	(P) SALES PROBABILITY	(a x P1) + (a x P2) + (a x P3) WEIGHTED $ VALUE OF EACH OPTION
1000 Units $10,000 Profit @ $10/Unit	Sell at $10	P1 – 85% Chance of No Change in 1000 Sales P2 – 10% Chance of 2000 Sales P3 – 5% Chance of 3000 Sales	$12,000
	Sell at $8	P1 – 10% Chance of No Change in 1000 Sales P2 – 60% Chance of 2000 Sales P3 – 30% Chance of 3000 Sales	$17,600 BEST OPTION
	Sell at $6	P1 – 5% Chance of No Change in 1000 Sales P2 – 75% Chance of 2000 Sales P3 – 20% Chance of 3000 Sales	$12,900

2. A *pessimistic time* in which everything that can go wrong, does go wrong—a very unlikely situation with an occurrence probability of 10 percent or even less.
3. A *most likely time* in which there is a fifty-fifty or better chance of occurrence probability.

DETERMINATION OF EXPECTED TIME

The PERT time technique assumes that actual completion time is more likely to *exceed the average* than to be less than the average time. Therefore, a statistical formula is used to weigh the three estimates to determine the expected time of completion for each step in a work project. The expected time is computed as the time period for which there is a fifty-fifty chance of completing the activity on time. The formula for calculating the expected time value is as follows:

$$\text{Expected time} = \frac{ot + 4(ml) + pt}{6}$$

$$\text{Where:} \quad \begin{aligned} ot &= \text{most optimistic time} \\ ml &= \text{most likely time} \\ pt &= \text{most pessimistic time} \end{aligned}$$

In Figure 10-3, for example, the expected time to complete the plans and specifications is twenty-eight weeks, which is the same as the estimated most likely time. The expected time and most likely time are not always the same as indicated in milestone event four where the expected time is $9\frac{1}{3}$ weeks and the most likely time estimated at eight weeks.

DEVELOPMENT OF A PERT NETWORK

There are four phases involved in the development of a PERT time network. As shown in Figure 10–3, these phases are as follows:

- *Identifying the key events involved in performing the activities or tasks required to complete a work project.*
- *Establishing the most optimistic, most pessimistic, and most likely times to complete each event.*
- *Establishing a task network showing the sequential flow in which activities and events must be performed.*
- *Establishing the time network for all activities and events.*

RULES OF PERT

Certain rules must be followed in constructing a PERT network. These rules are:

- *PERT events should normally be based on a product-oriented work breakdown structure as shown in Figure 10-3.*

FIGURE 10-3   Program Evaluation Review Technique (PERT)

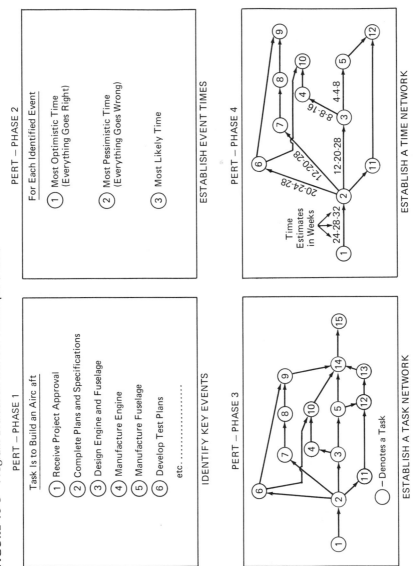

PERT – PHASE 1

Task Is to Build an Airc aft

① Receive Project Approval
② Complete Plans and Specifications
③ Design Engine and Fuselage
④ Manufacture Engine
⑤ Manufacture Fuselage
⑥ Develop Test Plans

etc. . . . .

IDENTIFY KEY EVENTS

PERT – PHASE 2

For Each Identified Event

① Most Optimistic Time
   (Everything Goes Right)

② Most Pessimistic Time
   (Everything Goes Wrong)

③ Most Likely Time

ESTABLISH EVENT TIMES

PERT – PHASE 3

ESTABLISH A TASK NETWORK

Denotes a Task

PERT – PHASE 4

Time Estimates in Weeks

24-28-32
20-24-28
12-20-28
8-8-16
4-4-8

ESTABLISH A TIME NETWORK

- *The task network should show all activities and events that must be accomplished and the sequence of their accomplishment.*
- *All significant interdependent activities and events must be shown in the network by linking activity arrows as shown in Figure 10-3.*
- *PERT does not reflect alternative courses of action, therefore, all activities required to accomplish key events must be completed in the sequence shown in the network.*
- *An event is not completed until every activity preceding it has been accomplished.*
- *An activity cannot be started until the event preceding it has been accomplished.*

If the EMC Company discussed earlier had developed a PERT time planning and control network, and applied the above rules, the following problems caused by premature actions would probably have been avoided:

1. The tearing down of the wall to the packing and shipping department
2. The early delivery of the materials handling equipment
3. The training of employees

PERT COST DEVELOPMENT

- *PERT COST*—The technique of PERT cost involves planning and controlling both time and costs on a common network. Figure 10-4 shows both the planning and control aspects of PERT cost. In addition to the four phases of work involved in developing a PERT time network, PERT cost requires that the following steps also be accomplished:

- *Development of a more* definitive work breakdown structure *for cost planning and cost accounting. This can be a significant difference between PERT time and PERT cost because the cost applications of all activities in the networking of a program* must *be very complete. In PERT cost there can be no program costs missing. In PERT time it is not uncommon to find only those elements of a program that have a major effect on time.*
- *Preparation of a cost collecting* account code structure *for the work breakdown structure. This facilitates the computer data processing of cost information.*
- *Establishment of* work schedules *with a breakdown of end items into elements of work whose beginning and ending points may be directly related to network events. This assists in the estimating and control of costs.*
- Estimation of costs *for all major tasks to include most optimistic, most pessimistic, and most likely.*

PERT COST IMPLEMENTATION

In the implementation of PERT cost, the work breakdown structure is the integrating device for both time and cost data. One of the primary objectives of PERT cost is to establish a time and cost correlation for tasks that are product-

FIGURE 10-4   PERT-cost planning and control

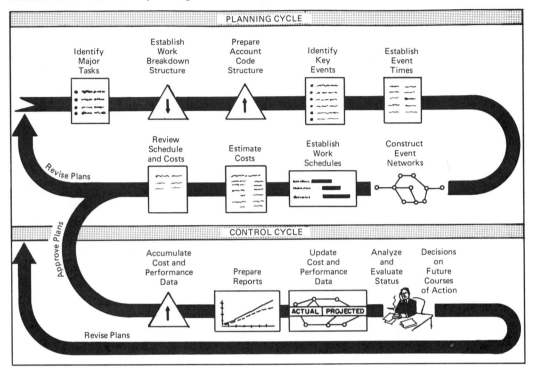

oriented. This is sometimes a problem because the work breakdown structure may be different from the cost structure of the company's standard accounting system.

PERT cost data is usually accumulated against the lowest-level components in the work breakdown structure and then progressively summarized by major items in the project. The cost estimates required by PERT cost serve as yardsticks for control of cost performance.

CRITICAL PATH NETWORK

• *CRITICAL PATH SCHEDULING AND CONTROL*—Critical path scheduling (CPS) is an arrow diagraming technique of highlighting the network events that require the greatest amount of time and/or costs in carrying out a work project. The technique can be used together with either, or both, time and cost control. Used with time control, CPS involves establishing those activities and events that require the greatest amount of time. Used with cost control, CPS involves establishing those activities and events that require the greatest costs to accomplish. The objective in both cases is to concentrate on the critical paths of events where the most time and the greatest costs are involved.

A "Deterministic" Approach

Critical path scheduling normally uses a single time or cost estimate for completion of a work project. The technique tends to be most used in the construction industry. If the EMC Company discussed earlier had used this technique of management, it might have been able to exercise better control over both the construction time and costs of its new building.

CPS and PERT

As shown in Figure 10-5, the arrow diagraming in critical path scheduling is similar to that used in PERT time. The major difference between the CPS approach and PERT time is that CPS generally uses just one time estimate—the expected time. Another difference between the two techniques is that CPS may only emphasize a single detailed network of activities. PERT time, on the other hand, coordinates and combines subnetworks involving the entire work breakdown structure. Figure 10-5 shows the critical path via the large arrow, as well as the other subnetworks in the total work project.

LINE-OF-BALANCE PLANNING AND CONTROL

PERT-LOB

The line-of-balance technique for planning and control is used primarily where repetitive production operations are involved. This management technique is sometimes referred to as PERT-LOB because it utilizes a PERT-type network and a line-of-balance chart. It is a simple graphical charting that involves no computations. As shown in Figure 10-6, line-of-balance charting consists of three items of information that can be made readily available:

- *An* objective chart *that presents in graphic form the planned schedule of work and the actual work accomplished (e.g., scheduled versus actual deliveries) against calendar dates.*
- *A* production plan *(PERT-type network chart) showing key control points. This chart shows the relative timing, within the production cycle, of a single unit of the major elements of the manufacturing process.*
- *A line-of-balance* progress status chart *that shows scheduled and actual quantities of work produced at each control point. The progress chart is developed by combining data contained in the objective chart and the network production control plan.*

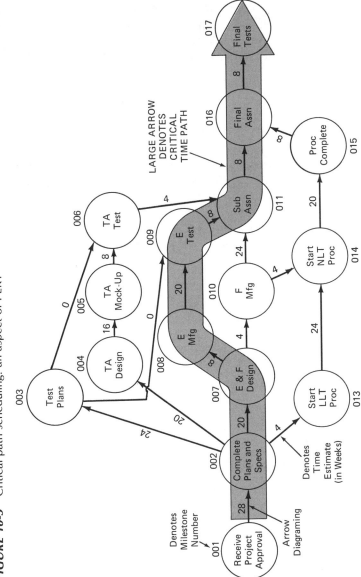

FIGURE 10-5 Critical path scheduling: an aspect of PERT

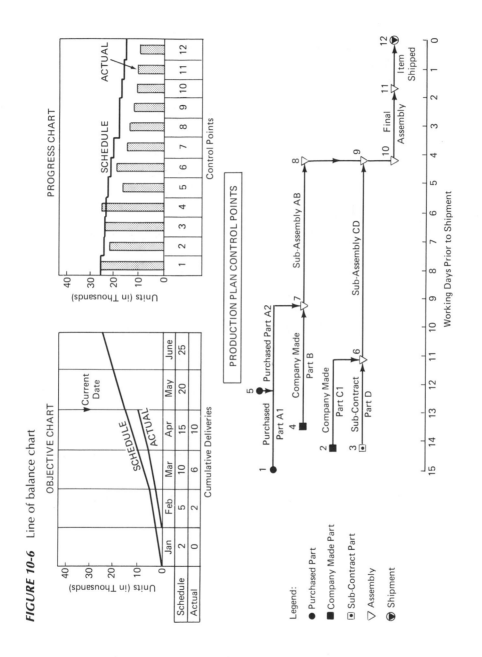

FIGURE 10-6 Line of balance chart

A Technique for Quickly Spotting Trouble

Line-of-balance charting enables a manager to spot quickly any production areas in trouble, and to take timely corrective action on a priority basis. For example, look at the progress chart in Figure 10-6. While 9 of 12 control points are lagging behind schedule, control points 2 and 5 are the two areas requiring immediate management attention. Control point 2 involves company-made part C1. Until that part is up on the schedule line, it causes slippages in control points 6, 9, 10, 11, and 12. Control point 5 involves purchased-part A2. Until that part is up to the schedule line, it causes slippages in control points 7 through 12.

GANTT CHART SCHEDULING AND CONTROL

Event and Time Planning and Control

One of the most comprehensive, condensed, and effective means for maintaining control of work activities is the Gantt charting technique. Gantt charts make use of two fundamental factors in scheduling and control. One factor is the *item or event* under consideration. The second factor is *time*. A wide variety of things can be scheduled and controlled through the use of a Gantt chart, including projects, products, functions, activities, tasks, machines, operations, customer orders, and training. A Gantt chart can be designed for the following purposes:

- *Scheduling the starting and completion dates for specific work activities*
- *Loading of work on specific machines or workplaces to achieve capacity utilization*
- *Scheduled versus actual production of specific items*
- *Scheduled versus actual deliveries of work or products to customers*
- *Scheduled versus actual machine idleness*
- *Scheduled versus actual assignment of jobs to workers*
- *Planned versus actual inventory levels*
- *Scheduling of employee vacations, training, and other events such as performance appraisals*

Gantt charts can be designed to serve office, manufacturing, commercial, and service operations. The flexibility in the use of Gantt charts is virtually limitless.

Henry Gantt (1861–1919) was a teacher, engineering draftsman, mechanical engineer, and consulting industrial engineer. He was concerned about the effectiveness of reflecting data through graphic means. His charting techniques for work scheduling and performance are widely utilized today in both industry and government. The Gantt charting technique provides a wealth of pertinent management information in a readily understandable format. It enables managers to see what the plan is and how it is progressing.

As shown in Figure 10-7, a typical Gantt chart is two-dimensional, with items or events listed on the vertical axis and time shown on the horizontal scale. A Gantt chart shows the starting time and the scheduled completion time. Times are specific as to date or even hours, if the latter are required for planning and control.

How To Use a Gantt Chart

In Figure 10-7, a horizontal bar [ ] shows when each event is scheduled to start and finish. As work is completed on each event, the bar is filled in [ ] to show current status. A glance at Figure 10-7 shows that all events are on schedule except the manufacture of the fuselage. A properly constructed Gantt chart readily provides for effective management by highlighting those events that require immediate manager attention. Gantt charts provide

FIGURE 10-7 Example of a Gantt time and event chart

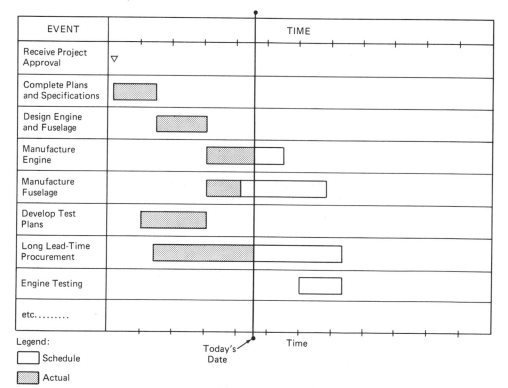

good record-keeping devices for monitoring projects. They are limited, however, in that they do not provide information about the interrelationships among the various tasks.

SIMPLIFIED PROCEDURE WRITING

Without written procedures, an organization tends to stumble and become both ineffective and inefficient in its work efforts. Many written procedures, however, are equally ineffective and inefficient because they are too wordy and therefore difficult to read and understand. A written procedure should clearly define two things: (1) *what* is to be performed, and (2) *who* is responsible for its accomplishment. These two things should be explained in concise and specific words that leave no questions of "what" or "who" in the minds of the individuals involved in the procedure.

EASY-TO-FOLLOW FLOW CHARTING

Figure 10-8 shows a technique for flow charting a procedure without the use of technical sign language. This technique is particularly useful in the writing of office paperwork procedures. As shown in Figure 10-8, the column entitled *action* identifies *what* must be done in a numbered sequence of actions. The

FIGURE 10-8   Procedure for staffing jobs

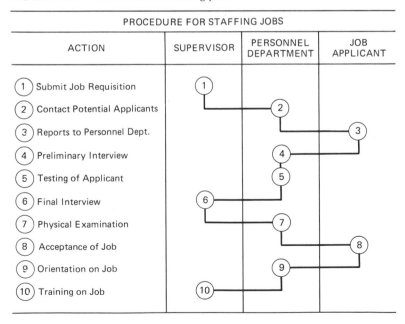

columns to the right show *who* is responsible for each numbered action. This charting technique is limited in that it does not show the physical distance between actions or delays in the flow of work.

TECHNIQUES OF REVIEW AND ANALYSIS

PERFORMANCE EVALUATION

Review and analysis is the comprehensive and critical examination of an organization's business operations to determine where things stand and where they appear to be heading. The objective of review and analysis is to determine whether or not the organization is doing what it planned to do and is doing it as well as it should. The intended results are timely decisions on what to do and how to do it.

MAJOR AREAS OF REVIEW AND ANALYSIS

The review and analysis of business operations looks at all significant deviations from established goals and then attempts to interpret the trend of future happenings. The scope of review and analysis can be very broad, with the major emphasis usually on financial and schedule status. Review and analysis generally includes the following priority items:

- *Achievement of planned objectives*
- *Budget planning and control*
- *Operational cost control*
- *Work program and/or project performance and accomplishment*
- *Resolution of schedule, financial, and technical problems*

Review and analysis focuses on such questions as: Are we accomplishing work according to our schedules? Are we expending resources according to our forecasts? Have we completed the proper amount of work for the resources that we have expended? Are we going to meet our work schedule and cost targets? To answer these questions, the review and analysis process makes use of various management tools such as performance standards, experience factors, past averages, trend charts, and experienced ratios. There is usually an abundance of sources of data that can be used for effective review and analysis. These sources are illustrated in Figure 10-9.

VERTICAL AND HORIZONTAL ANALYSIS

Review and analysis should be a continuous process at all levels of management. The essential steps involved in the process are shown in Figure 10-10.

FIGURE 10-9 Sources of data for review and analysis

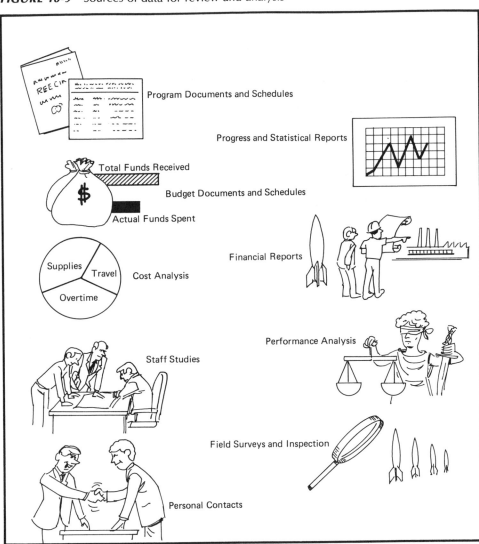

Maximum effectiveness is obtained if the review and analysis is performed on both a vertical and a horizontal basis, as indicated in Figure 10-11. Vertical review and analysis refers to the bottom-to-top appraisal of work activities within a specific organization. Horizontal review and analysis refers to a staff analyst's appraisal of the work activities that involve more than one organization, program, or project. It is a coordination and integration of vertical appraisals with a resulting comparative evaluation of activities in one program or organization against similar or dissimilar activities in other programs and organizations. Re-

FIGURE 10-10 Essential steps in review and analysis

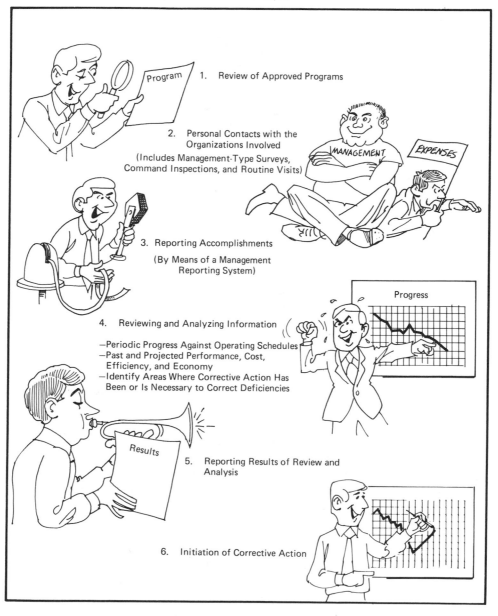

FIGURE 10-11 Vertical and horizontal review and analysis

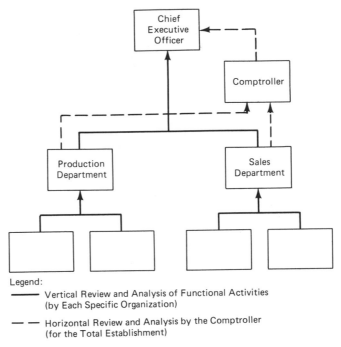

Legend:

———— Vertical Review and Analysis of Functional Activities
(by Each Specific Organization)

— — Horizontal Review and Analysis by the Comptroller
(for the Total Establishment)

view and analysis at the higher levels of management is mainly horizontal in nature. At the lower levels of management it is essentially vertical in nature. There are few organizations that do not require both vertical and horizontal review and analysis.

PREPARATION FOR REVIEW AND ANALYSIS

Effective review and analysis requires careful preparation and thinking before acting. As shown in Figure 10-12, the following things should be done in preparing for the review and analysis of an organization, operation, program, or project:

- *Study the purpose, functions, and resources of the organization whose operations are to be reviewed and analyzed.*
- *Develop a comprehensive checklist of the important work activities within the organization that should be periodically reviewed and analyzed.*
- *Find out what operational reports are already in use as well as any methods and yardsticks that can be used to measure accomplishment of work activities.*
- *Consult with subordinates and peers on effective methods of evaluating work performance.*
- *Consult with and keep the boss informed on what you are doing.*
- *Maintain close working relationships with appropriate staff specialists so that any review and analysis is performed on a coordinated basis.*

FIGURE 10-12 Preparation for review and analysis

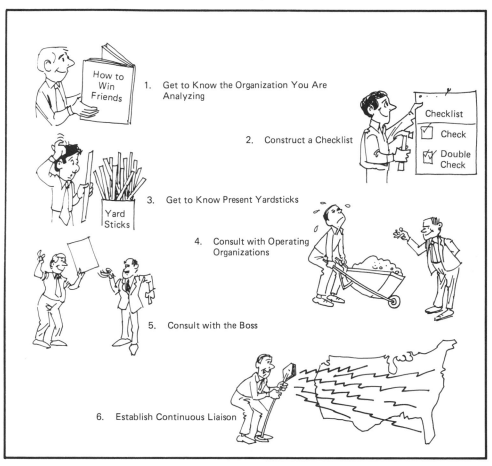

INPUT/OUTPUT CONTROL

There are many ways to present the results of an operational review and analysis. One method is Input/Output Control. A large aerospace corporation uses this in managing its multimillion dollar programs. The major work programs of the company are planned to reflect the sequence of events that will permit the cost-effective design, procuring, tooling, manufacturing, testing, and shipping of all items to the customer. Work planning reflects the inputs of funds, manpower, and other resources necessary to achieve the planned schedules of work. As shown in Figure 10-13, the input/output control integrates both financial and schedule data.

Input/output control plots actual monthly expenditures (inputs) and measures them against planned expenditures. This input curve of planned and actual expenditures is the controlling device for an output curve showing

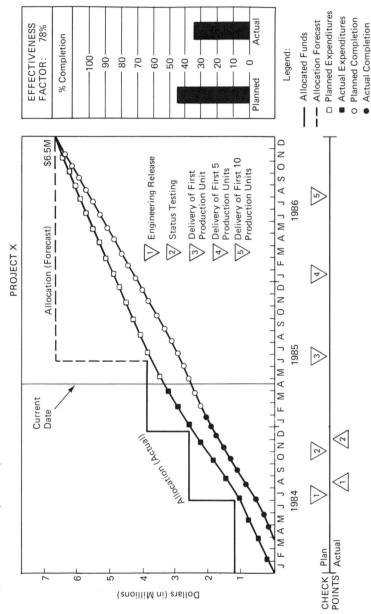

FIGURE 10-13 Input/Output control

planned versus completed work. When the production output curve is shown on the same chart as the resources input curve, management can immediately see if the trends in expenditures and completed work are acceptable. Input/output control can be very effective in detecting situations where the costs are exceeding the original budget or where there is an imbalance between inputs and outputs. In establishing the amount and value of work in process, it is possible to determine the likelihood of either cost overruns or underruns. The system enables management to find out early whether the costs or schedules are significantly deviating from original plans.

Input/output control charts can be prepared to show total project or product status as well as major subcomponents of a system. Both planning and execution data can be computer programmed to provide daily status of the project or product, if this is desired. Computer graphics (see Chapter 14) can be used to prepare input/output charts similar to the one in Figure 10-13. Correlated input/output control can enable managers to take timely action to reduce significant cost overruns or schedule slippages.

SYSTEM DESIGN

The design and operation of any system of review and analysis should be based on three rules:

1. Simplicity
2. Management by exception
3. Cost-effectiveness

If these three rules are not followed, the system will quickly become both ineffective and inefficient. To be effective, a review and analysis system must focus on the right things—those business operations that determine success or failure in the accomplishment of primary objectives. It must also be a system that is simple for managers to use. To be efficient, the review and analysis system must be structured to be cost-effective, and to provide enough benefits to justify its cost of development and operation. An important part of a cost-effective system is to focus primary attention on the most significant objectives and functional activities—the exceptional problems and management situations.

MANAGEMENT BY OBJECTIVES (MBO)

MBO MEANS PULLING TOGETHER

Various members of an organization perform different functions, but all should contribute toward the common objectives of the establishment. Members of an organization should pull in the same direction. Their contributions to the work effort must fit together to produce a whole operation. This means that a manager must know and understand what the organization's objectives demand in terms of work performance.

MBO IS RESULTS-ORIENTED PLANNING

The planning and control process of management by objectives (MBO) enables managers and workers to establish clearly defined and integrated goals for the work to be performed. As shown in Figure 10-14, MBO starts with the strategic planning done by top management. Throughout the chain of command, individual major areas of responsibility should be developed on a participative basis to reflect the work results expected by each member of the organization. The focus of effort in MBO is on clearly defined objectives with primary importance given to priorities—attention to the most significant things first. It is results-oriented planning. The focal point of *action* is at the level of the supervisor and the workers.

Managers at all levels must avoid including too many things in the list of objectives because the result would be a system which would fall under the weight of excessive "paper details." MBO should be applied on a selective ba-

FIGURE 10-14   The process of MBO

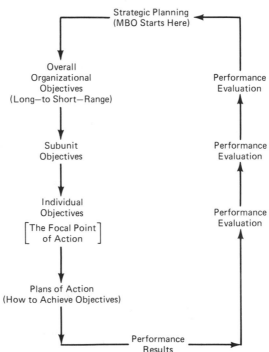

sis where it is most needed. Avoid trying to quantify all objectives in numerical terms. While quantifiable objectives are easier to develop and control, a preoccupation with "numbers" can result in attention being given to unimportant numbers rather than important actions. In many situations, the most important areas where substantial management improvement is needed are not easily quantified.

CONDITIONS FOR MBO

MBO can be applied to any type or size of organization. It tends to work best in organizations where there is a commitment on the part of management to improve the effectiveness of operations. MBO is a diagnostic technique which attempts to clarify the direction the organization is going and how well it is doing its job. To achieve its purpose, MBO requires that the following conditions be satisfied:

- *A well-designated organization structure which clearly defines the responsibilities of subunits and the authority of managerial personnel*
- *The managerial ability to delegate specific responsibility and authority and then give subordinates the freedom to act on their assigned tasks*
- *An organizational climate in which interfunctional cooperation is an accepted way of management*
- *The ability and desire of managers to communicate with subordinates on a continuing basis*
- *The establishment of a timely and accurate performance feedback system*
- *The recognition by management that MBO is not a cure for incompetence or uncontrollable events*

GUIDELINES FOR ESTABLISHING OBJECTIVES

MBO is a good system of management *provided* it is properly implemented. A vital factor in effective MBO is the establishment of the right objectives. The following are some guidelines for establishing work objectives:

- *Focus on the key things that are the most important in achieving maximum results.*
- *Develop objectives on a participative basis that involves both managers and subordinates.*
- *Develop objectives that are supportive and complementary of higher-level objectives.*
- *Develop objectives that interlock and complement those of other parts of the organization.*
- *Develop objectives that are specific and result-oriented—they are the best motivators of people.*
- *Develop objectives that are challenging, but achievable, without undue frustration.*

- *Wherever possible, develop objectives that are quantifiable and performance can be measured.*
- *As a general rule, provide deadlines for achieving objectives.*
- *Objectives should be approved and supported by the appropriate level of management authority.*
- *Objectives should include a system of feedback on their accomplishment.*

COOPERATIVE UNDERSTANDING

Cooperative understanding is important in MBO. Such an understanding starts with management openly communicating its concerns and priorities. MBO is at its best when it reflects the thinking of people at all appropriate levels in the organization. When properly implemented, MBO usually results in positive improvement in the attitude of subordinates. It gives them a work incentive that is greater than just making it through the workday.

MANAGEMENT BY EXCEPTION

MANAGEMENT BY IMPORTANCE

Management by exception is a highly recommended system of management because it focuses attention on the most important things. Some people refer to it as "management by importance." Whatever the name, it means not trying to manage everything but giving primary attention to the most important actions in the accomplishment of an objective.

People do not like to work under conditions which are confused, chaotic, and disorganized. Control by exception or importance recognizes that all things are not equally important and never will be.

ESTABLISH OBJECTIVES

Management by exception generally starts with the establishment of objectives. Once objectives have been established, the pattern of management should lean heavily on the concept of managing the exceptionally important matters. Why, for example, read detailed production delivery reports for every customer when all you really want to know is whether there were any failures to achieve the objective rate of 90 percent on-time delivery. Why impose a restrictive tardiness policy on *all* subordinates when only a *few* individuals are habitually late to work.

PROPORTIONAL VALUE DISTRIBUTION

Determining the most important things that require intensive management can be done through the use of a proportional value distribution. This involves listing the many things that require management attention and then ranking them in order of importance. Those items at the bottom of the list are given minimum attention or even eliminated. For example, the promotion of a low-revenue-producing product should probably be dropped so that more time, effort, and resources can be given to the most profitable products. Treating all things equally contributes to confusion rather than control.

SUMMARY

Many different management techniques have been developed to help managers perform the responsibilities of their position. In the handling of people to achieve higher productivity, much can be learned from the Japanese quality control circles. Many U.S. companies, such as IBM and the Chrysler Corporation, are using this technique very effectively in their management.

Network techniques such as PERT Time, PERT Cost, PERT Line of balance, and Critical Path Scheduling are useful in showing (1) milestone events to be accomplished, (2) time constraints, (3) funding limitations, and (4) critical decision points in planning and control. One of the most common methods of graphic planning and control is the Gantt charting technique. Gantt charts are used to compare scheduled starting and completion times against actual performance. These network or graphic techniques for planning and control are usually much more effective than having the same information presented in a narrative form.

Most organizations find it desirable to have a periodic, comprehensive, and critical review and analysis of business operations. The objective of review and analysis is to determine whether or not the organization is doing what it planned to do and is doing it as well as it should. The intended results are timely decisions on what to do and how to do it. A review and analysis system should be based on three rules—simplicity, management by exception, and cost-effectiveness.

Two highly recommended techniques of management are management by objectives and management by exception. In managing by objectives the supervisor and the workers jointly identify the most important tasks that must be accomplished. In managing by exception the supervisor and the workers give their work efforts to the highest priority tasks, including performance reports that focus on the significant accomplishments and/or problems and deficiencies. Both techniques concentrate on the most important matters first.

REVIEW QUESTIONS

1. Do you agree or disagree that Theory Z can be effectively implemented in the United States? Explain your answer.

2. Assume you are the manager of engineering development of new products. What techniques of planning and control can help you keep on top of those activities that are most critical in the development of a new product? How can these techniques help you?

3. If you had been the project manager at the EMC Company discussed at the beginning of the chapter, what techniques of planning and control would you have implemented? Why?

4. Describe the process of management by objectives and the guidelines for its use as a means of achieving effective management.

5. Discuss the future potential for adopting paternalistic management in the United States.

A CASE STUDY IN MBO PLANNING

Martha Chapman, the district supervisor of eight customer sales service representatives, decided to implement a management by objectives (MBO) program throughout her entire district. The program was to help all representatives in improving efficiency of operations and thereby increase profits. The objectives would also be used to evaluate the performance of the sales service representatives and provide the basis for salary increases and promotions.

Each sales-service representative was requested to develop the objectives that were deemed appropriate for his or her area of operation. This appeared to be a logical request since some representatives were located in highly urban areas while some operated in predominately small to medium-size communities. These objectives were to be reviewed and approved (or revised) by Chapman.

Chester Welsh, the sales-service representative in southern New Jersey, predominately a farming area, selected quantifiable objectives in sales, returns, and new accounts which were improvements from the past year but ones which he felt could be achieved with a minimum of increased work effort.

When Chapman reviewed Welsh's objectives, she merely scanned them briefly and stated that improvement in profits was really the only thing that interested her. Rather than monitor separate objectives for each sales-service representative, Chapman stated that she had already decided that a 15 percent profit improvement would be a reasonable objective for all sales service representatives.

QUESTIONS

1. What mistakes, if any, did Chapman make in establishing her MBO program?
2. Do you think the use of a single profit objective to measure the performance of each sales-service representative is the proper way to use MBO? Explain your answer.
3. Do you think Welsh had the right approach to setting MBO goals? Explain your answer.
4. What problems, if any, do you think Chapman may encounter in her approach to MBO?
5. How would you have set up the MBO program?

THE CASE OF "TALKING IS NOT ENOUGH"

Robert Smith is a mechanical engineer for the EMC Company, a manufacturer of electromechanical components for television, radio, and stereophonic equipment. Smith supervises ten people, seven of whom are engineers, two are technical assistants, and one is a clerk typist. Smith's group is responsible for providing product improvement services to all of the production lines of the EMC Company.

A mechanical part in one of the stereophonic phonograph products has developed a tendency to stick and thereby cause the record-changing mechanism to not operate properly. There have been many recent complaints from customers and Smith has been directed to redesign the faulty part. The instructions to Smith were to "do the job as quickly as possible."

Smith called in two of his best engineers and explained the problem. They came up with one design change that might correct the problem, but the redesign needed further evaluation and tests. Smith and his two assistants agreed to pursue the matter further.

One week later Smith followed up with each of the two engineers and found that one had done nothing and the other had only made a few rough sketches of a redesigned part. At that point Smith called a meeting with the two engineers and restated the importance of getting the job done before more customer complaints caused top management to "hit the panic button."

Four weeks and many meetings later, there was still very little progress on the redesign of the problem part—only complaints on how busy everyone was. Additional complaints had now caused the problem to become a crisis situation.

QUESTIONS

1. What should Smith do now?
2. How could Smith have prevented the crisis?

NOTES

1. Steve Lohr, "The Company That Stopped Detroit," *New York Times,* March 21, 1982, sec. 3, p.1.

2. William G. Ouchi, *Theory Z—How American Business Can Meet the Japanese Challenge* (Reading, Mass.: Addison-Wesley, 1981).

11

Supervision of Work and Productivity

THE SUPERVISOR'S CHALLENGE
IN WORK SIMPLIFICATION

The notion of work as an input in the process of production is a hollow entity until it is related to a product or a measured output of some sort. Work expressed as a manhour of effort, when identified as a ratio with units of output made in an hour, is an accepted expression of productivity. An increase in productivity means that output has increased relative to input. Or perhaps the same output is attained with less work input because work has been simplified, made lighter, or eliminated altogether with robots. Work simplification is an on-going activity of great national importance if we are to increase our share of satisfactions through distribution of a growing gross national product.

Inputs may be expressed as time units, dollars worth of wages, standard minutes of work, dollars worth of capital investment in plant and machinery, acres of land, or as wage dollars needed to produce a given quantum of value added in manufacture. However it may be expressed, the deliberate and disciplined simplification of the ways we use economic resources in production is indispensable to our being competitive in world markets.

Management is primarily responsible for the growth and prosperity of the firm. The supervisor is the responsible interface of management with those who produce. He or she is responsible both for assuring continuous improvement in productivity and gaining participation of the worker in the process. The supervisor provides leadership and training for a willing work force, to the end that all may share in the value that has been added in manufacture. The full weight of responsibility for economizing on applied resources rests heavily with the supervisor.

> John D. Dale, Ph.D.
> Chairman and CEO
> Dale, Elliott & Company, Inc.
> New York, New York

LEARNING OBJECTIVES

The objectives of this chapter on supervision of work and productivity are to enable the reader to

1. Relate the integrated nature of the many factors involved in the supervision of work and productivity
2. Show how a supervisor's involvement with productivity is both forward-looking and backward-looking
3. Identify the four basic elements of productivity
4. Use the following work simplification techniques:
   a. Work Distribution Analysis (division of work)
   b. Process Flow Analysis (sequence of work)
   c. Layout Flow Analysis (arrangement of the workplace)
   d. Operations Analysis (methods of doing work)
   e. Operator-Machine Utilization Analysis (idle time)
   f. Work Measurement Analysis (quantity of work)
5. Show how a supervisor can accomplish the following management tasks:
   a. Getting the most out of equipment
   b. Selling work simplification to workers
6. Describe the responsibilities of a supervisor in:
   a. Materials management
   b. Maintenance of facilities
   c. Human factors engineering

KEY WORDS

Automated Machine Tools Tools which perform certain tasks, such as cutting, drilling, and planing, by the use of magnetic or punched tape instructions.

Economic Analysis An objective comparison of costs in relation to benefits to be derived from alternative proposed actions.

Human Factors Engineering The linkage between the design and operation of tools and equipment and the ability, accomplishments, and satisfaction of the person who must operate and maintain the tools and equipment.

Layout Flow The identification of *where* work activities are performed.

Materials Handling The supportive functions involved in the procurement, supply, and provisioning of the materials necessary for work production.

Operations Analysis The detailed breakdown of a work activity into the *motions* of the worker doing the job.

Preventive Maintenance The systematic inspection and servicing of equipment to prevent malfunctions and breakdowns.

Process Flow The identification of *how* work activities are performed.

Regression Analysis The determination of the mathematical correlation between two or more variables.

Word Processing Equipment Electronic equipment that is capable of transforming written, verbal, or recorded messages to a typewritten form. The equipment consists of such components as (a) programmed instructions on magnetic tapes or cards, (b) units to store programmed instructions, and (c) a text-editing typewriter capable of making additions, deletions, corrections, and changes in the recorded text and producing a perfect finished document at a high rate of speed.

Work Measurement The determination of the *quantity* of incoming workload, work being accomplished, and work backlog.

Work Sampling Random observations of work activities to determine the percent of time spent in setup, operation, maintenance, and delays.

Work Simplification Analysis of work activities to identify and eliminate bottlenecks, conflict, backtracking, red tape, duplication, and waste.

A CASE ON IMPROVING PRODUCTIVITY

WORK FLOW PROBLEMS

The NFP Company manufactures products that involve various chemical processes. An increasing demand for the company's products has caused the production capacity of its Plant A to be expanded three times in the last ten years. These physical additions to Plant A have created work flow problems because the manufacturing process involves the use of so much immobile equipment.

Most of the raw materials used in Plant A are received in granular or powdered form. There is a large receiving warehouse that initially stores the many tons of raw materials used daily in the various production operations. The raw materials are loaded and moved by mechanical equipment to the second floor of the plant where the boxes and bags are opened by hand. Approximately 50 percent of these raw materials are then dumped through chutes into storage bins on the first floor. These bins are subsequently transported to another section of the second floor where the raw materials are processed through a continous-flow production line. The finished product is then returned to the first floor for filling, packing, final inspection, and shipping. Figure 11-1 shows the flow of raw materials through shipment of the finished product.

NO PRODUCTION STANDARDS

Management has never developed production standards for handling raw materials from the receiving of incoming shipments to the delivery to production processing lines. The steady flow of raw materials and semifinished products to the various production lines is critical to the continous processing of the products manufactured in Plant A. The warehouse workers, who are unionized, have established their own informal production standards as to how many items and/or tons of materials they will handle during an eight-hour shift. They almost always reach their self-imposed production quotos long before the end of their shift. The remaining shift time is spent in cleanup and other nonproductive tasks. The supervisors have given tacit approval to this work practice.

HIGH EMPLOYEE TURNOVER

The Filling, Packing, and Shipping Department of Plant A is where most newly hired production employees are first assigned to work. There are many mo-

FIGURE 11-1 NFP Company-Plant A production layout for product X (original layout)

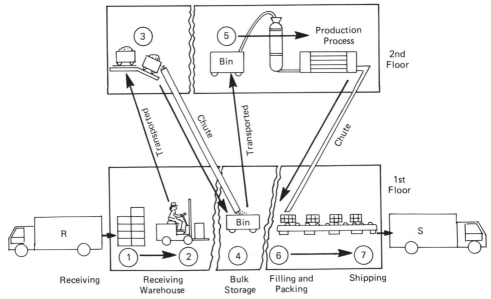

notonous and thereby boring jobs in this department. One job involves placing empty containers on a conveyer belt where they are filled by mechanical equipment. Another job involves inspecting the products as the filled containers move along the conveyor belt. A third job involves removing the filled containers from the end of the conveyor line. Still another job involves transporting the sealed cartons of filled containers from the packing area to the shipping area. There are other equally monotonous jobs, all of which pay the minimum hourly wage. Even though workers are frequently moved to manufacturing jobs in other departments, the Filling, Packing, and Shipping Department has a high turnover of workers who leave the company.

Plant A is a profitable operation, but the expansion of its operations has caused some personnel and production problems. To improve the situation, the plant manager contracted with a management consultant to implement a supervisory development program for all first-level and second-level managers. Based on what you have just read about Plant A, identify the areas where you feel the supervisors can improve the management of work and productivity in the plant. How would you go about making needed changes in the work environment? After you have developed your work improvement list and your recommended approach to making needed changes, check them with the guidelines found in this chapter.

THE TRUTH ABOUT WORK AND PRODUCTIVITY

WORK OUTPUT INVOLVES HANDLING MANY THINGS

Production involves the creation of something. It means obtaining work output by bringing interrelated parts of an undertaking into a state of effective (the right kind of) order. Productivity refers to the quantity of work output produced per hour, or for some other specified period of time. The supervision of work and productivity involves weaving many different factors into a single effort. As reflected in Figure 11-2, the diverse factors involved in the supervision of work and productivity include the following things:

1. Designing the product or service
2. Designing the process by which the product is to be made or the service performed
3. Planning the work tasks involved in the process
4. Organizing and laying out the work tasks to include:
   - Job design
   - Job description
   - Job evaluation

5. Developing the proper work methods and procedures for job performance
6. Staffing, training, and developing workers
7. Determining the work flow and materials flow into the production process
8. Establishing the balanced utilization of production facilities to include:
   - Physical space
   - Equipment
9. Simplifying the processes of work flow and materials flow
10. Controlling time, schedules, costs, and quality of work
11. Assuring effective maintenance of facilities
12. Maintaining good worker relations
13. Increasing productivity and utilization of equipment and other facilities through knowledge of the work process

Many Things Happen at the Same Time

Where there is good planning and organization, the control of production may seem deceptively simple and automatic. Experienced supervisors will tell you that it is anything but simple and automatic. There are just too many things happening all over the place at the same time. As reflected in Figure 11-3, when trouble strikes, it tends to have a "snowballing" effect that involves many areas of supervision. Poor work methods, for example, can affect worker relations, utilization of equipment, and maintenance of equipment.

FIGURE 11-2 Basic factors in productivity
(How many building blocks can you handle?)

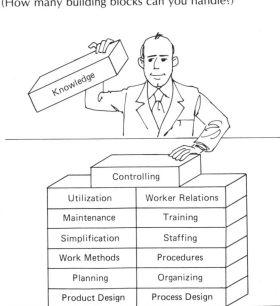

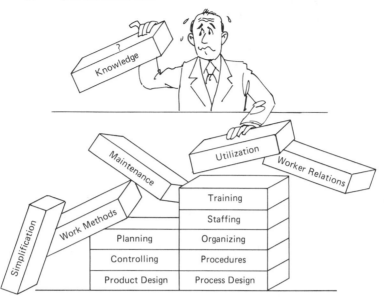

FIGURE 11-3 Supervision of work and productivity involves many things happening at the same time

THE SUPERVISOR'S INVOLVEMENT WITH PRODUCTIVITY

A SUPERVISOR MUST LOOK BOTH BACK AND AHEAD

The supervisor's involvement with productivity is both forward-looking and backward-looking. There must be projections into the future by developing financial budgets, labor utilization plans, equipment utilization plans, and production schedules; and by initiating actions on such matters as purchase orders, supply requisitions, and staffing of jobs. A supervisor must also take proper corrective action on such after-the-fact things as production output reports, cost reports, personnel performance appraisals, inventory status reports, and safety records.

BASIC ELEMENTS IN PRODUCTIVITY

Supervisory success in achieving high quantity and quality of work output at the lowest possible cost is closely related to the following basic elements involved in productivity:

- *Organizational management*
- *Personnel management*
- *Equipment and materials management*
- *Methods and procedures management*

Organizational and personnel management have been discussed in previous chapters. The remainder of this chapter will discuss the other two elements of productivity.

EQUIPMENT AND MATERIALS MANAGEMENT

Equipment and materials management involves the physical layout of work, utilization of equipment, materials management, and maintenance of facilities. If the work is to be accomplished at a profit, the use of energy must also be managed, because the costs of gas, oil, and electricity are major elements of expense in almost any undertaking.

- *LAYOUT OF WORK*—The layout of work facilities is both a management and a technical function. In a large organization there is usually an Industrial Engineering Department or similar group of specialists who have primary responsibility for developing the most effective and efficient layout of work. In a small organization, the supervisor may be the one responsible for developing the best possible work layout. In all situations, the supervisor should recognize the production problems and/or worker dissatisfactions that poor work layout can cause. The supervisor should be knowledgeable enough to recommend how work layout can be made more effective and efficient.

Layout of work includes planning the physical space requirements for people, equipment, and materials. Good work layout is important in both office and production facilities.

GUIDELINES FOR LAYOUT OF WORK

The layout of work is influenced by such factors as the type of business or production activity, the type of product, the type of work operations, and the type of workers. In developing the layout of work, there are certain guidelines that need to be considered:

1. Where appropriate, develop production centers with space allocated for people, machines, storage for materials, and storage for finished products.
2. Establish a proper work flow balance between production centers to eliminate bottlenecks and over or under capacity work situations.
3. Provide convenient service centers such as tool rooms, supply rooms, and lavatories.
4. Provide for short movements of work both within and between production centers.

5. Where applicable, allow enough space for movement of heavy materials, supplies, and/or products.
6. Don't try to save space at the expense of space for workers, equipment, or materials.
7. Allow for flexibility to modify the layout of work to fit changing conditions.
8. Provide for future expansion.

Referring to the case of the NFP Company at the beginning of the chapter, it is obvious that there was inadequate planning for handling future expansions. The result was a layout of manufacturing facilities that caused problems in the flow of materials between production operations. Figure 11-1 showed the layout and flow of work from the receiving warehouse to one of the production lines and finally to the Filling, Packing, and Shipping Department. During the supervisory training program that was conducted in Plant A, one of the supervisors suggested a work layout that would eliminate the flow of raw materials from the first floor to the second floor and back again to the first floor. Figure 11-4 reflects this suggested change which provides for a much more effective and efficient layout of work.

THE RIGHT MACHINE FOR THE RIGHT JOB

• *EQUIPMENT UTILIZATION*—Most office departments and all production departments have some kind of equipment to help get the work done. Some pieces of equipment are more efficient or have greater capacity for producing

FIGURE 11-4 NFP Company-Plant A production layout for product X (revised layout)

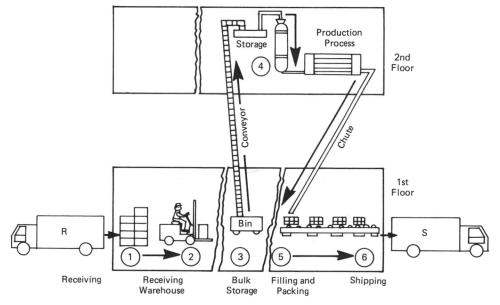

work than others. The qualities that make the difference in equipment are size, speed, power, design, electronics, ease of operation, and maintenance. A good supervisor knows the qualities of different pieces of equipment used or needed in the department. Whether the supervisor is in charge of an office or a production operation, he or she should strive to use the right machine for the right job. In an office operation, for example, this involves knowing the type of work that should be handled on a minicomputer versus that which would be more effectively handled by a large mainframe computer. It also means knowing the type of work that can be most effectively performed by hand.

TIME

Time is an important factor in equipment utilization. Idle equipment is unproductive, costly, and wasteful of capital investment. One of the primary causes of idle equipment is the tendency on the part of many managers to think that productivity can be increased and costs reduced merely by substituting a piece of equipment for manual labor. This type of thinking can result in equipment being installed that is not cost-effective—the benefits obtained from the equipment do not justify its costs. Acting before thinking things through can result in the installation of office computers, word processing equipment, highly automated machine tools, and other equipment that far exceed the work requirements of the organization. Underemployed equipment and operators are not the way to increase productivity and reduce costs.

UTILIZATION

Intelligent utilization of equipment, on the other hand, can produce faster and cheaper work. A machine that was right for a certain job yesterday may be obsolete and a bottleneck today. Cost-effective analysis can help determine which equipment wastes time and is expensive to operate and therefore should be replaced. Equipment technology—particularly in the use of computers, word processors, mechanical robots, and automated machine tools—is rapidly changing. This often causes yesterday's blockbusters to become today's broken-down old wrecks.

In some types of industrial operations, mechanical robots can work faster, steadier, and more accurately than human beings. As an example, the McDonnell Douglas plant in St. Louis has a million-dollar robot that controls a laser beam for cutting out sheets of graphite to be used in brake assemblies for jet aircraft. The robot also cuts parts for tail sections and wings that are welded together by another robot. With the help of robots, two workers can do the job once performed by thirty workers. In some high-volume, office-type operations such as purchasing, legal work, and handling of customer accounts, it is often cost-effective to install word processing equipment. This equipment can both increase work output and reduce the costs of adding, deleting, correcting, and typing involved in producing final written communications. The important thing for a supervisor to remember is to match the right equipment with the right job.

PRACTICALITY

Purchasing the newest and most technologically advanced equipment is sometimes not the best solution to productivity problems because of the high cost of purchasing or leasing. A supervisor, therefore, must often plan to get the most use out of existing equipment. This involves keeping equipment productivity at a high level by doing the following things:

1. Train workers in how to operate and maintain equipment properly to obtain the maximum use of its capabilities.
2. Keep records of equipment operations to help predict and plan operating and maintenance requirements (Figure 11-5).
3. Keep equipment in good condition by
   - Not overloading equipment
   - Encouraging operator care and maintenance
   - Establishing good relations with the Maintenance Department
4. Train workers only to make proper adjustments that will avoid damage to either or both equipment and product.
5. Plan ahead so that equipment cleanup, overhauling, and/or other maintenance can be performed during equipment idleness time.
6. Stress safety in the correct operation of equipment.
7. Communicate with workers on the utilization and maintenance of equipment.

ECONOMIC ANALYSIS

When it becomes necessary to replace old expensive-to-operate equipment or to add new costly-to-buy equipment, the supervisor should initiate an economic analysis study. In large organizations, the Industrial Engineering Department or cost analysis specialists can provide assistance in conducting such studies. The supervisor has a major role to perform in equipment studies because he or she is, or should be, familiar with equipment operating costs, equipment downtime, maintenance costs, equipment utilization, safety improvement, quality improvement, and many other operational factors. As a general rule, a supervisor should never recommend or initiate action to purchase expensive equipment without the benefits of an economic analysis study. Economic analysis helps prevent actions that are not cost-effective.

FIGURE 11-5 Equipment record

EQUIPMENT RECORD					
Type of Equipment:					Serial No.
Manufacturer:			Address:		
Description of Equipment:					
When Installed:			Where Installed:		

MINOR PERIODIC MAINTENANCE

Type	Frequency	Type	Frequency

MAJOR PERIODIC MAINTENANCE

Type	Date Sch.	Date Perf.	Type	Date Sch.	Date Perf.

CONDITION OF EQUIPMENT

Date	Excellent	Satisfactory	Poor	Remarks

MATERIALS MANAGEMENT: AN UNAVOIDABLE EXPENSE

● *MATERIALS HANDLING*—Materials handling involves the procurement, supply, and provisioning of the materials necessary for work production. Full utilization of equipment and personnel is highly dependent on the effective and efficient handling of supplies and materials. Industrial operations and, to a lesser extent, office operations, are contingent upon the proper requisitioning, purchasing, storing, and delivering of supplies and materials needed to perform the work. Without supplies and materials, both personnel and equipment are placed in a state of idleness. Supervisors have a responsibility for seeing that supplies and materials are available when and where needed and in the right quantities.

The handling of materials, from requisitioning to delivery to the job, is an unavoidable expense of business management. The costs of materials management can run to over 50 percent of the cost of manufacturing a product. A primary concern of supervisors is to keep the costs of materials management at the lowest possible level while still maintaining effectiveness and efficiency of operations. Materials handling is a management control function that affects inventory levels, facility costs, cash flow, productivity, and profits. If, for example, the inventory levels of materials are too high in relation to work production needs, the results are higher costs for storage space, insurance on inventory, interest on borrowed money to meet cash flow needs, obsolescence, wastage, and other administrative overhead costs. If inventory levels are too low in relation to normal work production needs, the results may be work stoppages due to lack of materials.

TECHNICAL PLANNING

Materials handling is also a technical function involving the proper movement of materials from storage to the work areas. The planning of a manufacturing or distribution facility usually starts with the layout of the flow of materials to and from the work production areas. This technical planning precedes the layout of the building itself. The importance of this technical planning is that the movement of supplies, materials, semifinished products, and finished products is wasteful and expensive. It therefore behooves management to set up the production process in such a way as to minimize the amount of materials handling.

The technical aspects of materials management includes providing the right types of handling equipment in the right quantities and in the right departments. In some operations major items of equipment are required for moving raw materials and work in process from one place to another. These can include equipment ranging from hand trucks and carts to motorized trucks, automated trucks, overhead cranes, power-lifts, forklift trucks, elevators, and conveyors. Too much materials handling equipment is not cost-effective. Too little materials handling equipment can cause costly production bottlenecks or stoppages.

EFFECTS OF GOOD MATERIALS MANAGEMENT

Materials management involves flow and control of materials as an integrated function of the production process. Good materials management results in more accurate control of capital investment, better utilization of production equipment, more efficient use of the work force, and avoidance of unnecessary movement of materials. First-level supervisors need to have a good understanding of the division of responsibility and authority for materials management. In a large organization materials management may involve the Industrial Engineering Department, the Purchasing Department, cost analysts, and other production departments. It is a function that entails good planning and coordination.

SUPERVISOR RESPONSIBILITIES

Some of the materials management responsibilities most frequently assigned to first-level supervisors are as follows:

1. Planning and scheduling the delivery of materials in accordance with department usage
2. Controlling loss of inventory within the department
3. Initiating requisitions for materials needed in the department
4. Controlling departmental wastage of materials used in the production process
5. Preventing inadequate or improper utilization of materials in the department
6. Avoiding unnecessary inventory investment in the department

Workers look to the supervisor for the planning and control that gets the right quantities of materials to the right place at the right time.

● *MAINTENANCE*—The maintenance of equipment and other physical facilities keeps things in good operating condition. The manner in which a machine is serviced and maintained affects both the amount of operational time and the quality of the equipment's performance. A machine that is well maintained has fewer breakdowns and fewer interruptions caused by operating complications.

MAINTENANCE FUNCTIONS

The functions in maintenance management are usually quite extensive. The Maintenance Department may have responsibilities including erecting buildings or partitions, rearranging equipment, designing tools and equipment, fabricating and installing tools and equipment, repairing and adjusting tools and equipment, and performing preventive maintenance tasks. Good maintenance management can eliminate many breakdowns of equipment, lengthen the usable productive life of equipment, and increase the productivity of the workplace through improved efficiency.

PREVENTIVE MAINTENANCE

Preventive maintenance is the systematic inspection and servicing of equipment to prevent malfunctions and breakdowns. It includes such routine and repetitive tasks as cleaning, lubricating, tightening, and making minor adjustments to equipment. It may in some cases include routine replacement of parts. Preventive maintenance can surface such situations as frayed wiring, overheating, noisy bearings, excessive belt tension, inadequate belt tension, improper pulley alignment, low water level, low oil level, loose bolts or screws, worn-out hoses, and low or high air pressure.

It is in the area of preventive maintenance that the supervisor plays the most important role in maintenance management. First, the supervisor should train the workers to conduct routine periodic inspections of equipment to determine if something might be wrong or is about to cause trouble. Second, the supervisor should train the workers *not* to make unauthorized adjustments or repairs but to report them to the supervisor for referral to the Maintenance Department. Haphazard adjustments or repairs to complex equipment can cause equipment breakdowns involving major repairs (Figure 11-6). Third, the supervisor should learn how to inspect equipment by looking at it, feeling it, listening to it, or testing it to determine if something might be wrong or is about to cause trouble. Last, the supervisor must develop cooperative relations with the Maintenance Department in their mutual execution of preventive maintenance.

FIGURE 11-6 Avoid haphazard repairs

METHODS AND PROCEDURES MANAGEMENT

MOST WORK CAN BE SIMPLIFIED

Supervisors who critically analyze their operations and apply work simplification techniques will become more effective and efficient in the performance of their overall job. Systematic analysis of operations can uncover work techniques that are taking a significant amount of work input and producing little output. After poor work techniques are uncovered, they can often be simplified to increase productivity. Most work can be simplified and made easier,

FIGURE 11-7 CSC procedure for processing invoices for payment Pittsburgh executive office (old method)

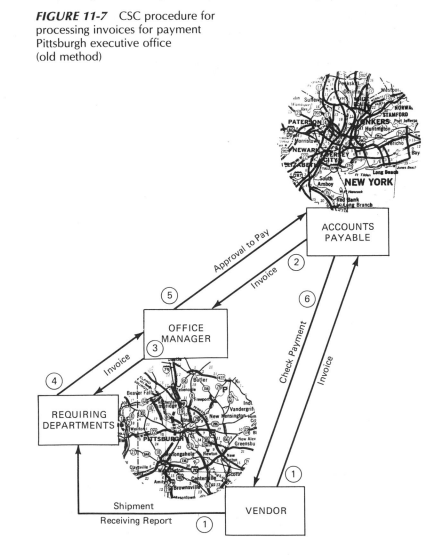

particularly the work methods and procedures related to administrative and clerical activities.

A large steel company had located some of its corporate executive offices, including the Controller and the Accounting Department, in New York City. The remainder of the executive offices, including sales, purchasing, order scheduling, and industrial relations, were located in Pittsburgh. The flow of accounting documents between the two cities presented many problems. Figure 11-7 shows the procedure that was followed for many years in processing invoices for payment. The time delays in the procedure caused the company to lose almost all discounts for early payment of invoices. A new office manager in the Pittsburgh office implemented the procedure shown in Figure 11-8.

FIGURE 11-8 CSC procedure for processing invoices for payment Pittsburgh executive office (new method)

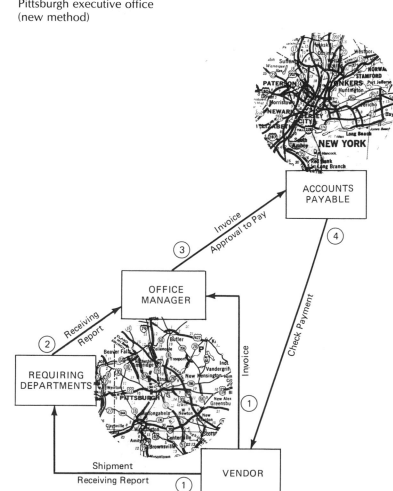

The improved procedure reduced the time lag in the payment of invoices, facilitated the taking of discounts for early payment, minimized the loss of correspondence between offices, and saved productive hours of clerical work in both offices.

ATTITUDE IS IMPORTANT

● *WORK SIMPLIFICATION*—The work methods and procedures used in performing a task can make a big difference in productivity. Managers, therefore, should develop a work simplification point of view in carrying out day-to-day supervision. The manager's attitude is a key factor in work simplification. For one thing, managers have to accept the fact that procedures they may have personally established yesterday need to be changed today. This is not always easy when the suggested improvement comes from a subordinate. Second, the best work simplification is a joint team effort of the Industrial Engineering Department, the first-level supervisor, and the worker on the job. Authoritarian management is usually not effective in methods and procedures improvement because many of the best work simplification suggestions come from subordinate employees. Last, work simplification must have the support of top-level management. When the top-level officials show their interest and active participation in improving the management of things, their attitude tends to spread to lower levels of management.

Work simplification techniques can identify and eliminate bottlenecks, backtracking, duplication, red tape, and waste. A supervisor needs to understand how work simplification techniques can help improve the productivity of the department. This includes knowledge and appropriate application of the following work simplification techniques (Figure 11-9).

Eliminate
Waste

FIGURE 11-9   Work simplification techniques

1.   Work distribution analysis (division of work)
2.   Process flow analysis (sequence of work)
3.   Layout flow analysis (arrangement of the workplace)
4.   Operations anlaysis (methods of doing work)
5.   Operator-machine utilization analysis (idle time)
6.   Work measurement analysis (quantity of work)

The paragraphs that follow will give the supervisor the familiarity needed to use these management improvement techniques.

ANALYZE THE TOTAL WORK PICTURE

●   *WORK DISTRIBUTION ANALYSIS*—The planning and control of work distribution involves analyzing the total work picture of the various tasks performed by each individual in an organization. In order to improve work performance, one needs to be able to clearly see in one place all the activities performed by the organization and the contribution of each employee to each activity.

   A work distribution chart is one of the easiest and best ways to arrange all

FIGURE 11-10 Task list

Date ______	TASK LIST (for Work Distribution Chart)		
Name	Job Title		
Organization	Supervisor		
DESCRIPTION		HOURS PER WK.	WORK COUNT
Prepared for Each Worker			

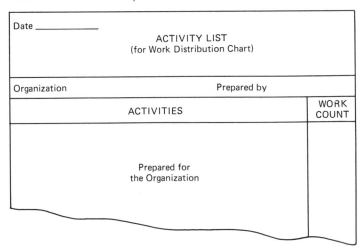

the activities and tasks of an organization on a simple form. There are three steps involved in preparing such a chart:

1. Prepare a list of the *tasks* performed by each worker and the estimated time spent on each task. This list can be prepared by the worker or by the supervisor (Figure 11-10).
2. Prepare a list of the *activities* that the organization is responsible for performing. (Figure 11-11).
3. Prepare a chart showing the organization's *activities* and the *tasks* related to each activity performed by each worker (Figure 11-12).

FIGURE 11-11 Activity list

Date ______	ACTIVITY LIST (for Work Distribution Chart)	
Organization	Prepared by	
ACTIVITIES		WORK COUNT
Prepared for the Organization		

FIGURE 11-12 Work distribution chart

ACTIVITY	WORK COUNT	HOURS PER WK.	NAME				POSITION			NAME				POSITION		
			TASKS				POSITION	WC	HRS.	TASKS				POSITION	WC	HRS.
Prepared from the Activity List			Prepared from the Task List							Prepared from the Task List						

Organization _____ WORK DISTRIBUTION CHART

Charted by _____

Approved by _____

WC = Work Count

Once the work distribution chart is prepared, it is analyzed to answer such questions as:

- *What activities take the most time?*
- *Where is effort being misdirected?*
- *Are skills being used properly?*
- *Are workers engaged in too many unrelated tasks?*
- *Are tasks spread too thinly?*
- *Is work evenly distributed?*
- *Is there unnecessary duplication of work effort?*

Analysis of the work distribution chart can identify discrepancies in the distribution of work to personnel. Once this type of situation is identified the supervisor can take corrective action where there is underutilization or overutilization of personnel in the work force. The work distribution chart and its analysis can systematically lead to further actions to simplify and improve work methods and procedures. It provides "clues" and points the way for further study of management improvement by showing where the bulk of the work in the organization is done.

FLOW DIAGRAMING OF PROCEDURES

- *PROCESS FLOW ANALYSIS*—Process flow analysis establishes *how* work activities are carried out. It is a graphic method of outlining the steps in a work process or procedure. Process flow charting, sometimes called flow diagraming, can be used to analyze work activities involving both materials and/or personnel, and applies equally to manufacturing, service, and office operations. Flow diagraming can show the what, where, when, who, and how of an entire work process. It permits the supervisor to ask "why" about each step. Only by asking about the purpose of each step can a supervisor find ways of simplifying procedures, getting rid of bottlenecks, and smoothing out rough spots in the flow of work.

SIGN LANGUAGE USED IN FLOW DIAGRAMING

As shown in Figure 11-13, flow diagraming makes use of sign language to show the steps that are taking place. Five simple symbols are used to reflect the basic actions of operation, transportation, delay, inspection, and storage. The use of these symbols in flow diagraming makes it easier to analyze the charted procedures. This simplifies achieving the objective of eliminating, combining, or rearranging the flow of work because the charting technique clearly shows what is happening in the work process. For example, Figure 11-14 shows the flow diagram of a manufacturing operation *before* unnecessary steps were eliminated. The chart clearly shows fifteen transportation actions and seven

FIGURE 11-13 Process charting sign language

FIGURE 11-13 Process charting sign language

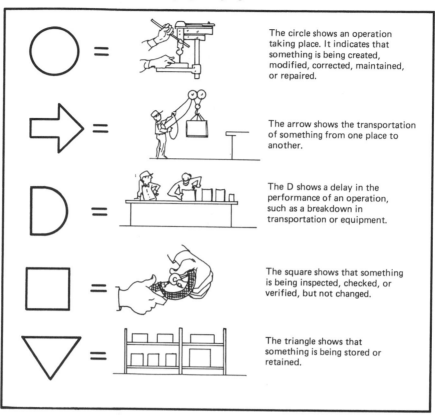

The circle shows an operation taking place. It indicates that something is being created, modified, corrected, maintained, or repaired.

The arrow shows the transportation of something from one place to another.

The D shows a delay in the performance of an operation, such as a breakdown in transportation or equipment.

The square shows that something is being inspected, checked, or verified, but not changed.

The triangle shows that something is being stored or retained.

delays. These phases of the job may be candidates for elimination. When we look at Figure 11-15 we see the same work process *after* eight transportation actions and five delays were eliminated.

ANALYZING AND QUESTIONING

The work simplification achieved in Figure 11-15 requires an analysis that focuses on such questions as:

- *What does each step in the process accomplish and is it necessary?*
- *When should the necessary steps be performed and is each step being done in the right sequence?*
- *Can any of the steps be combined or eliminated?*
- *Where is each step being accomplished? Is is being performed at the right place? Can the steps be done more easily with less time and transportation at some other location? Can the steps be done better on some other type of equipment?*

FIGURE 11-14 Flow process chart (present method)

FLOW PROCESS CHART

| Page No. 1 | No. of Pages 1 |

Process: Refinish Charger Housings

☐ Man or ☒ Material

Chart Begins: Dismantling Rack
Chart Ends: Assembly Bench

Charted by: D. Wilson
Date: 18 Dec 1984

Organization: Reconditioning Light Equipment Shop

SUMMARY

ACTIONS	PRESENT No.	PRESENT Time	PROPOSED No.	PROPOSED Time	DIFFERENCE No.	DIFFERENCE Time
○ Operations	6					
→ Transportations	15					
☐ Inspections	2					
D Delays	7	190				
▽ Storages	0					
Distance Travelled (Feet)	166					

DETAILS OF (X PRESENT) / (☐ PROPOSED) METHOD

#	Details	Symbol	Distance in Feet	Quantity	Time	What?	Where?	When?	Who?	How?	Notes	Eliminate	Combine	Sequence	Place	Person	Improve
1	From Dismantling to Rack	→	6						X			X					
2	Housing On Rack	D			30	X					Can Rack Be Moved To Cleaner Area	X		X			
3	To Solvent Cleaner Area	→	17						X			X					
4	On Floor Stack	D			30						Why?	X	X				
5	To Solvent Tanks And Spray	→	4			X			X								
6	Pressure Cleaned With Solvent	○				X											
7	To Dry Rack	→	6						X								
8	On Dry Rack	D															
9	To Paint Spray Area	→	28						X								
10	On Floor	D			15							X					
11	To Bench	→	2									X					
12	Determines Rust or Corrosion Checked (Rejects to Waste)	□				X	X	X	X		By Paint Spray Operator		X	X		X	
13	To Paint Spray	→	3														
14	Spray Inside of Housing	○				X			X	X	Both Utility Men Do Painting		X			X	X
15	To Truck Rack	→	6						X			X					
16	On Truck Rack	D			30							X					
17	4 Housings To Infra Drier	→	18						X			X					
18	Dry in Heater 1 Hour	○										X					
19	To Paint Spray	→	24						X			X					
20	On Floor	D			15							X					
21	To Spray Bench	→	2									X					
22	Spray Outside	○				X			X	X	Can Inside And Outside Be Painted At Same Time?		X			X	X
23	To Truck Rack	→	6														
24	On Truck Rack	D			30												
25	4 Housings To Infra Drier	→	18														
26	Dry In Heater 1 Hour	○															
27	To Assembly	→	20														
28	On Floor At Assembly	D			40							X					
29	Inspects Inside and Outside	□				X	X				Inspected By Mechanic		X	X			
30	To Assembly Bench	→	6									Rejects To Spray Booth						

346

FIGURE 11-15 Flow process chart (proposed method)

FLOW PROCESS CHART						Page No. 1	No. of Pages 1

Process: Refinish Charger Housings

☐ Man Or ☒ Material

Chart Begins	Chart Ends
Dismantling Rack	Assembly Bench

Charted By: D. Wilson	Date 18 Dec. 1984

Organization: Reconditioning
Light Equipment Shop

SUMMARY

ACTIONS	PRESENT No.	PRESENT Time	PROPOSED No.	PROPOSED Time	DIFFERENCE No.	DIFFERENCE Time
○ Operations	6		4		2	
→ Transportations	15		7		8	
☐ Inspections	2		2		0	
D Delays	7	190	2	60	5	130
▽ Storages	0		0		0	
Distance Travelled (Feet)	166		60		106	

DETAILS OF ☐ PRESENT / ☒ PROPOSED METHOD

#	Details	Symbols	DISTANCE IN FEET	QUANTITY	TIME	NOTES
1	From Dismantling To Rack	○ → ☐ D ▽	7			
2	Housing On Rack, At Solvent Tanks	○ → ☐ D ▽		30		
3	To Solvent Cleaner	○ → ☐ D ▽	4			
4	Pressure Cleaned With Solvent	○ → ☐ D ▽				
5	Determines Corrosion Checked	○ → ☐ D ▽				By Solvent Cleaner Operator
6	Transports To Dry Rack	○ → ☐ D ▽	6			Rejects To Waste Bin
7	On Dry Rack	○ → ☐ D ▽				
8	To Paint Spray	○ → ☐ D ▽	9			Lifts With New Painting Clamp
9	Sprays Inside And Outside	○ → ☐ D ▽				Holding With New Painting Clamp
10	To Truck Rack	○ → ☐ D ▽	6			
11	On Truck Rack	○ → ☐ D ▽		30		
12	4 Housings To Drying Heater	○ → ☐ D ▽	16			
13	Dry In Heater 1 Hour	○ → ☐ D ▽				On Truck Rack
14	Inspect On Truck	○ → ☐ D ▽				Rejects Back To Spray Booth
15	To Assembly Bench	○ → ☐ D ▽	12			

ANALYSIS WHY? — What? Where? When? Who? How?

ANALYSIS CHANGE — Eliminate, Combine, Sequence, Place, Person, Improve

- *Who is accomplishing each step? Is the right person handling it? Is it more logical to give it to someone else?*
- *How is the job being done? Can it be done better? If so, how?*

The development and analysis of flow diagrams can greatly assist a supervisor in planning and controlling work activities. The end results are usually better, more cost-effective, and more simplified ways of doing work. *In many organizations, if the supervisor does not analyze and improve operating processes and procedures there will be no simplification of work.* This is particularly true in the processing of paperwork involving overly complicated forms, unnecessary reports, and superfluous approvals. People tend to quickly establish paperwork requirements and then are quite reluctant to change or eliminate them. The result is an inefficient process that will continue unless the supervisor initiates work simplification action to change it.

FLOW PROCESS AND LAYOUT FLOW GO TOGETHER

- *LAYOUT FLOW ANALYSIS*—A layout flow chart is a scale drawing of the physical area or areas in which the flow of work shown on the flow process chart takes place. Complete work flow analysis is usually not possible until a floor layout flow chart is constructed to show *how* the work flows within the workplace. The flow process chart, for example, only shows the straight line flow of work from the top to bottom of the chart. It does not show how the flow of work may backtrack, cross itself, or move from area to area or from floor to floor. The process flow analysis of the NFP Company, mentioned at the beginning of the chapter, would not show the movement of product from the first floor, to the second floor, to the first floor, to the second floor, and finally back to the Filling, Packing, and Shipping Department on the first floor.

Figure 11-16 shows the layout of the work process reflected in Figure 11-15. Note that the same items are shown on both charts. The layout flow chart shows the locations of machines, equipment, and service areas as well as the actual distances between operations and storage areas. After the layout flow chart is completed, both it and the flow process chart should be analyzed together. The analysis should address the same questions of what, why, where, when, who, and how that were discussed with reference to the flow process chart.

Figure 11-17 shows how flow process and layout flow analyses can result in work simplification. Both flow process and layout charting should not be "one-shot" operations that are forgotten as soon as they are used. Keep the charts that have been prepared, and use them for future improvements as time, products, or other factors in the workplace change.

FIGURE 11-16 Layout flow chart

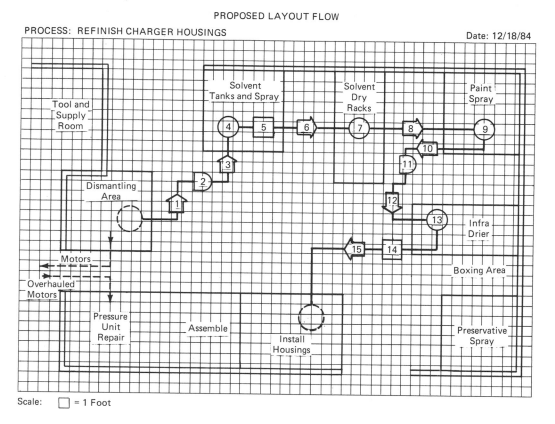

PROPOSED LAYOUT FLOW

PROCESS: REFINISH CHARGER HOUSINGS   Date: 12/18/84

Scale: ☐ = 1 Foot

ANALYZING WORK METHODS

• *OPERATIONS ANALYSIS*—The results of analyzing the work flow process
and the layout may indicate the need for a more detailed operations analysis.
The operations analysis involves a thorough breakdown of a work operation
into left-hand and right-hand actions and other specific motions of the worker
doing the job. The purpose of operations analysis, or motion study, is to find
the most efficient methods of doing work. The analytical observations in process and layout flow analyses give attention to the total work process. Operations analysis focuses on work simplification that involves the *best work methods* for the operator. This type of analysis can be very significant in arriving at
decisions to eliminate, combine, rearrange, or simplify actual work operations.

The techniques of performing an operations analysis are very similar to
those of a process flow analysis. Usually a form with standard symbols is used to
record the movements of the left and right hands and the times required for

FIGURE 11-17   Results of flow process and layout flow analyses

each hand action. The hand movements are identified by the basic motion elements of search, find, select, grasp, position, assemble, use, dissemble, inspect, transport loaded (moving a hand or the body with a load), pre-position, release load, transport empty (moving a hand or the body without a load), wait—unavoidable, wait—avoidable, rest—necessary for overcoming fatigue, and plan.

SELECTION OF JOBS FOR OPERATIONS ANALYSIS

The jobs selected for operations analysis should be those that appear, from the work process analysis, to be most in need of improvement. Pick jobs that seem to involve too much time, improper use of the worker's skills, too much effort, or too much waste. Operations selected should be those where you have already settled the overall questions of elimination, combination, or rearrangement of work activities. It is also important to select operations that are feasible and practical for an operations study. For example, don't pick jobs where the hand movements are faster than the eye, or ones that require mostly machine operations.

FIGURE 11-18 Operations analysis

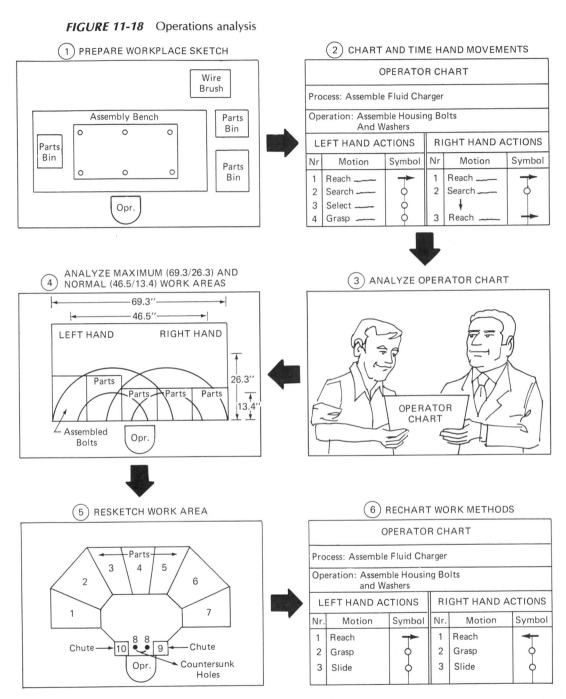

SIX STEPS

As illustrated in Figure 11-18, six steps are involved in an operations analysis:

1. Prepare a sketch to the scale of the workplace.
2. Record and time the movements of each hand on an operations chart, using standard motion symbols.
3. Analyze the hand movements shown on the completed chart, particularly the transportation motions and delays.
4. Analyze maximum and normal work area measurements for performing the job.
5. Resketch the improved work layout.
6. Rechart the improved work method.

After coming up with an improved method of work, defer implementation until after completing an operator-machine utilization analysis and a work measurement analysis. These two analyses may bring about still more improvements in the work operations.

REDUCE IDLENESS

• *OPERATOR-MACHINE UTILIZATION ANALYSIS*—A process flow analysis identifies work activities involving the use of machines. One of the aspects of work simplification is to further analyze machine activities to determine the operator's activities in relation to the machine. The purpose of such analysis is to determine and reduce idle machine time and idle operator time (Figure 11-19). Seeking a better method of improving operator-machine functioning must come after proper work distribution, good process planning, and efficient work layout. Overall machine utilization must be well supervised before time is spent refining operator-machine procedures. Maximum machine productivity and efficiency depend on all of the following:

• *Preventive maintenance of equipment*
• *Proper machine scheduling*
• *Proper materials and supplies scheduling*
• *Adequate training of operators*

The development and use of an operator-machine chart (Figure 11-19) can show the periods when the machine is idle while the operator loads it or removes finished work. It also shows the periods when the worker is idle while the machine is in operation. Analysis of the operator-machine chart can lead to improvement of methods in the workplace, particularly in the activities of getting ready and putting work away. Analysis can also lead to elimination of

FIGURE 11-19　Operator-machine chart

operator idleness time. It may be possible, for example, for the operator to do one of the following:

- *Perform an inspection while the machine is operating*
- *Perform another task while the machine is operating*
- *Operate several machines concurrently*

COUNT THE WORK

● *WORK MEASUREMENT ANALYSIS*—Work count shows how much has come in and how much has been accomplished (Figure 11-20). The benefits to be obtained from work measurement are

1. Balancing the volume of work and the number of workers
2. Determining the effect of volume of work on methods and procedures
3. Attaining realistic scheduling and routing of work tasks to workers and machines
4. Disclosing unusual ratios of errors and rejects
5. Highlighting workers who need help or training
6. Establishing a basis for developing standards of performance
7. Locating trouble spots needing analysis
8. Stimulating competition among workers
9. Providing the basis for work incentive plans

Work measurement does not report the quality of the work performed. Neither does it report the difficulties, obstacles, handicaps, methods, or resources utilized. It gives facts on results that can be used to examine and/or provide answers about work distribution, work flow process, layout flow, operations analysis, and operator-machine utilization. An analysis of work measurement data can help answer such questions as

● *Where are the bottlenecks?*
● *Where are the peaks and valleys in the production process?*
● *Is the volume of work sufficient to justify the number of workers?*
● *Does the volume of work support the use of the equipment?*
● *How much can be produced by changing the work methods?*
● *How many workers need to be assigned to the job?*

FIGURE 11-20 Work count

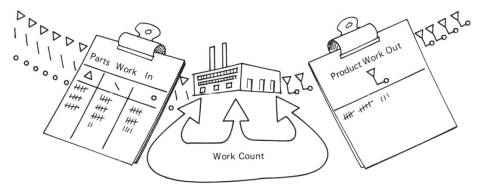

COUNT THE RIGHT THINGS

It is very important in work measurement to *count the right things*. The key to counting work is the selection of the proper work units that will show the real end results of productive effort. One should try to choose units that represent finished parts, end items, "do" work operations, line items, or materials used that are capable of being physically counted. Don't try to count everything. Focus on the significant end results of the productive effort.

Maximum productivity is usually encouraged when a worker is given (1) a definite task to do, (2) a standard prescribed method of doing it, and (3) a specific amount of time in which to do it. There are many ways to determine how much work an individual should be able to accomplish in a specific amount of time. One way is by time study with the use of a stop watch plus allowances for delays and rest periods. A second way is to collect work performance data and establish statistical standards from this data.

REGRESSION ANALYSIS

A third method of determining how much time a given job should take is through the use of regression analysis. This involves establishing the mathematical correlation between two or more key variables in the job. For example, if it takes x amount of time to make a batch of stainless steel with a 15-ton electric furnace, "$x + 5$" amount of time with a 20-ton electric furnace, and "$x + 10$" amount of time with a 25-ton electric furnace, it will probably take "$x + 15$" amount of time with a 30-ton electric furnace.

WORK SAMPLING

A fourth method of determining how much work an individual should be able to accomplish in a given amount of time is by work sampling. This involves random observations of work activities to determine the percent of time spent in setting up, operation, maintenance, and delays. It enables a supervisor to get facts without watching everything and everybody all the time. The key to the accuracy of work sampling is the number of observations. The principle involved in work sampling is that the average time reflected in the random observations, tends to equal the exact average time that would be found by continous observations.

Of these four methods of work measurement, work sampling requires the least amount of training—much less than the other methods, which should be carried out by qualified time study personnel, statisticians, or mathematicians. With a minimum amount of training, most supervisors can put work sampling to work for them.

WORK SIMPLIFICATION REQUIRES COMMON SENSE

• *SELLING WORK SIMPLIFICATION*—Each work simplification technique satisfies a particular management need. These tools should be used, *where appropriate*, to produce specific improvements in work and productivity. In many situations, all six techniques are necessary for a complete analysis and simplification of the work situation. When properly used, work simplification techniques can lead the way to the development of improved work distribution, better methods and procedures, more efficient layout, and effective utilization of both workers and machines.

Even though management of methods and procedures almost always pays for itself, it must be "sold" to the workers. Don't try to do too much, too fast, and without warning to the workers. New methods and procedures can lead to resentment, discord, and open antagonism if not handled properly. The supervisor, therefore, must obtain the willingness, cooperation, and interest of each employee involved in the development and implementation of work simplification.

In the case of the NFP Company discussed at the beginning of the chapter, there were several areas where improvements appeared to be feasible in the process and layout flow of work. For example, in the warehouse and materials handling work areas, there were many indicators that management could establish production standards and a financial incentive plan. These potential improvements could result in employees working smarter, not harder, and increasing their wages in the process. However, any changes involving work simplification should be developed on a participative basis involving management, the workers, and, in the case of the NFP Company, the union.

HONEST DISCLOSURE

To successfully implement any aspect of work simplification, there must be complete and honest disclosure of *what* is being done, *why* it is being done, and *how* the workers will benefit when it is done. *Work simplification, regardless of how significant the potential benefits, must be "sold" to the workers* to obtain their supportive suggestions and their willing cooperation.

HUMAN FACTORS ENGINEERING

EQUIPMENT DESIGN VERSUS HUMAN NEEDS

Human factors engineering considers the very important human needs of the individual worker in the handling of tools and equipment. It concerns the important link between the design and operation of tools and equipment and the ability, accomplishments, and satisfaction of the person who must operate and maintain them. Human factors engineering results in the design and operation of technological processes that increase the effectiveness and achievement of both machines and human resources in work productivity.

The primary focus in human factors engineering is to bring about compatibility between the capabilities and limitations of both people and machines. To achieve this compatibility involves analyzing the technological, sociological, and psychological factors of work and productivity. All three of these factors must be considered to achieve compatibility between people and machines in the accomplishment of work objectives.

NEW DEMANDS ON WORKERS

We have seen major accomplishments in such new technological developments as aerospace systems, nuclear power plants, word processing centers, post office operations, computerized accounting, communication systems, and computerized steel making. The advent of automation, computerization, and microminiaturization have made human factors engineering a very significant element in the supervision of work and productivity. It has created new functions for workers in the form of monitoring, operating, maintaining, and controlling technically complex machines. These functions have placed new demands on workers. *Human factors engineering focuses attention on the fact that no machine presently conceived has all the attributes and properties that the human being possesses.*

Supervision of work and productivity involves knowing the importance of using technology so that the best features of workers and machines are employed in the most effective manner. In the management of personnel the whole person should be employed on the job. A partially employed worker can become a bored and dissatisfied person who is not motivated to do good work.

SUPERVISOR RESPONSIBILITIES

Sometimes the engineer who designs new equipment does not see its full impact on the human beings who must work with it. The supervisor, who must work with both machines and people, is often in the best position to advise the design engineer on human factors engineering. In the supervision of work and productivity there must be an effective balance between people and machines. Such a balance is an important factor in achieving increased quantity and quality of work output, reduced operational costs, safety, and worker satisfaction. *Obtaining increased worker productivity is a management problem, and its resolution rests, to a considerable extent, with the first-level supervisor.* If the production system has basic problems, it is the fault of management not the worker.

SUMMARY

SUPERVISION OF WORK
AND PRODUCTIVITY IS A BIG JOB

Production efficiency depends on many variables and the supervision of many things. The production of anything means obtaining work output by bringing interrelated parts of an undertaking into a state of effective (the right kind of) order. These interrelated parts of the production process include product and process design, planning and organizing, work methods and procedures, staffing and training of workers, balanced use of production facilities and workers, maintenance of facilities, and good worker relations.

It is the supervisor's job to see that people and things are moving smoothly. To accomplish this, the supervisor must be both forward-looking and backward-looking. The supervisor holds a key management position in the achievement of productivity from workers and machines. Careful attention must be given to (1) organizational management, (2) personnel management, (3) equipment and materials management, and (4) methods and procedures management.

A supervisor has varying degrees of responsibility for work layout, equipment utilization, materials handling, and maintenance. The individual who can critically analyze work operations and apply work simplification techniques will become more effective and efficient in the performance of any job. To perform such analysis, the supervisor should have a basic knowledge of the following work simplification techniques:

- *Work distribution analysis*
- *Process flow analysis*
- *Layout flow analysis*
- *Operations analysis*
- *Operator-machine utilization analysis*
- *Work measurement analysis*

Having a knowledge of these techniques does not mean that the supervisor must be an expert in work simplification. It means that in a small organization the work simplification task may fall entirely on the supervisor. In a large organization the supervisor should know the importance of cooperating with the experts in work simplification.

In this age of technological development, the supervisor is often in the best position to help bring about the proper linkage between people and machines that is involved in human factors engineering. Supervision of work and productivity is a big job that requires giving balanced attention to many things.

REVIEW QUESTIONS

1. In what ways must a supervisor's involvement with productivity be both forward-looking and backward-looking?

2. What are the four basic elements involved in the achievement of productivity?

3. If you were responsible for developing a layout plan for a large office, what are some of the guidelines that you would follow?

4. Assume you are a supervisor in a company where funding limitations prevent the purchasing of new equipment in your department. What actions can you take to maximize the use of the existing equipment?

5. What are the benefits of good materials management?

6. If you were a supervisor in a manufacturing department, what are some of the preventive maintenance activities that you would perform?

7. Why is the manager's attitude important in work simplification?

8. Describe one work measurement technique that a supervisor can use.

9. There are problems in the office where you work regarding the central reproduction (copier) machine. Because of these problems—one of which is the waiting time to use the machine—several individuals want to have reproduction equipment in their own work area. How would you handle this problem?

10. Can a supervisor really make a contribution in human factors engineering? How?

THE CASE OF HELEN SMITH

Helen Smith is an office supervisor with FAAS, a large government agency. The agency's mission is to provide certain public services that benefit a large segment of the population. A new government administration recently approved a significant expansion in the implementation of one of the major programs administered by FAAS. This decision will cause a sizeable increase in the workload in Smith's office for at least the next eighteen months.

The government currently has a large funding deficit which, by its own regulations, is illegal. To correct the situation, the government has directed (a) a freeze on hiring new employees, and (b) a restriction on contracting out any "in-house" agency work to commercial business establishments. These restrictions are expected to remain in effect for an extended period of time.

Smith has a total normal work force of fifty employees. The expanded program workload will require approximately eight additonal employees in Smith's office. Because of this 16 percent increase in workload, Smith requested an exception to the restriction on hiring new employees. Her request for eight employees was denied. She then requested that some of her workload be contracted to an outside commercial establishment. This request was also turned down.

QUESTIONS

1. What should Smith do now?
2. Why is overtime *not* the solution? Why is dumping the additional workload on the current workforce *not* the solution?
3. After exhausting these nonviable solutions, Smith sat down and developed a detailed work simplification plan that she felt could solve her problem. If you were Smith, what kind of a plan would you develop?
4. How would you implement it?

12

Supervision of Money Resources

THE SUPERVISOR'S INVOLVEMENT IN FINANCIAL MANAGEMENT

Far too many supervisors fail to realize that they are also financial managers. Whether they are part of a profit-making organization, a non-profit institution, or a government department, they regard the budget-making process as a bore and as something imposed on them by an unknowledgeable bureaucrat. They do not see it as a means of getting the most productivity from a very expensive resource—money—as well as an extremely valuable planning mechanism. Mastering the process is a basic skill for anyone who wishes to become a manager, no matter what kind of an organization is involved.

Money is expensive, and even if an organization generates sufficient cash to support its own operations and does not have to borrow, there are always alternative uses for money. It can be rented out, even overnight, to help optimize the return on capital.

To do a good job in budgeting operations, whether for a small division or a whole company, the first essential is a clear understanding of the goals to be achieved during the fiscal year or whatever period is under review. Seldom is there only one way of achieving a goal. All the alternatives should be analyzed. Furthermore, no budget should be created in isolation. Each alternative should be studied for its impact on the rest of the organization and on the environment in which the institution is operating. Good budgeting is a challenge which requires careful planning and scheduling.

Once adopted, a budget cannot be set aside and forgotten until the next time around. Actual receipts and expenditures must be monitored to be sure that they are conforming to plan, and if not, why not. Integration of the form and content of the budget with accounting records provides regular feedback to management who then may be expected to manage better. The experiences of one cycle should be incorporated into the next to refine and improve the process. The budget is a blueprint for action.

Wherever you find an organization that is running smoothly year after year and meeting its goals, you will find good supervision of money resources.

> Madeline McWhinney Dale
> Assistant Director, Operations
> Whitney Museum of American Art
> New York, New York

LEARNING OBJECTIVES

The objectives of this chapter on the supervision of money resources are to enable the reader to

1. Relate how money management is important to all types of organizations and all levels of management

2. Establish the supervisor's responsibilities for controlling labor costs, reducing costs through value analysis, and maintaining effective budget management

3. Understand the following budgetary aspects of supervisory management:
    a. Factors to consider in arriving at capital investment decisions
    b. Steps to follow in developing an operating budget
    c. Methods of developing and managing an operating expense budget
    d. Development and use of manpower budgets, flexible budgets, and contingency budgets
    e. Use of quantitative data in the management of budget requirements

4. Identify the phases of financial management that involve most supervisors

KEY WORDS

Capital Expense Budget   A budget which plans the money resources required for purchase or construction of buildings and structures, major additions or revisions to existing buildings and structures, and/or purchase of major nonexpendable tools and equipment that are expected to be used for several years.

Cash Flow   The pattern of outflow and inflow of money resources.

Contingency Budgeting   Planning money resources for the possibility that something may go wrong with the initial budget estimates.

Correlation Analysis   The determination of how the behavior of one thing affects the behavior of something else.

Dependent Variable   An item with an unknown value.

Depreciation   Amortizing the costs of a major capital investment over its expected years of use.

Flexible Budgeting   Planning the money resources needed for various levels of workload.

Independent Variable   An item with a known value.

Manpower Budgeting   Planning the number of personnel required by an organization to perform its workload.

Operating Expense Budget   A plan of the money resources needed by an organization to perform its workload.

Payback   The length of time required for the earnings or cost savings from a capital investment to pay for itself.

Program Budget   A plan of the money resources needed to accomplish specific objectives and identifiable work outputs.

Time Value of Money   The future money value of a dollar invested today and allowed to accumulate interest at a given percent for a stated number of years.

Value Analysis   The process of looking for ways to reduce the costs, but not the quality and value, of a product or service by using less-costly materials and parts.

Zero-Base Budgeting   A planning, programming, and budgeting process which requires each manager to justify an entire budget in detail from scratch and to explain why any money should be spent at all.

A CASE OF "PENNY-WISE AND DOLLAR-FOOLISH"

Humanitarian Services, Inc. (HSI) is a nonprofit corporation engaged in a variety of community services designed to improve the welfare of humanity. HSI has a full-time paid professional staff as well as many volunteer workers who gratuitously give of their time and effort. Top-level decisions are made by a Board of Trustees who receive no salaries. They approve the educational, social, recreational, and health programs that HSI provides to the community.

BUDGETING BY ELEMENTS OF EXPENSE

The management of money resources is the Board of Trustees' biggest responsibility. Planning and control of money resources is accomplished through an annual budget and monthly reviews. Prior to the start of each fiscal year, the HSI professional staff prepares a proposed budget of planned income and expenses for the approval of the Board. The expense portion of the budget identifies the various amounts required for salaries, supplies, equipment, rental of buildings and equipment, maintenance of facilities, utilities, travel, telephones, insurance, cleaning services, and other elements of expense. These expense are *not* identified as to how much is spent on each of HSI's programs. The revenue portion of the budget shows expected income from county and state funding, contributions from the general public, and fees charged for certain HSI programs. Income is also *not* identified as to how much money comes in to each of HSI's programs.

MISCONCEPTIONS ABOUT BUDGETING

HSI's Board of Trustees has problems in managing the budget. Because the structure of the budget only provides information by elements of expense, the Board has no knowledge of what the various HSI programs cost in relation to the benefits derived. Another problem is caused by the adamant position of some Board members that actual expenditures for each and every line item in the budget should *never* exceed budgeted expenses. This unyielding attitude prevails even when the expenditures for some line items are below the budgeted amounts. At last month's Board meeting, for example, the agency manager pointed out the need to replace a photocopying machine that was frequently breaking down and disrupting work efforts. Repair of the equipment was not considered cost-effective because of its age and operating condition. The estimated cost of repair would also exceed the amount in the budget line item for equipment maintenance. Even though budget dollars could have been transferred from other line items to purchase a new photocopying machine, the Board deferred action on the matter.

As you read about this situation at HSI, what is your reaction? How does your own concept of managing money resources agree or disagree with that of the HSI Board of Trustees? As you read the remainder of this chapter, identify those things you feel might help HSI's Board of Trustees in its management of money resources.

THE IMPORTANCE OF MONEY MANAGEMENT

MONEY IS A LIMITED RESOURCE

Any organization—industrial, commercial, government, or nonprofit—must make effective use of its money resources. It is a rare situation where there is enough money to do all the things that are desired or needed. It is also very easy to waste money and end up without enough resources to do things that are necessary.

One of the most important actions in effective management is good financial forecasting and budgeting. The need for good money management is increasingly apparent in industry, government, and nonprofit institutions. All organizations must learn how to operate and accomplish their objectives by applying proper allocation of resources. In the industrial and commercial world there are problems of decreasing profits, spiraling costs, and pressures to reduce prices. At all levels of government, there is increasing pressure to avoid deficit financing, to reduce spending and taxes, and to eliminate services that are not cost-effective. In religious, educational, health, community service, and other nonprofit organizations, there are pressures caused by reduced sources of income and increased costs of operation.

BETTER FORECASTING MEANS GREATER FLEXIBILITY

The management of money resources is important to all types of organizations and to all levels of management. No organization and no manager can afford expensive wastefulness. Budgetary planning, by forcing all levels of management to think ahead, gives an organization flexibility. The more an organization is able to forecast its future needs for money, the greater is its ability to find sources of funding. The effectiveness of the organization's decisions regarding money requirements depends upon the accuracy and flexibility of its budgeting.

Money management enables an industrial or commercial organization to plan for and keep a close tab on profits. In a government organization, money management enables the managers to plan for and provide maximum services at a minimum expenditure of the taxpayers' money. Money management in nonprofit organizations enables the managers to plan for and accomplish their missions within money resource limitations.

THE SUPERVISOR'S RESPONSIBILITY FOR MONEY MANAGEMENT

PATROLLING OF COSTS

A supervisor is responsible for planning, organizing, directing, and controlling the work of others. The manner in which the supervisor executes these management functions has considerable influence on the expenditure of money resources. Supervisors, therefore, must accept the patrolling of costs as one of their continuing responsibilities.

DETERMINING SUPERVISOR EFFECTIVENESS

Many organizations use cost control as one of the measurement criteria for determining the supervisor's effectiveness. For example:

- *Were schedules met without incurring overtime?*
- *Were the resources of workers, materials, and equipment efficiently and fully utilized without costly waste?*

- *Did productivity increase? Did costs (after allowances for cost escalation) decrease?*
- *Were labor costs adequately controlled?*
- *Were labor turnover costs kept at an acceptable level?*
- *Was quality of work maintained while costs of waste were reduced?*
- *Were expenditures within approved budget limitations?*

Supervisors can influence the level of costs in their departments. Through such practices as work simplification (see Chapter 11), a supervisor can reduce direct labor and material costs. By prudent management, supervisors can contribute to lowering the costs of such overhead items as supplies, travel, postage, equipment rental or purchase, maintenance, and transportation.

Labor Costs Can Be Reduced

- *CONTROLLING LABOR COSTS*—A significant area in money management is the control of labor costs. This is particularly important in office and service operations where labor can account for 85 percent to 90 percent of the total costs. Four areas in which a supervisor can reduce labor costs are (1) not employing more workers than necessary to do the work, (2) keeping labor turnover at a minimum, (3) training workers to become more proficient in performance of their jobs, and (4) avoiding waste.

If a supervisor has ten workers employed at a minimum hourly wage of $3.35, the total labor costs are in excess of $100,000 a year. These costs include

- *Basic hourly wages*
- *Fringe benefits such as vacations, holidays, retirement, and various types of protective insurance*
- *Depreciation on equipment used on the job*
- *Training to the point where worker output is at an acceptable level*

Because of these costs, a supervisor should strive to keep the number of workers at the lowest possible level consistent with workload requirements. This can be accomplished through good planning and work simplification practices.

Labor Turnover Is Costly

Labor turnover can be very costly because of the time and money involved in training replacement workers. Figure 12-1 shows the economic costs of an employee earning $10,000 a year, working on a job that requires approximately a full year of on-the-job training before full productivity is reached. During the first few months on the job, the new employee is primarily engaged in learning to do the job. Even though the employee is receiving full pay, productive output is low. As a matter of fact, in the early months of employment, the employee's productive output may be at or near zero. When the first year of em-

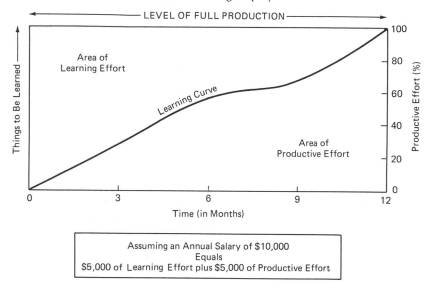

FIGURE 12-1 Economic costs of training employees

ployment on the job is averaged out, approximately $5,000 of the employee's wages may have resulted in no appreciable productive output. Keeping employee turnover at a low rate obviously saves money for the organization.

DEVELOP A COST-CONSCIOUS ATTITUDE

Another important way a supervisor can reduce labor costs is through the avoidance of waste. Skilled supervisors can see where wastefulness exists. The supervisor's attitude regarding cost-consciousness and the issuance of intelligent guidance on costs to subordinates are key elements in keeping labor costs down. Labor cost control starts with a supervisor's positive attitude that work simplification results in cost savings. The smart supervisor conveys this positive attitude to subordinates by

1. Setting the pace with specific attainable goals
2. Selling the workers on how the goals benefit them
3. Getting the workers involved in setting the goals
4. Following up on accomplishments
5. Giving credit to the achievers

A basic rule to follow in cost reduction is to make it an employees' program. When the workers are given an opportunity to participate in setting goals, they tend to set and accept higher targets than the supervisor might have set.

USING LESS-COSTLY THINGS

• *VALUE ANALYSIS: ANALYZE BEFORE TAKING ACTION*—It is easy to waste money on unnecessary "gold plating." The supervisor, therefore, should look for areas where less costly materials and parts can be used just as effectively as more costly ones. Value analysis (sometimes called value engineering) involves changing specifications, manufacturing practices, operating procedures, quality control standards, and expensive components to reduce costs and still maintain the quality and value of the product or service. By using less-rigid purchasing specifications, less-sophisticated packaging, and more-flexible tolerances and by increasing the number of units per package and reducing wastage of expensive materials costs can often be reduced *without* any loss of effectiveness. A careful value analysis should be conducted regarding products or services to include pertinent facts related to both costs and benefits. If the analysis shows that a reduction in costs will result in significant loss in product effectiveness, no changes should be made. On the other hand, if the analysis shows that changing to less costly methods will not decrease effectiveness, the changes should be made.

BUDGET RESPONSIBILITY CENTERS

• *BUDGET MANAGEMENT*—One of the practical and most used means of controlling costs is the budget. Budgets are commonly used as a means of control by designating organizations according to the type of responsibility center they fall under. As shown in Figure 12-2, the three most common types of budgetary responsibility centers are (1) Revenue Centers, (2) Expense Centers, and (3) Profit Centers.

REVENUE CENTERS

The *Revenue Centers* are responsible for the control of their *output*—that is, the income (revenue) they generate. The Sales Department (a Revenue Center), for example, has a sales budget that is expected to generate a certain amount of income. If the sales output falls significantly below the sales budget, there can be major impacts on production, inventory management, transportation, and other operations. Revenue Centers are usually held accountable for controlling their own internal operating costs. They, therefore, are also controlled as an Expense Center.

EXPENSE CENTERS

The *Expense Centers* are responsible for the control of their own *inputs* or expenditures. Departments such as security, maintenance, legal, and personnel in an industrial or commercial establishment do not normally generate revenues. They do, however, incur expenses. The input of labor, materials, and oth-

FIGURE 12-2 Budget responsibility centers

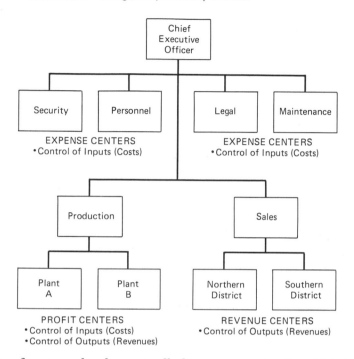

er elements of cost need to be controlled in any organization. This is commonly done by establishing an approved operating expenditures budget and controlling the inputs of costs by the Expense Center.

PROFIT CENTERS

The *Profit Centers* are responsible for both generating *revenues* and controlling the *expenditures* related to those revenues so that the Center makes a profit on its operations. The Profit Center is particularly found in large retail department stores and manufacturing plants. *Outputs* (revenues) are measured against *inputs* (costs) to determine if the operation or department is or is not profitable. The failure of a plant or department to operate at a profitable level may result in its discontinuance.

Supervisors should be familiar with the controls imposed by budgets that apply to their department because they are usually the ones held responsible for their implementation.

NOT NECESSARY TO BE A FINANCIAL GENIUS

Most supervisors do not look forward to preparing and presenting a budget of their operations. The primary reason for this is that they feel deficient in their knowledge of financial management. Supervisors who feel this way should change their attitudes because they do *not* have to be financial geniuses to develop and manage a budget. The essential ingredients for effective budgeting are: (1) obtaining and objectively analyzing facts, (2) using common sense, and (3) thinking things through. In the case of HSI at the beginning of this chapter, the Board of Trustees didn't do a good job in using any of these ingredients.

Managers at all levels should be involved in the budget process. This is a continuous process, not a one-shot action. Good budget management is the key to holding down increasing costs and finding ways to reduce costs. All managers, therefore, need to develop a positive attitude regarding the values to be gained from good budgeting.

• *A SUPERVISOR'S APPROACH TO INTELLIGENT BUDGETING*—A budget should be viewed as the reflection of *intention*—the intention to accomplish certain specific things within an estimated amount of resources. The budget, therefore, should be looked at as the challenge and opportunity to get things done within dollar limitations. A well-developed budget serves as a financial operating guide. It provides the supervisor with a measure of expected future results from proposed operational plans. It also provides a means of measuring and controlling the utilization of financial resources.

STEPS IN BUDGET DEVELOPMENT

Assuming that the current fiscal year still has three months remaining, how can a supervisor go about developing a budget for the next year, which is usually referred to as the budget year? The following ten steps show one way to develop a budget.

1. Obtain current year-to-date budget data, actual cost data, and past experience data.
2. Using step 1 as a computation base, estimate costs expected to be incurred for the remainder of the fiscal year.
3. Add the amounts arrived at in steps 1 and 2 to establish expected total costs for the entire current fiscal year.
4. Compare step 3 with the current fiscal year budget and analyze significant variances. Keep in mind that actual cost results will rarely match the budgeted costs exactly. Variances of plus or minus 1 percent to 5 percent are usually considered normal.
5. Identify any unusual events that occurred during the current fiscal year that had a significant effect on costs.
6. Analyze the objectives planned for the next budget year—both those that have come down from above and your own.
7. Determine and analyze the potential cost impact of any significant changes in objectives between the current fiscal year and the upcoming year.
8. Analyze, where appropriate, pertinent economic (including inflation), political, international, governmental, and financial factors that can have an impact on budget year costs.
9. Analyze, where appropriate, the potential cost impacts of competition, new missions, new policies, internal factors, and probable problems on budget year costs.

10. Using step 3 as the base point, develop the estimated costs for the budget year by applying, where appropriate, the information obtained in steps 4 thru 9.

In analyzing a current year budget and preparing a new budget, look for and make use of trend data. As previously mentioned, variances of plus or minus 1 percent to 5 percent between budget and actual costs are normal. However, if the trend on a given budget line item is consistently over or under month after month, there is probably something wrong that should be investigated.

TYPES OF BUDGETS

Most supervisors have some responsibilities in the development of the following two types of budgets:

- *Capital expense budget*
- *Operating expense budget*

These responsibilities, and the different methods by which budgets can be developed and managed will be discussed in the paragraphs that follow.

CAPITAL EXPENSE BUDGET

The capital expense budget involves planning for the purchase or construction of buildings and structures, major additions or revisions to existing buildings and structures, and purchase of nonexpendable tools and equipment that are expected to be used for several years. The determination of what tools and equipment are nonexpendable will vary with the passage of time, the policies of the company, and changes in Internal Revenue Service rules. For example, as inflation causes the costs of tools and equipment to increase, the cost threshold of items considered to be nonexpendable will also tend to increase. This means that certain low-value items once considered as nonexpendable become classified as expendable.

MAKING CAPITAL INVESTMENT DECISIONS

Budgeting for major capital expenses involves making crucial decisions. These decisions can commit financial resources over an extended period of time and thereby have a significant effect on long-range operations. In making capital investment decisions, managers should try to answer the following questions:

- *Should old facilities and/or equipment be replaced? If so, when and how?*
- *Should facilities and/or equipment be purchased or leased?*

- *How long will it take for new facilities and/or equipment to pay back the investment?*
- *Which is more cost-effective: expensive automated equipment with lower labor costs or less expensive manually operated equipment with higher labor costs?*
- *Should equipment be purchased for in-house work or would it be less costly to contract for the work with an outside organization?*
- *What type of equipment can best perform a certain operation?*
- *How much operating capacity is enough?*
- *What are the risks of replacing equipment versus not replacing it? Expanding facilities versus not expanding?*
- *What are the trade-offs in initial investment costs versus the expected reduction in operation and maintenance costs?*
- *What are the trade-offs in investment costs versus higher quality of work output and/or increased productivity?*
- *What are the comparative alternatives in facility and/or equipment investments?*
- *What are the possible interactions between different types of equipment in the total operating system?*
- *What is the outlook in future technology, operating changes, and obsolescence?*

CAPITAL INVESTMENTS SHOULD BE COST-EFFECTIVE

Operating managers, down to and including first-level supervisors, have an important role to play in capital investment decisions. These are the people who must get the work done. They are often the ones who initiate many of the proposals for altering facilities and purchasing equipment. Operating managers should be capable of evaluating existing facilities and equipment and proposing cost-effective changes. Proposals for expanding facilities and purchasing expensive tools and equipment should be based on economically sound facts. Evaluation should include looking at the comparative costs versus the benefits of alternative investment proposals.

Capital investment decisions are usually a mixture of technical, engineering, and economic factors. In manufacturing operations, environmental factors must be added to the list of elements that must be considered in making capital investment decisions. Managers involved in capital investment decisions should have a planned approach to the purchase of facilities and/or equipment. In the replacement or addition of equipment, for example, it is very easy to be pressured into buying things that are either not needed or are not cost-effective. Walk through almost any plant or office, and you will see a considerable amount of expensive equipment that is not being fully utilized. With the current rapid technological changes, many organizations have made the mistake of purchasing computer, word processing, communication, and other equipment with greater than necessary capacities. These situations reflect in-effective supervision of money resources.

Budgeting for capital expenditures is the most difficult and complex area of financial management for operating managers. In making capital expenditure decisions it is usually a good general rule to seek the guidance and assistance of personnel who are experts in such fields as accounting, cost analysis, and economic analysis. The average operating manager often has problems when it comes to evaluating capital investment alternatives in such terms as cash flow, depreciation, taxation, payback, rate of return on investment, time value of money, and risk.

FACTORS IN CAPITAL INVESTMENT DECISIONS

It is not the intention of this book to fully discuss the many financial management considerations involved in making capital investment decisions. However, operating managers need at least a cursory knowledge of the following factors that can be involved in a capital investment:

1. Cash flow
2. Depreciation
3. Impact of taxes
4. Payback
5. Time value of money
6. Rate of return on investment

• *CASH FLOW*—Cash flow in a capital investment refers to: (1) projected outflow of money resources for the initial investment plus the annual operation and maintenance costs, in comparison with (2) projected inflow of money resources through savings in operational costs. A cash flow chart shows the cash outflow and inflow involved in a capital investment. In the example shown in Figure 12-3, the initial capital investment is expected to be $150,000 and the annual operating costs (direct labor and operation-related indirect costs) are estimated to be $55,000. Current annual operating costs are $100,000. The investment, therefore, is expected to save $45,000 a year. The chart in Figure 12-3 shows the $150,000 initial investment as a cash outflow. Since the investment is expected to save operating costs, there is an annual cash inflow shown in the amount of $45,000. The chart shows this as inflow because the proposed investment, in reducing operating costs, has the same effect on profits as an increase in revenues. The chart also shows as cash inflow the expected terminal salvage value of the investment after an anticipated life of six years.

• *DEPRECIATION*—It is normal accounting practice to spread the costs of a major capital investment over its expected life. The process of amortizing the costs of a capital investment over its expected years of use is called deprecia-

FIGURE 12-3   Capital investment cash flow

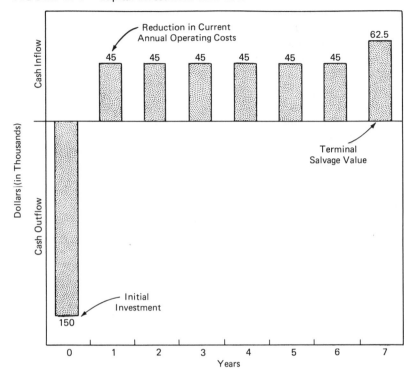

tion. The most common method is the straight-line annual depreciation which is determined by the following equation:

$$d = \frac{i - s}{n}$$

Where:
   d = annual depreciation costs
   i = investment costs
   s = terminal salvage value
   n = estimated number of years of use

Depreciation costs represent a decline in the value of items with the passage of time. Depreciation costs continue regardless of the utilization of the item. Just like any other costs, the annual depreciation on a capital investment is a factor in the computation of profits and is reflected in the taxes paid on those profits.

● *IMPACT OF TAXES*—In an economy where income taxes are levied at high rates, the impact of such taxes can be an influencing factor in capital investment decisions. For example, take the savings in operating costs reflected in the cash flow chart in Figure 12-3. As mentioned above, if the proposed investment reduces operating costs, it has the same effect on profits as an increase in revenues. Any increases in profits resulting from the capital investment are taxable. Since the increase in profits cause the total taxable income to move into a higher tax bracket, the expenses for taxes will probably be higher. It is usually a good practice to calculate the extra taxes which may be incurred and reflect these in the expected cash outflow. In most capital investment studies, taxable income will usually be the before-tax income less an allowance for depreciation.

• *PAYBACK*—Payback is the length of time required for the earnings or cost savings from a capital investment to pay for the cost of the investment. It is determined by the following equation:

$$p = \frac{i}{e}$$

Where:
p = payback
i = investment cost ($150,000)
e = annual earnings or cost savings ($45,000)
$$p = \frac{150,000}{45,000} = 3\frac{1}{3} \text{ years}$$

The above computation of payback is very misleading because it is only based on annual savings in operating costs. It does *NOT* reflect the loss of income from interest that could have been earned *if* the money had been invested in interest-bearing investments instead of facilities or equipment. The above computation also does not reflect the loss of income due to the increased taxes that may have to be paid as a result of an increase in taxable income caused by the savings. Under these circumstances, a more accurate computation of payback would be:

$$p = \frac{i}{e - t}$$

Where:
p = payback after taxes
i = investment costs
e = annual earnings or cost savings
t = taxes on savings

• *TIME VALUE OF MONEY*—Money has time value as indicated by the fact that people pay to use it. The person who needs to borrow money must usually pay interest to the lender for the use of his or her money. The lender of money usually charges interest to the people who use it. The interest charged on the use of money means that a dollar on hand today is worth more than a dollar to be received at a future date. The value of money compounds itself with time.

The following is an example of how the value of money increases with time. The example uses the data from Figure 12-3 in the discussion of cash flow.

$$fm = cm(1 + i)^t$$

Where:
  fm = future value of money
  cm = current value of money ($150,000 investment)
  1 = one year
  i = interest rate per year (10% or 0.1 as a decimal)
  t = number of years (6 years expected useful life)
  fm = $150,000 (1 + 0.1)^6$
     = 265,734

Simply stated, an investment of $150,000 today will be worth $365,734 in six years if it is invested at 10 percent interest per year with the interest allowed to accumulate.

• *RATE OF RETURN ON INVESTMENT*—An investment in capital equipment or facilities should generally include an analysis of the rate of return on the money invested. What is the potential return to the owners in terms that reflect cash-flow or profits? Which investment alternative will provide the greatest potential cash-flow or profit returns? There are at least five different basic formulas for arriving at an answer to these questions. One of these basic methods, the payback period, has already been discussed. A second method, and one of the least complicated, is the simple rate of return on investment. There are a number of variations in computing the simple rate of return. They are as follows:

1. Profit rate on investment before taxes

$$pr = \frac{e}{i}$$

2. Profit rate on investment after taxes

$$pr = \frac{e - t}{i}$$

3. Cash flow return on investment before taxes

$$cf = \frac{e + d}{i}$$

4. Cash flow return on investment after taxes

$$cf = \frac{e - t + d}{i}$$

Where:
  pr = profit return
  cf = cash flow
  e = annual earnings or cost savings
  t = taxes on savings
  d = annual depreciation costs
  i = investment costs

• *CAPITAL INVESTMENTS AND THE SUPERVISOR*—Many supervisors initiate proposals involving the expenditure of money resources for facilities and equipment. Before capital investment requests are approved, they should be quantitatively evaluated in such terms as cash flow, depreciation, impact on taxes, payback, time value of money, and rate of return on investment. If the supervisor does not have the capability to perform the necessary financial management analysis, he or she should exercise common sense and obtain the necessary expert assistance to perform such evaluation. Failure to properly evaluate the financial management considerations could easily result in an investment that is not cost-effective and wastes valuable money resources.

CONTINGENCY BUDGET

AN ALTERNATIVE PLAN OF ACTION

Contingency budgeting involves preparing for the possibility that something may go wrong with the initial estimates in the capital expense budget. It is a method of budgeting that makes allowances for the unexpected, such as equipment that must be replaced, and major investment in repairs to facilities. A contingency budget is based on the assumption that if something can go wrong, it will. It provides an alternative plan, budget, and schedule which the organization can put to use in the event the original estimate missed the mark.

BE PREPARED FOR THINGS TO GO WRONG

Nobody can predict the future with consistent accuracy. HSI, for example, did not forecast the breakdown of the photocopying machine, nor the fact that its repair would greatly exceed the budget line item for equipment maintenance. A contingency budget could have provided a plan of action to fall back on in the event of unforeseen happenings. The manager who has a contingency plan can react quickly, and in an organized and effective manner, to unexpected situations. Without a contingency plan, considerable time can be lost in adjusting to an emergency situation.

THREE-TIERED CONTINGENCY BUDGETING

There are several ways to prepare a contingency budget. The simplest, and probably most used, method of contingency budgeting is three tiered (Figure 12-4). The first tier is based on the expectation that if anything can go wrong, it will. This pessimistic budgeting, in the case of HSI, would have anticipated the

FIGURE 12-4

Humanitarian Services, Inc.
Contingency Budget
Period _____

SOURCES OF INCOME	MOST PESSIMISTIC	MOST LIKELY	MOST OPTIMISTIC
State Funding			
County Funding			
Contributions			
Fees			
Total Income			

PROGRAM ACTIVITY EXPENSES	MOST PESSIMISTIC	MOST LIKELY	MOST OPTIMISTIC
Educational Programs			
•			
•			
Social Programs			
•			
Recreational Programs			
•			
•			
Health Programs			
•			
•			
Contingencies			
•			
Total Expenses			

replacement of expensive equipment or major repairs to facilities due to age or other factors. The second tier reflects the most likely and expected workload, costs, and level of financing for the budget year. The third tier is based on the optimistic expectation that things will be better than projected in the most likely situation. This tier of budgeting, in the case of HSI, would have reflected their plans in the event that contributions from the general public were higher than expected and/or additional funding was forthcoming from either the county or the state.

When a contingency plan is a part of the budgeting process, it helps managers to know

- *Where and how much to adjust other budget line items to cover unexpected expenditures*
- *When and where to take actions to keep income and expenses in the proper balance*
- *When and how much money to borrow to finance an unexpected emergency situation*

OPERATING EXPENSE BUDGET

EXPENSE BUDGETING HAS UNIVERSAL APPLICATIONS

The operating expense budget involves planning for the money resources needed to accomplish a specific function, activity, task, project, or program. The usual period of time covered by an operating expense budget is one year. In a nonmanufacturing operation, expected income is only identified by its source and operating expenses are often only shown by expected elements of expense. An example of such a budget is shown in Figure 12-5. In a manufacturing operation, the budget usually reflects the expected revenues from sales forecasts (the sales budget) and the estimated costs of production (the production budget). An example of a production budget is shown in Figure 12-6. Notice in both Figures 12-5 and 12-6 that the method of budgeting is by elements of expense. There is one major difference, however. The operating budget in Figure 12-5 only shows planned expenses broken down by types of costs expected to be incurred. It does not show *why* or for *what purpose* these expenses are necessary. The production budget illustrated in Figure 12-6 shows planned expenses broken down by types of costs expected to be incurred to produce a *specific number* of a *given product.*

BUDGET VARIANCES

Budgeting for operating expenses is quite often a problem. The single-year aspect of the budget allows little margin for any management error in estimates. Operating expense budgets are also not too accomodating in handling unanticipated events such as abnormal cost escalation from inflation or catastrophic mishaps. The high percent of personnel costs usually found in an operating expense budget can create problems of inflexibility in making timely adjustments in the work force to meet budget-planned costs. Budget variances are a

FIGURE 12-5

Humanitarian Services, Inc.
Operating Budget
Period _____

SOURCES OF INCOME	J	F	M	A	M	J	J	A	S	O	N	D	TOTAL
State Funding													
County Funding													
Contributions													
Fees													
Total Income													

ELEMENTS OF EXPENSE	J	F	M	A	M	J	J	A	S	O	N	D	TOTAL
Professional Salaries													
Clerical Salaries													
Temporary Employees													
Employee Benefits													
Building Occupancy													
Business Insurance													
Office Equipment													
Office & Cleaning Supplies													
Printing & Publications													
Telephone & Telegraph													
Postage & Shipping													
Travel													
Meetings & Conferences													
Contractual Support													
Total Expenses													

fact of life. There is usually a cost variance in one or more line items in a budget. To conduct an operation of any magnitude with zero variances in all budget line items is very unlikely. Managers should assume that things will happen that necessitate changes to the budget. HSI, for example, should have managed their budget under a policy that permitted upward or downward adjustment up to a certain percentage factor on any single line item. Lacking a policy for flexible budgeting, they treated their budget as a rigid standard instead of a best available approximation.

FIGURE 12-6

XYZ Company
Production Budget
Period _____

Department _____   Product _____

PRODUCTION SCHEDULE	J	F	M	A	M	J	J	A	S	O	N	D	TOTAL
Number of Units													

ELEMENTS OF EXPENSE	J	F	M	A	M	J	J	A	S	O	N	D	TOTAL
Direct Materials													
Direct Labor													
Indirect Labor													
Supervision													
Clerical													
Materials Handling													
Overtime													
Supplies													
Maintenance													
Utilities													
Electricity													
Gas													
Water													
Equipment Rental													
Total Expenses													

BUDGET MISMANAGEMENT

The development and use of operating expense budgets are often not handled well. First, there is a great tendency for the manager who prepares a budget to overstate its requirements. Second, the manager who prepares a budget often fails to adequately justify and support budget requirements with quantitative facts. Third, the managers who *approve* budget requirements are prone to make arbitrary reductions without an adequate evaluation of the requester's real needs. This "cat-and-mouse" game of lower level managers overstating budget requirements and higher level managers arbitrarily reducing them creates distrust, confusion, and frustration.

Another mismanagement of budgets occurs when they are used as discriminating devices for determining who gets what resources. This happens when certain managers with either charismatic personalities or political influence get preferential treatment in the distribution of budgeted resources. Budget management should be based on supportable facts, not on manager personalities or politics.

SUPERVISOR BUDGET INPUT

The general practice of most organizations is to obtain budget input from all operating managers. The input to an operating budget is a reflection of what the manager intends to do during a specific future time period. It is up to the operating manager to accurately, concisely, and objectively present a budget supported with narrative justification that gives the best possible arguments for its approval. The achievement of budget approval, therefore, is highly dependent on the following management actions:

1. Knowledge of what needs to be done and why
2. Importance and priority of what needs to be done and why
3. Accurate supporting facts and, where possible, quantitative data
4. Concise and objective narrative justification
5. Avoidance of personal bias and interpersonal conflict
6. Understanding the budget needs of other organizations

COST VARIANCE REPORTS

During the execution phase of an approved budget, the operating manager should either maintain or obtain records that show what was actually accomplished in relation to what was intended to be accomplished. Figure 12-7 is a simplified example of a monthly cost variance report that shows the relationship between actual and budgeted expenses. A characteristic of the operational budget process is that its preparation, review, approval, and evaluation of results are recurring actions. The management of an operational expense budget requires exercise of common sense in determining when some items are getting out of control, or when revisions in the budget should or should not be made.

MANPOWER BUDGET

A MANPOWER BUDGET CAN BE SUPERFLUOUS

A manpower budget involves computation of the number of employees required and authorized by an organization to perform its workload. This meth-

FIGURE 12-7

XYZ Company
Production Budget
For the Month of _____

Department _____ Product _____

Number of Units Scheduled For Production _____

Number of Units Actually Produced _____

Production Variance _____

ELEMENTS OF EXPENSE	ACTUAL COSTS	BUDGET COSTS	VARIANCE
Direct Materials			
Direct Labor			
Indirect Labor			
Supervision			
Clerical			
Materials Handling			
Overtime			
Supplies			
Maintenance			
Utilities			
Electricity			
Gas			
Water			
Equipment Rental			
Total Expenses			

od of operational budgeting is usually employed by organizations with a high percentage of labor costs to total costs. It tends to be used where operating expense budgets are ineffective in controlling labor costs.

Once established, the manpower budget limits the number of employees that an organization is authorized to have. Most government and some non-government organizations require the development and use of a manpower budget to control the number of employees on the payroll and thereby control operating costs. If an organization is only authorized to have a specific number of employees, this effectively controls the operating costs for salaries and wages. However, if an organization has a well planned and controlled operating expense budget, it really doesn't need the superfluous manpower budget. In industrial and commercial-type operations, where the workload is directly related to sales and orders, it is a mistake to superimpose a manpower budget on an operational expense budget. To do so can result in sales and orders generating workload that cannot be accomplished due to the lack of sufficient personnel.

PROGRAM BUDGET

A More Meaningful Method of Operational Budgeting

A program budget is a more meaningful and supportable method of operational expense budgeting. For example, the elements of expense operating budget of HSI, discussed at the beginning of this chapter, was not an effective method of budgeting. Although HSI was engaged in many different program activities, the budget was strictly based on elements of expense shown in Figure 12-5. The management of money resources at HSI would be much more meaningful, and the job of getting funds would be easier if planned and actual costs were broken down according to the various educational, social, recreational, and health programs. With this type of budget structure, the various elements of expense would then be identified according to the different services provided by HSI. A program budget would provide HSI with a financial plan of its programs and services and would enable the organization to show the costs of each program they accomplish. The resulting budget would be both practical and understandable. It would also allow the Board of Trustees to allocate money resources to those programs that generate the greatest benefits.

Program Budgeting Focuses on Objectives

Program budgeting is a method of operational budgeting that identifies the outputs (program accomplishments) and the inputs (elements of expense) of an organization's operation. The emphasis in program budgeting is on the identifiable outputs that are the reason for the organization's existence. Follow-up emphasis is then placed on evaluation of output accomplishments in relation to input costs. Program budgeting focuses attention on the objectives that are to be achieved and their costs. This enables management to intelligently compare alternatives and program activities in a meaningful and practical manner. If the HSI operating budget were developed as a program budget, as shown in Figure 12-8, the organization would have a budget that is better understood and accepted. Simply stated, a program budget reduces alternatives to a simple calculation of gains (outputs) and losses (inputs) of each program. This enables the organization to determine what it is receiving for the money it spends.

FIGURE 12-8

Humanitarian Services, Inc.
Program Budget
Period _____

SOURCES OF INCOME	EDUC. PROGRAMS	SOCIAL PROGRAMS	REC. PROGRAMS	HEALTH PROGRAMS	TOTAL INCOME
State Funding					
County Funding					
Contributions					
Fees					
Total Income					

PROGRAM ACTIVITY EXPENSES	ELEMENTS OF EXPENSE				
	Direct Labor	Direct Materials	Other Direct	Shared Overhead	Total Expenses
Educational Programs					
•					
•					
Social Programs					
•					
Recreational Programs					
•					
•					
Health Programs					
•					
•					
Total Expenses					

ZERO-BASE BUDGET

IT IS EASY TO CONTINUE THE STATUS QUO

Although program budgeting is a more meaningful way of managing money resources than by elements of expense, there is still an even better way. In program budgeting, it is very easy for managers to continue to plan programs from year to year merely because "we did it last year." This attitude in budgeting can cause major problems where there is intense competition for funds to accomplish all the programs that every manager would like to undertake.

Therefore, it behooves management to find a better method of allocating and controlling the expenditure of funds. One effective way to tighten the controls between justification and allocation of money resources is the zero-base budgeting process.

The concept of zero-base budgeting, as we know it today, came about in the late 1960s when Texas Instruments was facing a budget decrease in the Staff and Research divisions of the company.[1] During the budget review process, the company identified three problems:

1. Objectives had not been established for some work activities, and certain stated goals were not realistic in relation to the amount of money budgeted.
2. Arbitrary operating decisions were being made that affected the amount of money required for their implementation.
3. Budget dollars were not strictly allocated in accordance with changing responsibilities and workloads. Some workloads had increased significantly while others had decreased, yet everyone had his or her budget cut 1 percent to 10 percent.

ZERO-BASE BUDGETING DEFINED

The Texas Instruments' review of their budget process led to the development of a new planning and budgeting methodology that they called "zero-base budgeting." It required each manager to justify budget requests in detail from scratch, and to provide a specific explanation of why any money should be spent at all. The zero-base approach to budgeting required that all work activities be identified in "decision packages" that could be evaluated by systematic analysis to establish their rank order of importance.[2]

STEPS IN ZERO-BASE BUDGETING

Zero-base budgeting involves six steps as outlined in Figure 12-9. *Step 1* is the determination of the programs, projects, products, services, and/or activities that are planned for the future. These are the decision packages. Zero-base budgeting can never be any better than the planning and development of the objectives that must precede the budgeting process. If you do not know what you want to do and why, you are embarking on a future of management-by-frustration.

Step 2 of zero-base budgeting involves the presentation and support of the following evaluation factors for each decision package:

- *Purpose of the planned action*
- *Importance of the planned action*
- *Consequences if the planned action is not performed*
- *Minimum level of effort required to get the planned action started*
- *Other possible levels of effort that could be given to the planned action*
- *Alternative courses of action for accomplishing the planned action*

- *Costs of the planned action*
- *Benefits expected to be gained from the planned action*
- *Method of measuring performance if the planned action is approved*

An example of a decision package format is shown in Figure 12-10.

Step 3 is the factual and objective analysis of the evaluation factors set forth in step 2. The primary focus of the evaluation should be in terms of the expected benefits (outputs) versus the required costs (inputs) to implement each decision package. The evaluation applies to *all* future planned program packages, both the continuation of current undertakings as well as the start of new ones. Even programs that were given high priority status in the past must be reevaluated. Nothing is taken for granted in zero-base budgeting, because every planned program is evaluated from "scratch" or "point zero."

Step 4 is the ranking of each decision package in the order of its evaluated priority importance. This step is the capstone of the zero-base budgeting process. The decision package that appears to offer the greatest benefits in relation to the money resources required should be given the highest priority ranking. The decision package that appears to offer the least benefits in relation to the money resources required should be given the lowest priority ranking.

FIGURE 12-9 Zero-base budgeting: the reevaluation of *all* programs and expenditures

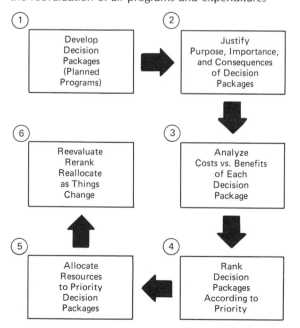

FIGURE 12-10 An example of a zero-base budget format

BUDGET REQUEST			
Department:	Date:		
Program Description:	On–Going Program ☐	New Program ☐	
Purpose:			
Importance:			Rank
Consequences if Not Performed:			
Alternatives:	RESOURCES REQUIRED	CURRENT YEAR	BUDGET YEAR
	Personnel		
	Facilities		
Benefits:	Equipment		
	Materials		
	Other Expenses		
	Total Funding		

Step 5 allocates money resources in accordance with the decision rankings of step 4. This means the highest priority programs will be the first to receive allocations of funds for their execution. Program packages receiving the lowest rankings will only be financed if money resources are still available after the higher priority actions have been fully funded. This step involves determination of the cutoff point at which those decision packages below a certain priority ranking will not be funded during the forthcoming budget year.

Step 6 involves appropriate reevaluation and reallocation of money resources to priority decision packages. The fact that a given package may have a high priority at the beginning of the budget year does not mean that it should automatically remain in that position for the following twelve months.

Many things can happen in the constantly changing environment to dictate a redirection in the priority ranking of decision packages. Astute managers should be prepared to reevaluate facts, rerank decision packages, and reallocate resources.

ZERO-BASE BUDGETING SHOULD BE SELECTIVELY USED

Zero-base budgeting, when applied to the right things, is a very effective device for planning and control in terms of "What am I going to get and what am I getting for my expenditure of money resources?" However, zero-base budgeting should only be applied in carefully selected areas. Most, if not all, staff functions are amenable to this type of budgeting. On the other hand, zero-base budgeting may not be appropriate for some line functions, such as field sales offices, field sales representatives, warehouse operations, and many manufacturing operations. Of the many companies that have used zero-base budgeting, 30 percent found that it gave them better control over allocation of resources, 25 percent felt that it improved decision making, and 20 percent said it facilitated planning. Only 12 percent claimed that it reduced costs.[3] Zero-base budgeting tends to be the most helpful in budgeting for overhead and administrative costs. The burden of proof in the zero-base budgeting process is on each budget center manager. Generally speaking, zero-base budgets are usually easy to understand, and help to identify inflated costs. The budget process really forces the first-level managers to "think things through."

FLEXIBLE BUDGET

BUDGETS MAY NEED TO BE REVISED

A flexible budget is a method of operational expense budgeting that makes allowances for such things as future upward or downward changes in workload, operations, and/or costs. Budgets are a reflection of planned intentions for the use of money resources in a future time period. All budgets include forecasts and estimates. The HSI budget had to include estimates of contributions from the general public and expected income from county and state funding. If significant differences occur between estimated and actual financing, the HSI budget would have to be revised. As another example, assume that a manufacturing concern based its production expense budget on estimated sales of $50 million. Midway through the budget year, there were many positive trend indicators that sales would exceed $60 million. Obviously, if production is to be revised upward to meet the new sales forecast, the production expense budget must also be increased.

Revising budgets to conform to upward or downward changes in actual funding, actual sales, actual workload, or other factors can present problems. One problem is that a complete revision of a budget takes time, effort, and costs money. This problem can be partly alleviated through flexible or variable budgeting. This type of budgeting is best accomplished at the time the initial budget for the budget year is prepared.

STEPS IN FLEXIBLE BUDGETING

Flexible budgeting involves doing the following three things:

1. Identify the *fixed costs* that are *not affected* by the amount of workload. These include such items as insurance, certain rentals, certain taxes, mortgage payments, interest on bonded indebtedness, and some administrative salaries.
2. Identify the *variable costs* that *are affected* by the amount of workload. These include materials, supplies, transportation, direct productive labor, and other expenses that vary directly with the volume of work that is accomplished.
3. Set up either a variable *cost schedule* (Figure 12-11) or a variable *cost chart* (Figure 12-12) to show the sum total of fixed and variable costs for different levels of workload.

In setting up a flexible budget it is often extremely difficult to clearly differentiate between fixed and variable costs because very often, many of the costs are really semivariable. For example, many labor costs tend to be semivariable because there is not a direct correlation on a day-to-day basis between the number of workers required in relation to the workload—such as the number of salespeople to sales, and production workers to production.

Flexible budgets can be developed through the correlation analysis of output data and costs. It is important that the correlation analysis be subjected

FIGURE 12-11 Variable cost schedule

XYZ COMPANY		PRODUCTION BUDGET			1984
		VARIABLE BUDGET			
ELEMENTS OF EXPENSE	Fixed Budget	100K Units	200K Units	300K Units	400K Units
Direct Materials					
Direct Labor					
Indirect Labor					
Overtime					
Supplies					
Maintenance					
Utilities					
Equipment Rental					
Total Expenses					

FIGURE 12-12   Variable cost chart

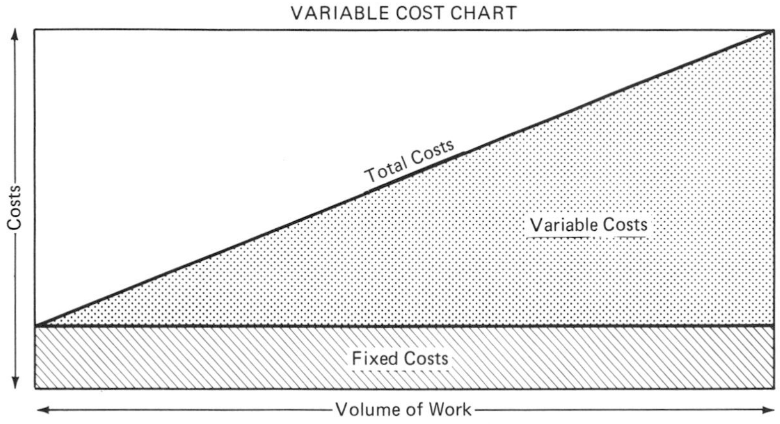

VARIABLE COST CHART

Total Costs

Variable Costs

Fixed Costs

Costs

Volume of Work

to supervisor judgment based on past experience. The organization that wants greater accuracy in flexible budgets should rely on studies performed by industrial engineers. Usually the relative accuracy to be obtained from good correlation analysis is more than adequate for the development of flexible budgets. For example, take a closer look at Figures 12-11 and 12-12 to see how one can easily determine the revised budget figures as funding or workload are increased or decreased by varying amounts.

REGRESSION ANALYSIS

DETERMINING CORRELATION BETWEEN THINGS

Correlation is the mutual relationship between two or more things. Correlation analysis is the determination of how the behavior of one thing affects the behavior of something else. It establishes the closeness of the relationship between two or more variables. When the value of an item is known, it is referred to as the *independent variable*. When the value of an item is not known, it is referred to as a *dependent variable*. Regression analysis is the determination of the average relationship or mathematical correlation between two or more variables. Establishing the mathematical correlation between two or more items means that knowledge of the value of the independent variable enables one to quickly establish the value of the dependent variable(s).

Regression analysis can be a very effective device in the planning and control of money resources. For example, there are certain logical relationships in budget management between (1) quantity of workload to be performed, (2) number of employees required to do it, and (3) costs to be incurred to accomplish it. Through regression analysis it is possible to establish the mathematical correlation between these three variables. Once this is established, the manager needs to know the value of only one of the variables to compute the other two.

QUANTITATIVE ANALYSIS

BUDGET COSTS SHOULD BE SUPPORTED
WITH QUANTITATIVE FACTS

Whenever possible, budget requirements should be supported by workload and productivity data. If a budget requirement is realistic because it is backed up with established facts, it usually establishes confidence with the managers who must approve it. However, some work activities are difficult to support with meaningful workload data. In these situations it makes sense to establish minimum-base cost budgets and not waste money trying to obtain and quantify meaningless statistics.

Effective quantitative analysis involves selecting the significant workload factors—the ones that involve the most workers and costs. The first-level supervisor is the most knowledgeable about operations in his or her organization, and thereby usually in the best position to identify the most significant

FIGURE 12-13 Procurement quantitative relationships 1980–1986

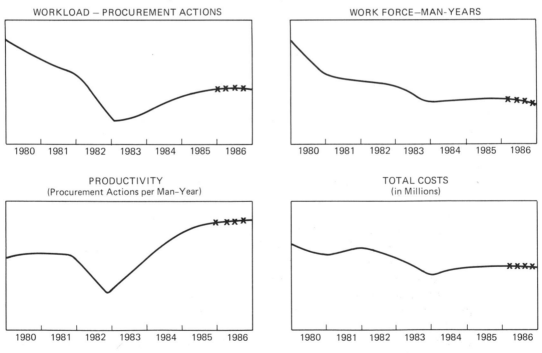

x Denotes Projections

FIGURE 12-14 Matrix for good/poor budgeting

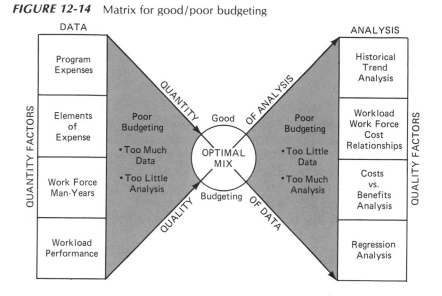

budget support workload data. Once the supervisor has identified these work-load factors, quantitative relationships such as those shown in Figure 12-13 can be developed.

THE OPTIMAL MIX

If intelligently developed and used, quantitative analysis can provide tremendous support to a supervisor in justifying budget requirements. The most realistic and supportable budgets result from an optimal mix of the quantity and quality of both data and analysis. Too much data usually results in too little analysis and results in poor budgeting. Conversely, too much analysis can be nonproductive and not cost-effective. Good budgeting is to be found somewhere between the two extremes shown on the matrix of Figure 12-14. The challenge for the supervisor is to achieve that optimal mix of neither too little nor too much budgetary data and analysis.

FINANCIAL MANAGEMENT IN PERSPECTIVE

FINANCIAL MANAGEMENT INVOLVES *ALL* MANAGERS

The supervision of money resources needs to be seen in the total perspective of financial management. The two major elements in financial management are planning and control. Cost information is used in planning to help determine money requirements and in choosing between alternatives. Cost information is also needed to assure the best and proper use of resources, which is control. Financial management is involved in almost every type of planning and control. To varying degrees, it is a responsibility of all levels of management.

INTERRELATIONSHIPS IN FINANCIAL MANAGEMENT

Financial management revolves around eight closely interrelated phases of management activity. These phases are schematically shown in Figure 12-15. With the exceptions of accounting and auditing, most supervisors are involved in every one of these phases of financial management. For example, economic analysis plays an important role in budgetary planning, particularly where major capital expenditures are involved. Figure 12-16 is a simplification of the

FIGURE 12-15 Interrelationships in financial management

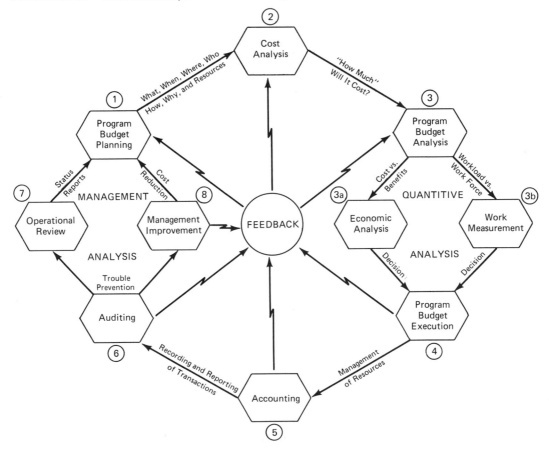

FIGURE 12-16 Economic analysis

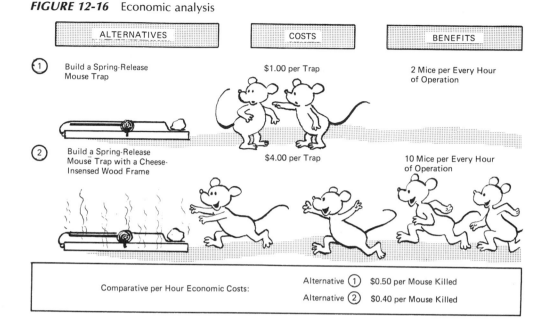

ALTERNATIVES	COSTS	BENEFITS
① Build a Spring-Release Mouse Trap	$1.00 per Trap	2 Mice per Every Hour of Operation
② Build a Spring-Release Mouse Trap with a Cheese-Insensed Wood Frame	$4.00 per Trap	10 Mice per Every Hour of Operation

Comparative per Hour Economic Costs:

Alternative ① $0.50 per Mouse Killed
Alternative ② $0.40 per Mouse Killed

economic analysis process. It reflects the three basic elements of (1) establishing alternatives, (2) estimating costs, and (3) determining benefits. Although the cheese-insensed mouse trap (alternative 2) costs four times as much as a regular spring-released trap (alternative 1), its effectiveness in killing mice is five times greater. On the basis of comparative per hour cost-effectiveness (costs benefits), the second alternative appears to be the most economical decision. There is one other important thing about conducting an economic analysis. It is very important to first clearly define the problem. In the mouse trap illustration, the decision-maker must first determine if there is a mouse problem. If there is not such a problem, there obviously is no need to conduct an economic analysis study.

A good manager cannot engage in the planning, execution, and review of a program, project, activity, or function without getting involved in financial management. The bottom line, therefore, is for all managers to *get involved!*

SUMMARY

Most officers, directors, trustees, managers, and supervisors in all types of organizations are involved to varying degrees in the management of money resources. These managers do not have to be accountants or economists to perform their money management tasks. They should, however, have a keen understanding of the importance of money management and have a basic knowledge of certain specific things that they can do to make effective use of money resources. This is very important because no organization or manager can afford expensive wastefulness.

One of the main areas where supervisors can carry out effective money management is the control of labor costs. A second area is the search for areas where less costly materials and parts can be used just as effectively as more costly ones. A third and very practical supervisory means of controlling money resources is the proper development and use of budgets. Most supervisors have some responsibilities in the development of capital expense budgets and operating expense budgets.

The capital expense budget involves planning for the purchase or construction of buildings and structures, major additions or revisions to existing buildings and structures, and the purchase of nonexpendable tools and equipment that are expected to be used for several years. In developing such budgets, it is a good practice to have a contingency plan and thereby be prepared for the unexpected.

The operating expense budget involves planning for the money resources needed to accomplish a specific function, activity, task, project, or program. Most operating expense budgets reflect the elements of expense expected to be incurred by the organization. A more meaningful and supportable method of budgeting is to show planned and actual costs of specific work objectives or programs. An even more effective method is zero-base budgeting. This requires each manager to justify budget requests from scratch, and to provide specific explanation as to why any money should be spent at all. In developing an operating expense budget, it is good practice to provide flexibility for future upward or downward changes in workload, operations, costs, and/or other factors that affect initial budget forecasts and estimates.

Even though most supervisors are not accountants, they need to be involved in the financial aspects of managing their organization. The scope of financial management involves every level of management.

REVIEW QUESTIONS

1. How do some organizations use cost control as a criteria for determining a supervisor's effectiveness?
2. Why is labor turnover so costly?
3. What is "gold plating" and what can a supervisor do about it?
4. What is meant by the statement that a budget should be viewed as the reflection of intention?
5. How can a supervisor go about developing a budget for the next year when there is still six months remaining in the current year?
6. Why can capital expense budgeting be so difficult?

7. How can operating expense budgets be mismanaged?

8. When can a manpower budget be a superfluous control?

9. What do you think is significant about program budgeting? What can be its weak point? Is there anything you can do to correct this weakness?

10. In what situations would you establish a minimum cost base budget and not waste time trying to do a quantitative analysis?

THE CASE OF PROJECT LEADER JONES

Ralph Jones is a project leader responsible for coordinating the management of selected major items of related communication equipment. As a project leader, Jones serves as a catalyst on items of equipment where there are serious troubles relative to engineering development, production schedules, use of resources, cost overruns, and technical problems. Items are assigned to or removed from Jones's intensive management as they either become or cease to be problems.

Jones, who works for the vice president of production, supervises a relatively small but highly paid staff of item managers, engineers, expeditors, and clerical personnel. Jones and his staff work very closely with the appropriate equipment managers in the engineering development and production departments. His responsibilities include the following tasks regarding items of equipment that are assigned to him:

- Evaluating the engineering development and production budgets
- Developing the budget for his own staff operations
- Monitoring equipment costs to prevent cost overruns
- Evaluating engineering changes which will affect the overall equipment performance, effectiveness, production schedules, and/or costs.
- Making sure that all affected personnel know about and/or participate in the evaluation of engineering changes
- Linking engineering design and manufacturing processes as well as materials to meet the practical exigencies of ongoing production
- Restraining costs by recommending standardized parts and by challenging superfluous technical requirements for items

The vice president of production has requested Jones to submit his organizational budget for next year. Jones was also requested to submit an evaluation of the engineering development and production budgets for the items of equipment being monitored by Jones's staff.

The major expense items in Jones's operating budget are salaries, employee fringe benefits, supplies, and travel. To assist his staff in obtaining timely management and technical information on the items being managed, Jones is planning to submit a budget request for $175,000 of computer terminal and communication equipment. The new equipment, if given budget approval, is expected to increase the productivity of the staff and enable them to keep on top of developing problems. Jones estimates that the equipment will not become obsolete for at least five years.

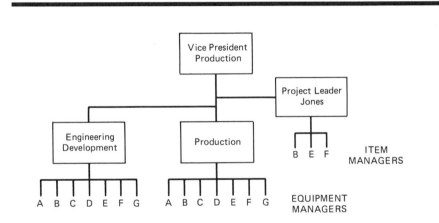

QUESTIONS

1. What different types of budgets should Jones prepare for the vice president? What should his rationale be for preparing certain budgets and excluding other types? What should Jones do to justify his budget requests? Why?

2. What should Jones request from the engineering development and production departments in order to evaluate the budgets for the items that Jones is monitoring? Why?

NOTES

1. Peter A Pyhrr, *Zero-Base Budgeting* (New York: John Wiley, 1973), p. ix.

2. Peter A Pyhrr, "Zero-Base Budgeting," an unpublished speech delivered to the International Conference of the Planning Executives Institute, Hilton Hotel, New York, May 15, 1972.

3. L. Allan Austin, "Zero-Base Budgeting—Organizational Impact and Effects," an American Management Association survey report, 1977, p. 2.

13

Understanding the Computer

LEARNING OBJECTIVES

The objectives of this chapter on understanding the computer are to enable the reader to

1. Relate the following distinctive features of a computer:
    a. How a computer operates with a binary numbering system
    b. The two basic types of computers and their general use
    c. The six functional elements of a computer
    d. The basic components of a business data processing system
    e. How the output of data is influenced by the way data is put into and filed within the computer
2. Delineate the following manager aspects in the use of computers:
    a. Reasons for ineffective use of computers
    b. Basic things a manager should know about computers and their use
    c. The classifications of computer business applications
    d. The steps in systems analysis
    e. Management's role in systems analysis and design
    f. The changing trends in business computers

KEY WORDS

Access Time   The computer time required to locate data and move it to and from storage.

Analog Computer   A computer which solves problems by translating measurable quantities (such as speed, temperature, and voltage) into numbers.

Arithmetic Element   That portion of a computer processing unit which performs addition, subtraction, multiplication, and division.

Binary Number System   An internal numbering system used by computers which uses the number *two* as a base (as opposed to the decimal system which uses the number *ten*).

Bit   A contraction of *binary digit;* a single pulse in a group of pulses such as a single hole in a punched tape or card. Bits comprise a character and characters comprise a word.

Cathode-Ray Tube (CRT)   A device similar to a television screen upon which data can be displayed.

Central Processing Element   The part of a computer containing the arithmetic, logic, control, and in some cases, the main storage units.

Console   The part of a computer used for manual control and observation of the computer system.

Control Element   The part of a computer containing the circuits for interpreting and controlling the carrying out of instructions.

Data/Data Processing   Basic elements of information such as facts, numbers, letters, and symbols that are processed (acted upon) to achieve a desired result.

Debug   To find and remove the mistakes from the design of a program or computer system.

Digital Computer   A computer that solves problems by using numbers to express all quantities and variables.

Hardware (Computer)   The physical equipment or devices which together comprise a computer and its associated data processing machines.

Input (Computer)   Data to be processed and the instructions to control the processing, which are moved into the internal storage of a data processing system.

Logic Element   The part of a computer processing unit that compares, matches, sorts, and performs nonarithmetic functions.

Magnetic Disk   A flat, circular plate with a surface that can be magnetized to store data.

Magnetic Drum   A rotating cylinder with a surface that can be magnetized to store data.

Magnetic Tape   A plastic strip coated with a metallic oxide upon which data can be recorded in magnetized spots.

Mainframe   The central processor of a large computer system.

Output (Computer)   Information transferred from internal computer storage to devices that produce cards, tapes, business forms, and the like.

Program (Computer)   A series of instructions which tell the computer in minute detail how to process data.

Programmer   A person who prepares problem-solving procedures and flow charts and writes and debugs computer programs.

Random Access Storage   A storage technique in which the computer can find one bit of data as quickly as any other, regardless of its specific location in storage.

Real-time   A method of processing data so fast that there is virtually no passage of time between inquiry and result.

Simulation   An exercise which usually uses a computer as a scorekeeper while people make decisions concerning a mathematical model of a real-world business situation.

Software (Computer)   All programs and routines used to extend the capabilities of computers, such as assemblers (machine-language coded instructions), compilers (devices that translate symbolic coded instructions into machine-language instructions), and subroutines (a sequence of computer instructions).

Systems Analysis   The examination of an activity, procedure, method, technique, or business to determine what must be accomplished and how the necessary operations may best be accomplished.

Time Sharing   Using a computer to process multiple requests by independent users, and providing responses rapidly so that each user feels that the computer is entirely at his/her disposal.

Transistor   An electronic device that performs functions similar to a vacuum tube.

ON/OFF—IS ALL IT KNOWS

BINARY NUMBERING SYSTEM

A computer is a mechanical or electronic device capable of rapidly performing repetitious and highly complex mathematical, logical, and manipulative operations on data. Data is represented in a computer by a binary numbering system that employs only two digits or *bits*—0 and 1. All numbers, letters, and special characters are expressed as a sequence of either zeros or ones. The number *12*, for example, is 1100 in the binary numbering system; and the number *13* is represented as 1101. The binary symbols *0* and *1* can be combined in strings, or *bytes*, to represent any numerical value or alphabetic character.

Modern-day computers operate with a large number of electrical circuits that are either "on" (corresponding to 1) or "off" (corresponding to 0). The more circuits it has, the more the computer can do. A computer is able to store information or perform a calculation because it is a system of electrical switches that are connected together in a precise and logical way. The computer performs according to the number of switches that are either "on" or "off." It is somewhat scary that a gadget that only knows the signals of "on" or "off" is drastically changing our lives and the way we manage things in business and government. Even more disturbing is the fact that the technological development of computers is running far ahead of our ability to use them in the most intelligent manner.

RAPID OBSOLESCENCE

FOUR GENERATIONS
OF COMPUTER TECHNOLOGY

The first big operational electronic computer was ENIAC (Electronic Numerical Integrator and Calculator). It was built in 1946, weighed over 30 tons, contained 18,000 vacuum tubes generating considerable heat, and filled a large room with its externally controlled switches and control panels. A year later ENIAC was obsolete because scientists at Bell Laboratories introduced the transistor, a tiny piece of material equipped with electrodes that performed functions similar to those of a vacuum tube. Transistors allowed the combining of many electrical circuits in a fraction of the space used by the old vacuum tube computer, and at much less cost. The development of the transistor established a second generation of computer technology.

In 1959 Texas Instruments and Fairchild Semiconductor simultaneously announced the successful production of integrated circuits. These were single silicon chips that contained several complete electronic circuits. The use of integrated circuits enabled computers to be built with thousands of electrical circuits on a single quarter-inch-square piece of silicon. With the development of integrated circuits came a third generation of computer technology. These microelectronic circuits were smaller, faster, and more reliable than the second-generation transistorized circuits. Their use significantly increased the speed, capacity, and type of computer storage and input/output devices. The new circuitry also greatly reduced the size as well as the costs of third-generation computers.

RECENT TECHNOLOGICAL DEVELOPMENTS

In the early 1970s the technological developments in electronic circuitry started a fourth generation of computers. The advancements in fourth-generation computers include the following technological developments:

1. One development is the use of large-scale microelectronic integrated circuitry for both the logic and the memory elements of the computer.
2. A second development is the microminiaturization of computer circuitry. This has greatly reduced the size and power requirements, while significantly increasing the processing speed of computers. In the fourth-generation circuitry shown in Figure 13-1, the microminiaturization of computer components has resulted in a million or more electronic circuits being placed on a tiny silicon chip.
3. A third development is the microprogramming of changeable computer instructions on magnetic diskettes, magnetic plastic cards, and other input media. This has greatly simplified the interpretation of machine-language instructions that enable the computer to perform the functions desired of it. The simplification in computer programming has facilitated "distributed processing" whereby electronic data processing can be dispersed to users throughout an organization.

The technological advancements in integrated circuitry, microminiaturization, and microprogramming have literally started a second computer revolution, with each day bringing about some new development.

TYPES OF COMPUTERS

ANALOG COMPUTER

There are two basic types of computers, the analog and the digital. The analog computer is a device that accepts continuous measurements and produces

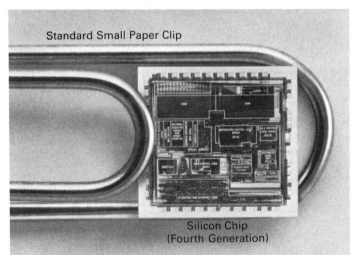

FIGURE 13-1 Four generations of computer components

SOURCE: Picture courtesy Bell Laboratories

continuous solutions to mathematical equations. This type of computer represents variables by physical analogies in a continuous form such as the amount of rotation of a shaft, the amount of voltage or resistance in an electric current, or the tracking of a missile or space vehicle.

DIGITAL COMPUTER

The digital computer is a device that represents information in a discrete form such as the presence or absence of an electrical pulse at a certain point in time. This type of computer is more versatile than the analog computer. The digital computer is used for such purposes as solving extremely complex mathematical problems, storing and performing calculations on large quantities of business data, and executing the fire control functions involved in the employment of military weapons.

The primary difference between analog and digital computers is that the analog "measures" and the digital "counts." All discussions in this chapter refer to digital computers.

Mainframe Computer

Differences in the characteristics of third- and fourth-generation computers have also brought about the classification of computers by size. The most common classifications are the large mainframe computer, the minicomputer, and the microcomputer. Mainframe computers are designed to handle the large volumes of numeric and alphabetic data that may be required by such business functions as payroll, billing, inventory, and accounting. These computers have extensive input, output, storage, and manipulation capabilities and are usually centrally located and controlled (Figure 13-2).

Minicomputer

Minicomputers are small desk-size computers which can perform all of the functions of a larger mainframe computer. Examples are computerized accounting machines and word processing equipment for automatic typing and

FIGURE 13-2 A large mainframe computer system

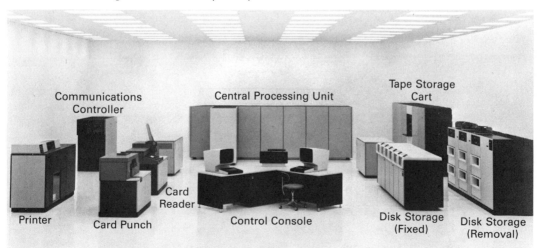

SOURCE: Picture courtesy of International Business Machines Corporation

text editing. Minicomputers usually have slower processing speeds, smaller memories, and less input/output capacity. Typical input/output capabilities include magnetic tape cassettes, magnetic "floppy disks," and cathode-ray tubes (CRT) with terminal keyboards. The CRT (with keyboard), which is similar to a television screen, is probably the most common input/output device used with minicomputers (Figure 13-3).

MICROCOMPUTER

Microcomputers are very small computers ranging in size from a complete computer on a "chip" to a small typewriter-size unit (Figure 13-4). An example is the programmable calculator that uses magnetic instruction and data cards as an input device. Many microcomputers can be purchased with a variety of ready-to-use programs available in cassette-tape cartridges. The typewriter-sized microcomputer can perform many data processing tasks without the aid of a central large computer. The use of "personal" microcomputers has accelerated the trend to "distributed data processing" at the worksite. This trend is having a revolutionary impact on the organization and operation of central computer facilities because it is decentralizing the storing and manipulating of data.

FIGURE 13-3 Example of dual minicomputer work stations showing the minicomputer used as an electronic text processing and filing system

SOURCE: Picture courtesy of International Business Machines Corporation

FIGURE 13-4   Progress in electronics: the microcomputer

A. The stamp of progress—this tiny silicon chip has the processing power of some minicomputers

SOURCE: Picture courtesy of Bell Laboratories

B. A self-contained microcomputer in use

SOURCE: Picture courtesy of Perkin-Elmer Corporation

FUNCTIONAL ELEMENTS OF A COMPUTER

COMPUTERS MUST RECEIVE INSTRUCTIONS

A computer is frequently referred to as an electronic brain. Since the human brain is capable of thinking and responding on its own, it is misleading to refer to a computer as a brain. Whatever semblance a computer has to the brain is found in the maze of electronic circuitry within its shell. The electronic computer performs tasks automatically, but only on the basis of what it is told to do, one thing at a time, step by step, and instruction by instruction.

COMPUTER HARDWARE
AND SOFTWARE

The hardware properties of computer equipment are one of the engineering marvels of the twentieth century. However, computer hardware cannot operate without the all important software of programmed routines and operating procedures that instruct the computer what to do. The technical capabilities of computer hardware tend to be far ahead of developed and tested software. The weak link is that the hardware user must be able to clearly define the problem to be solved and specifically state via the software what is wanted from the computer. What the user wants must be converted to a language that the computer understands. As shown in Figure 13-5, there are three significant relationships in understanding and using computers—the problem, the software, and the hardware.

BASIC FUNCTIONAL ELEMENTS

A computer system consists of six functional elements. They are input, storage, arithmetic and logic (processing), control, output, and communications. These six functional elements are schematically shown in Figure 13-6.
- *INPUT*—The input element consists of all devices and media that accept, convert, and transport data and instructions into the computer. Information may be fed into the computer from punched cards, punched paper tape, magnetic tape rolls, magnetic tape cassettes, magnetic strip cartridges, floppy disks, magnetic disks, magnetic drums, light pens, optical character readers, console typewriters, Touch-Tone telephone, or voice.
- *STORAGE*—The storage or memory element is the nerve center of the computer. This is where all data and instructions are stored until needed.
- *PROCESSING*—The arithmetic and logic or processing element is the heart of the computer. This is the element that adds, subtracts, multiplies, divides, and compares numbers and words at lightning speeds. It is here that the actual work of problem solving is done.
- *CONTROL*—The control element directs the computer in performing its operations. It is like a master dispatcher on a railroad. It sets switches and directs the flow of data and instructions through the computer system. The sequence of steps to be performed must be translated into detailed instructions which can be understood by the computer. These are the instructions or programs that are prepared by programmers. Figure 13-7 is an example of a coding form with the statements and flowchart of a simple computer program.
- *OUTPUT*—The output element consists of all devices and media that reflect computer processed data and information. Information may be fed out of the computer to microfilm, paper documents printed by line and character

FIGURE 13-5

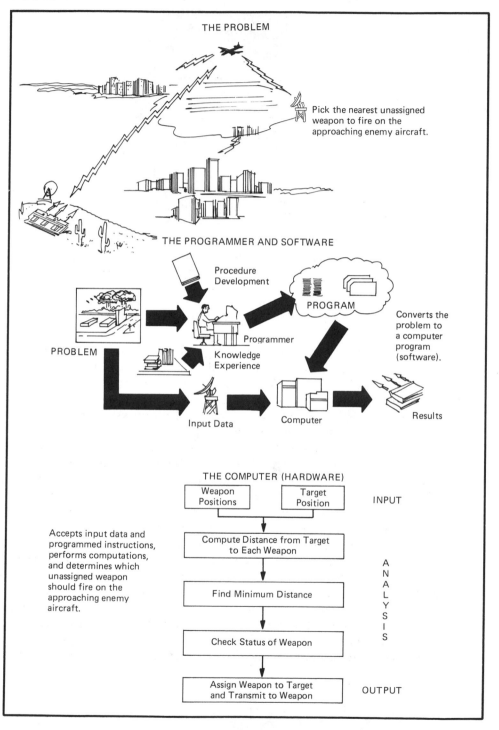

THE PROBLEM

Pick the nearest unassigned weapon to fire on the approaching enemy aircraft.

THE PROGRAMMER AND SOFTWARE

Procedure Development

PROGRAM

PROBLEM

Programmer

Knowledge Experience

Converts the problem to a computer program (software).

Input Data

Computer

Results

THE COMPUTER (HARDWARE)

| Weapon Positions | Target Position | INPUT |

Accepts input data and programmed instructions, performs computations, and determines which unassigned weapon should fire on the approaching enemy aircraft.

Compute Distance from Target to Each Weapon

Find Minimum Distance

Check Status of Weapon

A N A L Y S I S

Assign Weapon to Target and Transmit to Weapon

OUTPUT

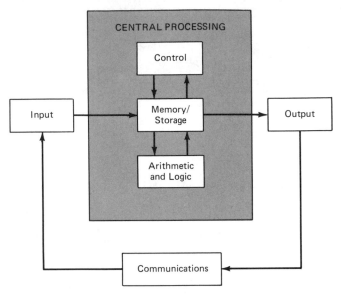

FIGURE 13-6   Functional elements of a computer system

printers, paper documents drawn by graphic plotters, video displays, and also by most of the same devices and media used to input data into the computer.

● *COMMUNICATION*—The communication element consists of the devices necessary to convert computer digital output signals into appropriate telephone, telegraph, and microwave radio transmission frequencies and vice versa. Data communication interface devices permit information to be transmitted to users, including the integration of one computer system with other computer systems. It is only when the sixth element—data communications—is added that a computer system can function as an integrated part of an overall management information system. The absence of a rapid automatic system for transmitting and receiving data between widely separated computer centers creates a bottleneck like closing down four of six lanes on the southbound New Jersey Turnpike on the Friday afternoon before Labor Day.

Electronic data transmission is an integral part of most distributed data processing installations. Public communications networks have been designed in the past to handle continuous analog signals such as the human voice. There are currently special communications channels that can be used for transmitting the digital output signals from computers. The ongoing conversion of telephone transmission systems to digital signals is making it possible to handle voice, data, video, and facsimile communications from one user point to another.

FIGURE 13-7 A simple computer program

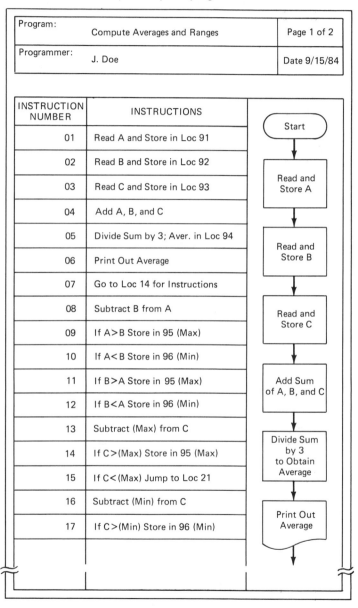

INSTRUCTION NUMBER	INSTRUCTIONS
01	Read A and Store in Loc 91
02	Read B and Store in Loc 92
03	Read C and Store in Loc 93
04	Add A, B, and C
05	Divide Sum by 3; Aver. in Loc 94
06	Print Out Average
07	Go to Loc 14 for Instructions
08	Subtract B from A
09	If A>B Store in 95 (Max)
10	If A<B Store in 96 (Min)
11	If B>A Store in 95 (Max)
12	If B<A Store in 96 (Min)
13	Subtract (Max) from C
14	If C>(Max) Store in 95 (Max)
15	If C<(Max) Jump to Loc 21
16	Subtract (Min) from C
17	If C>(Min) Store in 96 (Min)

Program: Compute Averages and Ranges — Page 1 of 2
Programmer: J. Doe — Date 9/15/84

Flowchart: Start → Read and Store A → Read and Store B → Read and Store C → Add Sum of A, B, and C → Divide Sum by 3 to Obtain Average → Print Out Average

THE DATA PROCESSING SYSTEM

Figure 13-8 shows the basic components of a business data processing system. The central component is the processing equipment and the personnel involved in developing the software and operating the hardware.

The key component is the input of data to the processing equipment. Input can be derived from many source documents such as employee time cards, sales slips, purchase orders, and contracts. This is the key component of a data processing system because the quality of the data base and the output can never be better than the quality and timeliness of the input.

The data base component consists of information derived from previous input records and files. It serves as a storage of file information for use in many different data processing applications. For example, data from employee time cards may be processed into payroll accounts, pay checks, labor cost reports, and other applications.

The objective of a business data processing system is the output component. The reason for inputing and processing data is to obtain such information output as sales analysis reports, inventory status, cash flow status, employee paychecks, and accounting reports. It is also common for the output of one data processing system to be the input to other systems (see the subsystem concept discussed in Chapter 14).

FIGURE 13-8   Business data processing system

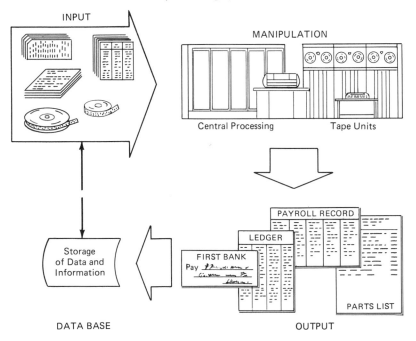

INPUT AND PROCESSING OF DATA

The output of data is considerably influenced by *how* data is put into and filed within the computer.

BATCH VERSUS REAL-TIME PROCESSING

- *BATCH PROCESSING*—In batch processing, data is usually put into the computer system in a sequential manner. The data is sorted, accumulated over a period of time into batches, and then processed periodically into the computer. Batch processing can be accomplished through a central input facility or at remote access terminal locations. The batch processing of input data is usually followed by batch processing of output data that is released on a planned periodic schedule. The logic for batch processing is that the accumulation and input as well as output of data on a planned schedule result in more efficient use of the computer. The negative aspect of batch processing is that the user of the data is denied immediate and timely access to information when it is needed.
- *REAL-TIME PROCESSING*—In a real-time processing system, data is put into the computer as it is originated or recorded without waiting to sort and accumulate it into batches. Under real-time processing, data is often fed directly into the computer from on-line remote terminals. Real-time processing results in up-to-date and accessible computer files, since the data is recorded whenever it is originated, regardless of its frequency of occurrence. The positive aspects of real-time processing are that the computer files can provide the user with information that is immediately accessible, timely, and up to date.

SEQUENTIAL VERSUS DIRECT ACCESS FILES

- *SEQUENTIAL FILES*—Computer files such as punched cards, paper tape, or magnetic tape require that data be stored and processed sequentially. This means that the computer must search an entire reel of magnetic tape, for example, in order to update a record stored near the end of the reel.
- *DIRECT ACCESS FILES*—Computer files such as magnetic disks, magnetic drums, and floppy disks allow direct retrieval of any record in the file. This means that the computer does not have to search an entire file in order to find a specific data record. As shown in Figure 13-9, the read/write head can go directly to a specific file in a way similar to selecting a particular song on a phonograph record. Direct access files may be on-line devices such as magnetic disks or drums, or they may be devices such as magnetic strip cartridges that are stored off-line until needed.
- *TIME SHARING*—A computer system that is designed to provide real-time processing of direct access files can be shared by many users. Time-sharing systems are possible because a computer can operate in nanoseconds (one bil-

FIGURE 13-9   Sequential versus direct access files

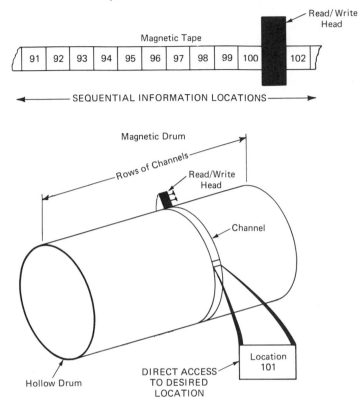

lionth of a second) and thereby process millions of instructions and data per second. The calculations that a computer can do in seconds would take years for humans to do. Because of the computer's fantastic speed, many users can be given time to process data into and out of the system. Time sharing relies on a good data communications system in order to provide instantaneous responses to many users operating remote input/output terminals.

USING COMPUTERS IN MANAGEMENT

REASONS FOR INEFFECTIVE USE OF COMPUTERS

Many computers, both large and small, are not being used effectively in providing management with the best information available for decision making. One of the reasons is that computer techniques which are very useful at the lower levels of management may not give higher-level managers what they really need. Second, certain types of information are not suitable for processing through a computer. This fact is not always understood, and the result is that computer programming and processing efforts are wasted, and all concerned are disappointed with the results. A third reason is the failure of managers to determine what they need from the computer. A fourth reason is the failure of managers to determine and correct the faults in data collection and processing *before* programming them into the computer. Faulty data collection cannot be corrected by a computer. A fifth reason is the tendency of some highly paid managers to play with computers as if they were toys. This situation is particularly true with microcomputers and computers using cathode-ray tubes with terminal keyboards. Managers should delegate the tasks of computer operations to their clerical assistants and spend their time performing the management functions of planning, organizing, directing, and controlling.

WHAT A MANAGER SHOULD KNOW

A computer can be a very helpful aid to good management. The effective use of electronic data processing for management purposes does not require that a manager know about the inner workings or the programming of the computer. However, there are several basic things that a manager should know about computers and their use.

First, a manager should have an understanding of what a computer can do.

- *It can accept and store large quantities of information—numbers, words, and instructions—and retrieve it at extremely rapid speeds.*
- *It can move information from one place to another in its internal memory.*
- *It can very rapidly and accurately perform arithmetic operations on the numerical data stored in its memory.*
- *It can very rapidly compare two pieces of information in its memory and tell whether they are equal or not. This is called the computer's* logic *operation.*
- *It can write or print out the information that is stored in its memory.*

Second, a manager should recognize that data processing problems may be symptoms of other management problems, with their roots far removed from the use of computers.

HOW TO USE A COMPUTER

Third, a manager should know how to use a computer effectively in management. This includes determining what information is needed. To do this:

- *Identify the key factors in the business operation which need to be controlled in order to achieve the objectives of the organization.*
- *Specify the basis for establishing standards of performance for each control factor such as forecasts, budgets, standard costs, turnover ratios, milestones, objectives, and lead time.*
- *Determine the information—accounting, operating data, and statistics—that must be accumulated to measure performance.*

- *Establish a reporting structure that identifies performance in each control area, relates causes and effects, signals significant trends, and identifies results by organizational responsibility.*
- *Monitor the system on a continuous basis to assure that the information focuses attention only on the crucial or significant events.*

WHEN TO USE A COMPUTER

Fourth, after a manager establishes what information is needed, he or she should determine which information is suitable for computer application. Generally speaking, a computer can be used to the best advantage if the information has the following characteristics:

- *Large quantity of data*
- *Repetitive computational operations*
- *Necessity for speed in obtaining information*
- *High number of interactive variables involving arithmetic and logic operations*
- *High degree of accuracy required*

Information which is relatively static, small in volume, and involving few interacting variables or repetitive computational operations may be handled best by *not* using a computer.

BUSINESS SENSE AND COMMON SENSE

The manager who exercises both business sense and common sense will find that computers can be very cost-effective devices (Figure 13-10). Business sense involves knowing the problem, performing a cost-benefit analysis of the alternative solutions, and selecting the action that provides the greatest benefits and cost savings. It also means getting the data processing people to think about such things as cash flow and return on investment in addition to talking about bits and bytes. Common sense involves recognizing that computers cannot solve all of management's problems. It also means programming computer output to reflect only the exceptional information to avoid voluminous output that is not used. Both business and common sense are involved in fitting the computer to the analyzed needs of the organization.

COMPUTERS REQUIRE PEOPLE

The effective use of computers requires much more than hardware. Above all else, computers require people. It is people who make computers work—who create the software, debug, fine-tune, and operate the hardware. People can be motivated by a computer or frustrated because they feel like a machine operating a machine. Thorough planning is the key to making the right decisions regarding the use of computers.

FIGURE 13-10   Business sense and common sense

BUSINESS SENSE:

①   Know the problem
②   Look at alternative solutions
③   Perform a cost-benefit analysis
④   Base decision on greatest
   • Benefits
   • Cost savings

SOURCE: Picture courtesy of International Business Machines Corporation

COMMON SENSE:

①   Computers can't do everything
②   Use the exception principle

COMPUTER APPLICATIONS

A MAJOR AIRLINE

A major airline receives daily operational reports at its corporation headquarters from all areas of its far-flung organization. Each morning the key operating executives meet for a fifteen-minute briefing session at which they review all significant operating irregularities for the preceding twenty-four-hour period. They also receive a forecast of operating problems for the next twenty-four hour period. At these short briefing sessions the managers are able to focus attention on the really important operations of the entire corporation—passenger and freight capacities versus load utilization, equipment availability, customer service (e.g., on-time flights, food, scheduling, baggage handling, mistakes, and complaints), maintenance operations, major parts rebuild schedules, operating personnel problems, and costs versus revenues. The daily reports are developed from a simplified real-time data processing system and the use of a relatively small computer. The computerized system makes it possible for the top-level managers to make timely decisions and to keep on top of one of the largest airlines in the world.

A DIVERSIFIED MANUFACTURER

On the eighth working day of every month, the vice-president and controller of a very large and diversified manufacturing company carries a set of forecasts into the office of the president in the company's mid-western headquarters. These forecasts for the month have been submitted by sixty-nine divisions via the company's highly developed "telecomputer" system. Before computerization, the review of forecasts was held infrequently, and top management was not able to make monthly comparisons of projections against corporate objectives and actual performance.

This company has learned to manage the computer in other business activities. Its data processing system handles more than 90 percent of all industrial orders, sending shipping instructions by teletype in just three seconds to the warehouse nearest the customer. Inventory records are on a real-time basis. This has enabled the company to reduce inventories by 50 percent and to close eight of thirty-five warehouses. Real-time cash management via the company's telecomputer system keeps a running balance on accounts in 230 banks and helps management make quicker decisions on short-term investments and borrowing. Computerization has changed both the accountant's and engineer's jobs because it greatly reduced manual calculations. The officials of this company feel that computerization requires a new type of manager. He or she must be able to *think* about *how* something is done rather than just doing it.

ORGANIZATION FOR COMPUTER SERVICES

A large metals processing company with many subsidiaries and plants exercises decentralized control down to the level of the plant manager. Corporate-level management has established a subsidiary company to plan and implement its computer information system for providing services to the entire corporation. The subsidiary company was formed because the people who had been running the computers, namely the accountants, had not been doing a total management information job.

ENGINEERING DOCUMENTATION

In the area of engineering data and scientific information, the Army Missile Command at Redstone Arsenal, Alabama, has a computerized scientific information center and a computerized engineering documentation storage and retrieval system. The latter enables the Command to handle thousands of engineering drawings, specifications, and manufacturing source lists. The system is used for such purposes as quickly determining if certain items are already available, whether new items must be designed, or if old items might be modified to serve other purposes without the need to start design from scratch.

BUSINESS APPLICATIONS

Figure 13-11 shows a breakdown of computer business applications into seven basic classifications. Within these broad categories one can identify potential applications that are as extensive as the number of diversified activities performed by a business organization. Learning to manage the computer involves analysis of the many interrelationships that exist among the various applications shown in Figure 13-12. Systems analysis plays an important role in establishing these interrelationships and their inclusion in the design of the computer system.

FIGURE 13-11 Computer business applications

(1) Management planning and control
  (2) Production scheduling and control
    (3) Research, development, and engineering
      (4) Financial management

(5) Marketing
  (6) Distribution
    (7) Personnel management

SOURCE: Picture courtesy of International Business Machines Corporation

FIGURE 13-12 Interrelationships in computer applications

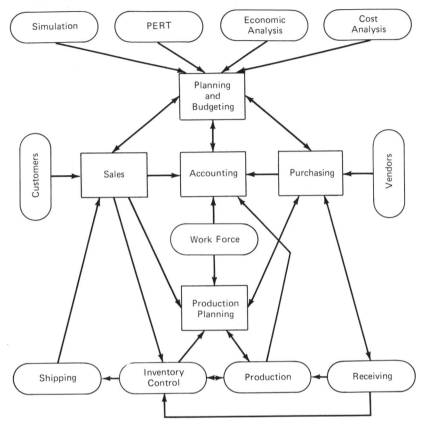

SYSTEMS ANALYSIS AND DESIGN

The overall process of developing a computer data processing system can be divided into three activities:

1. Design of the system
2. Implementation of the design
3. Operation of the system

DESIGN IS IMPORTANT IN PROBLEM SOLUTION

Design is primarily concerned with definition of the problem and devising a computerized data processing system that provides a workable solution. System implementation includes detailed procedure diagraming, coding, debugging, documentation, training, and conversion. The results obtained from computerized data processing depend more on the design of the system than on the specific equipment employed. The computer, while it is an extremely powerful data processing device, will not be effective unless the system that utilizes the equipment is properly designed.

MANAGERS ARE INVOLVED IN DESIGN

There are three major steps involved in the design of a computerized data processing system. The first step is to obtain an understanding of the business establishment as a total system and the configuration of the existing information system. Second, the results that should be obtained from the computerized information system must be specified. Third, the computer equipment to provide the data processing must be specified, and the procedures to obtain the desired results must be developed. Managers at all levels are involved in these three steps.

SYSTEMS ANALYSIS INVOLVES RETHINKING

Systems analysis involves (1) identifying the components and requirements of the present and proposed systems, (2) analyzing the needs of the various organizations for data and information, and (3) determining how these needs can best be satisfied. Systems analysis is a part of each of the three major steps involved in the design of a computerized data processing system. Managers at all levels are involved in systems analysis because it means rethinking the whole management process, not merely using computers to follow the same procedures once done by people.

Effective systems analysis requires an intensive and thorough study of the operations, problems, and informational needs of the organization. Detailed examination of the activity and its procedures is necessary to determine *what* must be done and *how* it can best be accomplished. A carefully conducted systems analysis may develop simplified procedures that enable the organization to do its job *without* a computer.

ONLY THE MANAGER CAN ANSWER CERTAIN QUESTIONS

It is not uncommon for the systems analyst to work in a partial vacuum. For example, a manager may want a management information system to provide data for decision-making purposes. However, when the analyst tries to find out what information is required, at what levels in the organization, and by whom, the situation becomes cloudy. The analyst may find that the manager expects to be told what information is required to make his or her decisions.

Another difficult area in systems analysis is the question of accuracy and timeliness of data. These two factors can have a considerable influence on the hardware and procedures that may be required—all of which affect the costs of implementation and operation of the system. The real questions are (1) How accurate *must* the information be? (rather than How accurate would I *like* it to be?) and (2) When is the information *needed?* (rather than When do I *want* it?) These questions can only be answered by the manager, not the systems analyst.

Only after a systems analysis has been conducted should a manager decide whether or not the use of a computer is justified. The general practice is to conduct the systems analysis as a team activity. This enables managers to obtain more than one point of view and to stimulate the development of the best solutions to the problem.

STEPS IN SYSTEMS ANALYSIS

Figure 13-13 shows one approach to conducting a systems analysis. The first step is to define the problem and the management objectives. The second step is for the analysts to get the current facts:

- *What is being done to process the work?*
- *What forms are used?*
- *What reports are prepared?*
- *What reports are needed but not available?*
- *What procedures are followed?*
- *What information files are maintained?*
- *How are files processed?*
- *How is input data generated?*

The third step is to analyze the current work methods and procedures, including the purpose and needs for information by all users. The fourth step is to determine the feasibility of using a computer. The fifth step is to develop a multitude of alternatives as to how to perform functions better. The sixth step is to evaluate each alternative as to its benefits and costs. At this point the analysts should be able to recommend the most cost-effective system for management's decision.

PARTICIPATIVE MANAGEMENT

Throughout the entire systems analysis study, there should be widespread participation by all levels of management. A systems analyst, no matter how competent, cannot set the objectives and define the problems of the entire organization. Neither can the systems analyst be given the freedom to redesign either the system or the organization to conform to a computer. Third, the systems analyst cannot specify what information is to be used for management decisions. Management, from top to bottom, must appropriately participate in the development of an information system, whether a computer is used or not.

FIGURE 13-13 Steps in systems analysis

① Define the problem and objectives   ④ Determine computer feasibility
② Get the facts of the situation   ⑤ Develop alternatives
③ Analyze the facts

Alternative A

Alternative B

⑥ Evaluate alternatives (costs vs. benefits)   ⑦ Make a decision

Alternative A installed

SOURCE: Pictures courtesy of International Business Machines Corporation

CHANGING TRENDS
IN BUSINESS COMPUTERS

ROUTINE TASKS

When computers began to be used in business management, the emphasis was on getting hardware to handle some of the most routine, repetitive, and time-consuming tasks such as payrolls and inventories. Most organizations had acquired computer capabilities that were far in excess of the simple routine tasks and workload that the equipment was assigned to do.

COMPUTER SIMULATION

One of the earliest and most important developments in the area of management science was the technique of computer simulation. This technique allowed complicated systems to be represented by mathematical and logical models that could be operated over time in the computer to test possible management decisions ahead of time. For example, a model could be developed to represent the internal cost structure of the company. The computer could then be used to manipulate the model to forecast a complete operating budget based upon product mix, price, and marketing program. Management could examine several alternative combinations of these variables to reduce the areas of uncertainty in making extremely important and complicated decisions.

PROBLEM SOLVING

As technology expanded, the use of computers in business operations extended into areas that required much more than just hardware. The use of computers to help solve business problems required extensive systems analysis and more sophisticated software programming. Technology has generated more versatile mainframes, new microprocessor-driven data terminals, powerful new minicomputers, and improved communication systems. The rapidly expanding technology has often moved far ahead of creative systems development for processing and communicating management information. However, the software aspects of input/output are starting to catch up with the hardware technology. For example, the large volume of printed output, so characteristic of earlier computerization of business management, can now be reduced by shifting to the use of microfilm or on-line inquiry via CRT terminals.

CENTRALIZED DATA PROCESSING

During the period from 1971 to 1977, data processing personnel became more involved in the business applications of computers. In many organizations this involvement was reflected in the consolidation of many computer sites into one or a few large ones with systems that many users claimed cost less but often did not produce the most beneficial results. Since 1977 more management attention has been given to the services and benefits that can be obtained from intelligent utilization of computers. This reflective thinking has caused many organizations to shift from central mainframe computers for certain business operations, to the use of minicomputers and microcomputers and the implementation of distributed data processing by users (see Chapter 14).

DECENTRALIZED PROCESSING

There is a developing trend toward low-cost, high-speed communications that will transfer some data processing from the domain of the computer specialists to the users. This trend does not indicate the demise of the central data processing department. Conversely, there are indicators that the data processing department of the future may include all communication functions—voice, data, and the conveyance of written documentation from place to place (electronic mail). However, the users of management data and information will have more control over input/output.

The following is one example of how new methods in the use of computers are changing business management. In the early 1970s, a large company engaged in manufacturing knitted fashion goods used manual methods for writing, processing, and scheduling orders on its various mills. In addition to these manual methods, the United States mail was the vehicle for communicating these orders from the marketing headquarters in New York City to customer services in South Carolina, and to the manufacturing mills in various locations. These manual methods resulted in significant built-in lag time in responding to the dictates of fashion clothing.

HANDLING DIVERSIFIED ACTIVITIES

Because of the lag time, as well as other problems, the company computerized its ordering, production scheduling, production reporting, and inventory control. The new method included implementation of decentralized distributed data processing wherein input/output terminals were installed in New York City and in the various mills, and all were hooked to the customer services operation in South Carolina. The computerized system enables the company to keep on top of ordering, scheduling, and production control as well as the monitoring of the condition of mill equipment, payroll incentive calculations, and status of orders. The lag-time problems of communicating by mail are now virtually a thing of the past.

SUPERVISOR RESPONSIBILITY

Current supercomputers are capable of performing up to 400 million calculations per second. This means that managers can work on an almost infinite variety of problems at every level of difficulty. However, the intelligent use of any computer requires that the manager first define the problem. In many situations the action must start with the first-level supervisor.

SUMMARY

The computer, which only understands the signals of "on" or "off," is drastically changing our lives and the way we manage things in business and government. There are two basic types of computers, the analog that measures and the digital that counts. The functional elements of a computer are input, storage, arithmetic and logic (processing), control, output, and communications. The technology in computer development has advanced from a thirty-ton device with 18,000 vacuum tubes to a million electronic circuits on a tiny silicon "chip." The computer with its great ability to add, subtract, multiply, divide, and compare must receive minutely detailed instructions. The weak link in the use of computers is that managers must determine what they want from the computer. These decisions must then be converted by computer specialists (programmers) into language that is understood by the computer—the signals of "on" or "off." The key component of a data processing system is the input of data—because the quality of the data base and the output can never be better than the quality and timeliness of the input. Output of data is also influenced by whether data is processed into the computer in batches or on a real-time basis. Timely use of data output is further influenced by whether data is filed sequentially or in a manner that allows direct access.

The greater a manager's understanding of the computer, the greater the potential for its effective use. The manager who exercises both business sense and common sense will find that computers can be used as very cost-effective devices. Above all else, it is people that make computers work. Making good use of a computer starts with management. It involves knowing the management problems, performing a systems analysis to determine the proper design and implementation of a computerized system, and being able to rethink the whole management process. The development of and conversion to computerized business operations must be accomplished on a participative basis, from the top to the lowest levels of management.

More management attention is now being given to the services and benefits that can be obtained from intelligent utilization of computers. This reflective thinking has caused organizations to implement such practices as distributed data processing by users. There are indicators that the use of minicomputers and microcomputers will transfer some data processing from the domain of the computer specialists to the users. Other indicators point toward an expansion of electronic business operations integrated with electronic means of communication.

REVIEW QUESTIONS

1. What is the meaning of the statement that a computer only understands the signals of "on" or "off"?
2. What is the basic difference between an analog computer and a digital computer?
3. Why is it misleading to refer to a computer as a brain?
4. What is the distinction between computer hardware and computer software?
5. Why is the arithmetic and logic element referred to as the heart of a computer?
6. What is the importance of the communication element in a computerized information system?
7. Why is input of data a key component of a data processing system?
8. Discuss the pros and cons of batch versus real-time processing of data into a computer.
9. Discuss how computer time sharing works.
10. What are the five things that a computer can do?
11. Discuss the manager actions involved in using a computer.
12. What are the five characteristics that determine whether management information is suitable for computer application?
13. Discuss the difference between business sense and common sense in the utilization of computers.
14. Discuss management's involvement in systems analysis and design.

A CASE STUDY IN UNDERSTANDING THE COMPUTER

Many managers, who have insisted on ten-year strategic business plans and five-year production and marketing plans, have not required similar planning for data processing. This lack of long-range planning is to be found in spite of the fact that information processing budgets are now getting to be as large as those of other corporate operations. Inadequate planning for computerized operations is to be found in both large and small organizations.

Commuterboro Township is a small rural community in New Jersey. Most of its working residents are employed in nearby New York City. There are a few small commercial businesses providing needed community services, but there are no manufacturing and few commercial establishments in the township.

The Commuterboro Township Council several months ago

announced that it expected to "enter the computer age" in forty-five days. It had authorized advertising for bids for its first computer. The equipment was expected to cost less than ten thousand dollars and would be used to handle budgeting, payment of bills, and other accounting functions. The Township officials stated, however, that it would continue to use outside services for payroll and accounting after the new computer system was operating.

The Township's business administrator stated that the new computer would serve the Township for two or three years. At that time the Township would then obtain a larger computer to handle the finance department and other areas. When the Township obtained its larger computer, the first computer would be used as a word processor. In making the decision to buy the computer, the Township did not have a computer consultant, but the mayor and business administrator conducted a survey to see what equipment was available.

Eighteen months after the computer had been purchased and installed, a concerned resident of Commuterboro made a visit to the Township office to see how the equipment was being utilized. She found that it was not being used at all for the purposes stated when it was purchased. Except for the Police Department using it to file reports, the equipment was idle and collecting dust.

QUESTIONS

1. Do you think that the mayor and business administrator had an understanding of what a computer can do? Explain your answer.
2. What actions should the Township officials have taken to assure that the new computer would be effectively used?
3. In view of the amount of the capital investment, do you think a systems analysis was necessary? Explain your answer.
4. Why do you think the Township computer is not being used for its intended purposes?

THE CASE OF THE PRODUCTION FLOW PROBLEM

Pat Lamborn is the supervisor of the final assembly, packing, and testing operations for the AC Company. The company manufactures major assembled components for the aircraft industry.

Lamborn is faced with two problems in his department. One problem involves meeting tight monthly customer shipping dates. The second problem is that of having all the many purchased parts,

company-assembled kits, and manufactured components in his
department at the right time and in the right quantities. Since the
production flow is on a job order basis, the assembled kits and
manufactured components come from all over the plant. It is not a
continuous production flow from the stock room to the final assembly
in Lamborn's department. The production flow of these purchased
parts, assembled kits, and manufactured components is a critical
problem in Lamborn's department. A single missing purchased part, for
example, can hold up the final assembly of the product.

The AC Company currently has no computers in its
manufacturing operations. The plant manager feels that they are not
needed.

QUESTIONS

1. What is your evaluation of the plant manager's position that computers are not needed
   in the AC Company's manufacturing operations?
2. In your evaluation of the situation, do you see where and how a computer could help
   resolve the production flow problem in Lamborn's department? If so, how?

14

Managing Information

THE SUPERVISOR'S INVOLVEMENT
WITH MANAGING INFORMATION

As managers, we cannot effectively
do our jobs without information. Computers and their related technology provide
the potential for providing us with the
necessary information we need. However,
we must tell the computer what we need. The managing of information goes far
beyond just dealing with computers. For one thing, we do not need to computerize
all of our information needs. We also have to face the fact that although the costs of
many computers have come down, the overall cost of information has gone up. The
reason is that as computers proliferate, so does the data they produce. Therefore,
our job as managers includes the control of expenditures for data processing and ensuring the effective development of both operational and management information.
The changing technology in computers and means of communication requires our
continual planning in the managing of any information system. We must strive to do
something about the disturbing gap between computer technology and our ability
to intelligently use that technology.

Robert C. Lowery
Former Comptroller
Army Electronics Command

LEARNING OBJECTIVES

The objectives of this chapter on managing information are to enable the reader to

1. Establish how managing information is a key element in good management
2. Describe flexible data processing methodology and its importance
3. Understand why business needs both operational and management information systems
4. Identify and describe the components of a computer-based information system
5. Delineate the three most misunderstood and misused areas in a computerized information system
6. Recognize what to do and not to do in the management of information
7. Delineate the importance of participative management in the development of management information systems
8. Establish the basic guidelines in the development of a good information system
9. Describe four effective systems for avoiding a costly business information paper avalanche

KEY WORDS

Aperture Card A standard tab card that has a hole cut in it for mounting a frame of microfilm.

COM (Computer Output Microfilm) A system in which microfilm images are prepared from digitized data stored on magnetic tapes or discs, or transmitted directly from a computer's central processor.

Cost-Effective Information System An information system in which the results or benefits derived from the use of the information more than justify the costs of obtaining it.

Data Measured facts, statistics, and/or observations.

Data Processing The conversion of data into information.

Distributed Data Processing Decentralizing the storing and manipulating of computerized data to the points where most of the work is done and the results needed.

Information Data that has been processed or converted into more meaningful and usable form.

Information System A mass of organized facts, statistics and/or descriptive words or numbers relating to specific identifiable things.

Management Information System   A network of feeding selected operational and other information to managers to support their decision-making responsibilities.

Microfiche   A sheet of film containing multiple microimages (photographic reproductions) in a grid pattern.

Microfilm   The photographic reproduction of alpha-numeric characters, drawings, and other printed materials in a miniaturized format.

Microfilm Jacket   Two clear sheets of separated acetate used for the storage of short strips of microfilm.

Operational Information System   The inputs, processing, and outputs of data pertaining to the day-to-day conduct of business activities by functional managers.

THE CASE OF THE DEVOURING INFORMATION SYSTEM

A $20 MILLION FIASCO

A large department of the federal government spent more than twelve years of development effort and expended over $20 million to implement a very comprehensive computerized management accounting and reporting information system. In addition to the costly development efforts, an estimated one million accounting manhours per year were spent to operate the system. These hours did not include computer processing time, the manhours spent in submitting input data to the accounting personnel, or the manhours spent in analyzing output data by managers and their staffs. The sad thing about this very costly management information system is that interviews with approximately ninety users of the system conclusively indicated that the system did not work.

The A & R system as we will call it (not its real title), was designed to be a single integrated total information system. It was to provide data covering thirty major management action areas including budget requirements, appropriations of funds to organizations, allocations of funds to programs, acceptances of customer orders, obligations of funds by programs, deliveries of hardware from production, and expenditures of funds by programs. Approximately seventy output reports covering between fifteen hundred and eighteen hundred items of data information were generated by the system. Some of the reports contained more than eight hundred pages of detailed data. The system, however, was not able to operate as a single source data bank, nor did it function without duplicate record systems.

WHERE WAS MANAGEMENT?

Managers from the top-level to the first-level found that the system was not structured to satisfy their informational needs. Attempts to redesign the system frequently failed because it sometimes required a thousand or more computer program changes to effect a revision to a single data element in the system. This situation was caused by the large number of closely integrated and interacting data information items that had been programmed into the system. A change in one item could interact and necessitate a program change to many other items which in turn could affect still other items. Several managers expressed their feelings that the system was designed for the computer, not for the human beings who must operate with the outputs of the system.

A DESIGNER'S DREAM

The concept of the single integrated total information system for an entire organization has been the long-term goal of many information system designers. Many government agencies and more industrial and commercial organizations than we will ever know about have attempted to implement this concept and failed. It is very easy to carry the single integrated information system to the extreme where it is unmanageable, unreliable, prohibitively expensive, and does not meet the needs of the users. The case of the A & R system is being used as an example in this chapter because it represents so many serious mistakes made by all levels of management. It is hoped that a study of this case will save some from making the same mistakes.

WHAT IS MEANT BY MANAGING INFORMATION?

INFORMATION IS A MANAGEMENT RESOURCE

Information refers to useful knowledge concerning some particular set of facts, events, or circumstances. Managers at all levels need usable information in order to effectively perform their jobs. One can look at information as another resource required in the process of managing a product, service, function, project, or organization. Timely knowledge of the right information can be a significant factor in making the right decision. Conversely, the absence of information when it is needed can cause a wrong decision to be made. Managers at all levels, therefore, have to obtain and use information properly in order to arrive at the right decisions at the right times. The managing of information is a key element in good management.

DATA PROCESSING METHODOLOGY

PROCESSED DATA BECOMES INFORMATION

Data in its usual form of measured facts, statistics, or observations may be of minimal value to a manager making a decision. It is usually after data has been "processed" into more useful "information" that it becomes meaningful and usable for management purposes. An important aspect of management, therefore, is the conversion or processing of data into information, hence the significance of the term *data processing.*

DIFFERENT DATA REQUIRES DIFFERENT PROCESSING

Information systems are a type of data processing. The primary purpose of an information system is to provide managers and others with the meaningful and usable knowledge needed to effectively perform their jobs. As used in this book, the term *information system* refers to any mass of organized facts, statistics, and/or descriptive words or numbers relating to identifiable things— events, objects, functions, projects, programs, and so on. These facts, statistics, descriptive words, and/or numbers can be related to the past, the present, and/or the future. They can be derived from highly accurate historical accounting data, or from mathematically developed data based on identifiable assumptions. This broad view of information systems recognizes that there are vastly different kinds of data and information requiring distinctly different processing methodologies.

DON'T COMPUTERIZE EVERYTHING

The designers of the A & R system would have done better if they had recognized that all types of data should *not* be subjected to the same processing methodology. One of the problems of the A & R system was caused by the fact that certain data and information, such as the President's budget request to the Congress, never should have been programmed into the system. This one-time, seldom-referred-to data would have been better placed manually in a file cabinet than programmed at the budget line-item level in the computerized A & R system. The system designers also would have come up with a better system if they had recognized that, while all managers need information, their requirements for different types of information are usually not the same.

The failure to recognize that different informational needs may require distinctly different data processing methodologies caused much of the A & R system output to be totally unusable to many managers. As one example, the system procedures were primarily written for the management of major items of equipment. The many managers involved with the procurement, production, supply, and maintenance of several hundred thousand minor or secondary items of equipment were not able to analyze and use the detailed, copious reports that they received. The system was not adequately designed to provide the proper information to secondary-item managers. There was insufficient flexibility in the data processing methodology.

TYPES OF INFORMATION SYSTEMS

DIFFERENT SYSTEMS FOR DIFFERENT PURPOSES

Different informational needs require different informational systems. As reflected in Figure 14-1, at the lower levels of management the need is for day-to-day information pertaining to control of operations and utilization of resources. At the middle levels of management the information needs tend to focus more on planning, budgeting, and allocation of resources. At the top levels of management the information needs tend to relate more to strategic planning and future sources as well as allocations of funding to achieve long-range goals. At all levels of management there is a need for current information regarding the status and trend of execution of plans and the utilization of resources.

FIGURE 14-1 Informational needs of management

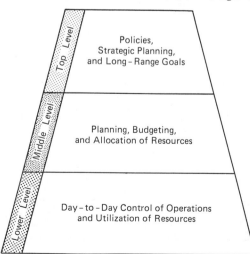

INTEGRATED SUBSYSTEMS

● *THE BUSINESS ESTABLISHMENT AS A TOTAL SYSTEM*—As shown in Figure 14-2, a business establishment must function as a total system. To achieve its objectives, the total business establishment must manage and control many operational functions. The most effective management of these many operational functions can be achieved by considering them as subsystems of the total system. These subsystems must be integrated and coordinated in order for the total system to operate smoothly in accomplishing its objectives. Managing information is a key factor in achieving total system integration and coordination. In the performance of functional operations, which are the foundation of the business establishment, there is a need for operational information. At all levels of management there is a need for manage-

FIGURE 14-2   The business establishment as a total system

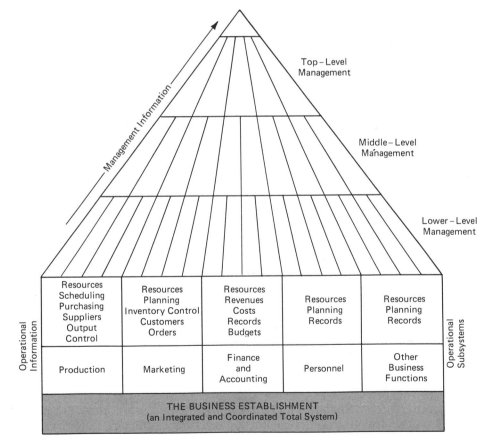

rial information for decision-making purposes. Both types of information are necessary in the administration of any business establishment.

DAY-TO-DAY OPERATIONS INFORMATION

- *OPERATIONAL INFORMATION SYSTEMS*—Operational information involves the input, processing, and output of data pertaining to such things as production results, sales transactions, accounting transactions, and other operational results. This data and information is needed for the day-to-day operation of business activities by the various functional managers. In production management, for example, first-level managers need operational information on such things as plant scheduling, receiving of supplies and materials, inventory control, materials movement control, machine control, quality control, and time reporting. In marketing there is the need for operational information on such things as advertising promotion, inventory control, orders placed, status of orders, dealer/branch operations, and customer services. In accounting there is the need for operational information for the purposes of handling such things as payrolls, accounts receivable, accounts payable, asset accounting, and general ledger accounting. While most of the operational information is used in the performance of day-to-day functional tasks, some is used to support the nonroutine decisions of managers at various levels in the business establishment.

DECISION-MAKING INFORMATION

- *MANAGEMENT INFORMATION SYSTEMS*—Management information is needed by managers in making decisions. The typical management information system is a network that feeds selected operational and other information to managers at various levels to support their decision-making responsibilities (Figure 14-3). In many business establishments the management information system also provides outside environmental information pertaining to customers, suppliers, competitors, stockholders, labor unions, financial institutions, government agencies, economic factors, and community relations. Any one or more of these informational factors can be of significance in the management decision-making process.

COMPONENTS OF AN INFORMATION SYSTEM

The components of an information system may consist of nothing more than a manually maintained diary, a loose-leaf notebook, or file folder of facts and information on events and/or circumstances pertaining to certain business oper-

FIGURE 14-3 A management information system

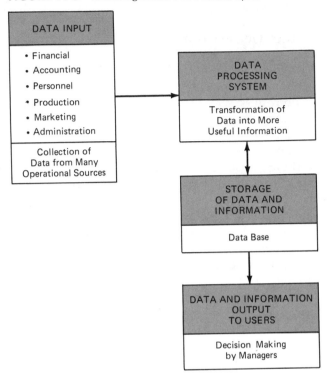

ations. However, with the advent of macro-, mini-, and microcomputers in many business establishments, most information systems are computer-based operations.

THE COMPUTER-BASED SYSTEM

What are the components of a computer-based information system? As shown in Figure 14-4, there are four component areas. The primary component area is the computer hardware with its capacity for receiving data input, processing data into the information desired, and producing information output. The second component area is the computer software or programs of input/output procedures and operating procedures that instruct the computer on what to do with the data it receives. The third component area is the data base or actual compiling of data and information that will be processed through the computer. The fourth component area is personnel. Depending on the type of computer hardware, it may include user personnel, computer systems personnel, computer programming personnel, and computer operations personnel.

USERS PLAY A DOMINANT ROLE

User personnel, including managers and supervisors, play a dominant role in computer-based information systems. First, they have a primary responsibility for determining what information they want from the system. Without user demands for information, there may be no need for computer information system analysts, programmers, or equipment operators. There may not even be a

FIGURE 14-4 Components of a computer-based information system

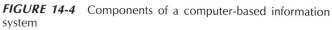

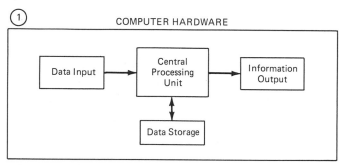

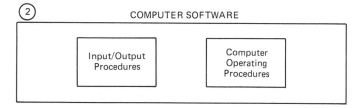

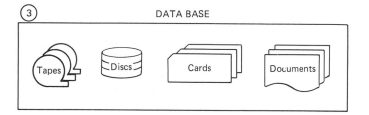

need for the computer. Remember that one of the problems with the A & R system was that many of the users did not know what they wanted from the computer. Second, user personnel may also have a major responsibility for providing data input into the information system. This is a very important responsibility because the quality of the computer output can never be any better than the quality of the input.

USE OF AN INFORMATION SYSTEM

Do Users Understand Computers?

Many computer-based information systems are not effective because the users do not understand the capabilities of the computer and do not know how to intelligently use computerized output. Three of the most misunderstood and misused areas in computerized information systems involve

1. The question of availability of information
2. The question of action versus information needs
3. The exception principle

These three areas will be discussed in the paragraphs that follow.

There Are Two Kinds of Knowledge

● *THE QUESTION OF AVAILABILITY OF INFORMATION*—A basic question in management is how to obtain assurance that information is available when it is needed. This question is partly answered by the way you define the term *available*. To some people, like Samuel Johnson quoted below, *available* means either available in one's mind or available in the sense that one knows where to go to obtain it.

> *Knowledge is of two kinds.*
> *We know a subject, or we*
> *know where we can find*
> *information upon it.*
> Samuel Johnson (1709–1784)

Johnson's philosophy makes practical sense. Possessing information about those things which are pertinent and significant in one's job is a required responsibility of a good manager. On the other hand, attempting to possess information in anticipation of every possible question that one's boss might ask at any uncertain time, if ever, can result in both ineffective and very costly management.

BE KNOWLEDGEABLE OF THE PERTINENT AND SIGNIFICANT THINGS

It is rather basic in management that you cannot accumulate and analyze the raw facts for each and every decision-making problem when it arises. Prudent judgment dictates that information which you believe may be helpful in expected situations be accumulated and properly stored. The important things are

- *That purposeful information be accumulated*
- *That information expected to be used be readily accessible when needed*
- *That every conceivable bit of information* not *be accumulated*

Purposefulness and accessibility of information appear to mean different things to different managers. There is a common malady that causes many managers to feel that they must personally possess a great abundance of both significant and detailed back-up data so that they can answer virtually any question without going to the source of the information. The result of this practice has caused data information to grow and grow in abundance to the satisfaction of scarcely anyone other than the recipient. Data information costs a great deal of money to produce, consumes valuable computer programming and operation time, ties up communication facilities, and often yields little in return. A manager, therefore, should restrict his or her informational needs to that which is purposeful and useful.

With regard to management attitude on availability of information, the lack of personal knowledge of all the details of any given subject is not necessarily a reflection of incompetence. The important things are to be knowledgeable of the pertinent and significant data and information and know where to go to get additional information.

CONCENTRATE ON WHERE THE ACTION IS

- *THE QUESTION OF ACTION VERSUS INFORMATIONAL NEEDS*—At all levels of management there should be a distinction made between the information needed as a basis for taking action versus that needed merely to keep informed. When the two needs are intermixed, there is the danger that the action information may be overlooked. Second, the information takes time to read, and this wastes managerial time, clerical time, and costs money. Third, the individual will be a better manager if he or she can concentrate on becoming thoroughly informed on those matters that require action. Obtaining informational copies of everything causes excessive distribution and unnecessary proliferation of paper.

Each manager must give substantial thought to the policy of controlling information they receive to that needed for management action. This involves

- *Identifying the key areas of action in the operations which must be controlled*
- *Specifying the means—forecasts, budgets, lead time, production schedules, standard costs, turnover ratios—for controlling the key areas of action*
- *Defining the accounting, operating, and statistical data that must be accumulated to measure performance in the key areas of action*
- *Establishing a reporting system that identifies performance and trends in the key areas of action*

Unless managers restrict the information they get to that needed for management action, they will soon be buried in information and find it even more difficult to control their operations.

CONTROL BY IMPORTANCE

- *THE EXCEPTION PRINCIPLE*—Information systems should be based on the principle of management by exception. Why, for example, read the entire budget report for ten organizations when all you really want to know is whether any of the organizations missed its budget, and if so, why? Why waste time and effort reading and trying to memorize reams of figures which are readily available in reference documents? Which is more important, the ability to impress management by rattling off strings of statistics at the drop of a hat, or effectiveness in getting things done?

ALL THINGS ARE NOT IMPORTANT

The management-by-exception principle recognizes that all things are not equally important and never will be; and that it is a serious mistake to develop control systems which make the error of treating all things equally. An information system which attempts to treat all things equally will be a major contributor to confusion rather than control. It has been said that it makes a lot of difference which end of the opera glasses you use to look at the characters on the stage. This strategy applies equally well to seeing and reacting to the big and important things rather than the little and unimportant things in management.

SOME MAJOR CONCERNS
ABOUT INFORMATION SYSTEMS

An evaluation of the A & R system, referred to throughout this chapter, provides many guidelines about things to do and not to do in managing information. The management action that should be taken *before* computerizing an information system is something that is often overlooked. Second, it is also important to know about and avoid the symptoms of a poor information system. Third, one needs an understanding of the pitfalls of the single-system concept. And fourth, on the positive side, one should know the merits of the subsystem concept of information.

AVOID COMPUTERIZING "GARBAGE"

● *INFORMATION SYSTEMS AND COMPUTERS*—Before thinking about computerizing an information system, the manager should first examine the adequacy of any currently existing information systems. A large expensive computer will *not* guarantee an effective information system. The development of the configuration and contents of the desired information system need to be established first and then, where appropriate, be computerized. There are three reasons why this sequence must be followed.

1. Not all information generated by a computer qualifies as management information, and no purpose is served by attempting to program the wrong things on a computer. It can be a mistake to assume that the same techniques used to provide operational information can always be used to provide higher-level management information. This unsound assumption was one of the failings of the designers of the A & R system.
2. Not all management information can be improved by the use of a computer. There are certain types of information that are really not suitable for processing through a computer. This also was one of the failings of the designers of the A & R system. Many of the computerized results of the A & R system were disappointing because the users did not receive output reports that they could use.
3. The biggest advantages to be gained from a computerized system come from the preliminary work of reevaluating and reengineering the types and processing of information really needed by the various levels of management. A computer cannot correct poor information processing procedures or improve the quality of the information it is given.

Computerization of information should be preceded by (1) adequate systems, methods, and procedures improvement; and (2) determination of the type of data desired and how it will be provided and used. If these things are not done, the resulting information system will provide data faster but not better, and all the managers will get is faster knowledge of conflicting data, erroneous data, unneeded data, and significant areas not covered by any data. Managers will also have to account for the expenses of

- *Procurement of additional computer capacity*
- *Proliferation of reports that were* not *used*
- *Clerical staffs that were* not *reduced as promised by the developers of the computerized system*

ABUNDANCE OF DATA DOES NOT CREATE
A COST-EFFECTIVE SYSTEM

● *SYMPTOMS OF POOR INFORMATION SYSTEMS*—The average computerized *operational information system* is probably cost-effective. Where on-line computer terminals are used, this system gives the user ready access to information needed regarding such things as reservations, inventory levels, status of customer accounts, and sales transactions. The average computerized *management information system,* on the other hand, is probably *not* cost-effective. That does not mean to say that such systems are not providing timely and important information for the users. What is being said is that many management information systems

- *Provide more data than managers have time to use*
- *Provide a considerable amount of data that some managers do not know how to use properly*
- *Provide some data that can be dangerous to use*
- *Provide a considerable amount of data that is useless*
- *Fail to provide data that is really needed*

In summary, most management information systems tend to be oversupplied with data. However, an abundance of data in itself does not make for a cost-effective management information system. More specifically:

- *Information systems tend to accumulate and report too much information to the point that the output is unwieldy, cumbersome, and too much for management to digest.*
- *Information systems tend to fail to include the significant data which management may need most for decision making.*
- *Information systems tend to provide a lot of "nice-to-know" rather than "need-to-know" facts.*
- *Information systems reports often tend to be in computerized formats that are difficult to read and understand because they are figure-oriented rather than situation-oriented.*
- *Information systems tend not to provide much, if any, analysis or interpretation of the data contained in output reports. This places the burden on managers who may or may not be familiar with the assumptions or other factors involved in developing the data.*

The A & R system possessed all of the above symptoms of a poor information system. In addition, the A & R system contained unintegrated information caused by separate, but related, input data that originated in different divisions of the department. The conflicting data was generated through different cutoff reporting periods, different definitions, different data units, and different bases of comparison. This situation enabled the originators of the data to show information which was most favorable and suppress that which might not be favorable.

PROLIFERATION OF REPORTS

Computerized information systems tend to bring about a proliferation of reports. First, the mere availability of data processing equipment encourages the establishment of elaborate and more frequent reports. Second, once a report is established, the law of inertia tends to keep it going long after its usefulness has been served or even its original purpose remembered. Third, nonselective distribution of computerized reports often swamps the recipients with huge reports that are of little to no value for management decision purposes. The originating office may consider that it is more economical to distribute the entire massive report than to pull out sections for selective attention and distribution. In the case of the A & R system, the receipt of twelve-inch-thick reports was a common occurrence. Many of the users destroyed most of the reports they received because the reports contained a great deal of data that had no relation to them. This practice was a deplorable waste of money. Also, it was not necessary because the computer could have been programmed to provide only that data needed by the users.

INTEGRATED REPORTING OF DIVERSIFIED INFORMATION

- *THE SINGLE-SYSTEM CONCEPT*—There was a tendency in the past to apply the computer in a piecemeal fashion to the handling of business activities. The earlier applications were concerned with the computerization of routine clerical and record-keeping tasks such as payroll and inventory control. Later applications of electronic data processing equipment focused attention on the need for integrated reporting of diversified management information. This attention has brought forth a considerable amount of thinking in terms of the single information system that provides data for many diversified purposes from one common data bank (Figure 14-5). The thought behind the single integrated information system appears, without close analysis, to be a good idea. Obviously management is at a disadvantage if it has reports that overlap, or different reports that deal with the same data but in an inconsistent way.

FALSE PROMISES

Advocates of the single-system concept are many, and their salesmanship is full of glib words and promises of untold wonders. The advocates of the A & R system wanted a system that would encompass capital acquisitions, inventory management, five-year planning, program and budget management, status of

FIGURE 14-5 Single system concept for management information

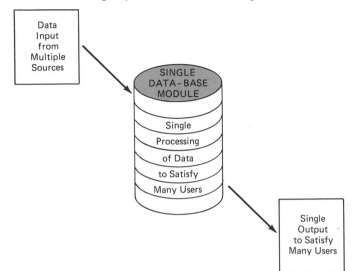

work in process, production costs, standard costs, deliveries, contractor performance, and all aspects of accounting and reporting. The various elements of data, they said, would be captured only once from a single source at the points of origin, and files would be updated on a timely transaction reporting basis. The A & R system never worked, however, in accordance with the dreams of its advocates.

Don't Try To Combine Too Many Things

Careful evaluation of the single information system, even in a single functional area, discloses that there are some obvious disadvantages in carrying the concept too far. A single information system for historical accounting data is one type of operation that is probably hard to find fault with—particularly if it provides timely, consistent, and reliable data. By the same logic, a single information system that provides technical data for engineers would likewise be welcomed by most users. However, a single system that tries to combine everything is usually doomed to failure—a victim of the weight of its own conflicting mass.

Operational Control and Management Control Are Not the Same

Different functions and different levels of management have varying needs for data information. Operational control needs exact data, whereas management control often needs only approximations. Management control is usually heavily built around a financial structure. Operational control is involved with many nonmonetary as well as monetary matters. Data in an operational information system are often in real time (e.g., reported as the event is occurring) and related to individual events. Data in a management information system are often retrospective and summarize many separate events. Planning at the highest levels of management is essentially applied economics, whereas planning at the lower operational levels primarily involves more tangible facts and figures. The focus of operational control is on individual tasks or transactions such as the scheduling and controlling of individual work orders. The focus of management control is on measuring the performance of the total organization.

LIMITATIONS OF THE SINGLE-SYSTEM CONCEPT

With so many variable needs for data information, there are severe limitations in the practicality of a large complex organization being able to provide all of its data from a single integrated management information system. Even the same type of data is often structured and used differently by various functional activities. For example, let us take the accounting and the purchasing departments. They both utilize some of the same financial data in their reports. However, their operational reporting cutoff dates may be different, and the way they structure and use the same data may not be the same. To further confuse the situation, the accounting personnel tend only to report a contractual obligation of money when the contractual document is actually received in the accounting department. The purchasing department, however, may have already reported the contractual obligation the moment that the contract was signed. The time lag in the reported data may be several days unless there is a direct real-time computer input terminal located in the purchasing department. There must also be a good control to prevent both the accounting and the purchasing departments from reporting different contractual obligation figures. The more organizations, functions, and transactions that are involved in a single information system, the greater the problems of communication, coordination, and reconciliation.

Various authors, such as Robert N. Anthony of Harvard University, have for many years expressed concern about the shortcomings of the single system concept. They have, for example, pointed out the consequences of failing to make a distinction between vastly different functional processes in management. Some have stated that an organization has an impossible goal if it plans to collect data in building blocks that can be combined in various ways to answer *all* conceivable management questions. The consensus of these authors and consultants is generally negative regarding the totally integrated single system that will provide management with all the data it needs for whatever problems it decides to tackle. Another author has stated that for most business firms, carrying systems integration to an extreme could result in systems that are costly, cumbersome, or unreliable and which do not effectively meet the information needs of users.[1]

PROHIBITIVE COSTS

The total system concept can lead an organization in precisely the wrong direction because the information system for an entire company can be too large and all-encompassing to be a meaningful and effective management "tool." The development of a single information system requires many different kinds of technical skills and implies a control of their system efforts. These situations also contribute to causing the single-system concept to be largely unsuccessful. The cost of a totally integrated system with fail-safe controls to prevent serious errors, loss or destruction of data, and unauthorized use is usually prohibitive.

● *THE SUBSYSTEM CONCEPT*—Each management information system proposal requires that the data be assembled in a way that best fits the requirements of all types and levels of management. In a large complex organization, the best way to satisfy these many varying requirements of different managers is probably the establishment of interrelated major subsystems.

The subsystem concept (Figure 14-6) involves establishing several information systems covering the primary and most extensive functional areas of

FIGURE 14-6   Subsystem concept for management information

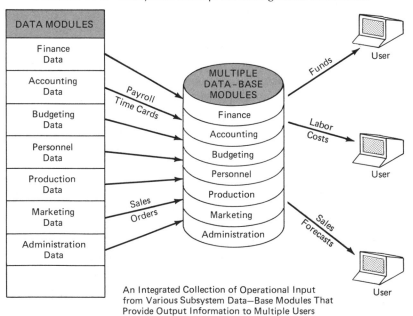

An Integrated Collection of Operational Input
from Various Subsystem Data–Base Modules That
Provide Output Information to Multiple Users

the total organization. The most common subsystems cover the areas of finance and accounting, production, marketing, and personnel. Under the subsystem concept there may be some duplication and redundancy in having relatively self-contained data banks for each major functional area.

INTEGRATED MODULES

As reflected in Figure 14-6, it is possible to establish a common data base as an integrated collection of the several subsystem data base modules. These subsystem modules can, with careful planning, be placed under the control of the central computer system. Only by placing these subsystem modules under central control can an integrated information system be achieved. Placing the various modules under central control allows each subsystem to access what becomes a common data base. The proper organization of the common data base, with the integrated subsystem modules, can minimize duplication in data collection, storage, updating, and deletion. The big advantage over the single integrated system is that each subsystem is a self-contained and usually easy-to-manage module.

DOES MANAGEMENT KNOW WHAT IT WANTS?

MANAGER RESPONSIBILITIES

A very basic and significant factor in any information system is for management to know what it wants and how it will use the information it gets. Each level of management must determine for itself the kind of information needed to plan and execute its responsibilities and to make the decisions necessary for a successful operation. One can get ideas from other organizations, but in the final analysis each manager must determine

1. *What* information is needed
2. *Why* and for *what purpose* it is needed
3. *How* it is going to be used
4. Whether the benefits from the information *justify the costs* of getting it

These decisions are necessary in the establishment of any information system if one wants the system to be effective, efficient, and economical to operate. Usually the purpose and use of information can be clearly defined in about two short sentences. If it takes more than two sentences, the need for the information is probably questionable.

UNREALISTIC VISIONS

In the case of the A & R system, the designers of the system, who didn't understand some of the complex business functions of the organization, determined the type of information that managers would receive. The designers in this case can only be partly faulted for making decisions that should have come from the managers and users of the system. Top-level managers, with visions of a single total information system, delegated the project of designing the system to the accountants and the data processing computer experts. However, when the system did not work, very few managers were able to state what information they really needed and how they would use it if they had it.

Another disturbing deficiency in the case of the A & R system was that many managers requested information that they could not use. For example, one relatively high level manager in procurement, with a very small staff, had requested and was receiving a monthly computer printout report that was approximately four feet thick. The information contained in the report was not structured in a format that was conducive to either effective or efficient manager use. In addition, the voluminous report was received too late after the end of the preceding month to be of much value for timely management decision purposes. This management practice was wasteful of computer processing and printout time, multi-copy printout paper, and the labor costs involved in the preparation and distribution of an unused report.

The top-level managers who directed the implementation of the A & R system were also to be faulted for not involving all appropriate levels of management in the development of the system and in not determining the estimated costs versus expected benefits of the system before they directed its implementation. When the government agency involved lost financial control over customer orders, the top-level managers stated that it was because the lower-level managers had not implemented the A & R system. They failed to realize that the system was so defective that, even if it had been implemented, it would not have prevented the problem from occurring.

PARTICIPATIVE MANAGEMENT

One of the many lessons to be learned from the A & R system is that managers at all levels should actively participate in the development of a major management information system. First, they need to specifically define what they need from the system and how they will use the information. Second, they should ascertain that the expected benefits justify the costs of developing and operating the system.

AN APPROACH TO GOOD INFORMATION SYSTEMS

There is no simple solution to the problem of developing and managing a good information system. There are, however, some basic considerations and guidelines that can at least provide a workable approach to take toward solution of the problem. These guidelines are discussed in the paragraphs that follow.

ORGANIZATION STRUCTURE

First, organize properly for the job. This is no easy matter because there is no one organization structure for the providing of management information that fits all possible situations. Much depends, for example, on the attitude, scope of vision, and objectivity of the personnel in the various organizational departments who would manage the information system. There can be problems because functional specialists often see only their own narrow activity and are thereby lacking in knowledge and understanding of the total organization and its information needs. The organization selected to coordinate and manage the information system should be staffed with personnel who have a broad understanding of management concepts and the importance of the various needs for information. These personnel should have an attitude that is flexible, adaptable, and objective.

MANAGEMENT PHILOSOPHY

Second, develop the right kind of management philosophy at all levels regarding the managing of information. It must be a "doing" not just a "talking and listening" philosophy. It means, for example:

- *Applying the principle of management by exception to the obtaining of information*
- *Recognizing the distinction between action needs and information-only needs for data, and reducing the latter to the absolute minimum*

PARTICIPATIVE MANAGEMENT

Third, develop the information system on a participative basis with specialists from involved functional activities. Also, get participative support at all appropriate levels of management. The participation by managers can have the following benefits:

- *It will tend to force the managers to determine exactly what they want from the system.*
- *It will enable the managers to see firsthand the costs of providing them with their informational needs.*

- *It will enable managers to check on unreasonable informational demands by their subordinates.*
- *It will help assure the development of an integrated and coordinated information system.*

MANAGEMENT REQUIREMENTS

Fourth, determine management's needs and uses for information during the design of the system. This determination should include:

- *Establishing what the significant issues are and the factual information that will enable managers to make sound decisions.*
- *Establishing the important areas of performance with which management at each level must concern itself. This includes recognizing that the areas of performance will vary with the type of function performed and its location in the management hierarchy.*
- *Establishing the specific types of information needed for different decisions by the various levels of management. This includes recognizing that the needs for information are not the same for different levels of management.*

PRINCIPLES OF GOOD REPORTING

Fifth, recognize and follow principles of good reporting.

- *Prepare reports against specific goals and objectives based on the exception principle.*
- *Use methods of approximation, where possible, because many reporting purposes are better served when managers are provided with timely close estimates of important developments that are revised later as more accurate information becomes available.*
- *Plan the contents of reports in conjunction with the people who are to use them as well as those who are to furnish the original data.*
- *Present reports in a language and format that are readily understood by the recipient. Prepare, if necessary, different versions for different users.*
- *Keep numbers and words to a minimum, and don't try to cover everything.*
- *Prepare reports to show, where possible, trends and/or comparisons with past performance, targets, forecasts, or performance standards.*
- *Use the principle of progressive synthesis (Figure 14-7) whereby each progressively higher level of management requests only the minimal significant data necessary for decision purposes.*

RULES OF FACT FINDING

Sixth, follow the simple rules of fact finding.

- *Get only salient information.*
- *Start with a broad look before getting into details.*

FIGURE 14-7 The principle of progressive synthesis

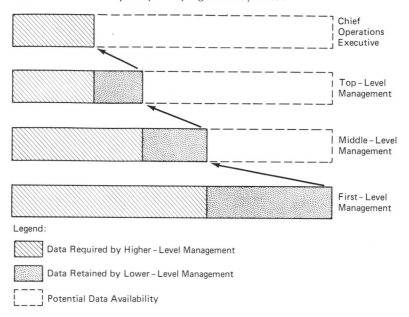

Legend:

Data Required by Higher-Level Management

Data Retained by Lower-Level Management

Potential Data Availability

- *Get directly to the problem.*
- *Don't go more deeply into details than necessary.*
- *Find the few facts that tend to account for the greatest part of the problem or situation.*
- *Don't generalize or make conclusions when there are insufficient facts.*
- *Learn to settle for something less than "all."*
- *Never lose sight of analyzing the relationship between the total costs of generating data and maintaining it versus the benefits served by having the data.*

CHANGING TRENDS IN INFORMATION SYSTEMS

SURVIVING THE PAPER AVALANCHE

The need for business information requires taking effective actions to survive the costly paper avalanche. Office activities may account for approximately 40 percent to 50 percent of a typical company's total operating costs. Analysis of these costs generally shows that most of an office's labor activities tend to be involved with handling information, the bulk of which is on paper. We have seen how the computer has led to a marked increase in reports generated for management's use in decision making and control. The manual operations (removing carbons, separating copies, binding, distributing, and filing) involved in the creation and handling of computerized reports is both time consuming and costly.

COMPUTER STORAGE IS NOT ALWAYS ECONOMICAL

In view of the need for and the costliness of business information, economy-minded managers need to evaluate and determine the best systems for the development, storage, and use of both operational and management information. Determining the best information system includes recognizing that computers are not always the most economical or efficient means of storing and retrieving data of medium- to long-term reference value. Some records, because of their format and reference requirements, cannot be economically reduced to a computer-processable form or be stored in computer memory. There are several alternatives in the handling of printed information. These alternatives include (1) source document microfilming, (2) computer-output microfilm, (3) distributed data processing, and (4) computer graphics.

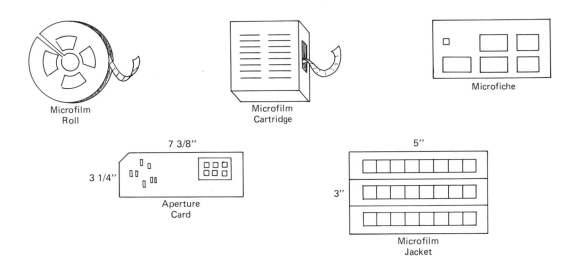

Microfilm Roll

Microfilm Cartridge

Microfiche

7 3/8″

3 1/4″

Aperture Card

5″

3″

Microfilm Jacket

• *MICROFILMING*—Microfilm is the photographic reproduction of alpha-numeric characters, drawings, and other printed materials in a miniaturized format. After developing, microfilm may be prepared in a variety of formats such as 16mm and 35mm rolls or cartridges, microfiche, aperture cards, and microfilm jackets. Microfiche is a relatively new technique consisting of a sheet of film containing multiple microimages in a grid pattern. Current concepts include updatable fiche where the original filmed record may be altered or added to after the first filming is complete.

An aperture card is a standard tab card that has a hole or aperture cut in it for mounting a frame of microfilm. It is well suited for applications in which such things as engineering drawings and material lists can be filed, retrieved, duplicated, distributed, and updated.

Microfilm jackets are an efficient and economical means of storing and retrieving records that must be periodically updated and duplicated. These jackets are comprised of two clear sheets of acetate separated into 16mm or 35mm channels and used for the storage of short strips of microfilm containing related images.

All microfilm formats are less expensive to store than equivalent paper documents. For example, the use of microfilm can reduce the space and equipment required for record storage by up to 98 percent. A four-drawer file cabinet containing 10,000 letter-size records requires six square feet of floor space. The same volume of records can be stored on four 100-foot rolls of microfilm measuring a total of $4'' \times 4'' \times 3''$—small enough to store in a desk drawer. Microfilm is also faster and less expensive to duplicate than paper. Improved indexing methods have made the retrieval of individual images faster and more economical than paper retrieval. For example, a duplicate microfiche containing approximately one hundred records may cost but a few cents to prepare. The same number of paper records reproduced by an office copier will cost several dollars. It is also cheaper to mail information on microfilm as compared with its paper equivalents.

• *SOURCE DOCUMENT MICROFILMING*—There are two basic types of microfilm processes. One process is called *source document microfilming* in which the microfilm images are prepared by photographing the actual paper records on roll film. After these 100-foot or 200-foot rolls of film have been developed they may be inserted in cartridges for future reference and communication. This type of system is commonly used by banks, utility companies, and retail stores for handling customer records pertaining to purchases, sales, returns, payments, debit and credit memos, and other business transactions.

• *COMPUTER OUTPUT MICROFILM (COM)*—The second basic type of microfilm process is called *Computer Output Microfilm* (COM) in which microfilm images are prepared from digitized data stored on magnetic tapes or disks or transmitted directly from a computer's central processor. No paper records are required with COM. The process enables the filming of computer-processable data on microfilm including the photographing of data as it is projected on the face of a cathode ray tube (CRT) which resembles a television screen. The CRT COM concept is simple. Computer output signals are sent to a CRT rather than to a printer. The image is reduced by a lens system, focused onto microfilm, and developed. The user accesses information by loading film or fiche into a reader/viewer. Most COM systems enable the user to obtain a printed copy of what he or she sees on the CRT screen.

AN ALTERNATIVE TO PAPER COMMUNICATIONS

The direct microfilming of computer-generated data replaces oversize computer paper output. COM has found considerable acceptance among computer users as a means of communicating statistics and other computer-generated data. A report in COM format will have about 1/500th the bulk of the equivalent computer-generated paper printout. Its use instead of paper copy usually reduces computer operating costs as well as the costs of duplicating, mailing, filing, and referencing copies of computer-generated output. A manager, for example, may utilize a compact reader in the office to review daily operational data or statistics and thereby eliminate the need to search for such records by wading through paper files. Figure 14-8 shows a picture of a desk reader/viewer.

Microfilm technology has now progressed to where the image quality approximates that of the printed original. Microfilm readers and readerprinters have also reached a uniformly high level of performance and operational simplicity. Where the volume of work justifies it, the use of microfilm technology can greatly reduce the paper avalanche in many types of business operations.

• *DISTRIBUTED DATA PROCESSING (DDP)*—Distributed data processing means putting business computers closer to their users. Where data processing was once conducted by professional computer technicians behind brick or glass walls, today staff and line managers have electronic connections into and out of the computers. DDP reflects the freeing of computer users from the

FIGURE 14-8 A microfilm reader printer provides an easy-to-read image. The push of a button delivers a print of the document.

SOURCE: Picture courtesy of Perkin-Elmer Corporation

grasps of technology. It involves putting data processing power where most of the work is done and the results are needed. It means storing and manipulating data at decentralized locations so that the data base is spread throughout the organization but is accessible to others as part of a total network system.

DDP is a network of computer processing modules that are functionally or geographically distributed and connected via a communication link. The communication link can be a direct tie-in with a central computer, or it can involve the recording of information on cassettes or diskettes which are then shipped to the central computer location. In a distributed processing network, much of the computing is performed at the point of origin with only summary information useful to higher level management being passed upward to the central computer. Figure 14-9 schematically shows a distributed processing network for a large retail department store with many widely scattered units. A small computer at each remote site provides source data editing to reduce

FIGURE 14-9   A distributed processing network

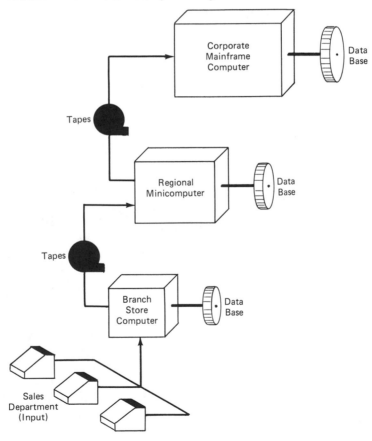

the cost of gathering information. As each small computer maintains its own local data base, each remote site can process orders, generate invoices, and produce inventory reports for local managers. One big advantage of the DDP concept of small computers running local operations is that if one computer goes down, the whole company isn't put out of commission until it becomes operational again.

POSITIVE ASPECTS

DDP is not suitable for all operations. It is most effective where most of the data generated at downline sites is useful only to those sites. The decision to implement DDP requires extremely careful planning. On the *positive* side, DDP can usually

+ *Reduce the costs of computer processing and memory*
+ *Offer more accurate and timely data to line departments*
+ *Reduce the overhead of centralized mainframe computer management*
+ *Provide greater reliability*

NEGATIVE ASPECTS

There are, however, several significant *negative* aspects of DDP.

— *Implementation tends to cut across established power structures within an organization and thereby create jurisdictional problems.*
— *Implementation may take years of development effort in a large diversified organization.*
— *Financial commitment to develop and maintain the system can be more than some organizations can afford. In addition to equipment costs and possible communication costs, there are significant training and support expenses.*
— *Control over information can suffer as more people get into the act.*
— *Less-experienced personnel running the information system can cause software development and equipment support to suffer.*

With new intelligent computer products and specialized data transmission techniques, management can readily pattern a computer/communications network to meet its particular needs. In distributing computer processing power to the points where it is most needed, managers are no longer "slaves" to centrally controlled computer systems.

• *COMPUTER-GRAPHICS*—Computer graphics enables managers to see in one picture what they might otherwise have to gather from a stack of computer printouts. As illustrated in Figure 14-10, computer graphics presents business data in a form that is easily understood. It also aids decision making because it presents trends and deviations in a graphic format. Most managers

FIGURE 14-10   Example of a computer-generated chart

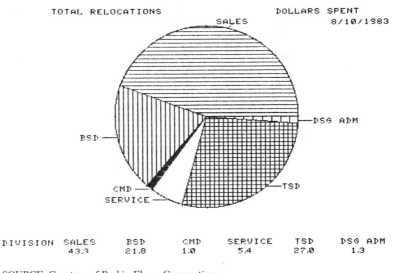

DIVISION	SALES	BSD	CMD	SERVICE	TSD	DSG ADM
	43.3	21.8	1.0	5.4	27.0	1.3

SOURCE: Courtesy of Perkin-Elmer Corporation

prefer scanning a single graphic chart to reading reams of statistical output printed in tabular form.

Computer graphics saves a manager's time by reducing the amount of effort expended to interpret data, digest facts, and communicate detailed statistical information to others. A computer-derived graph can readily show the trend of things and the location of the problems that most need management attention. In being able to see trends and the significant deviations from plans, budgets, and schedules, a manager can acquire a greater amount of pertinent information in a short period of time. It also facilitates implementation of the management-by-exception concept.

SUMMARY

Information is a resource and key element in good management. In the performance of functional operations which are the foundation of the business establishment, there is a need for operational information. At all levels of management there is a need for management information for decision-making purposes. User personnel, including managers at all levels, play a dominant role in determining what information they want from the system. User personnel may also have a major responsibility for providing data input into the information system. This is a very important responsibility because the quality of the output can never be any better than the quality of the input. Many computer-based information systems are not cost-effective because the users do not understand the capabilities of the computer and do not know how to use computerized output intelligently. Computerization of information should be preceded by providing adequate systems, methods, and procedures improvement as well as determination of what type of data is desired and how it will be provided and used. Most management information systems tend to be oversupplied with data, thereby creating a system that is unnecessarily costly to operate.

In developing an information system, don't try to combine too many things into a single system. It is generally best to establish interrelated major subsystems covering the primary and most extensive functional areas of the total organization. Managers at all levels should know exactly what they want from an information system; and the system should be developed on a participative basis. To minimize the proliferation of paper reports, consideration should be given to such systems as microfilm, distributed data processing, and computer graphics. Regardless of what type of information system is developed, it must be carefully planned and thought out before it is implemented.

REVIEW QUESTIONS

1. How can flexible data processing methodology provide for a more usable information system?
2. What is meant by the statement that a business establishment must function as a total system?
3. What is the distinction between operational information systems and management information systems?
4. In what ways do managers at all levels play a dominant role in computer-based information systems?
5. Do you agree or disagree with the position taken in this book regarding the question of availability of information? Why?
6. If you were a manager, what would be your working philosophy of controlling information?
7. What is meant by "control by importance"?
8. How do computerized information systems tend to bring about a proliferation of reports?
9. Why are operational control and management control *not* the same thing?
10. What is the subsystem concept of managing information?
11. What four things must each manager determine in the establishment of an information system?

12. If you were involved in the development and management of an information system, how would you approach the job?

13. Do you accept the concept of distributed data processing? If so, why? If not, why?

CASE STUDY IN MANAGING INFORMATION

JRL is a large company engaged in manufacturing a wide variety of diversified products in six plants. Each plant has a mixture of functional and manufacturing process departments. Within the product mix of the company there are currently two new high-risk/high-cost products being developed. These two new products have project managers assigned to provide intensive management (Figure 14-11).

FIGURE 14-11   The matrix organization structure of the JRL Company

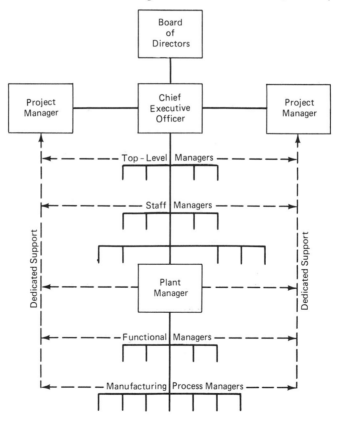

Each project manager has a small staff of personnel with dedicated groups of workers assigned from the various functional and manufacturing process departments.

The functional managers in the plants are required to process voluminously detailed planning, scheduling, and budgetary reports through their plant manager to the project managers. The project managers, in turn, are frequently called upon to brief top management, including the Board of Directors, on the status of their projects. Each level of management attempts to assimilate the massive details pertaining to their involvement in the high-risk/high-cost projects. Armed with these details, the manager then presents a report and, as called on, strives to answer any and all questions raised by the higher levels of management. During the information reporting process, the firsthand answering of questions by lower-level managers may or may not be requested above the level of the plant manager. On a fairly frequent basis, however, they are asked to remain on standby in case they are needed while their operations are discussed in the inner offices of top management.

QUESTIONS

1. What is your evaluation of JRL's approach to managing information pertaining to high-risk/high-cost projects?
2. If the opportunity presented itself, do you have any recommendations for improving JRL's approach to managing information?

NOTE

1. James A. O'Brien, *Computers in Business Management: An Introduction*, 3rd ed. (Homewood, Ill.: Richard D. Irwin, 1982), p. 403.

PART FOUR

MANAGING TIME AND DEVELOPING THE RIGHT ATTITUDES

TIME

PEOPLE

INNOVATION

ATTITUDES

ETHICS

WORK

COMPUTERS

EXPECTATIONS

The supervisor's attitude tends to be at the top of the management building-block process. It is reflected in most everything the supervisor does.

15

Managing Time

LEARNING OBJECTIVES

The objectives of this chapter on managing time are to enable the reader to

1. Relate how the effective use of time is particularly important for a manager
2. Identify guidelines for developing the proper attitude regarding time
3. Develop three diagnostic techniques for identifying time wasters
4. Identify twenty-two time wasters
5. Establish one way of evaluating time wasters
6. Recognize how to save time through planning one's work
7. Identify and describe at least five factors that can save time in organizing one's work
8. Describe at least eight factors that can save time in directing one's work
9. Recognize how to use time in controlling one's work
10. Establish a plan of action to help master the effective and efficient use of time

KEY WORDS

Briefcase-itis The compulsion of some people to take work home every night.

Management By Crisis Failing to act on something until it has become a major and urgent problem.

Meeting Log A diagnostic technique for identifying time spent in meetings.

Memo-itis The compulsion of some people to write memos about anything and everything.

Paper Bedding The compulsion of some people to generate paperwork that serves no purpose other than ego-building and/or justifying the positions of the people who generate it.

Perfectionism The compulsion of some people to demand perfection and to hold that it is attainable.

Telephone Log A diagnostic technique for identifying time spent in telephone conversations.

Time Inventory A diagnostic technique for identifying time spent in various activities.

Traditional-itis The compulsion of some people to do things today in exactly the same way they have been doing them in the past.

Word-itis The compulsion to proliferate unnecessary and/or unintelligible words in communicating.

THE CASE OF ALBERT STACKMORE

A Supervisor in Trouble with Himself

Albert Stackmore is a hard working and very conscientious supervisor. His work philosophy is that the harder you work, the more you get accomplished. This attitude is reflected in the fact that Stackmore works an average of ten or more hours of unpaid overtime each week, very seldom takes all of his vacation time, and carries a briefcase of work home every night. At work he is a perfectionist. It is not uncommon for Stackmore to redo reports and correspondence three or four times before he signs and releases them. His philosophy is that delaying actions for thorough analysis improves the quality of decisions.

Stackmore maintains an unrestricted open-door policy to his office because he feels it improves his effectiveness in dealing with his subordinates. Many of his workers take advantage of this policy and bring their work problems to him. As a general rule, he accepts their problems by saying: "Put it on the bottom of the pile and I'll take a look at it." Stackmore does this because he thinks that by doing the work himself, the task is achieved faster and better. The result of this omnipotent attitude is that there is always a mountain of paperwork stacked up on his desk. His preoccupation with details further clutters his desk. The proliferation of paperwork does not bother Stackmore. His method of work is simply to start at the top of the pile and work to the bottom.

After working in his current position for eight years, Stackmore applied for promotion to a vacant higher-level management position. He did not get the job. It was filled by a person with less seniority who was known to brag about never working more than forty hours a week. Stackmore was disappointed in not getting the job. He felt that his hard work efforts were not appreciated by his superiors.

Albert Stackmore is an example of a supervisor in trouble with himself. His own attitudes and work methods regarding the use of time are causing and will continue to cause him problems as a supervisor. Did you identify at least ten things that he is doing wrong? If not, they should surface for you in reading this chapter.

TIME: USE IT OR LOSE IT

Each of Us Has All the Time There Is

Albert Stackmore is *not* an uncommon type of supervisor. The world of management is full of supervisors who lose time by not properly using it. For example, many ambitious supervisors revel in the hours of overtime they have devoted to their job. These individuals confuse the characteristics of a good manager with those of the martyr. Working overtime, not taking vacations, and carrying home a briefcase of work are not necessarily synonymous with effective and efficient management. More often than not, these traits are an indication of improper use of time. While it is true that most managers are probably overworked, it is also probably true that many are underorganized and wasting time.

Ineffective use of time can be a "killer" for a manager because time is a very restricted and inelastic resource. There are only twenty-four hours in a day—no more and no less. The minute hand on the clock ticks away at a predetermined rate no matter what the manager does. Time management, to a certain extent, is a misnomer because no one can control the relentless forward movement of the clock and the calendar. The only thing we can do with time is to use it effectively by doing the right things with the amount we have. The bottom line is to either use time or lose it.

YOU CAN'T STOP THE CLOCK

Most managers have limited control over their time because so much of its use is directed by outside forces. For example, if the boss wants an important report finished by 5:00 P.M., the manager must drop other priority work and comply with this request. An important customer comes into the office while the manager is busy on a significant matter. What does the manager do? One thing is certain, the clock cannot be stopped, as is done in an athletic contest. Neither can time be accumulated or stockpiled, as can be done with money or materials. Time must be used on a minute-by-minute and day-to-day basis.

As will be discussed later, a manager can determine *where* his or her time goes. If the manager knows what happens to time, he or she can manage much more effectively the little time that is controllable. The manager can actually double or triple the effective available time by just *not doing things* that really don't have to be done.

Effective use of time is particularly important for a manager because the way he or she uses it tends to set the example for subordinates in their use of time. The planning, organizing, directing, and controlling of work activities by a manager has a multiplier effect because of the leverage that is exerted on the efforts of others. The manager who wastes time usually wastes the time of the subordinates as well. The manager must control each situation and thereby get things done without the frustration of unnecessarily long hours of work.

A PHILOSOPHY OF TIME MANAGEMENT

WORK SMARTER, NOT HARDER

The problem with time is not how much is available, but what the individual does with what is available. What the individual does with time is *his or her own choice*. Sometimes this choice is based on fear and sometimes on the inability to use time constructively. It is the individual alone who makes the decision on whether to use time effectively by doing the right things, or to lose it by becoming a slave to a cluttered desk, tradition, red tape, meetings, reports, memos, and the telephone.

Since the individual is the problem in the utilization of time, what can be done? Start by developing the proper positive attitude or philosophy regarding time management. The important thing is to develop an attitude that will achieve results. It is a myth, for example, to believe that the harder one works, the more will get done. The time management principles of planning have proven that every hour spent in effective planning saves three to four hours in execution and ensures better results.[1] The key to the hard work syndrome is to work smarter, not harder—it gets more done in less time.

ATTITUDINAL GUIDELINES

R. Alex Mackenzie has written an excellent book entitled *The Time Trap*. The following rational guidelines for developing the proper attitude regarding time management are largely a reflection of thoughts contained in this book.[2]

- *Work is not the thing one does to live but rather the thing one lives to do. When work is worthwhile, one finds fulfillment in it and gets more accomplished.*
- *Work should be judged by results achieved instead of time spent.*
- *Be honest and recognize that appearance of working hard may be a reflection of ineffectiveness and that intense work may be a protective reaction against insecurity.*
- *Time is on your side the moment you plan and organize it.*
- *Establish objectives as to what you really want to achieve in life.*
- *Work according to priorities; do the most important and urgent things first.*
- *Solve problems one at a time.*
- *Be adaptable to changes in the environment.*

In developing a philosophy of time management, a supervisor should learn to manage the present and foresee the future instead of looking back to the past. In managing the present, the supervisor must learn to say "no" to certain things such as outside distractions, unrealistic time estimates, and the confused priorities of working on second things first. The aim of time management should be to get important things done well. Developing a positive attitude regarding use of time is a good starting point.

IDENTIFYING TIME WASTERS

DEFINING THE PROBLEM

As previously stated, time management hinges on how well the supervisor manages himself or herself. If time is to be used effectively, first identify where time wasting occurs. In simple terms this means defining the problem in order to prescribe the cure. The supervisor should start by looking at the total scope of things that require attention and expenditure of time (Figure 15-1). This gives an overall appraisal of the areas of responsibility where time is a particularly important element.

DIAGNOSTIC TECHNIQUES

Having determined the areas that need time and attention, the supervisor should identify the time wasters. One way to do this is to maintain a diary or inventory of how time is spent over a representative period of several weeks. In this diary, describe and measure the things that take time and the purpose served. Figure 15-2 gives an example of one format to use to identify activities and the time spent on them. If telephone calls are a problem, the supervisor should periodically maintain a telephone log as a means of identifying where the problems might be and what can be done about them. In the same way, if meetings are a problem, the supervisor should periodically maintain a meeting log as a means of reducing time spent in meetings. The maintaining of time inventories, telephone logs, and meeting logs are *not* intended to be part of a supervisor's permanent routine. They should be used on a somewhat infrequent basis as a diagnostic technique to check on the supervisor's effectiveness in the use of time.

FIGURE 15-1 The division of a supervisor's time

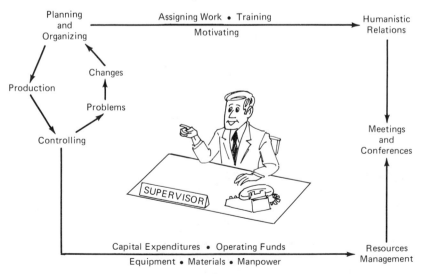

FIGURE 15-2 Time diagnostic techniques

DATE: TIME INVENTORY

TIME		ACTIVITY		WITH WHOM?	WHO INITIATED	ACTION/RESULTS
Start	End	Description	Purpose			

DATE: TELEPHONE LOG

TIME		TOTAL TIME	IN-COMING	OUT-GOING	WITH WHOM?	PURPOSE	COMMENTS
Start	End						

DATE: MEETING LOG

TIME		TOTAL TIME	WITH WHOM?	WHO CALLED IT?	PURPOSE	COMMENTS
Start	End					

EVALUATING TIME WASTERS

Having identified and measured the time wasters, rank them by significance and identify them as to whether they are self-generated or generated by others (Figure 15-3).

TIME WASTERS

The identification of time wasters may produce a listing such as the following:

- *Lack of planning and organizing*
- *Procrastination and indecision*

- *Mistakes*
- *Misplaced items and paper shuffling*
- *Poorly handled meetings*
- *Inadequate communication*
- *Failure to coordinate*
- *No priorities or objectives*
- *Inconsistency*
- *Poor filing system*
- *Clutter*
- *Socializing*
- *Failure to delegate*
- *Perfectionism*
- *Unnecessary correspondence and memo-itis*
- *Poor reading habits*
- *Failure to listen*
- *Too much attention to details*
- *Management by crisis*
- *Red tape (policies and procedures)*
- *Interruptions (telephone and visitors)*
- *Doing unnecessary things*

FIGURE 15-3   Evaluation of time wasters

TIME WASTER (DESCRIPTION)	RANK	SELF-GENERATED	GENERATED BY OTHER	PLANNED ACTION

CAUSES AND SOLUTIONS LIE WITH THE INDIVIDUAL

The usual conclusion drawn from the evaluation of time wasters is that the major causes and solutions of these problems lie within the individual. The important thing at this point is that once the individual knows where he or she is wasting time, the process of solving the problem can begin.

One suggested way of dealing with time wasters is to evaluate them according to the following list:

1. Time lost in *getting started*
    - socializing, including coffee breaks
    - reading
    - procrastination

2. Time lost through *disorganization*
   - too many things to handle
   - too many people to work with
   - clutter around the workplace
   - wrong priorities
3. Time lost through *diversion*
   - socializing
   - hobbies
   - unnecessary activities
4. Time lost in *paperwork*
   - excessive information
   - reports
   - correspondence
   - red tape
   - perfectionism

Using this evaluation of time usage, the supervisor can develop and implement a planned course of action to correct those areas where the greatest amount of time is wasted. Understanding and applying certain principles of management in the planning, organizing, directing, and controlling of work will help in using time effectively.

PLANNING ONE'S WORK

FIRST PLAN, THEN MANAGE

Effective time management is essentially a simple two-step operation. First, plan for the best use of the time available; then manage in accordance with the plan. The people who say they don't have time to plan are saying they don't have time to do it right. If that is the case, what happens when they have to do it over?[3] The person who fails to plan, is planning to fail.

Planning is the systematic and orderly arrangement for doing something. It involves a rational predetermination of where you want to go and how you intend to get there. Planning saves time by helping you get more done with better results in less time. Time management involves arranging to accomplish the things you choose to get done within the time available. It helps avoid wasting effort on unimportant things and increases the efficiency of getting the right things done.

DEFINE THE IMPORTANT OBJECTIVES

To use time effectively, first define the objectives and goals for the essential things that must be accomplished. You cannot intelligently plan without having something at which to aim. In establishing objectives it is very important to select the ones that are most significant to the work to be accomplished. Don't make every task or activity an objective. When too many things become objectives, hopeless confusion results. Good planning will eliminate time spent on nonessential tasks.

MANAGE BY OBJECTIVES

The supervisor must be able to plan his or her work as well as that of the workers. One significant time-saving technique is management by objectives (discussed in Chapter 10). As shown in Figure 15-4, it involves

1. Establishing the goals to be achieved
2. Establishing the criteria for measuring and determining progress
3. Establishing who is responsible for performing all necessary tasks
4. Establishing a reporting feedback system for determining progress in the achievement of goals
5. Maintaining follow up with the individuals responsible for performance
6. Taking corrective action on problems
7. Revising objectives where facts so dictate

Management by objectives, if intelligently used, can save time by focusing everyone's attention on the important things that need to be done first. It can

FIGURE 15-4 Managing by objectives

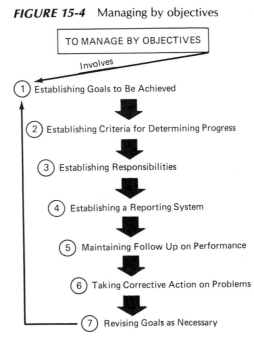

also prevent management by crisis by anticipating and taking action on matters before a problem situation occurs. Management by objectives lets people know and understand what is expected of them in terms of performance. Time is saved when people know what to do.

ASSIGN PRIORITIES

After establishing objectives, it is important to assign priorities to the tasks to be accomplished. Correctly assigning priorities results in doing the *right* things. It is very important to do the *right* things. To be efficient on the wrong task, or on the right task but at the wrong time, may be highly ineffective. Peter Drucker, author of numerous books on management techniques, has so aptly expressed the situation in these words: "What's the point in trying to do more cheaply what should not be done at all?"

STICK TO THE PRIORITIES

After identifying and assigning priorities to work objectives, a supervisor should do the following:

1. Allocate correct portions of time to each task.
2. Stick with a priority task until it is finished.
3. Accomplish tasks within established deadlines.
4. Avoid wasted effort in accomplishing tasks.
5. Allow for flexibility and change things when facts so dictate.

DAY-TO-DAY PLANNING

Within the framework of accomplishing objectives according to assigned priorities, a supervisor should plan his or her own day-to-day work schedule. A good practice is to take approximately fifteen minutes at the end of the workday and plan the next day's work agenda. This involves making a list of things to be done the next day in order of importance. Put the most important and urgent priority actions—the "must do" jobs—at the top of the list. At the bottom put the things that can wait until time becomes available. Many of these low-priority items may end up being ignored because of the lack of time. In between the high-priority and low-priority items should be the tasks that are important but not as urgent as the ones at the top. These include tasks with later deadlines.

Many supervisors find it a good practice to establish a separate file folder for

- *Urgent and important tasks*
- *Important but not urgent tasks*
- *Deferred tasks*

THINK THROUGH YOUR PRIORITIES

Each folder should have tasks arranged in order of priority, with highest-priority items on top. The backbone of this system is (1) to arrange work tasks every day in the order of their importance and urgency, and (2) to stick to the list as much as possible the next day. Planning the work schedule requires a supervisor to think through the priority actions and then firmly stick to them. Actions without thought usually result in costly time-consuming errors.

ORGANIZING ONE'S WORK

ELIMINATE CLUTTER

Organizing involves defining the work to be performed and the people responsible for doing it. Good organization results in efficiency and a savings of time in getting things done. As a supervisor, your organizing starts with yourself. It is reflected in how well you organize your work area, your desk or workbench, your work input, and output. The cluttered desk, for example, can mean a cluttered mind. If your desk is cluttered, piled high, and disorganized, you may be classified as a haphazard, inefficient, and untidy person. On the other hand, the clean desk may be evidence of efficiency in doing work, in avoiding it, or in getting others to do it.[4] Clutter tends to create tension, frustration, and a feeling of being disorganized. Clutter wastes the time of the person who lives with it because he or she can never find things. The manager who is trapped in the "stacked-desk syndrome" and says "Look how busy I am," is really saying "Look how inefficient I am."

ORGANIZE THE WORK LAYOUT

Figure 15-5 illustrates an efficiently organized desk. Some of its time-saving features are

1. A work tray for today's incoming urgent items
2. A work tray for today's incoming items that are not considered urgent
3. A work tray for today's outgoing completed items
4. A current-action file for important items being directed to each key subordinate
5. A file folder in the top drawer for each of the following action categories:
   - Urgent and important tasks (in priority order)
   - Important but not urgent tasks (in priority order)
   - Deferred tasks (in priority order)
6. A diary record book for recording important business transactions
7. A list on the desk fly leaf of most-used telephone numbers

FIGURE 15-5 The organized workplace

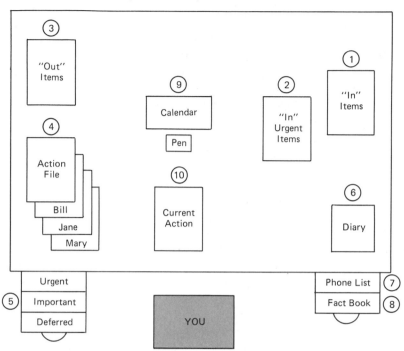

8. A reference fact book of information used on a frequent basis
9. A calendar with scheduled meetings, visitors, messages, and other reminders—the "reminder center" of the workplace
10. The one current action being handled

Figure 15-5 shows a desk that is clear of everything except those things related to the work at hand. This layout makes it easier to complete each action and send it on its way before starting the next priority project. It eliminates clutter and minimizes items being put in the work area of the manager's desk until he or she is ready for them.

MAKE USE OF PRIME TIME

A second key factor in accomplishing more work in the limited time available, is to make maximum use of the individual's prime time—the time of day when the individual is capable of doing the clearest thinking. In a book entitled *Getting Organized*, Stephanie Winston suggests that most people have high-energy periods and corresponding lows each day. Based on that theory, she advises that the person try to accomplish the most important jobs during the hours of peak efficiency.[5] The head of an advertising agency once told his staff that if they drank martinis for lunch, he wanted them to be made with gin rather than vodka. "I realize," he said, "that vodka is a little more difficult to detect on the breath—but that's just the point. When you call on our clients in the afternoon, I'd much rather have them think you're drunk than stupid."[6] The point here is that drinking martinis at lunch is a good way to transform early-afternoon prime time into secondary time because alcohol is a depressant and can diminish a person's effectiveness in both the quality of performance and in the time it takes. Determine your own high-energy periods and make the most use of those times.

CONCENTRATION

A third factor in using time is concentration. After planning and organizing of job priorities have been accomplished, concentration—doing one thing at a time—is a critical factor in time management. It helps avoid the wasting of time on a little bit of everything that only results in doing nothing well.

DO ONE THING AT A TIME

One of the great masters of concentrated effort was General George Patton of World War II fame. He had a capacity for deciding on the one most important thing to do and then doing it. Once he decided on doing something, he pursued it to the end without deviating. Nothing could deter Patton from doing one thing at a time. His power of concentration resulted in magnificent performance. By doing one thing at a time and working at it full time, he got jobs done quickly and was able to move on more rapidly to the next job.

DON'T BE A SUBORDINATE'S SUBORDINATE

A fourth factor in effective use of a supervisor's time is delegation. Albert Stackmore, mentioned at the beginning of this chapter, may have lost the promotion because he did not do a good job in delegating work to others. When subordinates brought their work problems to him, he accepted the problems and tried to solve them all himself. In doing this he literally became his subordinates' subordinate. Stackmore's inability to give authority to his subordinates to carry out assigned responsibilities was probably a key factor in his own high usage of unpaid overtime and in his not being able to find the time to take earned vacations. Supervisors should guide workers in the resolution of their problems, but it is wrong for the supervisor to try and solve all problems. The principle of delegation and its application (discussed in Chapters 2 and 7) applies in making effective use of time. Decisions should be made at the lowest competent level consistent with good judgment and the availability of relevant information.

OTHER PRINCIPLES TO THINK ABOUT

The following are additional principles that can be used in organizing work:

- *Schedule work activities around the key and most important events.*
- *Group related work activities together.*
- *Schedule the most difficult work activities to match the individual's peak energy level.*
- *Allow enough time for each scheduled work activity.*
- *Resist the temptation to leave the scheduled work activity to do more appealing tasks.*

DIRECTING ONE'S WORK

IF YOU DON'T KNOW WHAT TO DO: CALL A MEETING AND WASTE MORE TIME

A frequent cause of wasted time is the lack of clear communication between people (see Chapter 5). Sincere, honest, and direct communication is better for everyone. It avoids a lot of time being wasted in "wheel spinning"—much talk but little action.

Poor organization is one of the greatest time-wasters. The symptoms are easy to recognize. The moment you find that you spend a lot of your time in meetings, accept the fact that you are probably badly organized. A well-organized organization meets very rarely. People work or they meet. They can't do both at the same time. Excessive meetings are an indicator that the work is not being done where it should be done. Many managers should take heed of these statements of Peter Drucker[7] because poorly planned, organized, and conducted meetings are a terrible waste of time.

GUIDELINES FOR CONDUCTING MEETINGS

There are certain guidelines for conducting meetings that enable a group to accomplish the most in the least time.

1. There should be a specific purpose for any meeting and the chairperson should know when and when not to call a meeting.
2. There should be a specific and preferably written agenda prepared and distributed before the meeting.
3. Participants in a meeting should be chosen according to their ability to contribute to the subject matter. It is also desirable that participants be of relatively equal experience and status because it is easier for them to take part in the discussions.
4. Participants should prepare themselves before the meeting.

5. The chairperson should be a competent individual who knows how to effectively and efficiently conduct meetings.

6. Meetings should start on time, stick to the agenda, and end at the scheduled time.

7. The chairperson should lead the group to come to agreement, if possible, on each agenda item. The chairperson should have a participative, not an authoritarian, style of leadership.

8. At the end of the meeting, the chairperson should restate agreements or decisions reached and the assignments of tasks made to individuals.

9. The chairperson should send a memo to all participants confirming agreements, decisions, and task assignments.

10. The chairperson should follow through to see that agreements, decisions, and assignments are carried out.

Regularly scheduled staff meetings, if properly planned and conducted, can be a time-saving policy because staff meetings (1) allow people to accumulate items for discussion and (2) facilitate coordination.

MEMO-ITIS

Another time waster is what Robert Benchley called "The Memorandum Hour."

> When the mail is disposed of, one should have what is known as 'Memorandum Hour.' During this period everyone sends memoranda to everyone else. If you happen to have nothing in particular about which to dictate a memorandum, you dictate a memorandum to someone, saying that you have nothing to suggest or report. This gives a stimulating exchange of ideas, and also helps us to use up the blue memorandum blanks which have been printed at some expense for just that purpose.[8]

Memos, except where they serve to remind, clarify, or confirm, tend to postpone work. Memo-itis is an obsession to be avoided.

GUIDELINES FOR HANDLING CORRESPONDENCE

Much written correspondence can be avoided. Effective managers learn how to eliminate unnecessary correspondence by first not asking for it. They initiate action to discontinue it. They use the wastebasket. They use the telephone. A manager can save time in handling of necessary correspondence by following these guidelines:

1. Learn to read fast.
2. Screen and sort incoming correspondence by importance and priority.
3. Avoid repeated paper shuffling by making decisions on the disposition of correspondence at the time you *first* look at it.
4. Put brief handwritten replies on the bottom of routine letters and memos and return to sender.

5. Avoid frequent revisions of what you write. Many written communications with minor mistakes can be personalized by use of the "P.S."—postscript.
6. Get to the point by using short sentences and understandable words.
7. Avoid making and distributing unnecessary copies.
8. Keep away from the reproduction machines.

WORD-ITIS AND PAPER BEDDING

Word-itis and paper bedding are two major time wasters. Word-itis involves using terminology that others don't understand and using more words than necessary. Paper bedding involves generating paperwork that serves no purpose other than ego-building and/or justifying the positions of the people who generate it. Once established, paper bedding is extremely difficult to stop. Paper bedding is a primary reason for the existence of government bureaucracies.

OVERCOMING PROCRASTINATION

Another time waster—procrastination—is a close relative of incompetence and inefficiency. Supervisors who know their objectives and priorities have taken a big step forward in overcoming procrastination. A second big step in defeating procrastination is to remove the clutter and to organize one's workplace. The well-organized individuals who know where they are going and how to get there have less trouble in getting started.

One technique in overcoming procrastination is Norman Vincent Peale's philosophy. His power of positive thinking can overcome the fear which causes procrastination. Dr. Peale says to pick out one area where procrastination plagues you and conquer it. Don't duck the most difficult problems, he says, but learn to set priorities and focus on one problem at a time with deadlines that you have imposed on yourself.[9] Psychologist and philosopher William James suggested making habits work for you in conquering procrastination. His technique also involves positive thinking. First, establish new habits and launch the new practice as strongly as possible. Second, never let an exception occur until the new habit is firmly rooted.[10] Bjorn Secher, author of several motivational books and programs, recommends writing on a three-by-five card "DON'T PROCRASTINATE—DO IT NOW," and then looking at the card whenever you feel yourself wavering.

THE KEY IS GETTING STARTED

To overcome procrastination, break the problem task down into building blocks that can be accomplished one at a time. If you have something to write, for example, start putting thoughts on paper. It doesn't matter at first if they are well organized or even relevant. Just get started with notes, an outline, anything that gives you the feeling that you are on the way. You may change most of what you are doing later, but meanwhile you have something to build on. *Start now* and refine later.

AVOID INDECISION

Closely akin to avoiding procrastination is avoiding indecision. Albert Stackmore had a philosophy that delaying actions for thorough analysis improves the quality of decisions. Some observers have termed this "paralysis of analysis."[11] The longer a difficult decision is delayed, the more difficult it becomes to make. Also, each passing day reduces the time available for taking corrective action if something goes wrong.

BRIEFCASE-ITIS

Indecision is usually a major contributor to another managerial disorder which we will call briefcase-itis. When people such as Albert Stackmore take work home every night, it is an indicator that something is wrong. The individual may be trying to do too much and could be on the way to a serious stress-related illness. Taking work home may indicate managerial weakness, such as failure to delegate or failure to plan and organize.

AVOID PERFECTIONISM

Last, avoid perfectionism. There is a big difference between striving for excellence and striving for perfection. The first is attainable, gratifying, and healthy. The second is unattainable, frustrating, and a terrible waste of time.

CONTROLLING ONE'S WORK

CONTROLLING STARTS WITH PLANNING

Controlling starts with planning. If you say you don't have time to follow up on your plans, you are saying that your plans are not important enough to see that they are properly implemented. If that is the case, why did you waste time planning?

PROCEDURES CAN BE A "CRUTCH" FOR TRADITIONAL-ITIS

Procedures are necessary for good control and can be time savers. Procedures, however, can also become a "crutch" for supporting managers who have lost their innovativeness. Sticking to tradition can waste both time and money. We live in a constantly changing environment that places limitations on how long we continue to follow traditional customs, doctrines, policies, and procedures. Traditions do tend to be stabilizing factors in a society. They should, therefore, only be changed after careful evaluation of all pertinent factors and circumstances. Sticking to tradition, however, contributes to "red tape" by following excessive routine policies and procedures that can be a tremendous waste of time. A good manager learns to manage by objectives rather than by tradition. What happens when people are judged by how well they comply with procedures rather than by how well they accomplish work objectives? The answer is that there is usually a proliferation of memos and reports of little value except to prove that procedures are being followed.

WORK ON THE MOST ESSENTIAL TASKS

One of the most effective ways of saving time in controlling one's work is to *not* try to do everything. To conserve time, energy, and money, focus attention on the exceptional things. The number one priority is giving thought to the most significant deviations of actual from planned performance. Then work on the most essential tasks that need to be accomplished to correct the problem.

AVOID MANAGEMENT-BY-CRISIS

Working on the most essential tasks will help a manager avoid "crisis management." This type of management occurs when you fail to act on something until it has become a major and urgent problem. One cause of failing to act in a timely manner is trying to manage everything. A second cause is getting involved with a proliferation of managerial information of marginal value. Once you are trapped in management by crisis, you have to drop everything else and give full time to resolving the crisis. While you are doing this, other crises develop, and soon you are at least one crisis behind the power curve. Invariably, management by crisis involves more time than necessary to do the job, and often the additional time is costly overtime.

A POSITIVE PLAN OF ACTION

The following is an editorial statement by Mary Abrams, senior editorial assistant for the *Graduate Woman,* the official publication of the American Association of University Women:[12]

> Time is the raw material of your life. You can let it slip away on unimportant busywork and things you don't really want to do; you can let others commandeer big chunks of it for their own purposes; or you can take charge of it yourself to build the kind of life you genuinely want.

MANAGING OURSELVES

Unless we manage ourselves, no amount of ability, skill, experience, or knowledge will enable us to make effective and efficient use of time. We can master the best use of time by applying the following guidelines:

1. Get organized to work on the right things by having a plan of objectives with priorities and time values.
2. Work according to the priorities in the plan.
3. Try to overcome procrastination by establishing new habits and recognizing that perfectionism is not attainable.
4. Get motivated and off to a good start by matching physical and mental tasks to variations in the human energy cycle.
5. Learn to concentrate, to read and write rapidly, and to cope with interruptions and changes.
6. Develop work skills that will (a) reduce clutter, (b) minimize attention to minuscule details, (c) tactfully avoid prolonged telephone conversations, (d) avoid an overload of information, (e) save time in meetings, and (f) facilitate working with and through others including the delegation of responsibilities and authority.
7. Implement such principles of management as (a) management by objectives and (b) management by exception.

SUMMARY

The major causes of ineffectiveness (doing the *wrong* things) and inefficiency (doing *things* wrong) lie within ourselves. The solutions to mastering the effective and efficient use of time also lie within ourselves. We fail to make the best use of our time because we

1. Fail to plan and organize things before taking action and thereby waste time and effort
2. Fail to be sufficiently concise and precise and thereby overdo what we undertake to accomplish
3. Fail to be decisive and thereby lose time in deliberation and procrastination
4. Fail to use good principles of self-management and thereby do things the hard way

Time is a very restricted and inelastic resource. We cannot control time; we can only manage ourselves to make the best use of time. It's a matter of using it or losing it. What we do with our time is our own choice. We should start by first developing the proper positive attitude or philosophy regarding time management. By following certain positive attitudinal guidelines, such as working smarter and not harder, we improve our time management. Second, we should identify the areas where we are wasting time. Maintaining a time inventory, a telephone log, or a meeting log are some diagnostic techniques that can be used to identify time wasters. Once we know where we are wasting time, we can start to do something about it. Third, we can improve our effective use of time if we understand and apply certain principles of management in planning, organizing, directing, and controlling our own work.

REVIEW QUESTIONS

1. Why is "time management" a misnomer?
2. Why is the effective use of time particularly important for a manager?
3. How can the development of a philosophy of time management help one to use time more effectively?
4. How can a person identify his or her time wasters.
5. What is meant by the words *stacked-desk syndrome*?
6. What is a subordinate's subordinate?
7. What are some of the undesirable aspects of memo-itis?
8. How can you overcome procrastination?
9. How can procedures be a "crutch" for sticking to tradition?
10. What is management by crisis?

A CASE STUDY IN MANAGING TIME

Dorothy Morestack is a hard working, very conscientious, but not too happy supervisor. In talking with Morestack one gets the impression that she constantly feels the pressure of not having enough time to do her job.

On a typical work day Morestack arrives at her office approximately an hour before her subordinates come to work. She goes to the filing cabinet and removes a tray of work left over from the preceding day and places it on her desk. One look at the overflowing work tray and Morestack feels she needs a second cup of coffee at the cafeteria. After having the coffee and reading the morning paper, she returns to her desk and starts going through the items in the work tray. These are the first items she looked at:

1. A memo from another division requesting some data for a report. Since this was a job that Mary could do, Morestack wrote a memo telling her what to do.
2. A shipping notice for materials that had been ordered and received by Morestack's office.
3. A letter from a customer expressing satisfaction with service received.

4. A memo from the boss requesting attendance at a meeting next Tuesday at 9:00 A.M.

5. A catalogue describing office supplies. Morestack looked through it and put it back in the work tray since she didn't want to make a decision at this time.

6. A letter from a customer that requires immediate action. Since this was a job that Mary could do, Morestack wrote her a memo and attached it to the letter.

7. A letter from a customer complaining about service received.

8. A revised regulation from the Purchasing Office.

9. A current issue of a trade journal with articles worth reading.

10. A memo from another department requesting some assistance on a project. The memo isn't clear so Morestack feels she should call the supervisor who sent the message. She makes a calendar note of this and then writes a memo to Jane to handle the request.

11. A request from Bill for personal leave.

12. A letter describing the merits of certain word processing equipment. Morestack puts this back in the bottom of the work tray.

13. A directive from the Personnel Department.

At this point Morestack's subordinates have been at work for some time, the telephone is constantly ringing, people are coming into her office on various matters, and additional items are being put on top of the stack in the work tray. At the end of the work day, a tired Dorothy Morestack puts the full work tray in the filing cabinet, locks it, and goes home.

QUESTIONS

1. How would you have handled each of the above transactions?

2. What suggestions could you give Morestack to help her in doing her job?

NOTES

1. R. Alec Mackenzie, *The Time Trap* (New York: AMACON, a division of American Management Associations, 1972), p. 41.

2. Ibid., pp. 11–13.

3. Ibid., p. 49.

4. Excerpt from *How to Get More Done in Less Time* by Joseph D. Cooper, p. 130. Copyright © 1962, 1971 by Joseph D. Cooper. Reprinted by permission of Doubleday & Company, Inc.

5. Mary Abrams, "Seize the Moment—It's Yours," *Graduate Woman*, September–October 1979, p. 15.

6. Edwin C. Bliss, *Getting Things Done—The ABC's of Time Management* (New York: Scribner's, 1976), p. 4.

7.   A reflection of statements made by Peter Drucker in an address to students at the Industrial College of the Armed Forces at Fort McNair, Washington, D.C., on February 6, 1970.

8.   Robert Benchley, *The Benchley Roundup "From Nine to Five"* (New York: Harper & Row, Pub., 1954), p. 28.

9.   Excerpt from "You Can Stop Being A Procrastinator" by Norman Vincent Peale, *Reader's Digest,* January 1972.

10.   Excerpt from "Making Habits Work for You" by William James, *Reader's Digest,* August 1967 and from the book *Psychology: Briefer Course* by William James, published by Holt, Rinehart and Winston.

11.   R. Alec Mackenzie, "Myths of Time Management," *The Business Quarterly,* Spring 1974, published by the School of Business Administration of the University of Western Ontario.

12.   Mary Abrams, an editorial in the *Graduate Woman,* September–October, 1979.

16

Attitudes and Ethics

MEETING THE MANAGEMENT CHALLENGES OF TOMORROW

In our attempt to meet the management challenges of today and tomorrow, it is important that we first recognize and understand the challenges themselves, their interrelationship of one to another, their impact on our business and, finally, on our specific roles as managers.

As I reflect on the successful managers with whom I have been associated during my career, they universally had similar success characteristics. First, they understood specifically their role in managing and developing people in their organization and, second, they were effective role models.

As role models, they personally modeled the behaviors that would lead to personal and organization growth. Whether in an individual discussion or a group environment, they consistently and constructively exhibited the following qualities:

- *Established and nurtured a working climate that was conducive to personal growth.*
- *Functioned as a coach instead of a directive manager. They worked hard at and encouraged two-way communications.*
- *Acted as agents of change as well as adapting to change.*
- *Established high performance standards and helped their subordinates achieve those standards.*
- *Practiced good listening.*
- *Expected subordinates to adapt to other people's needs within the organization.*
- *Provided frequent and consistent, positive feedback on accomplishments.*
- *Strived to pass on their personal managerial skills to their subordinates.*

Looking back at these successful managers and the positive behaviors they modeled, I see and expect the same formula for success in the future. Our operating environment may be more complex, the business conditions more unpredictable, our employees more sophisticated with higher expectations—but managing by utilizing these basic and highly desirable qualities will continue to identify the successful manager in the 1980s.

> Stanley C. Gault
> Chairman of the Board
> and Chief Executive Officer
> Rubbermaid Incorporated

LEARNING OBJECTIVES

The objectives of this chapter on attitudes and ethics are to enable the reader to

1. Relate how attitude tends to be the most significant factor in the management building-block process
2. Describe how unethical management practices can destroy the individuals who commit them
3. Identify fourteen expectations of the future which supervisors should be prepared to handle

KEY WORDS

Attitude   A reflection of an individual's state of mind or opinion.

Ethics   The rules of moral conduct including the values of honesty, fairness, justice, and the right or wrong of the motives involved in certain actions.

Flexitime   A time and attendance policy that requires all employees to work during a core period, such as 9:00 A.M. to 3:00 P.M., but lets them choose when to work the remaining hours of their schedule.

Robotics   The field of robot technology, which includes the design and use of robots to perform routine mechanical tasks on command.

Teleconferencing   The use of advanced electronics and other technology that enables several people in various locations to conduct a meeting or conference without leaving their place of work or home.

A CASE OF SELF-DESTRUCTION

Robert Burnwall had many things going for him. He was young, handsome, intelligent, talented, and possessed a marvelous personality. Burnwall was also ambitious and fortunate in being with the right company at the right time. Be-

neath the infectious smile that was part of his charming personality, Burnwall
had a vindictive attitude toward any individual who might be a threat to his
personal advancement.

Burnwall's company had gone through a tremendous expansion that resulted in many internal personnel transfers and promotions. He was one of the
fortunate individuals who moved up very rapidly. After being with the company a relatively short time, he was progressively promoted from the position of
accounting clerk to chief accountant, passing on his way several older employees with more seniority. Probably because of his pleasing personality, most of
the employees he bypassed had great admiration for him. Robert Burnwall appeared to be on his way to even higher management positions. Why did he
find himself, five years later, a prisoner in a state penitentiary?

The answer to what happened to Robert Burnwall is very clear. He destroyed himself through his own lack of good moral principles, both on the job
and off. Burnwall was a "big spender" as reflected in the expensive clothes he
purchased, his gourmet eating and drinking habits, and his love for the "hors-
es" which did not cooperate in winning at the racetracks. He also spent considerable money on women other than his wife, including his secretary. Even
though he earned a very respectable salary, he apparently was living beyond
his financial means. This was partially reflected in the fact that he constantly
borrowed money from his subordinates and others and never repaid it—a very
unethical personal practice.

Burnwall got his secretary pregnant and was more or less "blackmailed"
into paying for her problem situation. This was evidently the breaking point in
his financial status. He started writing bad checks; was fired from his job; and
was indicted, convicted, and sentenced to serve time in the state penitentiary.
What an ending for a young manager in his midthirties who at one time appeared to have so much going in his favor. Burnwall's case is not fictitious. It's
one of too many cases where people destroy themselves through their attitudes and ethics.

MANAGERIAL ATTITUDES

Attitude is a reflection of an individual's state of mind or opinion regarding
such things as other people and personal conduct. In supervisory management, attitude also includes the feeling and position of the manager toward
such matters as organizational objectives, work actions, innovation, humanistic
relations, and ethics. Attitude tends to be at the top of the management building-block process, as shown in Figure 16-1. The manager's attitude can greatly
strengthen or weaken the other building blocks in the entire management
process. Attitude is a very powerful force.

ATTITUDE AND CONSIDERATION OF OTHERS

• *ATTITUDE AND PEOPLE*—The manager's attitude regarding people is a
key factor that determines style or type of leadership. If the manager has the

FIGURE 16-1 The management build-ing-block process

MANAGEMENT STEPPINGSTONES

attitude that most people are *not* competent, the style of leadership will usual-ly be authoritarian. On the other hand, if the manager has the attitude that most people are responsible individuals, then the style of leadership will most likely be either consultative or participative. In participative management the prevailing attitude is that wisdom can be obtained from subordinates and peers.

A manager's attitude influences his or her humanistic relations with oth-er people. This attitude is reflected in how orders and instructions are given, in job performance appraisals, in career development plans, in disciplinary ac-tions, in labor-management relations, and in helping others with problems. The way a manager communicates and interacts with others provides an indi-cation of the manager's attitude. It is primarily because of their attitude that some managers take unilateral actions affecting people without really caring how these actions will affect the people involved.

ATTITUDES CAUSE RECIPROCITY

The supervisor's attitude toward subordinates results in a reciprocal situation. If the supervisor shows an attitude of indifference regarding subordinates, they, in turn, will show a lack of concern for the supervisor's problems or de-sires. In response to a supervisor's orders to expedite a certain work activity, workers will probably be indifferent and unresponsive. Attitude regarding people tends to be a give-and-take exchange, as seen in the following true situ-ation.

Bob Hyatt had been a supervisor in his organization for twelve years. He showed his attitude toward fellow workers by never saying anything compli-mentary about them, and also by making frequent caustic and cynical com-ments. When there were promotions, retirements, or events where fellow em-ployees were leaving, Bob never attended and never contributed to a gift for the person involved. When Bob announced his retirement, no one made ar-rangements for a going-away party or gift. Because of his attitude toward oth-ers in these situations, his fellow workers thought no one would attend even if they did plan a retirement event. The message in this case is that whatever attitudes we develop regarding other people, we can expect similar ones in return.

ATTITUDE AND SCIENTIFIC MANAGEMENT

● *ATTITUDE AND INNOVATION*—Supervision in the ongoing turbulent environment requires the courage to implement new and different management strategies. To some individuals, innovation requires the employment of unconventional approaches to problem prevention and solving. For example, operations research involves applying the scientific method of mathematical and statistical techniques to the solution of problems involving probabilities, uncertainties, and/or unknowns. The use of and confidence in the results obtained from various operations research techniques is largely influenced by the manager's attitude. Because a manager may not understand the use of higher-level mathematical equations in problem solving, there is often an unwillingness to trust the results of the analyst's work. The failure to use scientific management in management problem solving is often the result of the negative attitude of the manager.

ATTITUDE AND WORK SIMPLIFICATION

Work simplification is another area of management that is greatly influenced by the supervisor's attitude. Some supervisors are perfectly content to follow the same outmoded work methods and procedures forever. If the supervisor favors continuing things as they are, you can't expect the subordinates to implement better work methods on their own. The leadership in work simplification must usually come from the supervisor. Attitude is a key factor in the leadership exercised by the supervisor.

ATTITUDE AND FINANCIAL MANAGEMENT

● *ATTITUDE AND WORK*—Many different techniques and aspects of management have been discussed in this book. Their effective use is very dependent on the attitude of the manager. For example, take the supervision of money resources. Many managers, particularly at the first and middle levels, have had little or no education or training in financial management. Their attitude regarding financial management is often expressed in their statements that (1) they are not bookkeepers or accountants, and (2) accounting is not their area of expertise. Such attitudes reflect several erroneous assertions—all without factual support or reason and all detrimental to good management. First, accounting is but one of many elements of financial management. Second, managers are very much involved in budget development and execution, in cost control, and in decisions pertaining to the expenditure of money. Third, managers do not have to be accountants to be intelligent managers of financial resources. Because of their negative attitudes regarding financial management, many managers do not give the necessary balanced attention to all aspects of their job. As a result, they tend to be both ineffective and inefficient in their management. What is really bad about this is that the supervisor's attitude becomes that of the subordinates. This compounds the poor management.

ATTITUDE AND MANAGEMENT PRACTICES

Other areas where attitude plays a role in how things are done are (1) management by objectives, (2) management by exception, (3) participative management, (4) delegation of work to others, (5) management of information, and (6) utilization of time. The extent to which these management practices are implemented as well as how they are put into effect, can be greatly influenced by the manager's attitude regarding them.

ATTITUDE AND THE COMPUTER REVOLUTION

● *ATTITUDE AND COMPUTERS*—Supervisors in today's management environment need to have computer literacy. This literacy is necessary so that managers can develop the proper attitude regarding effective use of computers. Some managers think that computers can automatically simplify and make work easier, and that computers can make decisions. The end result of this attitude is the attempt to use computers in work areas where they are not effective or efficient. The following are significant work areas where attitude adjustment to computer utilization is needed:

1. Robots and robotics
2. Replacement of drafting tables
3. Elimination of office paperwork
4. Elimination of staff meetings and conferences

ROBOTS AND ROBOTICS

Robots are no longer a thing of the future. The first industrial robot was produced in 1961, and by 1979 there had been 1,300 units built in the United States. The projection of robots built per year by 1900 is 31,000.[1] Robotics, the study of robots, is a new area that managers must adjust to and understand. They must adjust to the fact that robots can replace many of the human workers, particularly those in the unskilled category. On the other hand, robots create new job opportunities for robot installers, repairers, programmers, design technicians, applications technicians, and mechanics. The possible future uses of robots are limitless. Managers must adjust their thinking to meet these challenges.

THE CHANGING WORKPLACE

In other areas of management, computerization is drastically changing things: in drafting work, office work, staff meetings, and out-of-town meetings. The use of computer assisted drafting (CAD) is virtually eliminating the use of drafting tables. The employment of microcomputers and distributed processing (see Chapter 14) makes it possible to eliminate a considerable amount of office paperwork and staff meetings. The advancing technology in teleconferencing, such as the use of lasers and conversion of voice communication from analogue to digital transmission, makes it possible for people in various locations to conduct conferences and meetings without leaving their office or plant. Effective use of these technological breakthroughs requires continuing attitude adjustment. The bottom line is that "the old workplace ain't what it used to be."

RAPID OBSOLESCENCE

The changes and advances in computer and communication technology are mind-boggling matters in achieving the most effective management. We must keep up with advancing technology to know what, where, when, and how to employ it in the appropriate areas of management. This is and will continue to be a very difficult task. Past experience in working with computers has shown that they do not always work as expected. The technology has always been far ahead of our ability to use it in management. With computers costing as little as a few thousand dollars, they are purchased and put to use in many operations where the people do not fully understand how to operate them properly. This is a frightening situation because it can result in bad decisions being made faster. There is a tremendous challenge to managers to know where, when, and how to use a technology that is experiencing a full cycle turnaround from development to obsolescence every eighteen to twenty-four months.

WE LIVE IN A CHANGING WORLD

• *ATTITUDES AND EXPECTATIONS*—Attitude adjustment to meet the expectations of the future is a vital aspect of effective management. Today's manager must be forward-looking and prepared to adjust to (1) the ongoing revolution in computer and communication technology, (2) the changes in economic conditions, (3) the unpredictable changes in the social environment, and (4) the values in accepting new principles of management.

CHANGES IN ECONOMIC CONDITIONS

The changes in economic conditions dictate attitude adjustment on the part of both managers and workers. The pressures of inflation, competition, energy consumption, international trade, and a leveling of the growth in the standard of living in the United States, challenge all managers to find better ways to reduce costs and increase productivity. These pressures call for more effective labor-management coordination, cooperation, and participation in resolving problems of waste and inefficiency.

CHANGES IN SOCIAL ENVIRONMENT

The entire social environment has been and is continuing to undergo significant changes that affect humanistic relations in the workplace. The changing style of working and living, particularly where both husband and wife work, places pressures on management to change the "quality of working life." Flexible work scheduling policies are becoming more prevalent to accommodate workers' individual needs and family responsibilities. With increasing computerization of work, it becomes a management responsibility to find ways of making work more appealing, interesting, and rewarding to the worker. Management must also give more aggressive attention to reducing covert discrimination against certain workers, particularly females and blacks. More pressure needs to be exercised in the community, particularly in the schools, to teach *all* people the importance of being responsible individuals. With *rights* there are commensurate *responsibilities* that we all have to develop and adopt. Both our social and economic environments will suffer if we place irresponsible workers in responsible positions.

ACCEPTING NEW PRINCIPLES OF MANAGEMENT

To be continuously effective, a manager must be on the alert to discover, accept, and implement new principles of management. Many of the participative management practices of the Japanese offer an effective means of increasing both job satisfaction and productivity. These practices should be studied and applied wherever possible. The entire area of labor-management negotiations needs to be studied and analyzed in order to achieve more cooperative, constructive, practical, and intelligent agreements. Our society cannot afford continuation of unrealistic and uneconomical labor-management agreements. There is no reason why future agreements cannot be worked out on a truly participative basis that results in benefits to labor, management, and society.

MANAGERIAL ETHICS

ATTITUDE AND MORALITY

Ethics are the rules of moral conduct that recognize the values of honesty, fairness, justice, and the rightness or wrongness of the motives involved in certain actions. The most effective managers have a positive and long-range attitude that reflects concern about the ethical consequences of management decisions. In today's turbulent environment, there are many moral obligations to be fulfilled by individuals in managerial positions:

MORAL OBLIGATIONS

- *Responsibility to employees in the form of good humanistic relations*
- *Responsibility to customers in the form of safe and useful products and services*
- *Responsibility to stockholders in the form of dividends from profits*
- *Responsibility to the community in the form of economic stability*
- *Responsibility to the government in the form of compliance with laws and regulations*
- *Responsibility to society in the form of actions that do not unfairly benefit some while hurting others*

The manager's ethical values can be significant factors in sins of omission and commission. The actions that unfairly benefit some while hurting others include discrimination in personnel practices, personal prejudices that lead to unfair treatment, failure to inform about a known safety hazard, kickbacks, and theft from the company (cheating on travel vouchers, embezzlement, and so on).

IT IS NOT EASY TO CHANGE

It is not easy to develop a change in ethical standards of conduct. Unfortunately, by the time many individuals become managers, their ethical values are firmly established. The process of learning ethical values is a growth process that starts in childhood. By the time we reach adulthood, our ethical values are a reflection of our family, religious, social, and educational background.

Ethics implies personal behavior. In business management, a manager must constantly make decisions that have ethical implications. Sometimes the ethical aspects are not obvious or seen from the viewpoint of their long-range impacts. The following case situation may help illustrate the importance of ethical behavior in the making of decisions.

THE CASE OF GENERAL J.B.

A military Lieutenant General, whom we will call General J.B., allowed gross mismanagement to occur in his own office in the handling of money resources. The mismanagement involved such irresponsible actions as spending money that wasn't available. The situation was unbelievable. General J.B.'s office received sales orders from customers and used them as cash available to be spent *before* the customer received the materials and paid for them. When faced with explaining the situation to Congeess, General J.B. covered up the mismanagement in his own office and attempted to use an executive-level civilian comptroller as the "scapegoat."

Instead of retiring, which is what General J.B. demanded, the civilian comptroller initiated an investigation. The subsequent investigation report indicted General J.B. and many other managers for wrongdoing and mismanagement. General J.B. was officially reprimanded and "retired" from the military service. The civilian comptroller continued in his position. General J.B.'s unethical actions to blame an innocent subordinate resulted, in the long run, in bringing about his own downfall. The lesson to be learned from this case is that unethical actions are not the recommended solution to problems at any level of management.

UNETHICAL BEHAVIOR IS A LOSER

The New York City, New Jersey, Philadelphia, and Washington, D.C. areas are centers of industrial and government business activity. It seems that almost every day there is disclosure of unethical behavior on the part of some prominent leader. The following examples are but a small sampling of people who have literally destroyed themselves by their own unethical behavior:

- *A former U.S. President resigned rather than face possible impeachment for allegedly lying and covering up deceitful practices while in office.*
- *A former U.S. Attorney General was convicted and imprisoned for deceitful practices while in office.*
- *A U.S. Senator resigned rather than face almost certain expulsion after being convicted, fined $50,000, and given a three-year prison sentence for conspiracy, bribery, and conflict of interest.*
- *A U.S. Congressman was expelled from Congress after being convicted, fined $20,000, and given a three-year prison sentence for conspiracy, bribery, and interstate travel for racketeering.*
- *Five other U.S. Congressmen were convicted, fined, and given prison sentences for bribery, conspiracy, conflict of interest, accepting unlawful gratuities, and other charges.*
- *A New Jersey State Senator and former mayor of a large city was convicted, fined $40,000, and given a six-year prison term for bribery, conspiracy, and interstate travel in the aid of racketeering.*
- *A Philadelphia City Councilman was convicted, fined $20,000, and given concurrent three-year prison terms for conspiracy, bribery, and interstate travel for racketeering.*
- *A New Jersey Superior Court Judge found leaving the courtroom with $12,000 in cash, was indicted for bribery.*
- *A New Jersey State Senator and city mayor was convicted and sentenced to seven-years in prison for racketeering.*
- *A New Jersey Police Sergeant and his supervisor were convicted on charges of altering a blood test report on the son of a borough official so that he would not have to be charged with driving while intoxicated.*

- *A former forty-two-year-old executive vice-president and acting president of a New Jersey College was indicted and convicted on three counts of conspiracy, illegally obtaining money as a public employee, and official misconduct in cashing bad checks.*
- *A former thirty-one-year-old director of accounting of a New Jersey College was indicted and convicted on three counts of conspiracy, illegally obtaining money as a public employee, and official misconduct in cashing bad checks.*

MORE UNETHICAL PRACTICES

The above listing might give the misleading impression that unethical practices are found primarily in government. Before making that conclusion, consider the fact that in the late 1970s more than 500 U.S. corporations had disclosed to the Securities and Exchange Commission that they made improper or illegal payments either at home or overseas. In almost every case, the payments were disguised by falsifying or making improper entries in company books. For example, a large steel corporation pleaded guilty to maintaining a "secret-source fund" that was used for bribes to obtain ship repair work. In another corporation, an investigation into illegal political contributions led to a jail sentence for the company's chief financial officer for stealing company funds. All of this leads to the question: If 500 corporations admitted unethical actions, how many didn't confess their sins?

There is a considerable amount of unethical business conduct in both industry and government. Disclosures of unethical practices in government are usually widely publicized, while those in industry are often covered up. After all, it's not good advertising to publicize unethical or illegal business actions. As a matter of fact, many unethical practices are never even reported to the Board of Directors of the corporation.

A DISTURBING SITUATION

The very disturbing thing about unethical practices in both industry and government is that they are so prevalent. Hopefully, this discussion of business ethics will cause more managers and students of management to recognize the long-term benefits of honesty, fairness, justice, and the rightness or wrongness of their actions. Sooner or later most unethical practices cause the downfall of the person who engages in it.

PREPARING FOR TOMORROW'S CHANGES

The most effective supervisors not only keep up with the changes in the work environment, they look ahead and anticipate tomorrow's changes.

EXPECTATIONS OF THE FUTURE

What are some of the things that a supervisor can reasonably expect in the foreseeable future? One thing is change. The next ten years will probably be different in many ways from the past ten years (Figure 16-2). Some of the expectations of the future are as follows:

1. The continuing pressures of inflation, competition, and a leveling of the growth in the U.S. standard of living will compel supervisors to find more ways to reduce costs and increase productivity.
2. The pressures of near-zero growth in productivity will call for better and more effective labor-management coordination and cooperation with emphasis on cutting wastes, reducing costs, and using technological improvements in work methods.
3. The continued expansion of computerized and mechanized operations will cause supervisors to spend less time observing actual work performance and more time analyzing and interpreting information reports.
4. The continued energy-shortage problems will compel supervisors to find more ways of reducing energy consumption.

FIGURE 16-2   Preparing for tomorrow

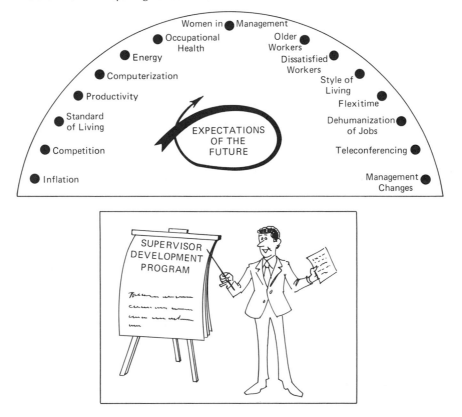

5. The continued high incidence of accidents and occupational health hazards will compel supervisors to find ways and means of achieving greater safety in the work environment.

6. The continued increase of women in the workplace will call for more concerted management efforts to have affirmative action programs that result in more women promoted to managerial positions.

7. The increase of women in the workplace will bring pressure on management to establish an "affirmative duty" to prevent and eliminate sexual harassment at all levels of the organization.

8. The expectation that more people will be living to an older age and working longer before retiring will compel management to develop and implement changes in human resource planning and utilization. The percent of workers over sixty is increasing, while the percent of young people under twenty is decreasing. This dwindling number of young workers will make it more difficult to fill many entry-level jobs.[2]

9. The expectation that increasing numbers of workers will become restless and dissatisfied with dull, routine, and repetitive jobs will put pressure on management to make work more appealing, interesting, and rewarding to the worker.

10. The changing style of working and living, particularly where both the husband and wife work, will bring pressures on management to change the "quality of working life." One of the changes expected is an expansion of flexible schedules that allow employees' work times to be in harmony with their individual needs and family responsibilities.

11. The use of "flexitime" mentioned above requires all employees to work during a core period, such as 9:00 A.M. to 3:00 P.M., but lets them choose when to work the remaining hours of their work schedule. While the flexible work schedule may improve worker morale and reduce turnover and absenteeism, it will create work-scheduling problems for the supervisor.

12. The dehumanizing effects of computerized work will make it necessary to find ways to put group socialization in the workplace.

13. The use of teleconferencing in communications will cause managers to make significant changes in the conducting of conferences and meetings and in their methods of decision making.

14. The increased use of computers and changing modes of communication will necessitate adjustments to the need for fewer middle-level managers.

A SUPERVISOR MUST PREPARE FOR THE FUTURE

The changes in the future work environment give many indications that the supervisor must be prepared to meet tomorrow's challenges in management. Many companies are now requiring their supervisors to have a college education. Still other companies are seeing to it that their supervisors are trained in humanistic relations, which is probably the weakest area of management for many supervisors. Tomorrow's changes appear to place more emphasis on supervisors who can think, who are innovators, who can handle people, who see beyond their own responsibilities, and who are effective managers not just upgraded workers.

SUMMARY

The emphasis in this book has been to provide managers, and people with aspirations of becoming managers, to see and understand the broad scope of work activities and responsibilities involved in such positions. Primary attention has been given to the lower levels of management which include the greatest number of individuals. We have discussed various aspects of management at all levels to avoid conveying a "tunnel-vision" learning approach to those who work at the lower levels of supervision.

In obtaining an understanding of the broad scope of supervisory management, we have discussed the basic fundamentals of management, the handling of interpersonal relations, the supervision of the workplace, and meeting the challenges of the future. The "key point" of our discussions focused on our attitudes. We should never lose sight of the fact that the attitudes we have about people, innovation, work, computers, expectations, and ethics can greatly strengthen or weaken the other building blocks involved in effective and efficient management.

NOTES

1. Joe Kaiser, "Robots and Industrial Education," *Industrial Education*, February 1983, pp. 14–16.

2. Neal H. Rosenthal, "The United States Economy in 1985: Projected Changes in Occupations," *Monthly Labor Review*, December 1973, p. 18; and Jeffrey Sommerfeld, "Dealing With the Aging Work Force," *Harvard Business Review*, November–December 1978, pp. 81–92.

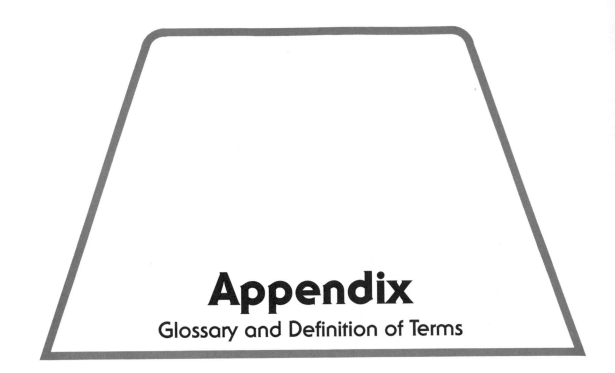

Appendix

Glossary and Definition of Terms

A

Access Time The computer time required to locate data and move it to and from storage.

Accountability The obligation to explain or justify the performance of assigned responsibilities.

Acronym A word formed from the first (or first few) letters of a series of words, such as IRS for Internal Revenue Service.

Administrative Skills The ability to plan, organize, direct, and control a task, function, project, or organization.

Affirmative Action Plans and programs designed to achieve results in the avoidance of discrimination against any person.

Analog Computer A computer which solves problems by translating measurable quantities (such as speed, temperature, and voltage) into numbers.

Aperture Card A standard tab card that has a hole cut in it for mounting a frame of microfilm.

Arbitration The use of a third party to make decisions for disputing persons and resolve their differences.

Arithmetic Element (Computer) That portion of a computer processing unit which performs addition, subtraction, multiplication, and division.

Attitude A reflection of an individual's state of mind or opinion.

Authoritative Leader A leader who is self-ruling and dictatorial, and makes unilateral decisions without any consultation with or participation from others.

Authority The designated right to act and make decisions on assigned responsibilities.

Automated Machine Tools Tools which perform certain tasks, such as cutting, drilling, and planing, by the use of magnetic or punched tape instructions.

B

Binary Number System   An internal numbering system used by computers which uses the number *two* as a base (as opposed to the decimal system which uses the number *ten*).

Biofeedback   An electronically recorded technique of obtaining information about vital body functions (blood pressure, heart rhythm, muscle tension, and skin temperature) to determine an individual's stress level (the point at which stress is triggered). Once the stress level is established, avoidance skills are put into practice to help the individual achieve stress reduction when faced with stressful situations.

Bit   A contraction of *binary digit;* a single pulse in a group of pulses such as a single hole in a punched tape or card. Bits comprise a character and characters comprise a word.

Briefcase-itis   The compulsion of some people to take work home every night.

C

Capital Expense Budget   A budget which plans the money resources required for purchase or construction of buildings and structures, major additions or revisions to existing buildings and structures, and/or purchase of major nonexpendable tools and equipment that are expected to be used for several years.

Career Appraisal   The evaluation of an employee's potential future for promotion to a higher position.

Cash Flow   The pattern of outflow and inflow of money resources.

Cathode-Ray Tube (CRT)   A device similar to a television screen upon which data can be displayed.

Central Processing Element (Computer)   That portion of a computer containing the arithmetic, logic, control, and in some cases, the main storage units.

Chain of Command   The hierarchy of supervisors and subordinates.

Civil Rights   The rights to full legal, economic, and social equality established by the Thirteenth and Fourteenth Amendments to the United States Constitution and by certain Congressional Acts.

Civil Service   Those branches of public service concerned with all governmental functions except the military services.

COM (Computer Output Microfilm)   A system in which microfilm images are prepared from digitized data stored on magnetic tapes or discs, or transmitted directly from a computer's central processor.

Computer Output Microfilm   (*see* COM)

Conciliation   The use of a third party to bring disputing persons together in order to resolve their differences.

Console (Computer)   The part of a computer used for manual control and observation of the computer system.

Consultative Leader   A leader who seeks advice, guidance, information, suggestions, and recommendations from others.

Content Theories of Motivation   The theory that people are motivated according to their needs.

Contingency Budgeting   Planning money resources for the possibility that something may go wrong with the initial budget estimates.

Control Element (Computer)   The part of a computer that contains the circuits for interpreting and controlling the carrying out of instructions.

Controlling   The process where a manager determines progress toward work objectives, identifies deviations and their causes, and initiates action to correct problem situations.

Coordination Ensuring that all work efforts are aimed toward a common objective.

Correlation Analysis The determination of how the behavior of one thing affects the behavior of something else.

Cost Analysis The process of developing cost estimates and predicting the consumption of resources under conditions of uncertainty.

Cost-Effective Accomplishing something at the lowest possible cost and with the greatest benefit. Sometimes called cost-benefit analysis.

Cost-Effective Information System An information system in which the results or benefits derived from the use of the information more than justify the costs of obtaining it.

Cost-Effectiveness The comparative costs of various alternatives versus the expected benefits or effectiveness.

Critical Path Scheduling (CPS) An arrow diagraming technique that highlights the critical path of events requiring the most time and/or costs to implement.

D

Data Measured facts, statistics, and/or observations.

Data Processing Recording and handling of basic elements of information such as facts, numbers, letters, and symbols.

Debug (Computer) To find and remove the mistakes from the design of a program or computer system.

Decision Tree A linear (using lines only) means for outlining objectives, alternatives, and consequences of a series of interrelated decisions.

Delegation Assigning to others the responsibility and authority for accomplishing work activities.

Departmentalization Grouping work functions in a systematic and logical way.

Dependent Variable An item with an unknown value.

Depreciation Amortizing (spreading) the costs of a major capital investment over its expected years of use.

Digital Computer A computer that solves problems by using numbers to express all quantities and variables.

Directing The management process of assigning, instructing, and correcting people in the work efforts required to achieve objectives and plans.

Distributed Data Processing Decentralizing the storing and manipulating of computerized data to the points where most of the work is done and the results needed.

Division of Labor Dividing a work task into specific subtasks so that each person may become more efficient in the performance of his or her job.

E

Eccentric Management A leadership characterized by the belief that management is best achieved through putting workers under pressure or placing trust in a small exclusive group of people. The two most common styles of eccentric management are probably management by crisis and management by clique.

Economic Analysis An objective comparison of costs in relation to benefits to be derived from alternative proposed actions.

Effective Doing the *right* things that result in achieving desired objectives.

Efficient Doing *things* right that result in achieving desired objectives with the best methods and procedures and the lowest costs.

Employee Turnover The number of employees being replaced on jobs within a specified period of time.

Encounter Group An informal group of people, usually with similar backgrounds and problems, who engage in rough-and-tumble confrontation where each member airs his or her emotions without holding back, thereby eliminating stressful situations.

Equal Employment Opportunity The avoidance of discrimination against a person because of age, nationality, race, sex, or disability.

Equal Opportunity The right of every person, regardless of race, color, sex, age, religion, nationality, or disability, to equal treatment on the job.

Equal Opportunity Laws The Equal Pay Act of 1963, the Civil Rights Act of 1964, the Age in Discrimination Act of 1967, and the Federal Rehabilitation Act of 1973.

Ethics The rules of moral conduct including the values of honesty, fairness, justice, and the right or wrong of the motives involved in certain actions.

F

Filter The term *filter* in the communication process refers to the tendency of each individual to read into a situation what he or she wants to read into it.

Flexible Budgeting Planning the money resources needed for various levels of workload.

Flexitime A time and attendance policy that requires all employees to work during a core period, such as 9:00 A.M. to 3:00 P.M., but lets them choose when to work the remaining hours of their schedule.

Functional Authority Authority that is limited to a specific specialized activity or function.

Functions Work activities to be performed.

G

Gantt Chart A charting technique that shows specific scheduled starting and ending times versus actual work progress.

Gobbledygook Vocabulary characterized by jargon peculiar to a particular trade, profession, or group that tends to be unintelligible or meaningless to others.

Grievance A formal complaint alleging that some unjust act has been committed against a person.

Group Dynamics The active forces that exist when groups of people get together.

H

Hardware (Computer) The physical equipment or devices which together comprise a computer and its associated data processing machines.

Human Factors Engineering The linkage between the design and operation of tools and equipment and the ability, accomplishments, and satisfaction of the person who must operate and maintain the tools and equipment.

Humanistic Relations A method of dealing with people that shows an interest in and a concern for the liberty, rights, welfare, and dignity of human beings.

Humanistic Relations Skills The manifestation of interest and concern for the liberty, rights, welfare, dignity, and other values of human beings in the performance of work activities.

Hypothesis An unproved theory presented as a possible explanation for the occurrence of something or as a potential solution to some problem.

I

Independent Variable   An item with a known value.

Industrial Engineering   The discipline that involves research in developing the most effective and efficient methods and procedures for performing work.

Information   Data that has been processed or converted into more meaningful and usable form.

Information System   A mass of organized facts, statistics and/or descriptive words or numbers relating to specific identifiable things.

Input (Computer)   Data to be processed and the instructions to control the processing, which are moved into the internal storage of a data processing system.

Intermediate-Range Planning   Planning for the period of time extending from two to five years beyond the current year.

J

Job Content   The characteristics of a job, such as responsibility and potential for growth.

Job Context   The characteristics (such as pay and working conditions) found in the job environment.

Job Description   An explicit statement of the duties, responsibilities, and authority of a job.

Job Design   The process of prescribing the work required of a person to accomplish a specific undertaking.

Job Enlargement   Assigning additional work tasks of the *same level* of responsibility.

Job Enrichment   Assigning additional work tasks of a *higher level* of responsibility.

Job Evaluation   The comparison of jobs to determine their relative value to the organization.

L

Labor Relations Laws   The National Labor Relations Act of 1935, the Fair Labor Standards Act of 1938, and the Taft-Hartley Act of 1947.

Layout Flow   The identification of *where* work activities are performed.

Leadership   The act of showing the way and guiding others in the achievement of an objective.

Life-Cycle Management   The management of a product or project from its initial engineering development, through its procurement, production, testing, marketing, distribution, supply, and maintenance.

Line Authority   Authority over all work-related activities of subordinates.

Line of Balance   A charting technique that shows scheduled versus actual quantities of work produced at each key control point.

Line Organization   An activity that contributes work directly related to the purpose of the organization.

Logic Element (Computer)   The part of a computer processing unit that compares, matches, sorts, and performs nonarithmetic functions.

Long-Range Planning   Planning for the period of time extending from two to ten years, or more, beyond the current year.

M

Magnetic Disk   A flat, circular plate with a surface that can be magnetized to store data.

Magnetic Drum   A rotating cylinder with a surface that can be magnetized to store data.

Magnetic Tape   A plastic strip coated with a metallic oxide upon which data can be recorded in magnetized spots.

Mainframe (Computer)   The central processor of a large computer system.

Management The planning, organizing, directing, and controlling of the activities necessary to get something done.

Management By Crisis Failing to act on something until it has become a major and urgent problem.

Management By Exception An approach to management that emphasizes that the most important actions be accomplished first and then gives priority attention to these actions.

Management By Objectives (MBO) The process of establishing and performing work activities in accordance with clearly defined and integrated goals.

Management Hierarchy The successive ranking of managers, one above another.

Management Information System A network of feeding selected operational and other information to managers to support their decision-making responsibilities.

Manager An individual who plans, organizes, directs, and controls the activities involved in achieving the objectives of an organization. Sometimes called administrator, director, executive, general manager, or superintendent.

Manpower Budgeting Planning the number of personnel required by an organization to perform its workload.

Materials Handling The supportive functions involved in the procurement, supply, and provisioning of the materials necessary for work production.

Matrix Organization A hybrid organization in which some workers report directly to two supervisors. One supervisor is function-oriented and the other is project- or task-oriented.

Mediation The use of a third party to offer suggestions to disputing persons in order to resolve their differences.

Meeting Log A diagnostic technique for identifying time spent in meetings.

Memo-itis The compulsion of some people to write memos about anything and everything.

Microfiche A sheet of film containing multiple microimages (photographic reproductions) in a grid pattern.

Microfilm The photographic reproduction of alpha-numeric characters, drawings, and other printed materials in a miniaturized format.

Microfilm Jacket Two clear sheets of separated acetate used for the storage of short strips of microfilm.

Mission An organization's reason for existence or main objective for the future.

Model An abstract representation of real-world phenomena by means of mathematical equations, symbols, or statements.

Motivation Whatever causes a person to act or behave in a certain way.

N

Network Techniques A logical arrangement of geometric symbols, interconnecting lines, bars, or arrows that shows significant operations, occurrences, sequences, and interrelations in the accomplishment of a work program.

O

Objective The expected goal to be achieved in an organizational undertaking.

Open-Door Policy A manager's practice of making him- or herself readily available to workers for discussion of problems or other matters.

Operating Expense Budget A plan of the money resources needed by an organization to perform its workload.

Operational Information System The inputs, processing, and outputs of data pertaining to the day-to-day conduct of business activities by functional managers.

Operational Planning The continuous process of preparing plans, budgets, schedules, and/or forecasts for specific actions on a short-range basis.

Operations Analysis The detailed breakdown of a work activity into the *motions* of the worker doing the job.

Operations Research The scientific method of applying mathematical and statistical techniques to solving problems involving probabilities, uncertainties, and/or unknowns.

Organizing The management process of identifying, dividing, and grouping the work activities; and then defining the responsibilities, authority, and accountability of the workers required to best achieve these objectives.

OSHA (Occupational Safety and Health Administration) A government agency that assists employers in providing a safe and healthy workplace.

Output (Computer) Information transferred from internal computer storage to devices that produce cards, tapes, business forms, and the like.

P

Paper Bedding The compulsion of some people to generate paperwork that serves no purpose other than ego-building and/or justifying the positions of the people who generate it.

Participative Leader A leader who has others take an active part in the development of objectives, plans, and work methods prior to making a decision.

Participative Management A team approach to management problem solving and decision making where managers and subordinates work together to establish objectives, make plans, and determine ways to get jobs done.

Payback The length of time required for the earnings or cost savings from a capital investment to pay for itself.

Perfectionism The compulsion of some people to demand perfection and to hold that it is attainable.

Performance Appraisal The evaluation of an employee's past and current work performance on the job.

Personnel Management The area of management concerned with procurement, development, and maintenance of personnel.

PERT An acronym for a planning network technique called Program Evaluation Review Technique.

PERT Cost A network charting technique that shows major events and estimated costs for performing a work program.

PERT Time A network charting technique that shows major events and estimated times for performing a work program.

Plan The end product of planning.

Planning The management process of determining the what, when, where, how, who, and why in the accomplishment of work activities.

Policies General principles or rules of action for the conduct that managers and employees are expected to follow.

Preventive Maintenance The systematic inspection and servicing of equipment to prevent malfunctions and breakdowns.

Principle An accepted rule of action or conduct.

Procedures The series of steps to follow to accomplish a work activity.

Process Flow The identification of *how* work activities are performed.

Process Theories of Motivation The theory that people are motivated according to their expectancies.

Productivity The quantity of work produced per hour (or other specified period of time).

Program (Computer) A series of instructions which tells the computer in minute detail how to process data.

Program Budget A plan of the money resources needed to accomplish specific objectives and identifiable work outputs.

Program Planning The translation of broad goals of strategic planning into definitive objectives, policies, directives, and work programs to be accomplished within an intermediate-range time schedule.

Programmer (Computer) A person who prepares problem-solving procedures and flow charts and writes and debugs computer programs.

Proportional Value Distribution Listing the many things that require management attention and then ranking them in order of importance.

Q

Quality Control Circle A team of supervisors and workers who study work problems and their causes, and suggest corrective actions.

R

Random Access Storage A storage technique in which the computer can find one bit of data as quickly as any other, regardless of its specific location in storage.

Real-time A method of processing data so fast that there is virtually no passage of time between inquiry and result.

Regression Analysis The determination of the mathematical correlation between two or more variables.

Reliability The degree to which data is trustworthy and consistent in a cost or economic analysis.

Report-itis The tendency of some managers to require detailed reports on anything and everything regardless of their significance in the management process.

Responsibility The assigned obligation to perform a certain work task.

Review and Analysis The critical examination of an organization for the purpose of establishing where things stand and where they appear to be heading.

Robotics The field of robot technology, which includes the design and use of robots to perform routine mechanical tasks on command.

Role Perception The inclination of people to see other individuals as they want to see them or as they expect them to be. Role perception exists when people stereotype other people according to age, sex, race, national origin, or other factors and then attribute certain characteristics to everyone who falls within the group. Role perception also involves the tendency of people to say or do what they *think* someone else wants them to say or do.

S

Semantics The different meanings of words or other symbols.

Seniority The status obtained as the result of a person's length of service.

Sensitivity The degree to which certain facts or data are susceptible to various stimuli or changes.

Shop Steward The first-level representative of a union.

Short-Range Planning Planning for the time span of the current year and the next year (the budget year).

Simulation An exercise which usually uses a computer as a scorekeeper while people make decisions concerning a mathematical model of a real-world business situation.

Software (Computer)   All programs and routines used to extend the capabilities of computers, such as assemblers (machine-language coded instructions), compilers (devices that translate symbolic coded instructions into machine-language instructions), and subroutines (a sequence of computer instructions).

Span of Control   The extent of a manager's control: the number of persons who report directly to a manager.

Staff Assistant   An individual responsible for providing technical assistance and support in a specialized functional activity such as accounting, law, or personnel management.

Staff Organization   An activity that contributes work in support of other parts of an organization. Its efforts do *not* contribute directly to the mission or purpose of the organization.

Staff Planning   Providing guidance, instruction, assistance, review, and coordination to the planning efforts of others.

Staffing   The selection and placement of personnel to perform each job in an organization.

Strategic Planning   Long-range planning by top executives to identify important problems requiring decision for future operations.

Stress   Anything that arouses or provokes a person to the point where it disturbs or interferes with the normal functioning of the human body. A stressful situation, such as a frustrating job, can increase blood pressure, pulse rate, and/or muscle tension to the point where it can damage both physical and mental health.

Supervision   The act of overseeing the accomplishment of the work to be done.

Supervisor   A manager at the lowest managerial level in the organization hierarchy. Sometimes called foreman, group leader, team leader, project leader, unit chief, section chief, or department manager.

Systems Analysis   The examination of an activity, procedure, method, technique, or business to determine what must be accomplished and how the necessary operations may best be accomplished.

T

Technical Skills   The specialized knowledge in a particular profession, trade, or type of work.

Teleconferencing   The use of advanced electronics and other technology that enables several people in various locations to conduct a conference or meeting without leaving their place of work or home.

Telephone Log   A diagnostic technique for identifying time spent in telephone conversations.

Tension   The reflection of mental or emotional anxiety caused by situations involving suspense, excitement, or a strained relationship between individuals.

Theory X   A human behavior theory formulated by Douglas McGregor that assumes people to be lazy, to dislike work, and to be driven to work only by coercion or threatened disciplinary action by the supervisor.

Theory Y   A human behavior theory formulated by Douglas McGregor that assumes that people have a psychological need and desire to work and that they will seek responsibility in the right work environment.

Theory Z   A concept of management formulated by William G. Ouchi that considers workers as the key to increased productivity through the development of trust, discernment, coordination, and intimacy between managers and subordinates.

Time Inventory A diagnostic technique for identifying time spent in various activities.

Time Sharing Using a computer to process multiple requests by independent users at remote locations, and providing responses rapidly so that each user feels that the computer is entirely at his or her disposal.

Time Value of Money The future money value of a dollar invested today and allowed to accumulate interest at a given percent for a stated number of years.

Traditional-itis The compulsion of some people to do things today in exactly the same way they have been doing them in the past.

Transcendental Meditation A technique for reducing tension and stress through the act of concentration without interruption for an extended period of time (twenty minutes). The meditation is executed by thinking of some meaningful and pleasant word.

U

Uncertainty The difference between the value of predicted data displayed in a management study and the true value that actually occurs in the real-world situation.

Unity of Command A management principle that each employee should have only one boss.

Unity of Direction A management principle that each employee should receive only one set of directives from one boss pertaining to the same objective.

V

Validation The development of data that is sound and produces the desired results in a cost or economic analysis.

Value Analysis The process of looking for ways to reduce the costs, but not the quality and value, of a product or service by using less-costly materials and parts.

W

Word Processing Equipment Electronic equipment that is capable of transforming written, verbal, or recorded messages to a typewritten form. The equipment consists of such components as (a) programmed instructions on magnetic tapes or cards, (b) units to store programmed instructions, and (c) a text-editing typewriter capable of making additions, deletions, corrections, and changes in the recorded text and producing a perfect finished document at a high rate of speed.

Word-itis The compulsion to proliferate unnecessary and/or unintelligible words in communicating.

Work Ethic The value of exerting effort to accomplish something.

Work Measurement The determination of the *quantity* of incoming workload, work being accomplished, and work backlog.

Work Sampling Random observations of work activities to determine the percent of time spent in setup, operation, maintenance, and delays.

Work Simplification Analysis of work activities to identify and eliminate bottlenecks, conflict, backtracking, red tape, duplication, and waste.

Z

Zero-Base Budgeting A planning, programming, and budgeting process which requires each manager to justify an entire budget in detail from scratch and to explain why any money should be spent at all.

Index

CASE STUDY/SITUATION LIST
(by chapter)